THE NEW EUROPE

An A to Z Compendium
on the
European Community

Other Books by the Author

Automation, Manpower and Education
The Computer Prophets
The Death of Privacy: Do Industrial and Government Computers Threaten our
    Personal Freedom?
Dictionary of Business and Management, 2nd Edition
Dictionary of Banking and Financial Services, 2nd Edition
Inside the Wall Street Journal: The History and Power of Dow Jones & Company
    and America's Most Influential Newspaper
Dictionary of Computers, Information Processing and Telecommunications, 2nd
    Edition
The Investor's Dictionary
Dictionary of Artificial Intelligence and Robotics

THE NEW EUROPE
An A to Z Compendium
on the
European Community

Jerry M. Rosenberg
Professor
Graduate School of Management
and
Department of Business Administration
Rutgers University

The Bureau of National Affairs, Inc., Washington, D.C. 20037

Library of Congress Cataloging-in-Publication Data

Rosenberg, Jerry Martin.
   The new Europe: an A to Z compendium on the
European Community / Jerry M. Rosenberg.
      p.   cm.
   Includes bibliographical references and index.
   ISBN 0-87179-669-4
   1. European Economic Community—Dictionaries.
I. Title.
HC241.2.R59   1990
341.24′22′03—dc20   90-48878
                                          CIP

Published by BNA Books
1231 25th St., NW, Washington, D.C. 20037

Printed in the United States of America
International Standard Book Number: 0-87179-669-4

This book is affectionately dedicated to
Lauren and Bob
"All I can give them are love, roots, and wings"

Preface

The New Europe: An A to Z Compendium on the European Community gives detailed information on the most significant aspects of the E.C., which include the issues involved and the language people will need to understand them. It is more than a dictionary and easier to use than an encyclopedia. *The New Europe* contains over 2,500 definitions answering questions about the European Community, the Single European Act, the European Free Trade Association, and Eastern Europe . . . from the E.C.'s founding over thirty years ago, to the day the last trade barriers are expected to fall.

This *Compendium* identifies and explains the people, places, and events that have paved the way to a "Europe Without Frontiers." It also features a useful section on the structure and institutions of the European Community, plus a comprehensive chronology of the European Community from its creation in 1957 to the present day.

By 1992, Europe plans to be the largest single market in the world. Business leaders and decision makers in the United States must be prepared for the impact of the New Europe by first, understanding what the recently enacted rules, recommendations, directives, and policies are; and second, making certain that in responding to the challenges of the future, clear communications should lead the way when using terminology of this newly envigorated European Community. Drawing from a wide-range of sources, including official documents, news releases, formal conferences and contemporary practices, the definitions in this *Compendium* are complete and detailed, clear and concise, keyed to current usage, extensively cross-referenced, and grouped by concept for easy comparison.

This volume covers events of the European Community through October 1990. As the next two years unfold the dust will have settled bringing on this monumental moment in Europe's history—Post 1992.

Acknowledgments

No reference book can be the exclusive product of one person's effort. Even when written by an individual, such a work requires the tapping of many sources, which is especially true of this book. By the very nature of the fields included, I have had to rely on the able and extensive efforts of others.

As best I can discern, I have not deliberately quoted descriptions from any copyrighted source, except where permission has been granted. Any apparent similarity to existing, unreleased descriptions in these cases is purely accidental and the result of the limitations of language.

Much assistance has come indirectly from books, journal articles, official documents, copies of original proposals, opinions, recommendations, regulations, directives, etc. They are too numerous to be named here. Various organizations have aided me directly by providing informative source materials, in particular the Washington, D.C., and New York Delegation of the Commission of the European Communities.

Of the many sources, most helpful in the preparation of this work have been numerous copies of the following publications. I am most appreciative of the authors and publishers of these works.

Bulletin of the European Communities, Supplements. Commission of the European Communities. Belgium.

Cecchini, Paolo. *The European Challenge—1992: The Benefits of a Single Market*, Commission of the European Communities. Newcastle-upon-Tyne: Wildwood House Ltd., 1988.

Completing the Internal Market. Commission of the European Communities. New York: Ernst & Whinney.

Eurecom, Commission of the European Communities. New York.

Eurobarometer, Commission of the European Communities. Brussels.

Europe—Magazine of the European Community. Delegation of the Commission of the European Communities. Washington, D.C.

European Community News. E.C. Office of Press & Public Affairs. New York.

European Documentation, Commission of the European Communities. Periodicals. Federal Republic of Germany.

European File, Commission of the European Communities. Brussels.

European Information-External Relations. Commission of the European Communities. Brussels.

Fourth Progress Report of the Commission to the Council and the European Parliament—concerning the implementation of the Commission's White Paper on the completion of the internal market. Commission of the European Communities, Brussels: June 20, 1989.

A Journey through the E.C. Commission of the European Communities, Brussels-Luxembourg: 1986.

ix

Morris, Brian, P. Crane, and K. Boehm. *The European Community—A Guide for business and government.* Bloomington: Indiana University Press, 1981.

On a more personal level, I thank the various individuals I used as a sounding board to clarify my ideas and approach; they offered valuable suggestions and encouraged me to go on with the project. Harriet Berlin, product development manager at The Bureau of National Affairs, Inc. had the foresight to initiate this book; and my editor, Cheryl Drew, followed it through to publication with the help of freelance editor Mary Hughes. I thank, again and again, my wife Ellen, my daughters Elizabeth and Lauren, and my son-in-law Robert, who showed understanding and offered full support during the preparation of this work. Time away from them, whether spent researching an article or struggling with a complex regulation or directive, is more than compensated by their affection.

Finally, to my reader—the ultimate jurist—I welcome critical comments bringing errors to my attention, to make it possible to correct them in later editions, thus evolving a greater conformity of meaning for all.

New York, NY   J.M.R.
November 1, 1990

Contents

Preface   vii

Acknowledgments   ix

Introduction   xiii

Guide to the Compendium   xix

The New Europe Compendium   1

Chronology   185

Index of Major Subjects   201

Introduction

Institutions of the European Community

The four principal institutions of the European Community (E.C.) are the European Commission, the Council of Ministers, the European Parliament, and the Court of Justice.

The Commission is the E.C.'s executive body. It submits drafts for new policies, implements those already decided upon, and watches over the correct application of the E.C. rules. The Council of Ministers decides or legislates on policy on the basis of Commission proposals.

The power of the Parliament, which has been directly elected by the citizens of all member states since 1979, has been increased by the Single European Act, and it now plays a more significant legislative role than in the past. The Court interprets E.C. law and gives rulings in the event of disputes.

By their composition or function, the Commission, the Parliament, and the Court are free from the direct control of E.C. governments. The Council of Ministers, made up of representatives of the member states themselves, is the exception. Therefore, the member states have made sure that the Council remains the most powerful of the E.C. institutions.

The European Commission

Only the Commission can initiate E.C. policy, and the Council of Ministers cannot take decisions on specific policy issues without a Commission proposal. The Commission is responsible for implementing decisions taken by the Council, and it also has the power to enforce the E.C. treaties and legislation derived from them, which gives it the informal title of "guardian of the treaties." It is the Commission's duty to take action against member governments who it believes have violated their treaty obligations.

The Commission has considerable autonomy, by dint of the treaties and by exercising powers conferred on it by the Council. This is particularly true in the cases of the E.C.'s antitrust regulations and agriculture policy. The Commission also draws up the draft of the E.C.'s annual budget and negotiates international agreements on behalf of the Community.

There are currently 17 commissioners, two from each of the five larger member states (West Germany, France, Britain, Italy, Spain), and one each from the other seven. All are nominated by their national governments and appointed for a four-year term by the Council, and may be reappointed. They act in the E.C.'s interest, independently of member governments, and upon appointment swear an oath to this effect. Decisions within the Commission, are if necessary, taken by simple majority.

The President of the Commission and the six vice-presidents are chosen nominally for two years, but their tenure has always been extended to four years. They also can be reappointed.

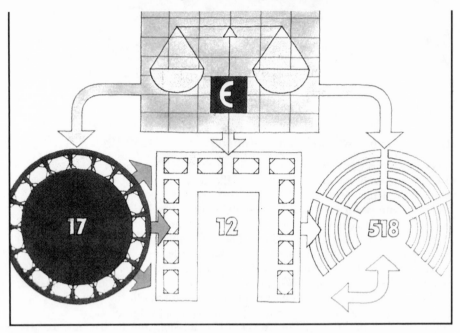

The four institutions work closely together to make the Community function. The Commission (left) drafts new policy, which the Council of Ministers (center) can approve into E.C. law only after the Parliament (right) has agreed. The Court (above) ensures that E.C. law is upheld in the member states.

Source: "Demystifying the E.C. Institutions," Europe: Magazine of the European Community, No. 29 (Nov. 1989).

The President is nominated first, giving him the chance to influence the choice of his fellow commissioners. He has no power to turn down a candidate nominated by a member government, however; nor can he fire a colleague appointed by the Council.

The Council of Ministers

The Council is composed of ministers from the 12 member states and is the final E.C. decision-taking body. Its meetings are also attended by at least one member of the Commission. Ministers have the difficult task of representing and defending the interests of their countries while framing agreements that promote E.C. goals.

Participants at Council meetings change according to subject matter. Thus, if the theme is finance, the E.C.'s 12 Finance Ministers attend; when industrial policy is discussed, Industry Ministers will participate.

The "senior" Council formation is that of the foreign ministers. They deal with external relations, but can also take on particularly urged issues in other sectors. The foreign ministers coordinate the work of other council formations and prepare the twice-yearly sessions of the European Council.

The European Council (or E.C. Summit) is described as the Council of Ministers meeting at head-of-state and government level. It is the top authority both on Community matters and on political cooperation issues. The Single European Act gave it legal recognition but did not define its powers.

Beginning in 1975, when the first European Council met, it has sometimes made difficult decisions when the Council of Ministers was unable to find a solution. More recently, the European Council's prime role has been to set the policy priorities for the E.C.'s future development. The presidency of the Council of Ministers (and of the European Council) rotates among the member states every six months.

In one of its most important reforms, the Single European Act provided for majority voting by the Council of Ministers on issues that formerly required unanimity. This facilitated decision-taking in areas covered by the single market program, in which all decisions, with the exception of fiscal matters, can be taken by majority vote.

The European Parliament

The European Parliament is the E.C.'s only directly elected body. Its 518 members, elected every five years by voters in all member states, scrutinize draft E.C. legislation, question the Commission and the Council of Ministers on their conduct of E.C. affairs, and debate topical issues. Most pieces of draft legislation cannot be formally adopted by the Council until they have received the Parliament's opinion. The Parliament, largely because of the national governments' reluctance to increase its power, has less legislative authority than national parliaments, although this is changing.

The European Parliament can dismiss the European Commission and the E.C.'s annual budget cannot be adopted without Parliament's agreement. The Single European Act increased its legislative role by giving it the right to a "second reading" and more scope for amending new E.C. legislation before it is formally adopted. The Parliament must give its assent to important agreements the E.C. enters into, such as cooperation agreements with third countries, or the accession of new members.

The Parliament meets in plenary session once a month in Strasbourg. Sessions last one week and much of the rest of the members' time is taken up by committee work mainly in Brussels. The Members of the European Parliament (MEP) form political rather than national groups.

The Court of Justice

The Court of Justice is the E.C.'s equivalent of the U.S. Supreme Court. It interprets Community law for national courts and rules on legal questions pertaining to E.C. treaties that are raised by Community institutions, member states, companies, or individuals. Its rulings are binding.

The Court's judgments have helped consolidate the E.C. by ensuring that private citizens, companies, and governments are both protected by, and subject to, the provisions of E.C. law. It has been particularly important in building up case law in specific areas of E.C. activities, thereby setting precedent for policymakers and other parties concerned.

The Court has been instrumental in making governments respect the obligations they accept when signing the treaties. Although it cannot impose sanctions on member governments, its ruling have invariably been complied with. The Court also serves as a court of appeal in antitrust cases, where a company has been fined by the Commission for violating E.C. fair competition rules.

The Court is composed of 13 judges, one from each member state plus one other, who are assisted by six Advocates-General. Both are appointed for six-year renewable terms by the Council of Ministers. The Court is located in Luxembourg.

The Legislative Process

The E.C.'s legislative process generally involves the Commission, the Council, and the European Parliament. Draft legislation is sent from the Commission to the Council of Ministers for a decision. Prior to the Single European Act's implementation, the Council did not need to take into account the Parliament's opinion. The Single European Act, however, has introduced a second reading procedure. Consequently, if the Parliament rejects in its second reading a "common position" reached by the Council in the latter's first reading, the Council can only overrule the Parliament's rejection by unanimous vote. The Parliament also has greater scope than before for amending draft legislation prior to formal adoption by the Council.

The most complex legislative procedure concerns the E.C. budget. The Council of Ministers and the European Parliament share authority for the budget, and a conciliation procedure exists in case of disagreement. On several occasions, however, disagreements have been such that the E.C. has begun a new financial year without a budget. In 1986, the Court of Justice ruled that an attempt by the Parliament to impose a budget without the consent of the Council of Ministers was illegal: the budget must be approved by both before it can be adopted.

A major obstacle in the run-up to 1992 was removed in February 1988 when the Twelve agreed to a comprehensive reform of the budget's size and structure. Funding is being raised by 50 percent between 1987–92, which means that long-running budget disputes, relatively common in the past, will no longer put a brake on the whole range of E.C. activities.

Decisions taken by the Commission and the Council of Ministers are directly applicable in the member states, and must be applied by both national administrations and national courts. These decisions may be challenged before the Court of Justice, which ensures that E.C. law is interpreted uniformly throughout the Community. E.C. law overrides national law when they are in contradiction.

THE LEGISLATIVE PROCESS IN THE EUROPEAN COMMUNITY Stages in the Decision Making Process

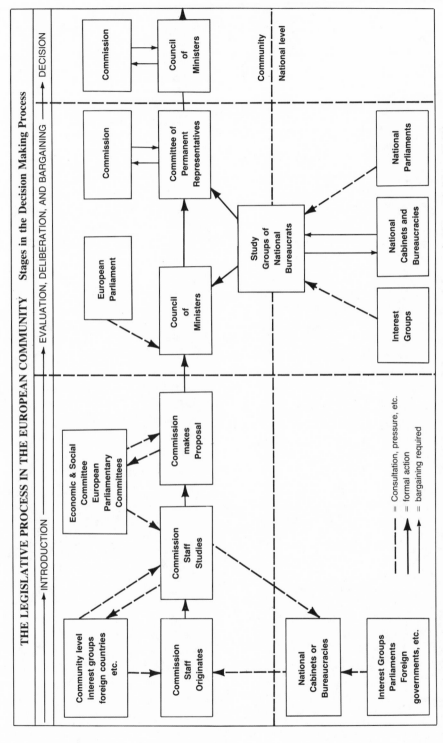

Source: "Demystifying the E.C. Institutions," *Europe: Magazine of the European Community,* No. 29 (Nov. 1989).

Guide to the Compendium

Organization

The entries in this volume offer the most recent information taken from contemporary practices, official documents, news releases, and formal conferences. This book opens with an Introduction describing the European Community structure. A reader unfamiliar with the institutions of the E.C. may wish to first scan these pages. A Chronology of the European Community since 1957 closes the book.

Alphabetization

Subjects are presented alphabetically, word-by-word, e.g.,

COST   Costa Rica
cost savings   costs of non-Europe

Some compound terms are inverted and entered under their most distinctive component. For example, Consultative Committee for Coal and Steel is alphabetized under Coal and Steel, Consultative Committee for; likewise, the Standing Committee on Employment is found under Employment, Standing Committee on.

Entries containing mutual concepts are usually grouped for comparison. For example, following the entry for agriculture, one would find

agriculture, Common Agricultural Policy (CAP)
Agriculture 1980
agriculture, processing and marketing
agriculture, production grouping
agriculture, right of establishment

Entries

The current popular subject is usually given as the principal entry, with other terms cross-referenced to it. Some entries have been included for historical significance, even though they are no longer in common use.

Cross-References

Cross-references run from the general to the specific. Occasionally SEE references from the specific to the general are used to inform the user of subjects related to particular entries. The use of CF. suggests subjects to be compared with the original entry.

Synonyms

The phrase SYNONYMOUS WITH following a description does not imply that the entry is exactly equivalent to the principal topic under which it appears. Frequently, the subject only approximates the primary sense of the original entry.

A

AASM The Associated African States and Madagascar. These were the 18 states associated with the E.E.C. under the Yaoundé Convention in 1963. They were formerly dependent territories that had gained independence since the signing of the Treaty of Rome. *See* YAOUNDÉ AGREEMENTS.

abattement forfaitaire *Synonymous with* MONTANT FORFAITAIRE.

Abnormal Occurrence Reporting System (AORS) *See* NUCLEAR ENERGY.

Academy of Science, Technology and Art As proposed by the Commission, it would be an institution with international influence dedicated to highlighting the achievements of European science and the originality of European civilization in all its wealth and diversity. As an independent body, its role would be to award prizes in the main areas of science, technology, and art and to give opinions in these fields for the different Community institutions. The Academy would be composed of personalities eminent in the various disciplines and independent from political authority. The first College would be composed of two members designated by each head of state or government. These members would themselves select their peers to make up the Academy which would comprise about 40 members. The member states, assisted by the Commission and in close cooperation with the group of the first members nominated by the heads of state or government, would draw up the framework for the organization of the Academy.

Accession, Treaty of *See* TREATY OF ACCESSION.

accident hazards *See* MAJOR ACCIDENT HAZARDS.

Accord Relatif Aux Services Occasionnels Route *See* ASOR.

Accords of Luxembourg *See* LUXEMBOURG COMPROMISE.

accountants The European Commission presented a proposal to achieve mutual recognition of qualifications for accountants. The proposal was adopted in 1978 and expanded in March 1984. It is designed to permit freedom of establishment for the self-employed in the economic, financial, and accounting areas.
See AUDITORS; WORK AND EMPLOYMENT.

acid rain The E.C. Commission issued a directive on air pollution and acid rain in December 1983. It imposes restrictions on the volume of emissions from the chimneys of large combustion plants, chiefly power plants.
See AIR POLLUTION.

ACP (states) African, Caribbean, Pacific (states). The nations from Africa, the Caribbean, and the Pacific signatory to the Lomé Conventions. The Treaty of Rome set up the mechanism for special association agreements with non-European nations and territories that had special relationships (through former empires) with the Community member nations. Sixty-six states signed the Lomé Convention that was launched in 1975 and renewed in 1984 and 1988. In July 1989, the E.C. agreed on a revised offer for a new five-year trade and aid pact (later changed to 10 years) to the ACP group of nations to replace the current Lomé Convention (Lomé III), including a plan to compensate these nations (69 by 1990) for losses in earnings from commodity exports because of world market fluctuations. On October 23, 1989, third world countries asked the E.C. to forgive $200 billion of African debt under the new Lomé Convention (Lomé IV) trade agreement to go into effect in 1990. *See* LOMÉ CONVENTIONS.

ACPM Advisory Committee on Program Management.

acquis communautaire The body of 1,000-odd regulations and directives of the European Community.

acquisitions *See* MERGERS.

Action Committee for United States of Europe (Monnet Committee) This Committee was formed in 1955 on the instigation of Jean Monnet, the distinguished French statesman, by the principal political parties and non-Communist trade unions of France, Germany, Italy, Luxembourg, Belgium, and the Netherlands. Its purpose was "to ensure the unity of action of those organizations which are its members and on the basis of those concrete achievements, progress towards the United States of Europe." It played a major role in the evolution of the Treaty of Rome and was disbanded in May 1975.

addiction *See* DRUG TRAFFICKING.

additives *See* FOOD ADDITIVES.

admission temporaire *See* ATA CARNET.

Adonnino Committee *See* CHRONOLOGY (JUNE 25 AND 26, 1984; JUNE 20, 1985) IN APPENDIX.

ADR Agreement on the International Carriage of Dangerous Goods by Road. It became effective in 1968 and was signed by 14 nations, including all E.E.C. countries. ADR ensures that dangerous goods being conveyed by road can cross international frontiers without hindrance, provided that goods are packed and labeled in accordance with the Agreement. Tanker vehicles carrying inflammable substances are subject to technical inspection.

Advanced Informatics and Medicine program *See* AIM.

advanced manufacturing equipment This refers to computer-integrated manufacturing, automation, computer-aided design, and a host of other forms of advanced technology equipment. These devices will have an impact on

the quality of production and the efficient use of Community resources in the European industrial area (see European Area of Development entry) and will advance the objectives of a prosperous E.C. Consumers and producers will be able to benefit from standardization and automation, with producers being able to lower production costs—provided they can achieve production on a continental or even a world scale.

There remains a need to make the various systems compatible through standardization of interfaces, design rules, systems architecture, and other elements making up automated systems.

advertising As declared by the Community consumer protection policy, consumers have the right to be protected from misleading and unfair advertising. Nineteen eighty nine approved legislation defines unfair and misleading advertising, and provides that the courts may, without proof of fault, demand that such advertising cease and that the offender publish a corrective statement.

It is expected that the single market of 1992 will usher in mega-Eurobrands to appeal throughout the 12 member states. Many advertising specialists believe that mass-market regional brands selling in just one or two nations will become obsolete, with international marketing and advertising as the wave of the future. Global or Pan-European campaigns will be appropriate when the same product specification is sold in each nation to the same target consumers, for the same end use, against competition that offers the same mix of advantages and disadvantages, and with a similar market maturity.

The E.C. Court of Justice decided in a 1990 case that the principles of the common market are compromised if consumers are denied the right to receive advertisements published just across the border from their country, even if the advertising contravenes national legislation.

See CONSUMER PROTECTION; TOBACCO.

advisory committee The Commission listens to the opinions of representatives of the member states. While it has promised to take the fullest account of the views expressed during these consultations, it is in no way bound by them and the committee has no influence on the further course of the procedure. The declarations annexed to the Single European Act recommend the use of advisory committees for measures relating to the completion of the internal market.

Cf. MANAGEMENT COMMITTEES; REGULATORY COMMITTEE.

Advisory Committee on Foodstuffs This Committee was established in 1970 to advise the Commission on problems relating to the harmonization of laws on foodstuffs.

See CONSUMER PROTECTION.

AELE The Association Européene de Libre-Échange.

See EUROPEAN FREE TRADE ASSOCIATION.

aeronautics *See* AIRCRAFT INDUSTRY.

aerosol An optional common standard that makes both present intra-E.C. trade in aerosols and any future E.C. environmental restrictions easier. It was adopted on May 20, 1975, by the Council of Ministers. Aerosol manufacturers whose products conform to the specification are assured that their goods will have unimpeded passage across Community frontiers. Products manufactured and sold in the same market are not affected, and products which do not conform may still be traded but run the risk of incurring bureaucratic and nontariff barriers. Aerosols conforming to Community standards carry a special sign—an inverted epsilon.

AFNOR *See* EUROPEAN STANDARDS INSTITUTE.

Africa, the Caribbean, and the Pacific *See* ACP (STATES).

aging In 1978, the Community began its first research program on the aging process, on improving heart-lung machines, and on congenital defects. It included studies on the liver, immunology, and the crystalline lens of the eye. Research into improving heart-lung machines for extending the duration of treatment during heart and lung operations was supported. The improvement of registration and study of congenital abnormalities throughout the Community was coordinated.

Agreement on the International Carriage of Dangerous Goods by Road *See* ADR.

AGREP *See* DATABASES AND DATABANKS OF THE E.C.

agriculture Some 10 million people work in agriculture either as farmers or farm workers or as processors of agricultural products, and together they produce some 3.4 percent of the wealth of the Community. Differences exist between member states, for example, 16.9 percent of the Greek national income is produced by agriculture compared with only 1.4 percent in the United Kingdom. Farming accounted for only 2.7 percent of the European economy but cost E.C. consumers and taxpayers some $93 billion in subsidy in 1989.

agriculture, Common Agricultural Policy (CAP) This critical policy was designed to improve productivity, secure fair living standards for farmers and farmworkers, stabilize markets, and secure supplies at reasonable prices for the consumer. These were the objectives set by the Treaty of Rome in 1957. CAP was adopted in January 1962 to carry out these objectives, following the recommendations of the Stresa Conference.

In 1984, the Community began to replace the system of border subsidies or levies known as MCAs (Monetary Compensatory Amounts) with a new mechanism where the MCAs were to be calculated in connection with devaluations or revaluations, on the basis of the currency revalued most. Adopted in 1985, a new policy on agricultural structures is expected to run until the middle of the 1990s. It makes allowances for the current economic and social constraints and the problems confronting European farmers, such as government subsidies, which vary considerably in the 12 member states.

The Commission set out a number of options for reform of the Common Agricultural Policy which remain "on the table." Under pressure, primarily from the United States, which insists that CAP gives unfair advantage to the E.C., debate continues well into the 1990s.

Reform of the CAP is essential before 1992 when the Single European Act's provisions take full effect. Milk quotas were introduced in 1984, and later reduced. Limits were imposed on market support (intervention) for cereals and milk products in 1986 and 1987; and in 1988, stabilizers were introduced in all market organizations, accompanied by very strict budgetary provisions. Approved in June 1989, the Community's farmers will follow the 1989–1990 agricultural prices. These entail a two percent sugar price cut (instead of the proposed five percent) and a slight tightening on cereal prices.

The CAP today consumes some 70 percent of the E.C. budget and through its complicated network of protection, price supports, and subsidies, it has created large surpluses of many agricultural products. E.C. export subsidies, used to dispose of some of these surpluses, have helped to create an unstable market in agricultural commodities. Sales to nonmember nations increased more than fourfold from 1973 to 1984 on commodities produced by nearly 10 million farmers and farm workers within the Community. Over the years, E.C. products benefiting from the CAP have displaced some U.S. farm exports. The 1992 single market program however, will have only a small direct effect on the CAP. Indirectly, the impact will come as other sectors seek funds to ease the adjustment brought about by the program. An E.C. budget package adopted in the winter of 1987, aimed at balancing the budget and reducing growth in agricultural expenditures over the next four years, resolved short-term budgetary problems by basically resorting to supply management techniques. While the package may reduce agricultural oversupply within the E.C. and help limit new pressure on international agricultural markets, it does not contribute significantly to the fundamental reform needed to create a system where farmers produce in response to market signals. The global reform of agricultural policies remains a U.S. objective and a major task of the current round of multilateral trade negotiations.

See BUDGET; FARM FUND; FINANCE; FISH; FRAUD; MAXIMUM GUARANTEED QUANTITY; STRESA CONFERENCE; SUBSIDIES.

Agriculture 1980 *Synonymous with* MAN-SHOLT PLAN.

agriculture, processing and marketing Assistance comes from the Farm Fund under the Common Agricultural Policy, assuming that projects are part of national or regional programs.

See AGRICULTURE, COMMON AGRICULTURAL POLICY; FINANCE; FRAUD.

agriculture, production grouping Subsidies for established producer cooperatives exist for certain products, e.g., fruits and vegetables, hops, and for certain areas where cooperative development is inadequate. Subsidies come from the Farm Fund and may, in general, be granted equivalent to three percent in the first year, two percent in the second year and one percent in the third year of the value of products placed on the market.

See AGRICULTURE, COMMON AGRICULTURAL POLICY; FINANCE.

agriculture, right of establishment A series of directives, initially adopted by the Council of Ministers in 1963, established the right of workers in one member state to work in agriculture, including forestry and horticulture, in other member states. These directives cover employed and self-employed persons, and include the right to transfer holdings, the right of access to farmers' cooperatives, and the right to the same services accorded to nationals, including access to credit and various other forms of government assistance.

AIDS *See* DRUG TRAFFICKING.

aid to developing countries Financial assistance is available for developing nations under the Community's Generalized System of Preferences, and a large number of developing countries benefit from trade and cooperation agreements with the Community.

See EXTERNAL TRADE; FINANCE.

AIM Advanced Informatics and Medicine (Advanced Information in Medicine). The E.C. launched AIM in 1987 to sustain qualitative growth in health care in the Community for the 1990s by exploiting the potential of medical and bio-informatics within economically acceptable limits. The projects center around research on medical databases, work stations, artificial intelligence, and fast or parallel information processing.

air cargo In the spring of 1990, the Commission drafted a regulation to cover the air cargo services sector, providing for free access to the market for every Community operator and fixing criteria and procedures for air cargo tariffs within the Community. Under the regulation, member states would allow air traffic rights to be exercised between state airports without discrimination. Therefore, transporters would be able to change aircraft in an airport according to their requirements.

airbus *See* AIRCRAFT INDUSTRY.

aircraft industry A consortium of aerospace companies from France, Britain, Spain, and West Germany that has become the world's No.2 manufacturer of passenger aircraft. Programs exist for European aircraft and air transport industries, and for aeronautical research. In 1978, the European Commission urged the development of European aircraft based on the Airbus. In June 1988, the E.C. announced a major research drive in aviation technology covering both civil and military aeronautics. Research began in 1990 following a two-year pilot phase.

The E.C. aeronautics industry has grown in 15 years from a world market share of five percent to 25 percent. In March 1989, the E.C. approved a West German subsidy package for the European Airbus that could increase the United States' frustration over government aid for the aircraft project. In addition, Europe is home to six of the world's eight major commuter aircraft manufacturers.

See ARIANESPACE, AIRLINE SECTOR, AIR TRAFFIC CONTROL.

airline sector In 1987, the E.C. agreed to liberalize air transport somewhat and to push for increased freedom before 1992. In July 1988, the E.C. Commission adopted three competition regulations laying down strict new conditions for various types of agreements in the air transport sector. They relate to commercial agreements between airlines such as coordination of capacity and schedules of revenue pooling, computer reservation systems operating in the Community, and the provision of ground handling services at airports. In April 1989, the European Court of Justice ruled that almost all pricing contracts between airlines, including routes within the 12 member nations and to non-European Community destinations, could violate European competition rules. In July 1989, the E.C.'s Ministers of Transport proposed the second phase of deregulation that would give airlines wider latitude in fare pricing and prohibit E.C. members from limiting routes to only one of their national carriers. Other provisions would give airlines increased freedom to compete for market share and start new routes. E.C. members would be prevented from refusing traffic rights in the E.C. to their own airlines, if the carrier meets the financial and technical standards to fly. In addition, the number of routes that two airlines from each country would be able to serve would increase. Furthermore, the complicated ticket price plan would be scrapped for a more liberal system in which any nonpredatory air fare would be allowed unless it was vetoed by the governments on both ends of the route.

Also in 1989, the E.C. transport ministers, in an attempt to lower air fares, proposed a system that would reduce a Community nation's share from the current 40 percent to 25 percent in relation to the total number of seats available on a given European route. In December 1989, transport ministers approved guidelines allowing carriers more freedom to set fares and secure market share after 1992. The 12 ministers also said states shouldn't be allowed to refuse traffic rights in the E.C. to their own airlines and that exemption to E.C. antitrust rules granted to airlines should come to an end. The guidelines would permit airlines to fly to other E.C. states via intermediate stops in third E.C. nations. The new rules would also abolish by 1993 anti-competitive arrangements between governments. The ministers also agreed that final regulations should permit airlines more freedom to establish themselves in other E.C. nations, and that from July 1, 1992, governments should not discriminate against their own airlines, applying both to a nation's smaller airlines and to subsidiaries of other E.C. carriers.

In March 1990, the Commission said it would seek rules to protect consumers caught by overbooking of flights from E.C. airports. The Commission suggested airlines should first seek volunteers to abandon seats in return for a transfer to another flight and a financial incentive. In addition, the E.C. plans to harmonize and restrict airline pilots' working hours. New regulations, proposed in the spring 1990, if accepted, would limit pilots to flying eight hours a day, 72 hours in any 28-day period, 200 hours a quarter and 720 hours a year. The new limits would be applied even to non-E.C. airlines, but only when they are flying between points within the 12 member states.

Europe's top 10 Airlines are:

Airlines*	Passengers carried in 1988	Miles flown
British Airways	22.5 million	35.3 billion
Lufthansa (W.Germany)	17.8 million	21.1 billion
Air France	14.8 million	21.3 billion
Iberia (Spain)	14.5 million	12.7 billion
SAS (Scandinavia)	13.3 million	8.7 billion
Alitalia (Italy)	9.2 million	9.7 billion
Swissair	7.1 million	8.9 billion
Olympic Airways (Greece)	6.7 million	4.7 billion
KLM (The Netherlands)	6.2 million	14.5 billion
JAT (Yugoslavia)	3.9 million	3.4 billion

*Association of European Airlines

See AIRCRAFT INDUSTRY; AIR TRAFFIC CONTROL; TRANSPORT.

air pollution The Community adopted its first legislation designed to reduce or avoid pollution of the environment, in 1972; other environmental measures have subsequently been adopted.

See ACID RAIN; CAR POLLUTION; ENVIRONMENT; PCBs; VEHICLES.

air traffic control In September 1989, 21 European airlines proposed an air traffic control system throughout Europe to replace the national systems now in place. The present fragmented approach, based on 22 national air traffic control systems with 42 control centers, is costly and inefficient. The new system could mean direct savings of $500 million a year at present air traffic levels and $800 million a year when future growth is considered.

See AIRLINE SECTOR.

air transport See AIRLINE SECTOR; TRANSPORT.

Albania This nation is a member of the Council for Mutual Economic Assistance.

See COUNCIL FOR MUTUAL ECONOMIC ASSISTANCE.

alcohol See EXCISE DUTIES.

Algeria This nation has had a cooperation agreement with the Community since January 1976.

See MAGHREB AGREEMENT; MEDITERRANEAN POLICY; MNCs.

Alliance for Progress This agreement was signed in 1961 at Punta del Este by 20 American States, giving a more comprehensive institutional expression to the attempt by the United States to stimulate economic cooperation in Latin America through multilateral assistance. This was the goal of the Inter-American Development Bank founded in 1958.

Andean Pact An association of five countries—Bolivia, Columbia, Ecuador, Peru, and Venezuela—signatory to a cooperation agreement with the E.C. The Pact was designed to promote closer trade and economic ties. The five countries have agreed to encourage regional economic development in Latin America by merging their economies. The Pact provides a framework for industrial, scientific, and technical cooperation between the two parties.

See LATIN AMERICA.

Andorra In 1990 for the first time in 700 years, Andorra signed an international treaty. The treaty, made with the E.C. makes the territory a member of the E.C. customs union, allowing industrial goods to freely flow between Andorra and the E.C. Andorra will apply the E.C.'s external tariffs on such goods to third countries.

Angola The nation has observer status with the Council for Mutual Economic Assistance.

See COUNCIL FOR MUTUAL ECONOMIC ASSISTANCE.

animal health and meat inspection A 1968 resolution established the basic policy for the adequate protection of animal and human health within the Community. It secures the free movement of animals and animal products (including meat) and identifies common measures to combat disease. Approved legislation covers internal E.C. trade in fresh meat from domestic animals.

In the field of veterinary controls, further harmonization of national laws and regulations on essential veterinary requirements are needed for the single market of 1992. This harmonization must reach the point where it is possible for animals and animal products, destined for export across the Community's internal frontiers, to be controlled and certified at the point of departure, requiring no further inspection. This certification would then be accepted throughout the Community. Intra-Community trade across borders of animals and animal products would thus become equivalent to national trade in these products. Imports from non-E.C. countries would, upon arrival at a Community border, be checked to ensure compliance with Community regulations. Once certified, these products would then be able to move within the Community in the same way as any other Community product. The areas covered are: transport of animals, embryos of farm animals, trade in shellfish, labeling rules for food, game and game meat, trade in horses, live poultry and eggs, trade in dogs and cats, and the extension of Community rules to the national markets.

Numerous directives dealing with the protection of animal and human health have been issued. They include:

(1) a 1985 directive on hygiene in fresh meat;
(2) a 1985 directive on the harmonization of health requirements for heat-treated milk;
(3) a 1985 directive on the harmonization of health requirements for egg products;
(4) three 1985 directives on improving hygiene in establishments where fresh meat, poultrymeat, and meat products are handled;
(5) a 1985 directive on measures for the control of foot-and-mouth disease, Aujesky's disease, and swine vesicular disease;
(6) 1985 directives on proper training of personnel for carrying out health inspections; on public health and animal health problems affecting the impor-

tation of meat products from third countries; and on harmonizing requirements for producing and marketing minced meat;
(7) 1985 and 1988 directives on restricting the use of hormones for the fattening of livestock;
(8) a 1986 directive to eradicate brucellosis, tuberculosis, and leucosis in cattle;
(9) a 1986 directive on the spread of animal disease of semen in pigs and cattle;
(10) a 1986 directive concerning the examination of animals and fresh meat for the presence of residues;
(11) a 1986 directive on free competition in the keeping and rearing of farm animals;
(12) a 1986 directive on facilitating the import of glands and other organs, including blood, for the pharmaceutical processing industry;
(13) a 1987 directive on elimination of classical swine fever from the Community;
(14) a 1987 directive on heat treatment of pork products;
(15) a 1987 directive on harmonizing the pedigree requirements of cattle and their semen for breeding purposes;
(16) 1987 directives on harmonizing standards for breeding pigs and for breeding sheep and goats.

A proposed directive would harmonize health requirements to prevent the consumption of fish and fish products contaminated by nematodes. In 1989, the E.C. announced an 18 to 24 month moratorium on the use of the controversial hormone bovine somatotropin (BST) which can boost cows' milk production as much as 25 percent.

See AGRICULTURE, COMMON AGRICULTURE POLICY; FEEDINGSTUFFS.

animal testing *See* COSMETICS.

Annecy Round *See* GENERAL AGREEMENT ON TARIFFS AND TRADE.

annual accounts *See* BANKING; INSURANCE.

annual general meetings *See* PUBLIC LIMITED COMPANIES.

annual report As required by the Merger Treaty, a General Report on the activities of the European Communities must be published annually in the Community languages for Presentation to the European Parliament in the first half of the month of February.

Antarctica Territory *See* OCT.

anthem *See* SYMBOLS.

anti dumping policy *See* DUMPING.

Antigua *See* CARIBBEAN BASIN.

antitrust policy *See* COMPETITION POLICY.

AORS (Abnormal Occurrence Reporting System) *See* NUCLEAR ENERGY

Apollo In 1985, the E.C. Commission and the European Space Agency joined forces to develop a high-speed document delivery system allowing the rapid transmission of long-data messages throughout Europe by using a new European communications satellite. The system allows about 10 information sources to provide documents rapidly to a large number of widely distributed users throughout Western Europe.

Arab League On December 21, 1989, the E.C. and 22 members of the Arab League decided, after a six-year lull, to resume a formal dialogue on political, economic, technical, social, and cultural issues.
See NEAR EAST.

architects The Council of Ministers in 1978 was set to accept an updated 1967 European Commission proposal on the freedom of architects to practice their profession anywhere in the Community, subject to minimal training requirements and mutual recognition of qualifications as applies to other professions. The proposal was finally adopted in 1985.
See WORK AND EMPLOYMENT.

Argentina Imports into the Community from this nation are subject to Community commercial rules dealing with third (non-E.C.) nations. A nonpreferential trade agreement went into effect on January 1, 1972. Negotiations between the E.C. and Argentina, with a view to the conclusion of a classic trade and economic cooperation agreement, began on January 11, 1990.
See LAFTA; LATIN AMERICA.

Arianespace (Ariane) This is an 11-nation European launch consortium. In 1980, it created the world's first commercial space transportation company from a consortium of 36 European aerospace and electronics houses, 13 major banks, and the French Space Agency.
By 1989, Ariane had launched 58 satellites.
See AIRCRAFT INDUSTRY; EUROPEAN SPACE AGENCY.

ARION The aim of the ARION program is to improve the knowledge of each of the E.C. member states' education systems by fostering exchanges between persons designated by education authorities at national, regional, or local levels. Study visits of one week are organized for small groups from different member states.
See EURYDICE.

arms legislation A proposal for a Council directive on the control of the acquisition and possession of weapons was submitted in 1988. Its purpose is to abolish controls on the possession of weapons at intra-Community frontiers. It does not affect the right of member states to take other measures to prevent illegal trade in weapons.
See CONTROL OF INDIVIDUALS.

arsenic *See* TOXIC EFFLUENT.

Article 100A This article is part of the 1986 Single European Act that amended the Treaty of Rome. It is the legislative heart of 1992 because it permits rule by "qualified majority," meaning 54 votes out of the total of 76 of the European Council, eliminating the prior unanimous vote requirement.
See SINGLE EUROPEAN ACT.

Article XXXV It is the Article in the General Agreement on Tariffs and Trade whereby, at the time of accession, the acceding nation can elect not to apply the General Agreement in its relations with any other contracting party. Similarly, any contracting party can invoke this Article against any newly acceding nation.
See GENERAL AGREEMENT ON TARIFFS AND TRADE.

artists In 1977, the E.C. Commission proposed a plan to improve the plight of impoverished artists. The plan, never adopted, attempts to encourage trade in art works by simplifying requirements so that artists would not have to engage agents to help them in other nations. There are proposed tax reforms geared to an artist's income. The E.C. has requested a system of royalties for duplication of works through modern techniques such as photocopy and recorders. Improvements were suggested for social security and unemployment benefits, aid for young artists and craftspeople seeking training in other states, and development of cultural exchanges.

Arusha This city in Tanzania is the center of a coffee-growing area and headquarters of the East African Community. The Arusha E.E.C. Convention was signed there in 1969.
See EAST AFRICAN COMMUNITY.

Arusha Convention This is a four-year agreement of association between the E.E.C. and Kenya, Uganda, and Tanzania that was signed on September 24, 1969. Its provisions were similar to those in the Yaoundé agreements except that there is no arrangement for development and the preferential agreement for E.E.C. goods is more limited. The Agreement terminated in 1975 and was replaced by the Lomé Convention.

asbestos In June 1983, the E.C. Employment Ministers adopted new E.C.-wide rules designed to protect workers from exposure to asbestos, a fire-proof material linked to various forms of cancer. This regulation requires firms producing or processing asbestos to provide their workers with protective masks and clothing if the amount of asbestos fibers in the air exceeds certain set levels. In addition, new rules require workers to undergo annual medical checks to detect any harmful effects from their exposure to asbestos. It places stiff limits on the maximum airborne concentration of "blue asbestos" fibers permitted in the workplace, but establishes a wider tolerance for other varieties.
See CHEMICALS.

ASEAN *See* ASSOCIATION OF SOUTH EAST ASIAN NATIONS.

Asian nations *See* ASSOCIATION OF SOUTH EAST ASIAN NATIONS.

ASOR (Accord Relatif Aux Services Occasionnels Route) The agreement on the international carriage of passengers by road by means of occasional coach and bus services.

assembly *See* EUROPEAN PARLIAMENT.

association agreement This agreement was concluded in the early years of the E.E.C. with Greece, Turkey, Cyprus, and Malta. It was designed to accommodate the economies of signatory countries with the Community Customs Union and Common Customs Tariff (CCT), pending full Community membership at a future time.

Association Européene de Libre-Echange *See* EUROPEAN FREE TRADE ASSOCIATION.

Association of South East Asian Nations (ASEAN) Indonesia, Malaysia, the Philippines, Singapore, and Thailand formed an association in 1967, agreeing to work together to accelerate economic growth, social progress, and cultural development, and to promote peace and stability within the area. The Community in 1979 formed a cooperation agreement with ASEAN to consolidate, deepen, and diversify commercial relations between the two regions, and to provide for a Joint Cooperation Committee to supervise and promote a variety of activities. It was the first time the Community had signed such an agreement with a Third World regional unit. Agreements with India and Pakistan were extended to cover economic and development cooperation, the first in 1981 and the second in 1986. The Sultanate of Brunei joined in the agreement on January 7, 1984. In 1984, E.C. imports from ASEAN were 9,662,000 ECU and E.C. exports to ASEAN were 9,886,000 ECU. The percentage of manufactured products in ASEAN exports to the Community had risen to 46 percent by 1982 from 25.4 percent in 1973 (Japan remains the EC's principal trading partner, followed by the United States). The rate of growth in the value of exports from the ASEAN nations to the Community was 139 percent over the period from 1978 to 1984. The volume of E.C. Asian imports and exports (including Japan) reached $70 billion in 1988, a 10 percent increase over the previous year's levels. Exports to the E.C. constitute two-thirds of that figure, resulting in trade deficits.

See CHINA, SOUTH ASIAN DELEGATION.

ASSUC (Association des Organisations Professionnelles de Commerce des Sucres pour les pays de la CEE) The Association of Sugar Trade Organizations for the E.C. Countries.

ATA (Admission temporaire) carnet This is an international customs temporary importation document that is used for exhibits for international trade fairs, samples, and professional equipment. It can be used in all E.C. member nations and many other countries in Europe.

Athens European Council See CHRONOLOGY (DECEMBER 4–6, 1983).

audio-visual policy The single market of 1992 will introduce the prospect of a Europe without frontiers, opening up the audio-visual sector. The challenge is great since the film and television industries of E.C. member nations have all developed in an essentially national, if not State framework. The 1992 goal of the Commission is to have a European audio-visual space without frontiers in which producers would be able to work on a European scale and in which consumers would have the widest possible choice, both in terms of quality and quantity. New measures include those designed to create a truly common audio-visual market by eliminating existing obstacles and those designed to promote the European technical and cultural content of the emerging market without frontiers. A directive on "television without frontiers" is designed specifically to allow for free circulation of programs from one Community country to another within the framework of the internal market, to promote European production and employment in the sector, and to help audio-visual enterprises adjust to the strong growth in demand resulting from technological developments.

In 1988, the European Cinema and Television year, a European Academy of Cinema and the Audio-Visual Arts was established. During that year plans were made for drawing up a European charter for the audio-visual industry emphasizing the political and dem-ocratic aspects of the rights of creators, and for encouraging the production of the first high-definition television programs, to enable creativity to keep up with technology. In March 1989, broad agreement was reached on common standards for television broadcasting in the satellite era. The accord sets curbs on pornography, violence, and racism, and seeks, where practical, to devote a majority of air time to European programs. While member states can show as many commercials as they want in programs broadcast in their own country, advertising is limited to no more than 15 percent of daily transmission time for cross-border transmissions. On June 14, 1989, the plan for "television without frontiers" fell apart after 6 of the 12 member countries refused to accept it at a meeting in Luxembourg, although curbs on pornography, racism, and violence in domestic and cross-border television broadcast and restrictions limiting advertising to 15 percent of transmission time were approved.

In October 1989, the E.C. approved a measure to create a single market in TV broadcasting with more than $254 million to be provided over five years for audiovisual projects. The E.C. ministers also approved the "Television Without Frontiers" directive which takes effect in October 1991 aimed at allowing E.C. television stations to broadcast without restrictions throughout the Community. The same directive also establishes a single set of rules governing TV advertising. The directive has drawn criticism from the United States because it recommends that television stations devote a majority of their broadcasting time to programs made in the E.C. This recommendation is not legally binding.

See MEDIA, TELEVISION.

auditors A 1978 Commission proposal for harmonizing the minimum qualifications required of auditors who audit the annual accounts of limited liability firms in Community nations was adopted in 1978 and expanded in March 1984. It specifies the content of the qualifying examination, and includes provisions to permit individuals already practicing as auditors but who do not fulfill conditions set down in the draft directive to be exempted from passing the examination of competence.

See ACCOUNTANTS; COMPANY LAW; WORK AND EMPLOYMENT.

Aujesky's disease *See* ANIMAL HEALTH AND MEAT INSPECTION.

Australia When the United Kingdom joined the E.C. in 1973 it resulted in the termination of Commonwealth Preferences (reduced taxes for products from Commonwealth nations imported by the U.K.) and subjected Australian products to levies and quotas under the Common Agricultural Policy. In 1981–82 Australia's main exports to the Community were wool, iron ores, and coal. In September 1980, agreement was reached by both parties on an arrangement for annual self-limitation by Australia of sheepmeat exports to the Community, fixed at 17,500 tons as of January 1, 1981, in exchange for a reduction of the Community's tariff duty. In one year some 15 percent of total Australian mineral and energy exports went to the E.C.

See AGRICULTURE, COMMON AGRICULTURAL POLICY; GENERAL AGREEMENT ON TARIFFS AND TRADE; PACIFIC RIM.

Austria This nation is a founder member of the European Free Trade Assocation (EFTA). A preferential agreement establishing a free-trade area between the E.C. and Austria went into effect in January 1973. Austria's long-expected application for European Community membership was made in July 1989, with formal talks not to begin until after the internal market barriers are eliminated by the end of 1992. Austria's economy is closely tied to the E.C., with 66 percent of the country's exports going to Community nations and 70 percent of its imports coming from them. Austria's 1988 exports to the E.C. were worth $20 billion and its imports about $27 billion.

automation *See* ADVANCED MANUFACTURING EQUIPMENT.

automobile *See* CAR INDUSTRY; CAR PRICES; JAPAN.

aviation *see* AIRCRAFT INDUSTRY.

B

Bahamas One of the ACP states that is a signatory to the Lomé Convention of 1988.

See CARIBBEAN BASIN.

Bahrain Its imports are subject to Community commercial rules pertaining to third (non-E.C.) nations.

See GULF COOPERATION COUNCIL.

Baker Doctrine On December 12, 1989, U.S. Secretary of State James Baker urged a strengthened E.C. to act in partnership with the United States. He outlined a concept of a new Europe and a new Atlanticism.

balanced response *See* LOMÉ CONVENTIONS.

bands *See* VALUE ADDED TAX.

Bangladesh The nation entered into a non-preferential commercial cooperation agreement with the Community in 1976 and signed a bilateral agreement in 1977 on the restriction of textile exports to the Community. The E.C. is Bangladesh's principal trading partner. In 1979, it took some 32 percent of the country's exports.

See NON-ASSOCIATED STATES.

Bank for Europe First proposed by French President Mitterrand at the European Parliament October 25, 1989, meeting in Strasbourg to channel development money to Eastern Europe. The institution, which would function along the lines of the Asian Development Bank or the Inter-American Development Bank, would have capital of about $10 billion and would be controlled by the governments of the 12 E.C. nations. The Bank would lend money for development projects and help provide technical expertise. On December 9, 1989, the E.C., meeting in Strasbourg, approved in principle the formation of a Bank for Europe.

See EASTERN EUROPE.

Bank for International Settlements (BIS) An international institution founded in Basel (Basle), Switzerland, in 1930. BIS is designed to foster cooperation among world central banks, to seek opportunities for development of financial activity among governments, and to serve as an agent involving the transfer of payments.

banking The E.C. Council of Finance Ministers adopted a directive in November 1977 (First Banking Coordination Directive) on the coordination of laws and policy over banking and credit institutions. This was seen by international banking executives as the first step toward a common market for banking. This proposal, first made in 1974, provided procedures for financial institutions and their subsidiaries in other member states, rules for monitoring their solvency and liquidity, and standards for third country credit institutions. By 1992 various directives will be in place to prepare the Community for new banking procedures and regulations. These will include: a directive on the coordination of laws, regulations, and administrative provisions relating to the reorganization and winding-up of credit institutions operating in several member states; establish a directive on common standards for the "own funds" (funds which are the property of a bank and are used by regulatory bodies in calculating the bank's lending level) of authorized credit institutions for the purpose of supervision by the regulatory authorities; a directive concerning the introduction of deposit guarantee schemes in the Community to establish harmonized minimum requirements for such schemes and encourage the introduction of deposit guarantee schemes by all member states; and a directive on the freedom of establishment and the free supply of services in the field of mortgage credit across frontiers and to improve cooperation between supervisory bodies in the member states.

The E.C.'s Second Banking Coordination Directive, adopted on December 15, 1989, allows banks in one European country freedom to do business in any other E.C. member state, with the introduction of a single banking license. It remains conditional on setting common capital-adequacy rules which will require E.C. banks to have capital equivalent to eight percent of risk-weighted assets. The license would be granted by the banking regulators in the country in which a bank is incorporated and it would enable the institution to operate E.C.-wide, either through foreign banks or simply by selling banking services across national frontiers. Private customers and companies would be able to open bank accounts throughout the E.C. with banks of their choosing. The freedom granted by the single banking license covers not just lending money, but also leasing, fund management, mortgage lending, money brokering, and trading in securities. This directive was approved by the E.C. in June 1989. In April 1989, the E.C. adopted a less protectionist approach to granting access to American and other foreign banks. The E.C. called for allowing a foreign bank to start doing business in Europe so long as the bank's home country gives European banks the same rights it gives its own banks. The concept of "home authorization" is the core of the banking directive that permits a bank, once licensed to do business in its home country, automatically to be allowed to do business in any other part of the E.C. In Madrid, at the end of June 1989, the 12 agreed that by July 1, 1990, they would broaden the European Monetary System, to coincide with an end to exchange controls and obstacles to community-wide banking, securities, and insurance operations.

The dawning of the single market is forcing the banking industry to develop new strategies, with talk of mergers, alliances, and takeovers, which will in time lead to a new breed of superbanks. The borders that once protected national banking giants in West Germany, France, and Britain will be abolished, clearing the way for invasion by the Americans and Japanese. The single market year of 1992 promises a greater upheaval in banking than in other businesses in Europe. The opening of competition across product and geographic lines will squeeze margins faster than business will grow. By far, the greatest changes will come in retail banking, which presently provides as much as 65 percent of European bank profits and has so far served to subsidize the deregulated free-for-all of wholesale and investment banking. Most experts believe that Europe, with 20 percent more bank branches and only half the deposits per capita as the United States is overbanked. When completed, the number of European commercial banks may be halved, down to about 800. Eventually, Europe will be dominated by 15 groups made up of the 22 European banks now ranked in the world's top 50. On December 15, 1989, E.C. Finance Ministers approved the last step for creating a single banking license to allow a bank licensed in one Community nation to open as many branches as it would like anywhere within the Community. At its semi-annual European Council meeting held in Strasbourg, the E.C. leaders agreed to hold a special conference in 1990 to deal with the questions of a central bank and a common currency. As a result of the Second Banking Coordination Directive adopted in December 1989 producing the emergence of a unified banking market in the Community, member states must transpose the directive into national law within specific time limits. National laws implementing the Second Directive must be in place at the latest by January 1, 1993. January 1, 1991, is the deadline for implementing the directive fixing the solvency ratio of credit institutions. The Solvency Ratio directive provides for a weighing of assets and elements not included in the balance sheet of credit institutions in accordance with the degree of credit risk and an 8 percent ratio which will lead the institutions in question to strengthen their capital level, and thus provide improved consumer protection through better banking sector supervision.

See CAPITAL ADEQUACY DIRECTIVE; CENTRAL BANK, CHRONOLOGY (JANUARY 13, 1988; DECEMBER 8–9, 1989); EUROPEAN CURRENCY UNIT; EUROPEAN ECONOMIC UNITY; INTERBANK AGREEMENTS; LEASING; MADRID MEETING.

bankruptcy There are conditions under which a firm's financial position is such as to cause actual or legal insolvency. The E.C. developed a preliminary draft of a Convention of Bankruptcy, Winding-up Arrangements, Composition and Similar Proceedings, that was issued by the European Commission in 1970. It comprises a set of rules dealing with jurisdiction and applicable law to enable the insolvency laws of member nations, although different, to operate in harmony. It was revised in 1979.

See COMPANY LAW; HARMONIZATION; WORK AND EMPLOYMENT.

banks *See* BANKING; CAPITAL, FREE MOVEMENT OF; FINANCIAL SERVICES; MADRID MEETING.

BAP (Biotechnology Action Program) Research within the E.C. extended to cover new areas such as the study of protein structures, the application of biotechnology to industrial micro-organisms, *in vitro* methods of analyzing the pharmacological and toxiocological properties of molecules, and the identification of risk due to genetic manipulation. BAP also encourages the development of the infrastructure for biotechnological research in Europe.

See BIOTECHNOLOGY.

Barbados One of the ACP states that is a signatory to the Lomé Convention of 1988. A Protocol annexed to the Convention protects its sugar exports to the Community.

See CARIBBEAN BASIN; SUGAR.

Barre Plan One of the steps toward economic and monetary union within the E.E.C., it was presented to the Council of Ministers in February 1969 by Raymond Barre, then vice-president of the E.E.C. Commission. The Plan advocated that each member nation undertake to place part of its reserves at the disposal of the other members so that, should difficulties arise, any member could call on its partners for assistance up to a fixed amount. Then joint consultations would occur to re-establish equilibrium. If no agreement could be reached the indebted nation would have to repay the borrowed funds within a three-month period, but should agreement occur this would lead to medium-term assistance.

At the same time, there would be a move towards greater alignment of economic policies of the member nations involved. It advanced the concept that negotiations and arrangements were to be between the central banks rather than with governments. The Plan was approved by the Council of Ministers in July 1969.

barriers *See* COSTS OF NON-EUROPE; MARKET INTEGRATION; EUROPE WITHOUT FRONTIERS.

base agreement *See* EUROPEAN MONETARY UNION.

basic price The price fixed each year under the Common Agricultural Policy's method of price supports applying to fruits, vegetables, and pork. Once the average market price is below the basic, or cost of production price, action is taken to support the market by buying up surplus output.

See INTERVENTION PRICE, TARGET PRICE.

Basic Research in Industrial Technologies for Europe *See* BRITE.

basket of currencies *See* UNITS OF ACCOUNT.

Basket Units of Account *See* UNITS OF ACCOUNT.

Basle credits European and certain other central banks gather regularly at Basle for Bank for International Settlement meetings. This term is applied to the ad hoc mutual arrangements between central banks for rendering each others foreign exchange assistance.

See BANK FOR INTERNATIONAL SETTLEMENTS.

bathing waters *See* BEACHES; ENVIRONMENT; MARINE POLLUTION.

BCR (Bureau Communautaire de Reference). A five-year program initiated in 1988 in an attempt to improve the reliability of chemical analyses and physical measurements (applied metrology) so as to achieve agreement of results in all member states. Research deals with the analyses of food and agricultural products, environment-related analyses, biomedical analyses, analyses of metals, and applied metrology.

14

beaches In 1975, Community legislation was adopted setting a 10-year period in which to ensure that all Community bathing waters are free of pollutants that are deemed to be harmful to health, such as sewage, pesticides, and most detergents. Exceptions are granted where bathing is prohibited, or where geographical or natural soil conditions have created unique problems. The directive required that member nations inform the European Commission by the end of 1979 of the beaches falling within the boundaries of the law.

See ENVIRONMENT; WATER.

beef and veal Under the Common Agricultural Policy or common market rules of 1968, regulations contained a guide price for producers. An intervention agency assisted when market prices fell to 90 percent of the guide price. In 1974, a system of seasonal payments for beef cattle began in an effort to encourage more orderly marketing. There are customs duties of 16 percent on imported live cattle, and of between 20 and 26 percent on imported beef, depending on types. Levies are fixed each week, comprising the difference between the imported price (plus duties) and the guide price.

See REFERENCE PRICE; GUIDE PRICE.

beef mountain *See* MOUNTAIN.

beer Following protests by some member states that a proposal for harmonization was "taken to an extreme," a proposal to introduce Community standards for beer was withdrawn in 1976. Later other proposals were introduced to permit consumers to have a larger choice in buying beer, so that no nation would be able to ban the import of beers from another member state if Community standards were met.

See CONSUMER PROTECTION; INDUSTRIAL STANDARDS.

BEI (Banque Européene d'Investissement) *See* EUROPEAN INVESTMENT BANK.

Belgium This nation signed the Treaty of Paris (E.C.S.C.) in 1951, the Treaties of Rome (E.E.C. and Euratom) in 1957, and the Treaty of Brussels (Treaty of Accession) in 1972. The headquarters of the European Commission is located in the Belgian capital, Brussels. The Belgians are the world's biggest per capita exporters, with U.S. companies accounting for 23 percent of all of its exports and directly or indirectly providing work for about 10 percent of the total labor force. Belgium only attracts about five percent of new American investment, down from seven percent in 1980. Economically, Belgium is stronger than at any time since the mid-1970s, with business investment and its stock exchange flourishing. In 1988 the real economic growth of 4.2 percent, together with an inflation rate of only 1.2 percent, mark the best results achieved by Belgium in 12 years. Most impressive has been the dramatic growth in business investment, which soared by more than 20 percent in 1988 with projections for a continued investment prosperity.

Belgo-Luxembourg Economic Union *See* BLEU.

Belize This nation is a former U.K. overseas territory included in the Lomé Convention.

See ACP (STATES), CARIBBEAN BASIN.

Benelux An acronyn, formed from Belgium, the Netherlands, and Luxembourg. It is used to describe the customs union of these nations and applies to their concerted actions. A customs union between the Kingdom of Belgium and the Grand Duchy of Luxembourg was concluded at Brussels on July 25, 1921, and ratified on March 5, 1922; the customs frontier between the two countries was abolished on May 1, 1922. The union was dissolved in 1940 but reestablished on May 1, 1945. A customs union was signed on March 14, 1947, between Belgium and Luxembourg and the Netherlands. The total union became effective on January 1, 1948, and is known as the Benelux Economic Union. A joint tariff was adopted but import licenses were still needed. A total economic union came into practice on November 1, 1960.

See MESSINA CONFERENCE.

Benelux Economic Union *See* BENELUX.

Benin This nation was formerly the Republic of Dahomey and a French West African Territory. It was a signatory to the Yaoundé Agreements, and is now a signatory to the 1988 Lomé Convention. Benin is one of the ACP states.

BEP (Biomolecular Engineering Program) A Community Research effort, especially in genetic engineering, encompassing the body of techniques which enable the genes determining certain properties of living organisms to be identified, isolated, transferred, and expressed in other organisms.

See BIOTECHNOLOGY.

BERD European Bank for Reconstruction and Development.

See EUROPEAN DEVELOPMENT BANK.

Bermuda A United Kingdom dependency that is subject to U.K participation with the E.C.

Berne Union
(1) An international copyright convention ratified in 1886. It provides copyright protection to literary or artistic works published in a nation signatory to the Convention.
(2) A Union established in 1934, with 26 member nations, to work for "the international acceptance of sound principles of export credit and investment insurance."

BIAC Business and Industry Advisory Committee. The joint management and trade union advisory body in association with the OECD (Organization for Economic Cooperation and Development).

See COMMON DECLARATION OF EUROPEAN BUSINESSES.

bicycles The E.C. in 1989 began a campaign to encourage the building and use of bicycles, noting that this means of transportation would help reduce noise and air pollution, lessen traffic jams, conserve energy and natural resources, and improve the health of its citizens.

BIE *See* BRITAIN IN EUROPE.

biomolecular engineering In December 1981, the E.C. Council of Ministers adopted a $7 million five-year program to encourage innovations in agri-food products through a Community-wide research and development program. The program included suggestions to improve patent laws to better protect European inventors; harmonize members' regulations covering pharmaceuticals and chemicals; and ameliorate the negative effects of certain E.C. policies—for example, the Common Agricultural Policy hampers market access by E.C.-based biotech firms selling agri-food products.

biotechnology The Council of Ministers in the summer of 1988 approved an amendment to the research and training program in this field, increasing funding by 20 million ECU through the end of 1989. This increase, in small part, allowed Spain and Portugal to join the program and permitted greater assessment of the risks such research involves and enabled researchers to process more data electronically.

In April 1989, the Commission passed guidelines that would regulate the research and marketing of certain gene-spliced products. Each of the 12 states have until October 1991 to pass implementing legislation. In the spring of 1990, E.C. environmental ministers adopted two pieces of legislation designed to protect the environment and to assure a single unified market for biotechonology. The two directives—*Contained Use of Genetically Modified Microorganisms* and *Deliberate Release to the Environment of Genetically Modified Organisms*—introduce regulatory oversight of both experimental and commercial operations that use organisms created by genetic modification. The new laws cover, respectively, activities where modified bacteria are intended to be kept under physical containment, and activities where modified bacteria are intended to be used in the open environment. In addition, the new laws oblige firms to assess the risk their organisms pose to the environment and to follow appropriate approval procedures for experimental work, industrial production, and marketing of these products.

See BAP; BEP; BIOMOLECULAR ENGINEERING; BRIDGE

Biotechnology Research for Innovation, Development, and Growth in Europe. *See* BRIDGE.

birds *See* WILDLIFE.

BIS *See* BANK FOR INTERNATIONAL SETTLEMENTS.

BRIDGE (Biotechnology Research for Innovation, Development, and Growth in Europe) A 1989 biotechnology program to promote cross-border research for the purpose of speeding up the production of biological data, materials, and processes necessary for the optimal use of natural organisms. In addition, BRIDGE will establish Community regulations for biotechnology.

Bleeping *See* EUROPEAN RADIO MESSAGING SYSTEM.

BLEU Belgo-Luxembourg Economic Union. Founded in 1921, BLEU was intended to integrate the two diminutive economies of Belgium and Luxembourg. It includes a common currency, a common economic policy, the elimination of internal trade barriers, and the formation of a common external tariff wall. Although modified twice to accommodate the Benelux customs union and the E.C., BLEU still exists as Europe's most complete economic union.

block exemptions Acting under the Council of Ministers, the E.C. Commission identifies broad categories of agreements that may be exempt from the ban on restrictive trade agreements. Such agreements are known as block exemptions.

blue asbestos *See* ASBESTOS.

Blueprint for Cooperation *See* SINGLE EUROPEAN ACT.

BN Brussels Nomenclature.
See BTN.

Bolivia This nation has an agreement on trade with the Community on hand-made products.
See ANDEAN PACT; LATIN AMERICA.

bonds *See* CAPITAL, FREE MARKET OF; EUROPEAN CURRENCY UNIT BONDS; FINANCIAL SERVICES.

border checks *See* VALUE ADDED TAX.

Botswana One of the ACP states, this nation is a signatory to the Lomé Convention of 1988.

bovine somatotropin *See* ANIMAL HEALTH AND MEAT INSPECTION.

branches, bank *See* BANKING.

Brazil This country is the Community's largest export market in Latin America. In 1968 it took 23.3 percent of the Community's exports to that region, principally machinery and transport equipment. The E.C. is Brazil's largest export market accounting for nearly 30 percent of its exports.
See LAFTA; LATIN AMERICA.

bread A 1973 draft directive from the Commission would have ensured that certain types of bread baked according to Community composition and rules could be sold through the Community. It was rejected in December 1976.
See CONSUMER PROTECTION.

Bretton Woods A resort in the White Mountains of New Hampshire where the United Nations Monetary and Financial Conference convened in 1944. Those assembled agreed to establish the International Monetary Fund and the International Bank for Reconstruction and Development, also known as the World Bank. Articles of agreement were adopted by the international monetary conference of 44 nations. The Fund's major responsibility is to maintain orderly currency practices in international trade, while the Bank's function is to facilitate extension of long-term investments for productive purposes. Periodic meetings are held at Bretton Woods to amend the original agreement.

Britain In Europe (BIE) The pro-Common Market "umbrella" organization that is active in the United Kingdom referendum campaign.

BRITE Basic Research in Industrial Technologies for Europe. A four-year program begun in 1985 to increase the use of advanced technologies in the traditional sectors of industry. Research is designed to be precompetitive in nature, with commercial product development being left entirely to industry. Present projects cover a wide range of industrial sectors and technical disciplines, often making surprising use of techniques developed in one area to make new applications in another. A few key technological fields (including laser technology, membrane science, catalysis, and particle technology, new material joining techniques, and so on) have been priorities. Under the first phase of the BRITE program, 1,000 firms, research centers, and universities have worked on 200 projects. The second phase, begun in 1989, combines BRITE with the EURAM program, dedicated to new materials development. BRITE/EURAM is a four-year program that seeks to use E.C.'s resources efficiently to support industrial research and development at the precompetitive stage and within the framework of Europe-wide collaboration. The program has been allocated $722 million until 1992.

British dependent territories As stipulated in the Treaty of Accession, all British dependent territories except Gibraltar and Hong Kong were offered association with the E.E.C. under Part IV of the Treaty of Rome.

British Standards Institution *See* BSI.

broadcasting *See* AUDIO-VISUAL POLICY; TECHNOLOGIES; TELEVISION.

brokerage *See* SECURITIES.

BROKERSGUIDE *See* DATABASES AND DATABANKS OF THE E.C.

brucellosis *See* ANIMAL HEALTH AND MEAT INSPECTION.

Brunei A former U.K. overseas dependency, this nation is covered by the Lomé Convention of 1988.
See ASSOCIATION OF SOUTH EAST ASIAN NATIONS.

Brussels The capital of Belgium and the administrative center of the European Communities.

Brussels Tariff Nomenclature *See* BTN.

Brussels, Treaty of *See* TREATY OF ACCESSION.

BSI The British Standards Institution. It is the official organization for the preparation of national standards in the United Kingdom. BSI cooperates with other national organizations in preparing recommendations for common standards.
See EUROPEAN STANDARDS INSTITUTE.

BST *See* ANIMAL HEALTH AND MEAT INSPECTION.

BTN Brussels Tariff Nomenclature. Established in 1950, it is the system for the standard classification of goods for custom tariff purposes used by the majority of nations. In 1987, the E.C. Council of Ministers adopted a new harmonized system of customs classification replacing the BTN. The new system has been used since then in the Community and other nations around the world. The new system also serves as the basis of the integrated Community tariff known as TARIC, which was introduced in January 1988.
See NIMEXE.

budget The E.C.'s budget is controlled jointly by the European Parliament and the Council of Ministers. Each calendar year the Commission prepares a preliminary budget, which the Council and Parliament then consider in two readings. Community expenditure is classified as either "compulsory" or "noncompulsory." According to the Treaty of Rome, compulsory expenditure is "expenditure necessarily resulting from this Treaty or from acts adopted in accordance therewith"; all other expenditure is noncompulsory. The European Parliament has the power to reject the budget as a whole. Within the budget, it has the last word on noncompulsory expenditure, while the Council has final word on compulsory items. Usually, in the exercise of these powers, a wide measure of agreement is needed between the two. Also, in addition to responsibility for the final adoption of the budget, Parliament gives the Commission the ultimate authority to spend money. Parliament can influence only the noncompulsory expenditure. The bulk of the Community's revenue is composed of customs duties and agricultural levies charged on imports of products from nonmember countries, and a proportion of member states' VAT receipts— up to the equivalent of a one percent rate— with more than 90 percent of revenue distributed to the member states. Its expenditure on administration and staff accounts for between five and six percent of the budget.

The Court of Auditors, established in 1977, keeps a close watch on the implementation of the budget. At the Stuttgart compromise meeting in 1983 and Fontainebleau summit of June 1984 the Council of Ministers approved agreement on budgetary imbalances and the financing of the 1984 budget. At 45 million ECU, the 1989 E.C. budget represents scarcely 1 percent of the combined gross national product of the 12 member states. In February 1988, agreement evolved on budgetary reform to allow the Community to have additional resources (1) to enable it to meet the obligations arising from the Single European Act establishing the large market of 1992; (2) to gradually double the European structural Funds (social, regional, and agricultural); and (3) to spread more fairly the burden of financing the Community.

For 1989, the General Community Budget was forecast as:

Customs duties	9,954,000 ECU	22.2%
Agricultural levies	2,462,000 ECU	5.4%
VAT	26,219,000 ECU	58.5%
GNP resource	3,907,000 ECU	8.7%
Miscellaneous	274,000 ECU	0.6%
Balance from previous financial year	2,025,000 ECU	4.5%
total	44,841,000 ECU*	

*representing 1.03 % of Community GNP

The Community can no longer be concerned with agriculture alone. Budgetary reform has introduced a more equitable distribution of expenditure in preparation for the internal market of 1992. Budgetary appropriations for new policies envisaged by the Single European Act (structural activities, research, internal market, environment), account for 24 percent of total expenditure and are programmed into the 1988–1992 financial projections. The reform provides the Community with sufficient resources to implement its policies, with prudent limits extending until 1992. The mechanisms employed take account of the economic situation of the member states and allow for a more equitable distribution of the burden of financing the Community budget.

See CHRONOLOGY (JUNE 25–26, 1984), COST SAVINGS.

Budgetary Policy Committee of the E.C. Founded in 1964, its meetings are attended by senior officials of member countries. In-

formation on each nation's forthcoming budget is exchanged at these sessions.

budgetary procedures The E.C. procedures are defined in Articles 202–205 of the Treaty of Rome.

See BUDGET; EUROPEAN PARLIAMENT; POWERS OF INVESTIGATION.

bulbs and cut flowers When placed for sale, bulbs and flowers are subject to Community quality standards, requiring that they be fresh, free from defects, parasites, and residues, and must be properly packaged and marked.

See AGRICULTURE, COMMON AGRICULTURAL POLICY.

Bulgaria This nation is a founder member of the Council for Mutual Economic Assistance. It has a bilateral agreement on textiles with the Community. Events of the fall 1989 may significantly alter Bulgaria's relationship with the E.C. Negotiations for a trade and cooperation agreement began in April 1989, but were interrupted. New informal discussions began in December 1989. Bulgaria has also asked to benefit from the E.C. system of generalized preferences.

See CHRONOLOGY (APRIL 1989); COUNCIL FOR MUTUAL ECONOMIC ASSISTANCE; EASTERN EUROPE.

Bulletin of the European Communities This monthly periodical is published in the official languages of the Community. It records the activities of the Community and supplements the Annual Report. The Bulletin is designed for a wide readership in government departments, universities, the press, political groups, employers' and workers' associations, and other organizations. It is purchased on subscription.

Bureau Communautaire de Référence *See* BCR.

Burundi This country is one of the ACP states and a signatory to the Lomé Convention of 1988.

See ACP (STATES).

Business and Industry Advisory Committee *See* BIAC.

Business Cooperation Center This center was established in 1974. It concentrates on a limited number of sectors, essentially construction and related industries, transport, processed chemicals, furnishings, and plastics. The Center is allowed to take the initiative in contacting firms rather than waiting to be approached, and it extends its activities to non-E.C. countries in certain circumstances. Its role is to facilitate contacts between small- and medium-sized businesses, which do not have the market research facilities of large companies, in search of joint ventures, tie-ups, or takeovers.

Synonymous with MARRIAGE BUREAU.

See SINGLE EUROPEAN ACT; SMALL BUSINESSES.

butter   This product is subject to Common Agricultural Policy legislation and price support for milk items.

See DAIRY PRODUCTS; MILK AND MILK PRODUCTS; MOUNTAIN.

butter mountain   *See* DAIRY PRODUCTS; MOUNTAIN.

Buy Europe   *See* PUBLIC WORKS CONTRACTS.

C

cabinet Within the E.C., each Commissioner has his or her own Cabinet, a group of chosen advisers, usually of the same nationality. The Cabinet is headed by a Chef-de-Cabinet. It acts as a liaison between the Commissioner and colleagues in the Commission and as a general secretariat.

See EUROPEAN COMMISSION.

cabotage *See* TRANSPORT.

CACM *See* CENTRAL AMERICAN COMMON MARKET.

CACTUS An E.C. project that is testing the feasibility of developing a computerized data based on import and export regulations in order to assist E.C. traders.

CADDIA (Cooperation in the Automation of Data Documentation for Import/Export and Agriculture). The Commission pioneered an action plan, launched in 1985, aimed at replacing paper documentation with more efficient and cost-effective electronic data interchange. This E.C. project is designed to establish the infrastructure and data-processing hardware needed to provide the E.C. with the information essential for the smooth functioning of the customs union and the common trade policies.

See HARMONIZED COMMODITY DESCRIPTION AND CODING SYSTEM; SINGLE CUSTOMS DOCUMENT; TEDIS; TELECOMMUNICATIONS.

cadmium *See* TOXIC EFFLUENT.

Cairns Group *See* GENERAL AGREEMENT ON TARIFFS AND TRADE.

Cameroon This country is one of the ACP states and a signatory to the Yaoundé Conventions of 1963 and 1969 and the Lomé Conventions of 1984 and 1988.

Canada In 1976 the Community and Canada concluded a framework agreement for commercial and economic cooperation. This non-preferential agreement establishes mechanisms for cooperation in areas such as trade, industry, and science.

Canary Islands On January 17, 1990, the Commission adopted a paper proposing three possible scenarios for future relations between the Community and this archipelago which had refused total integration with the Community during Spanish accession.

cancer An agreement in principle in June 1985 resulted in a European program against cancer to determine how a substantial number of cancers can be avoided and to publicize the fact that early detection of some types of cancers can lead to a better chance of cure. By the year 2,000 the aim is to reduce mortality from cancer in Europe by 15 percent. A European Code Against Cancer has been approved by health ministers of the 12 member states. Posters, television programs, and a cartoon character called Euro-Jim are used to spread the message through the 12 E.C. member states in an anti-cancer campaign. Nineteen eighty-nine was designated as the "European Information on Cancer Year" and included plans to train health-care workers and to boost cancer research. In the summer of 1989 the Commission adopted a proposal for a 1990–1994 action plan to strengthen and continue the activities of the first action plan (1987–1989) in the fields of prevention, information, health education, and training in the medical professions.

See ASBESTOS; PCBs.

CAP (The Common Agricultural Policy) *See* AGRICULTURE, COMMON AGRICULTURAL POLICY.

Cape Verde This nation is one of the ACP states and a member of the Lomé Convention of 1988.

capital This is the amount invested in a venture; a long-term debt plus owners' equity; the net assets of a firm, partnership, and so on, including the original investment, plus all gains and profits.

capital adequacy directive In the spring of 1990, the Commission proposed a directive on the minimum capital requirements of investment firms wanting to operate throughout the E.C. The new capital adequacy directive would apply to all firms that carry out financial investments on the behalf of clients, including banks or specialized securities houses, dealers, brokers, or investment managers. The directive calls for a basic capital requirement of at least 500,000 ECU for investment institutions. For firms that act as agents or portfolio managers, but do not hold trading positions of their own, member states could reduce the requirement to 100,000 ECU. For institutions that are not authorized to hold customers' money or securities (nor to act as a market maker) the requirement could be reduced to 50,000 ECU. Investment advisors are not treated as investment firms for the purposes of this directive. The directive ensures a high level of consumer protection by requiring all investment service businesses to maintain a safety net of "own funds" equal to one quarter of their previous year's overhead. For banks, banking supervisors would be able to apply the existing eight percent solvency ratio to all the bank's activities, or they could separate their investment trading books from other activities and subject them to the investment services' capital adequacy provisions.
See BANKING.

capital, adequacy rules *See* BANKING.

capital, free movement of Under Articles 67–73 of the Rome Treaty member nations shall, in the course of a transitional period and to the extent needed for the proper functioning of the Common Market, gradually abolish as between themselves restrictions on the movement of capital belonging to individuals living in member nations and also any discriminatory treatment based on the nationality or place of residence of the parties or on the place in which such capital is invested. Current payments connected with movements of capital between member nations are freed from all restrictions not later than at the termination of the first stage of the transitional period. Member nations must grant in the most liberal manner possible such exchange authorizations as are needed following their ratification of the Treaty. By 1992 the Community expects a strengthening of the European Monetary System, the harmonization of national supervisory structures to facilitate complete freedom for financial services, measures to combat tax evasion, and the implementation of the full liberalization of capital movements.

In 1986, a directive reduced from four to three the number of categories of capital movements. This list includes, besides direct investments or investments in real estate made since 1960, all credits related to commercial transactions, the purchase of shares and bonds, and the admission of a company's securities to the capital market of another Community member state. In June 1988, finance ministers of the Community agreed on a timetable for progressive removal of all the remaining restrictions on the movement of money in or out of their countries. By July 1, 1990, the richer eight E.C. nations are to abolish capital controls, when all the E.C. nations are committed to repealing any restrictions on the movement of capital within the 12 member states. By 1992, the four poorer states are due to do the same thing.
See COMPETITION POLICY; FINANCE; FINANCIAL SERVICES; HOT MONEY; TRADEMARKS; WHITE PAPER.

capital gains *See* TAX BARRIERS.

carcinogens *See* PCBs.

Caribbean Basin The E.C.'s relationship with the countries of the Caribbean Basin is governed by several distinct agreements. Thirteen Caribbean countries—Antigua, Bahamas, Barbados, Belize, Dominica, Grenada, Guyana, Jamaica, St. Christopher, St. Lucia, St. Vincent, Suriname, Trinidad and Tobago—are partners of the Community under the Lomé Convention. The five countries of Central America—Costa Rica, El Salvador, Guatemala, Honduras, and Nicaragua—and Panama have an Economic Cooperation Agreement with the E.C.

car industry The E.C. automobile industry accounts for one-third of world output and nearly 10 percent of E.C. industrial production and employs some 10 million people. Demand for cars rose by six percent in 1987 and by four percent in 1988. Automobiles are the only manufacturing industry where the European market is the largest in the world: automobiles account—directly or indirectly—for more than 8 percent of total European manufacturing output and close to 11 percent of total manufacturing-related investment. On December 6, 1989, the Commission announced that it would push to remove all internal E.C. trade barriers on automobiles by the end of 1992. The Commission also called for restraint from Japanese manufacturers of automobiles. Britain, France, Italy, Spain, and Portugal presently limit imports of Japanese cars. Removal of quotas will start in 1991 and end at the close of 1992.

In March 1990, the E.C. Environment Commissioner proposed regular, mandatory checks on vehicles' catalytic converters. Industry estimates project a market of 20 million vehicles with converters by the mid-1990s.

See CAR PRICES; HARMONIZATION; JAPAN; TRUCK INDUSTRY.

car pollution In June 1989, the E.C. adopted the pollution standards used in the United States for small cars sold in its 12 member nations. It will become compulsory on July 1, 1992, for new models and on December 12, 1992, for existing models. The Community has already adopted pollution limits for medium-sized and large cars. Cars will be fitted with catalytic converters and electronic fuel-injection systems. The pollution standards were set at 19 grams a test for carbon monoxide and 5 grams a test for hydrocarbons and nitrogen oxide.

In May 1990, the E.C. proposed tougher emissions standards for trucks (trucks can cause 10 times more pollution than other forms of transport) that would cut pollution from such vehicles by up to 60 percent.

See LEADED GASOLINE; VEHICLES.

car prices In 1985, the E.C. Commission adopted new legislation that guarantees the right to buy a car in any E.C. member state and goes some way towards reducing price differentials for cars in different E.C. countries. Car prices vary by as much as 30 percent for the same car in different states. The E.C. regulation, effective July 1985, is designed to rationalize existing car manufacturers' distribution systems by giving them certain exemptions from E.C. rules on restrictive practices. In return, the firms will have to supply any car ordered, whether left- or right-hand drive, at reasonable prices.

See CAR INDUSTRY.

carryover of losses This is an E.C. method to harmonize and liberalize member-state laws governing the carry-over of losses because of its effect on the investment capability and competitiveness of businesses. A firm can choose from one of two alternative approaches. The first is that losses from a given financial year may be offset against the profits of one or more of the three preceding financial years. If not completely offset in this way, the balance may be set against the profits of the following financial years in chronological order. The second alternative is that the loss may be offset against the profits of the following financial years in chronological order.

See TAXATION.

cartel A group of separate business organizations formed to regulate competition by influencing prices, production, or marketing.

Cassis de Dijon case This 1979 European Court of Justice case developed from difficulties by a German firm wishing to import Cassis liqueur into West Germany. Cassis is a low-proof blackcurrant liqueur that does not meet the requirements of German law that only drinks containing at least 32 percent of alcohol by volume can be sold as liqueurs. The European Court of Justice concluded that an importing Community country cannot justify prohibiting the sale of a product from another Community nation simply on the ground that the way the manufacturer nation applies regulations affecting consumer protection is different from that imposed on a domestic product. The Court believed that the idea of the Euro-product, i.e., Euro-beer,

Euro-loaf, was negated. No longer will member states be able to keep out competing products from other member states because they are slightly different from their own.

See NON-TARIFF BARRIERS TO TRADE.

castor beans A product having an annually fixed target price set by the Council of Ministers. The difference between the market price and the target price is payable to oil mills. To receive this price support payment, the mills must meet the requirement that a contract be concluded with producers, who must receive a specified guaranteed minimum price.

See TARGET PRICE.

catalytic converters *See* CAR INDUSTRY.

cats *See* ANIMAL HEALTH AND MEAT INSPECTION.

Cayman Islands These islands are a U.K. dependent territory and are covered by the Lomé Conventions.

See OCT.

CBR
(1) *See* COMMON BUREAU OF REFERENCES.
(2) *See* COMMUNITY BUREAU OF REFERENCE.

CCC *See* CONSUMER CONSULTATIVE COMMITTEE.

CCITT (Comité Consultatif International Télégraphique et Téléphonique) (The International Telegraph and Telephone Consultative Committee). It is a committee of the International Telecommunications Union (ITU) with responsibility for public telecommunication services standardization.

CCT *See* COMMON CUSTOMS TARIFF.

CEC The Commission of the European Communities.

See COMMISSION, THE.

CECA Communauté Européenne du Charbon et de l'Acier.

See EUROPEAN COAL AND STEEL COMMUNITY.

Cecchini Report Paolo Cecchini headed a team of researchers who produced "The European Challenge—The Benefits of a Single Market," published in 1988. They showed that the failure to achieve a single market within

the E.C. has been costing European industry millions in unnecessary costs and lost opportunities. The study identified what will be achieved by the 1992 program through cutting out red tape, breaking down protectionism, and removing blocks on cross-border activities.

See COSTS OF NON-EUROPE; INTERNAL MARKET.

CECUA The Confederation of European Computer User Associations. It is an independent consultative and advisory body to the E.C.

CEDEFOP *See* EUROPEAN CENTER FOR THE DEVELOPMENT OF VOCATIONAL TRAINING.

CEEA (Communauté Européenne de l'Énergie Atomique) *See* EUROPEAN ATOMIC ENERGY COMMUNITY.

CELEX *See* DATABASES AND DATABANKS OF THE E.C.

cellular phones *See* TECHNOLOGIES.

CEN (Comité Européen de Normalization) *See* EUROPEAN COMMITTEE FOR STANDARDIZATION.

CENELEC (Comité Européen de Normalisation Électrotéchnique) *See* EUROPEAN COMMISSION FOR ELECTROTECHNICAL STANDARDIZATION.

Center for European Policy Studies (CEPS) Launched in 1982, CEPS is an E.C. "think tank" dealing with a range of policy-oriented research programs falling into three broad categories: economic and social affairs, foreign policy and security questions, and political and institutional problems. The center's regional groups cover the United States, Canada, Japan, Latin America, ASEAN, and the African, Caribbean and Pacific countries linked to the E.C. through the Lomé Convention. It chooses its researchers and academics from all over the world.

Center for Research and Documentation on the European Community (CERDEC) Situated at the American University in Washington, D.C., CERDEC sponsors courses on the Community for undergraduate and graduate students interested in European development.

Central African Empire This nation is one of the ACP states and a signatory to the Yaoundé Conventions of 1963 and 1969 and the Lomé Convention of 1988.

Central America In 1979, 39 percent of the Community's banana imports and 17 percent of its coffee imports derived from the region. The Community in 1985 signed a five-year cooperation agreement with the countries of the Central American isthmus agreeing to grant each other most favored-nation trade status, to cooperate in technological, agricultural, industrial, and other fields, and to promote European investment. In 1989, the Commission allocated six million ECU for small- and medium sized industries in Central America to assist the region in its drive for regional integration. The E.C. announced in April 1990 plans to increase its aid to Central America by half. The E.C. now gives Central America about 100 million ECU ($120 million) a year.

See CENTRAL AMERICAN COMMON MARKET; LATIN AMERICA.

Central American Common Market (CACM) Guatemala, Honduras, Nicaragua, and El Salvador signed the General Treaty of Central American Economic Integration on December 13, 1960, with Costa Rica joining in 1962. This Treaty established a number of measures aimed at an eventual economic union, namely the establishment of a common customs tariff (in 1988, more than 90 percent complete), a degree of unity in productive investments, and the coordination of economic policies and monetary schemes.

central bank A banker's bank. This bank holding institution is the main body of bank reserves of a nation and the prime reservoir of credit (e.g., Bank of England, Bank of France). On December 8, 1989, leaders of the E.C. agreed to call a special conference for 1990 that will make economic and monetary union possible with the establishment of a Central Bank of the E.C. This has been opposed by British Prime Minister Margaret Thatcher.

See BANKING; DELORS COMMITTEE; EUROFED; MADRID MEETING.

Central Banks, The Committee of Governors of Established with advisory status by the Council of Ministers on May 8, 1964, its aim is to facilitate cooperation among the Central Banks of the member nations. It is composed of Central Bank Governors. The Commission, though not a member, is invited to send a representative. It has no decision-making power with the E.C., but is involved in the preparation of all decisions and resolutions of the Council of Ministers concerning monetary policy and the proper functioning of the E.C. exchange system.

The full economic and monetary union of Europe awaits the formation of a European central bank and the free use of the European Currency Unit by companies, banks, and consumers in all 12 E.C. member states. This would involve setting up a system along the lines of the U.S. Federal Reserve System. The common central bank would be run by a board of independent members, but would make market intervention and system financing decisions jointly with representatives of the 12 national central banks, which would become the equivalent of the U.S. regional reserve banks. As proposed, but bitterly fought by some member states, the 12 nations would also agree to accept as legal tender in addition to their own national currencies, the ECU, currently a theoretical basket of currencies, but with a central bank coordinating these multiple currencies.

In April 1989, the E.C. released a report urging that the Community members harmonize their economic and monetary policies before they move closer toward forming a European central bank. Instead of setting a deadline for the establishment of a central bank, it left it to government officials in the 12 member nations to decide how fast to move toward this goal.

See EUROPEAN CURRENCY UNIT; EUROPEAN ECONOMIC UNITY; FINANCIAL SERVICES; MADRID MEETING.

Central Europe *See* EASTERN EUROPE.

CEPS *See* CENTER FOR EUROPEAN POLICY STUDIES.

CEPT (Conférence Européenne des Administrations des Postes et des Télécommunications, The European Conference of Postal and Telecommunications Administrations).

See TELECOMMUNICATIONS.

CERD *See* COMMITTEE FOR EUROPEAN RE-SEARCH AND DEVELOPMENT.

CERDEC *See* CENTER FOR RESEARCH AND DOCUMENTATION ON THE EUROPEAN COMMUNITY.

cereals Under the Common Agricultural Policy, there are marketing arrangements for cereals and their annual fixed price levels. A target price is determined for each type of cereal based on the level expected by producers in the open market where grain will be in shortest supply. The price is not an on-farm price, but a price when delivered. Levies are determined daily in Brussels for bridging the gap between import prices and the threshold price, and are payable as each cargo arrives at an E.C. port to ensure that Community prices are not undercut. Grain not sold on the home market is usually exported and export subsidies or export restriction payments can be paid from the E.C.'s Farm Fund to cover differences when world prices are below Community prices. When world prices are higher than those in the Community, levies are imposed on cereal exports.

See AGRICULTURE, COMMON AGRICULTURAL POLICY, FARM FUND, INTERNATIONAL WHEAT AGREEMENT; MAXIMUM GUARANTEED QUANTITY; PLANT HEALTH CONTROLS; SUGAR; THAILAND.

CERN Centre Européen de Recherches Nucléaires, The European Organization, formerly Council, for Nuclear Research, based in Geneva. It's European Laboratory for Particle Physics is a 14-nation research project that has built the world's largest atom smasher, the 17-mile-long Large Electron-Positron Collider, at a cost of $700 million.

certificates *See* STANDARDS.

certification Products satisfying specified tests are awarded certificates.

See CONFORMANCE TESTING; INFORMATION TECHNOLOGY; STANDARDS.

CET The Common External Tariff.
See COMMON CUSTOMS TARIFF.

CFCs Chlorofluorocarbons.
See ENVIRONMENT.

CFP The Common Fisheries Policy.
See FISH.

Chad This nation is one of the ACP states and a signatory to the Lomé Convention of 1988.

Channel Islands These Islands have free trade in agriculture and industrial goods between themselves and E.C. members, as agreed upon under the Treaty of Accession. The Islands are exempt from other E.C. rules and regulations, including VAT, free movement of labor, freedom of establishment, and competition policy.
See MAN, ISLE OF.

Charlemagne Prize The Commission of the European Communities won the 1969 international Charlemagne Prize for outstanding services to European unity. It was the first time since the city of Aachen (W. Germany) introduced the prize in 1950 that it had been awarded to an institution and not to an individual.

Charter of Basic Social Rights *See* SOCIAL CHARTER.

Charter of Tourism Rights *See* TOURISM.

cheese *See* DAIRY PRODUCTS; MILK AND MILK PRODUCTS; INDUSTRIAL STANDARDS.

cheese war The E.C., bowing to U.S. government requests, temporarily suspended export refunds on Guryere and Emmenthal cheese bound for the U.S. market. The suspensions, on April 23, 1975, were the last in a complex series requested by the United States following the Commission's February 5 reintroduction of export refunds on certain cheeses destined for U.S. markets. The refunds had been suspended in July 1974 after a U.S. complaint that E.C. export refunds had caused a large loss in U.S. domestic cheese sales.

chef-de-cabinet *See* CABINET.

chemicals The Community first adopted a directive on the classification, packaging, and labeling of dangerous substances in 1967. It has been amended nine times, with other directives passed in the 1970s. The White Paper timetable for 1992 provides for amendments in directives to take into account recent technical advances. Examples of new or amended directives include those covering polychlorinated biphenyls and terphenyls and asbestos within the directive that restricts the marketing and use of dangerous substances and preparations; the classification, packaging, and labeling of dangerous preparations; and detergents and fertilizers. In December 1988, the E.C. Commission fined most major European chemical companies for fixing prices and arranging to share markets.

See DETERGENTS; ENVIRONMENT; PCBs.

Chernobyl nuclear accident *See* NUCLEAR ENERGY.

chicory *See* COFFEE AND CHICORY.

children The E.C. Commission announced on May 7, 1987, a campaign to prevent the deaths of thousands of children in home accidents each year. The new program, aimed particularly at those in charge of children, is designed to warn people of the dangers of accidents in a bid to cut injuries and deaths by 10 percent to 20 percent a year.

Chile This country has an agreement with the Community on trade in hand-made products.

See LAFTA; LATIN AMERICA.

China (People's Republic of) The Community, acting on behalf of the Nine (the six original members, plus Denmark, the Irish Republic, and the U.K.), developed guidelines that led to negotiations for a trade agreement between China and the Community. The negotiations began on January 30, 1977, and the trade agreement was signed on April 3, 1978, effective June 1, 1978. A textile agreement sets out a five-year framework for imports into the Community of Chinese textiles and garments of cotton, wool, or synthetic and artificial fibers.

Overall trade between the Community and China doubled between 1975 and 1979. In 1975 total trade between China and the E.C. amounted to 1.8 billion ECU with a balance of 486 million ECU in favor of the Community. By 1981, trade had risen, to 4.2 billion ECU and the balance had swung in China's favor with a net surplus of 390 million ECU. In 1985, trade passed 10 billion ECU, with a huge leap in European exports, almost doubling 1984 exports, and giving the E.C. a

surplus of 2.7 billion ECU. China's exports to the E.C. represents only 1.3 percent of the Community's external trade.

A nonpreferential agreement, which defines a number of rules aimed at development of trade was signed in 1985 with the E.C. The Committee on Development and Cooperation of the European Parliament concluded in 1986 that "a fair and consistent" policy of cooperation with China "is a positive option for the future from the point of view of both East-West and North-South relations." The Community's and China's two-way trade has increased substantially and become more balanced after 1987. By the late 1980s long-term agreements on trade in textile products had also been concluded.

The E.C. imports more manufactured items from China than any other industrial nation. In 1987, the E.C. Commission's announcement that it intended to open an office in Beijing illustrates the growing importance of trade between the E.C. and China. E.C.-Chinese trade has risen fourfold since 1978, when it stood at $3 billion. Yet investment by the E.C. in plants and equipment represents only $2 billion of the $25 billion by all foreign investors in 1988. Since the turmoil in China in the spring of 1989 the E.C. and member states are likely to be more cautious in the future. At its Madrid meeting in June 1989, the 12 European leaders issued a special statement expressing dismay at China's execution and repression of political dissidents. These leaders announced a series of new reprisals against Beijing, including a suspension of military cooperation and arms sales.

See ASSOCIATION OF SOUTHEAST ASIAN NATIONS; PACIFIC RIM.

chips *See* COMPUTERS.

chlorofluorocarbons *See* ENVIRONMENT.

chocolate *See* COCOA AND CHOCOLATE.

Christian Democratic Parties, Federation of In April 1976, delegates of seven of the nine E.E.C. nations, representing thirteen Christian Democratic and centerist parties, met in Brussels and agreed to establish the "European People's Party—Federation of Christian Democratic Parties of the European Community." Its principal goal was the preparation for direct elections to the European Parliament.

cigarettes *See* EXCISE DUTIES.

CIRD *See* RESEARCH AND DEVELOPMENT INTERSERVICE COMMITTEE.

CIUTS *See* UNIT TRUSTS.

civil protection Since 1977 the Commission has provided emergency aid to help natural disaster victims within the Community. Between 1977 and 1987 more than 95 million ECU in relief was granted to help with earthquakes, floods, snowstorms, cyclones, and severe cold spells. In May 1987, Community civil protection cooperation began. The Community program calls for a continental-European-level strategy to include all resources for fighting disasters, the establishment of a permanent network of liaison officers, more effective use of data banks, and the holding of simulation exercises. The development of the "People's Europe" towards European Union includes an intensification of activities in the civil protection area.

See PEOPLE'S EUROPE.

classic voice services *See* TELECOMMUNICATIONS.

CMEA *See* COUNCIL FOR MUTUAL ECONOMIC ASSISTANCE.

coal *See* ENERGY.

Coal and Steel, Consultative Committee for This committee was formed in 1952 under Articles 18 and 19 of the European Coal and Steel Community treaty. It is a parallel body to the Economic and Social Committee for the two industrial sectors. It has 81 members appointed by the Council of Ministers on the proposal of the member governments. Coal and steel trade unions, employers, and users are represented. It is located in Luxembourg.

See ENERGY; EUROPEAN COAL AND STEEL COMMUNITY; FINANCE.

coal gasification *See* GAS.

cocoa and chocolate A 1973 directive defines and sets rules in respect to the composition, manufacturing specifications, packaging, and labeling of cocoa and chocolate for human consumption. The aim of the directive is to protect the consumer and to allow for free movement across the Community of cocoa and chocolate.

See CONSUMER PROTECTION.

Code against Cancer *See* CANCER.

CODEST *See* EUROPEAN DEVELOPMENT OF SCIENCE AND TECHNOLOGY.

coffee and chicory A 1977 directive is designed to protect and educate consumers and eliminate misleading sales of products. It established the rules to be observed regarding definition, composition, and substances that can be used in the manufacture of related products, packaging, and labeling.

See CONSUMER PROTECTION, FOOD.

Collective Investment In Transferable Securities (UCITS) *See* SECURITIES.

collective investment undertakings *See* SECURITIES.

Colombia A nation having a bilateral agreement with the Community on textiles.

See ANDEAN PACT; LAFTA; LATIN AMERICA.

Columbus *See* EUROPEAN SPACE AGENCY.

COMECON *See* COUNCIL FOR MUTUAL ECONOMIC ASSISTANCE.

COMETT (Community Program in Education and Training for Technology) A Community youth program that provides a favorable environment for the assimilation and diffusion of new technolgies and strengthens links between higher education institutions and the business sector. It fosters the joint development of COMETT training programs by improving the availability of training in the Community. A minimum of $258 million has been allocated by the E.C. through 1994.

See EDUCATION; ERASMUS; PEOPLE'S EUROPE; YOUTH FOR EUROPE.

COMEXT *See* DATABASES AND DATABANKS OF THE E.C.

Comité de Coordination des Industries Textiles de la CEE (COMITEXTIL) *See* COORDINATING COMMITTEE OF THE TEXTILE INDUSTRIES OF THE E.E.C.

Comité de Recherche Scientifique et Technique (CREST) *See* COMMITTEE ON SCIENTIFIC AND TECHNICAL RESEARCH.

Comité des Organisations Professionelles Agricoles de la CEE (COPA) *See* COMMITTEE OF AGRICULTURAL ORGANIZATIONS IN THE EUROPEAN COMMUNITY.

Comité Européen de Normalisation (CEN) *See* EUROPEAN COMMITTEE FOR STANDARDIZATION.

Comité Européen de Normalisation Electrotechnique (CENELEC) *See* EUROPEAN COMMITTEE FOR ELECTROTECHNICAL STANDARDIZATION.

Comité Européen de Recherche et de Developpement (CERD) *See* COMMITTEE FOR EUROPEAN RESEARCH AND DEVELOPMENT.

COMITEXTIL (Comité de Coordination des Industries Textiles de la CEE) *See* COORDINATING COMMITTEE OF THE TEXTILE INDUSTRIES OF THE E.E.C.

commercial agents A 1986 directive attempts to deal with the coordination of national legislation concerning relationships between self-employed commercial agents and their principals, including rights and obligations of a commercial agent, remuneration, and context, and termination of agency contracts.

commercial vehicle fuel *See* VEHICLE FUEL.

Commission, The (Commission of the European Communities) (CEC) The Commission originally consisted of 13 members: two each from France, the Federal Republic of Germany, Italy, and the United Kingdom; one each from Belgium, Denmark, the Irish Republic, Luxembourg, and the Netherlands. The executive and policy-proposing body of the Communities and its members must act, throughout their period in office, in full independence both of the member governments and of the Council of Ministers. The Council may not remove any member from office; the European Parliament can, should it wish, cause a vote of censure, which would compel the Commission to resign en bloc. The Commission sees to the proper functioning and development of the Common Market and has the right to initiate Community policy. Its present 17 members, appointed for four years by agreement between the governments, are entirely independent both of the governments and of the Council. The president of the Commission and the six vice-presidents are chosen nominally for two years, but their tenure has always been extended to four years. The president is nominated first, giving him or her the chance to influence the choice of fellow commissioners. The president has no power to reject a candidate nominated by a member government, nor can the president fire a colleague appointed by the Council. The Council has no power to remove the Commission from office. In performing their tasks, the Commission makes regulations, issues directives, takes decisions, makes recommendations, or delivers opinions. In E.C. and Euratom affairs they are supported by the Economic and Social Committee, made up of 189 representatives of business and labor. A Consultative Committee delivers opinions on E.C.S.C. (coal and steel) matters. The draft Community budget is established by the Council and Parliament on a proposal from the Commission. Final adoption of the budget rests with the president of Parliament. The Parliament can also reject the budget, in which case a new draft must be brought forward.

See DIRECTIVES.

Committee for European Research and Development (CERD) (Comite Europeen de Recherche et de Developpement) Established in 1973, this Committee is composed of 21 independent scientific experts selected by the European Commission to advise in setting research and development goals and priorities, taking into account the socio-economic needs of the Community.

See COMMITTEE ON SCIENTIFIC AND TECHNICAL RESEARCH; NUCLEAR ENERGY; RESEARCH AND DEVELOPMENT INTERSERVICE COMMITTEE; SCIENCE AND TECHNOLOGICAL COMMITTEE.

Committee of Agricultural Organizations in the European Community (COPA) (Comité des Organisations Professionnelles Agricoles de la CEE) A committee whose primary priority is to promote the farmers' view in the

European Community. It serves as a forum for national farming and related organizations to communicate their views and as a vehicle for processing these views to the European Commission, the Council of Ministers, and the European Parliament. Members monitor proposals or legislation affecting different commodities.

See EUROPEAN COMMUNITY; REPRESENTATIVE ORGANIZATIONS.

Committee of Permanent Representatives (COREPER) (Comité des Représentants Permanents de la CEE) This Committee attempts to ease passage of Community legislation. It consists of Permanent Representatives or Ambassadors from each member nation who, with attendant delegations, represent in Brussels a continuing national interest in the activities of the Community. It provides a means for testing national reactions to European Commission proposals and in facilitating final Council adoption of legislation.

See EUROPEAN COMMUNITY; LEGISLATIVE PREPARATION.

Committee on European Cooperation in the Field of Scientific and Technical Research (COST) (Coopération Européene dans le Domaine de la Recherche Scientifique et Technique) This Committee is composed of senior bureaucrats from 19 European countries (including non-E.C.-members) who have responsibility for scientific and technical research. An intergovernmental organization, it was established in 1971 to offer scientific and technical collaboration in specific areas, such as telecommunications, data-processing, new means of transport, oceanography, meteorology, pollution, agriculture, and food technology. COST is serviced by the Council of Ministers Secretariat with meetings held in Brussels.

See COMMITTEE FOR EUROPEAN RESEARCH AND DEVELOPMENT; COMMITTEE ON SCIENTIFIC AND TECHNICAL RESEARCH; NUCLEAR ENERGY; RESEARCH; SCIENCE AND TECHNOLOGICAL COMMITTEE.

Committee on Scientific and Technical Research (CREST) (Comité de Recherche Scientifique et Technique) This Committee was established by a Council of Ministers Resolution on January 14, 1974. Its goal is to develop a common policy in the field of science and technology for coordinating national research policies and jointly implement projects of interest to the Community. It has its origins in the discussions of the American challenge and the technology gap in the early 1970s. The Committee is comprised of 19 European countries, including the member states of the E.C. The project is coordinated at the Commission of the European Communities. The areas of cooperation are currently limited to data processing, telecommunications, oceanography, metallurgy and materials science, environmental protection, meteorology, agriculture, food technology, medical research, and health.

See COMMITTEE FOR EUROPEAN RESEARCH AND DEVELOPMENT; RESEARCH; SCIENCE AND TECHNOLOGICAL COMMITTEE.

committees The Treaties creating the European Communities provided for a limited number of committees to assist the Council of Ministers and the European Commission in their work. Others committees have since been created. There are working committees and expert groups (working on an ad hoc basis) whose existence can be terminated at short notice.

See EUROPEAN PARLIAMENT.

Common Agricultural Policy *See* AGRICULTURE, COMMON AGRICULTURAL POLICY; STRESA CONFERENCE.

Common Agricultural Policy, Accession of the Three to This agreement was adopted by the three new member nations—Denmark, the Irish Republic, and the United Kingdom—on February 1, 1973. The terms under which they agreed to become members of the European Communities provided for the implementation of the common agricultural policy in six equal stages over a five-year period beginning on February 1, 1973.

See AGRICULTURE, COMMON AGRICULTURAL POLICY.

common border posts The European Parliament approved a proposal to reduce significantly customs formalities at internal land frontiers by requiring only a single customs check (instead of one on exit and one on entry), and by enabling officials of one member state to act in the place of officials of an adjoining member state with no loss of legal effect. The single check will be at the office of entry into a member state.

See CONTROL OF GOODS.

Common Bureau of References (CBR) Backed by 59.2 million ECU and approved by the Council of Ministers for five years, CBR creates a scientific basis for the E.C.'s standardization policy, and involves researchers from the E.C.'s industrial companies, scientific laboratories, and universities.

See STANDARDIZATION.

Common Central Bank *See* CENTRAL BANK.

common currency On December 8, 1989, the leaders of the E.C., meeting in Strasbourg, agreed to hold a special conference in 1990 to deal with the prospects of a common currency throughout the E.C. British Prime Minister Margaret Thatcher has opposed this proposal.

See BANKING.

Common Customs Tariff (CCT) A tariff which represents the duty paid on goods entering the Community Customs Union at any point. The level averages about six percent, but certain specific duties are levied on agricultural and other products. CCT requires harmonization of national customs laws; it is an ongoing process for which the Commission is responsible, with administrative power delegated to it by the Council of Ministers.

Synonymous with COMMON EXTERNAL TARIFF (CET).

See CHRONOLOGY (JULY 1, 1968); EUROPEAN FREE TRADE ASSOCIATION; FINANCE; NON-TARIFF BARRIERS TO TRADE.

Common Declaration of European Businesses The first summit meeting of European business leaders was held in Paris in December 1988. The heads of the leading European industry associations signed a 16-point charter calling for speeding up the process of deregulation to help Europe compete more effectively when trade barriers are lowered at the end of 1992. The charter was signed by representatives from all 12 European Community countries as well as from eight other nations.

common European house *See* UNION OF SOVIET SOCIALIST REPUBLICS.

Common External Tariff (CET) *See* COMMON CUSTOMS TARIFF.

Common Fisheries Policy (CFP) *See* FISH.

Common Market *Synonymous with* EUROPEAN COAL AND STEEL COMMUNITY, EUROPEAN ECONOMIC COMMUNITY, EUROPEAN ATOMIC ENERGY COMMUNITY. It is often applied to the entire European Community.

common policy The complete alignment, usually by stages, of objectives, planning, and execution pertaining to a specific branch of national life, such as agriculture or transport, usually in accordance with the Treaties of Paris or Rome.

common position *See* COOPERATION PROCEDURE.

common taxation *See* TAXATION.

common technical specification A technical specification drawn up with a view to uniform application in all member states of the E.C.

See PUBLIC PROCUREMENT.

Cf. EUROPEAN TECHNICAL APPROVAL.

Commonwealth preferences *See* AUSTRALIA.

Community Bureau of Reference (CBR) An agency of the Community since 1973 with a program on reference materials and methods for promoting collaboration and coordination between bodies involved in research. The agency disseminates parallel reports to sponsors and researchers in an attempt to keep all parties well informed of each other's work.

See RESEARCH.

Community Information Center *See* SINGLE EUROPEAN ACT; SMALL BUSINESSES.

Community law Community law evolves from the Community constitutions as established by the Treaty of Paris and the Treaty of Rome. Community legislation (regulations, directives, decisions) is binding on member states, with implementation of the law varying according to national custom and institutions. Enforcement is traditionally the responsibility of national governments, but the

European Commission has the power to take direct action against companies or governments that break rules against restrictive trade practices. There are no sanctions under the Treaty of Rome available against governments that disregard Court of Justice rulings, and it is a generally accepted custom that rulings will be obeyed. The Community is a legal reality in three different senses: it is created by law, it is a source of law, and it forms a legal order—that is, it provides co-operation between Community law and national law, has primacy over conflicting national law, and confers rights and imposes obligations directly not only on the Community institutions and the member nations, but also on the Community's citizens.

See EUROPEAN COMMUNITY; LEGISLATIVE PREPARATION.

Community Patent Convention *See* EURO-PEAN PATENT CONVENTION; PATENT LAW.

Community preference A concept where domestic agricultural products are priced below imported items. Threshold prices or minimum import prices, together with subsidies for domestic production, are set at levels to guarantee that non-E.C. country imports will be somewhat more expensive than the domestic item.

Community Program in Education and Training for Technology *See* COMETT.

Community reform With the enlargement of the Community in the 1980s, the European Commission advocated reducing the number of Commissioners by appointing one only from each member state rather than continuing to allow the largest nations each to have two appointees.

See EUROPEAN COMMISSION; EUROPEAN COMMUNITY.

Community resources Originally the E.E.C. budget was financed totally from direct contributions by member nations. In the early 1970s it was replaced by an independent revenue system which will ultimately comprise 90 percent of all food-import levies, 90 percent of import duties and a proportion of the value-added tax levy of up to one percent.

See BUDGET.

Community's identity *See* SYMBOLS.

Community trademark The European Commission commenced work on the harmonization or unification of industrial property law in 1959. In 1973, the Trademark Registration Treaty was signed. In November 1980, a proposal was made for legislation harmonizing national laws on trademarks, and for the establishment of a Community trademark and a Community Trademark Office. The legislation would ensure that trademarks enjoy uniform protection under the laws of all member nations, and would, through regulations, govern registration of trademarks directly affecting the movement of goods and services within the Community.

See COMPANY LAW; TRADEMARKS.

Comoros This nation is one of the ACP states and signatory to the 1988 Lomé Convention.

company accounts The Fourth Directive on company law is concerned with the harmonization of the annual accounts (reports) of public and private limited firms. Its purpose is to make annual accounts comparable throughout the Community, with the physical presentation of accounts conforming to prescribed layouts, and assets and liabilities set out in accordance with fixed rules. Annual accounts became subject to an audit through legislation effective in 1982 for registered firms, and in 1985 for unregistered firms. Exemptions exist for small and medium-sized firms.

See COMPANY (GROUP) ACCOUNTS; COMPANY LAW; SMALL BUSINESSES.

company (group) accounts A proposal seeking to ensure comparable accounting procedures for groups of firms (multinationals) whether based internally or internationally. Such firms would have to publish group accounts relating to their subsidiaries throughout the world, clearly stating the relationships and activities within the group. The purpose is to give a true and fair view of multinational company activity, including the group's assets, liabilities, financial position, and results.

See COMPANY ACCOUNTS.

Company capitalization A 1989 directive aims to regulate the formation of public firms and the maintenance and alteration of their capital. It provides for specific responsibility for preincorporation liabilities, with a virtual prohibition on the issue of shares at a discount, and strict controls on the issue of shares for consideration other than cash. Dividend payments and interim dividends are also subject to certain restrictions.

company law Legislation harmonizing company law is authorized under Article 54 of the Treaty of Rome as part of Community policy of the right of establishment and the removal of obstacles to cross-frontier cooperation. Legislation already adopted deals with company capitalization, mergers, company accounts, and stock exchanges. New directives permit existing companies to restructure across borders without being subject to differing national laws. By 1992, laws will be harmonized to permit cross-border mergers, protect the interests of shareholders, ensure employee participation, and bring member state laws closer together. Foreign branches of firms will be relieved of the need to publish separate branch accounts. By 1988, proposals were presented on the liquidation of companies, takeover bids, and amendments to the European Company Statute.

See CROSS-BORDER MERGERS; EUROPEAN COMPANY STATUTE; EUROPEAN ECONOMIC INTEREST GROUPING; MERGERS; POISON PILL; PUBLIC LIMITED COMPANIES.

compensation payments *Synonymous with* RESTITUTION PAYMENTS.

Competition Directorate In preparing for the single market of 1992, the Directorate was given a mandate by the E.C. to concentrate on larger cross-border mergers, leaving smaller ones to national governments. The mandate makes it easier for Europe's major companies to know whether a merger will be approved by the E.C. and minimizes those regulations that traditionally exist with national governments. The Competition Directorate will have up to four months to review cross-border mergers of newly created companies with sales exceeding $1 billion a year.

See CROSS-BORDER MERGERS; MERGERS; RULES OF COMPETITION.

competition effect *See* COST SAVINGS.

competition law *See* COMPETITION POLICY, POWERS OF INVESTIGATION.

competition policy This policy, as stated in the Treaty of Rome, prohibits agreements among enterprises which adversely affect trade between member nations, and which have as their purpose or outcome the prevention, restriction, or distortion of competition within the common market; or in the case of any enterprise in a dominant position, prohibits it from abusing that position. Competition rules also apply to state monopolies, nationalized industries, discriminatory pricing, patents and trademarks.

See COMPANY LAW; DAWN RAIDS; DECISIONS; DE MINIMIS RULE; INDUSTRIAL POLICY; KNOW-HOW LICENSING; POWERS OF INVESTIGATION; RULES OF COMPETITION; SMALL BUSINESSES; SUBSIDIES.

complex program Adopted in July 1971 at Bucharest, the Complex Program for Further Cooperation and Integration evolves long-term goals for the Council for Mutual Economic Assistance (COMECON) to be implemented in the next two decades. It seeks to extend COMECON activity beyond the harmonization of investment plans towards creating conditions for multilateral trade through the introduction of true exchange rates, alignment of domestic and foreign trade prices, and credits to finance payments disequilibria.

See COUNCIL FOR MUTUAL ECONOMIC ASSISTANCE.

Computer Information Network *See* EURONET DIANE.

computers In 1989, the E.C. imposed a mechanism for calculating floor prices in Europe for member-produced computer chips. The aim is to prevent prices for dynamic random-access memory chips from falling below manufacturing costs, as they did earlier when E.C. officials contend that Japan dumped chips in Europe at half their cost. The E.C. is urging foreign firms to do more advanced chipmaking in Europe. E.C. antidumping decisions already require that Asian products, from copiers to electronic typewriters, have a 40 percent European content. Earlier, a chip was considered European-made even if only its final packaging was done in the E.C. Under the new rules introduced in February 1989, a more sophisticated chipmaking process, called wafer fabrication, must take place in the Community for chips to be considered "made in the E.C."

Several E.C. companies plan to spend up to $500 million annually on JESSI (Joint European Submicron Silicon), a program to develop future memory chips, with the E.C. and various governments paying half the costs. In June 1989, the E.C. threw its weight behind this $4 billion research and development program intended to counter Japan's dominance in the computer chip industry.

In August 1989 an agreement among 11 Japanese semiconductor makers agreed to meet E.C. demands for, among other things, price floors on dynamic random-access memory chips, or DRAMS, which had been the subject of a two-year dumping investigation. To confront the Japanese, the E.C. altered some customs rules. As a result, American chips not fabricated in Europe have been subject to a 14 percent duty. To avoid paying dumping penalties, some Japanese firms agreed to put at least 45 percent European content into the products they sold in Europe. In late September 1989, the United States Trade Representative Carla A. Hills, received assurances from the E.C. that it would not discriminate against American manufacturers in setting rules of origin for DRAMS.

In January 1990, the Commission and Japan settled their three-year inquiry into the dumping of Japanese computer chips on the E.C. market. Eleven Japanese firms agreed to set a minimum price on their chips equal to average production cost plus a profit margin of 9.5 percent. The agreement also applies to new generation computer chips.

See ESPRIT; JESSI; REPETITIVE STRAIN INJURY; SEMICONDUCTORS.

Confederation of European Computer User Associations *See* CECUA.

Confederation of Industries of the European Community (UNICE) (Union des Industries de la Communauté Européenne) An organization of major employers and industrial federations of 17 European nations. Its mission is to follow the development of various issues of interest to industry, to organize contacts with the trade unions and other associations, the Commission, the Council of Ministers, and the European Parliament.

See EUROPEAN COMMUNITY; REPRESENTATIVE ORGANIZATIONS.

Conference on Security and Cooperation in Europe (CSCE) This meeting was first proposed by members of the Warsaw Pact in 1966. It reached the stage of preparatory talks in November 1972. Including all European nations, the United States and Canada, it was meant to deal with, among other things, the political aspects of security, economic cooperation, and the freer movement of persons and ideas between East and West.

conformance testing A technical task of testing a product to determine whether it meets the requirements defined in a particular standard. The tests are conducted by the supplier of the product (first-party testing) or an independent body (third-party testing).

See CERTIFICATION; INFORMATION TECHNOLOGY; STANDARDS.

Congo This nation is one of the ACP states and signatory to the Yaoundé Conventions of 1963 and 1969 and the Lomé Convention of 1988. A protocol annexed to the Convention guarantees its sugar exports to the Community.

See SUGAR.

Conscience of the Community *See* EUROPEAN COMMISSION.

conscientious objectors The European Parliament suggested in 1989 that conscientious objectors be allowed to replace national military service with community service in an E.C. country other than their own.

consolidated profits To reform the tax system to aid cross-frontier mergers, the Commission in 1969 proposed and then approved plans enabling firms to opt for a system of consolidated profits when a parent company has major holdings in other companies. Under this system, profits of the subsidiaries would be taken over by the parent company and included in its profit calculations. Double taxation would be avoided by a corresponding reduction in the tax burden borne by the parent company. The system would give the parent company an opportunity to deduct any losses suffered by its subsidiaries from its own taxable profits, making it a suitable means of easing industrial mergers through acquisition of major holdings. It was the logical counterpart, in respect to foreign subsidiaries, of the world profits system proposed for affiliates.

Cf. WORLD PROFITS.

construction The Community's largest employer, with 8 to 10 percent of the active labor force, the E.C. advocated in 1975 joint efforts to ensure comparability of national statistics and forecasts, the elimination of technical and legal barriers, and technological research in order to create the conditions indispensable for achieving a common market in construction and building materials and an increase in productivity.

construction products Two problems have long existed—the free movement between member states of construction equipment and differing standards for buildings, which can mean different levels of protection for occupants. Safety requirements are essential not only for construction equipment but also for buildings and hotels. Two proposed measures dealing with noise levels of tower cranes and safety in hotels remain in debate.

consultation procedure One of the two distinct procedures for the adoption of a directive. The Council requests an Opinion from the European Parliament, and in most cases, from the Economic and Social Committee. Once these have been given, the Commission then has the opportunity to amend the proposal if it so wishes. The proposal is then examined by the Council which may adopt it as proposed, adopt it in an amended form, or fail to reach an agreement, in which case the proposal remains "on the table."

Cf. COOPERATION PROCEDURE.

Consultative Committee (European Coal and Steel) The E.C.S.C. Consultative Committee advises the Commission on a large number of economic and social questions. It is composed of 30 to 51 members, representing producers, labor, consumers, and dealers, who are appointed by the E.C.S.C. Council of Ministers.

Consumer Consultative Committee (CCC) The CCC was established by the European Commission in 1973 to represent consumers' opinions. It is consulted about food standards, health and safety, and other matters which it or the Commission considers appropriate. Its publication lists major consumer organizations in Community countries. In 1990, new measures were proposed by the E.C., including introducing comparative advertising throughout the E.C., providing standards contracts with product guarantees after purchases, removing unfair contract terms in sales between two E.C. member states, and protecting consumers in general.

See CONSUMER PROTECTION; REPRESENTATIVE ORGANIZATIONS.

consumer credit Consumer credit laws are not uniform among Community nations. A proposal recommends the establishment of a minimum standard in consumer/credit relations, including a requirement for written contracts, licensing of credit suppliers or making them subject to inspection by the appropriate public authority, and other safeguards. Consumers would then be free to dissolve the credit agreement by repaying any outstanding credit before the due date, and the consumer would not be permitted to sign away his or her rights. Any clause in the agreement suggesting the removal of such rights would be ineffective. In the spring of 1990, the Council of Ministers adopted legislation providing a uniform method of calculating the costs to the consumer who borrows anywhere within the E.C. The legislation uses a mathematical formula, which applies to credits of between 200 ECU ($240) and 2,000 ECU ($2,400). It excludes credit for the purchase of new cars, apartments, and houses, all of which are covered by national legislation protecting consumers. The new European method of calculating costs will be effective January 1, 1993, although nations using a formula other than the Council's may continue to do so until the end of 1995.

See CONSUMER PROTECTION.

Consumer Price Index The measurement of the cost of living. The Community's Consumer Price Index rose three-tenths of a percent in December 1988, with Portugal, Greece, and Spain posting the largest increases.

See INFLATION.

consumer protection In 1973, the European Commission established an Environment and Consumer Protection Service, responsible for action programs incorporating the basic consumer rights: protection of health and safety and of economic interests; the right of redress to information and education; and the right to be heard. The Consumer Consultative Committee is responsible for putting forward consumers' opinions on work undertaken at the Community level. Consumer redress required the introduction of simplified judicial proceedings, defense and law of collective interests, conciliation and arbitration, and consultation centers.

See CONTRACT TERMS; DOOR-TO-DOOR SELLING; FOOD; FOODSTUFFS LABELING.

consumer surveys *See* PUBLIC OPINION POLLS.

contact materials *See* FOOD.

Continental Can Company On January 8, 1972, the Commission invoked Article 86 of the Rome Treaty against the Continental Can Company of America charging it had abused a dominant position which it held in the E.E.C. by acquiring control of one of its leading Dutch competitors, Thomassen Drijver-Verblifa. In February 1973, the European Court of Justice upheld the Continental Can's appeal against the Commission on the grounds that the Commission had failed to prove specifically which sections of the market had been abused to the detriment of consumers.

contracts *See* CONTRACT TERMS; GOVERNMENT CONTRACTS; INSURANCE.

contract terms The Community believes that all consumers should enjoy a high standard of protection against unfair contract terms. Regional disparities should be eliminated as far as possible; consumers should be able to make their purchases in the place where they can obtain the most favorable terms, with rules providing the same protection to consumers in respect of guarantees and after-sales service including protection against unfair contract terms. According to the Commission, a directive is needed to provide a clearer definition of what is meant by unfair. A list of unfair, and therefore void, contract terms could aid in quick identification of offending language and provisions in a directive dealing with possible control and enforcement procedures would further the community's consumer protection goals.

See CONSUMER PROTECTION.

control of goods Under the Single Administrative Document, there is now one single document which is to be used for all consignments of goods crossing internal frontiers. The abolition of exit formalities for goods travelling under TIR carnets was the first step to achieving a single land border post at frontiers, to be extended to include all goods. The Community has partially adopted a measure which allows the duty free admission of fuel in standard tanks of coaches and a measure which abolishes postal fees for customs presentations. The completion of the internal market will result in the total abolition of controls and formalities for all goods at internal frontiers and for Community goods in connection with the trade between member states. At that time, the Single Administrative Document will cease to apply to dispatch, transit (except in certain limited cases), and arrival formalities for Community goods in intra-Community trade. Other proposals deal with the means of transport, harmonization or abolition of all remaining import formalities and controls on goods between member states.

See COMMON BORDER POSTS; CONTROL OF INDIVIDUALS; FISCAL CONTROLS; FRONTIER BARRIERS; SINGLE ADMINISTRATIVE DOCUMENT; TIR CARNETS; TRANSIT PROCEDURE; VEHICLE FUEL.

control of individuals By 1992, directives will allow Community citizens to cross borders unchecked. However, there are numerous problems with the free movement of citizens across internal frontiers, including terrorism, drug smuggling, and crime. Frontier controls also serve the purpose of performing checks on the taxable goods carried by travellers.

See ARMS LEGISLATION; CONTROL OF GOODS; INDUSTRIAL COOPERATION; TAX RELIEF; VALUE ADDED TAX; VALUE ADDED TAX EXEMPTION.

Cooperation in the Automation of Data Documentation for Import/Export and Agriculture *See* CADDIA.

cooperation procedure This is one of the two distinct procedures for the adoption of a directive. The Council requests Opinions from the Parliament and the Economic and Social Committee as in the *consultation procedure*. Once these Opinions have been received, the Council has to adopt a common position. Failing any common position being reached the proposal will remain "on the table." On a common position being reached, this is transmitted to the Parliament which has three months to accept, reject, or propose amendments to it, on its second reading. At this stage the Commission may again amend the proposal if it wishes. The proposal is then returned to the Council which has three months to take a final decision. In the absence of a decision, the proposal lapses.

Cf. CONSULTATION PROCEDURE.

Coordinating Committee of the Textile Industries of the E.E.C. (COMITEXTIL) (Comité de Coordination des Industries Textiles de la CEE) An organization that represents textile manufacturers from all Community nations except Luxembourg. It coordinates its members' views and lobbies at the Community level on behalf of the textile industry.

See EUROPEAN COMMUNITY; REPRESENTATIVE ORGANIZATIONS.

COPA Comité des Organisations Professionnelles Agricoles de la CEE. *See* COMMITTEE OF AGRICULTURAL ORGANIZATIONS IN THE EUROPEAN COMMUNITY.

Copenhagen report *See* CHRONOLOGY (July 23, 1973).

copiers *See* COMPUTERS.

copper President Reagan launched his third trade restriction in December 1988 on E.C. export quotas on copper, focusing on whether Europe is unfairly restricting its own exports.

See TOXIC EFFLUENT.

COREPER *See* COMMITTEE OF PERMANENT REPRESENTATIVES.

coresponsibility levy This is a deduction from the price farmers receive for milk which then is used, in part, to finance specific projects such as the Community subsidy for milk provided in schools. The levy's objective is to hold down the cost of the Common Agricultural Policy.

See GRAIN SECTOR; MILK AND MILK PRODUCTS.

corporate breakup rules This is a 1983 E.C. rule designed to protect the interests of employees, creditors, and stockholders of public corporations undergoing a breakup, or division. Aside from safeguarding stockholders and other interested parties, it simplifies the process of splitting up or restructuring a publicly held firm. The directive enables an existing firm to transfer all of its assets and liabilities to two or more existing or newly created companies (in exchange for stock in those companies) without having to go through costly, complex, and often lengthy legal proceedings. It allows member states to relax certain procedural requirements in cases where a breakup, or division, takes place under close court scrutiny. The directive stipulates that the successor companies are jointly liable if one of their number fails to satisfy one of the divided company's creditors. For the protection of shareholders, the directive mandates a report by independent experts on whether the share exchange ratio at which the split took place was justified, and it requires a report from management on the transaction's effect on workers.

corporate statute *See* COMPANY STATUTE.

cosmetics The Community passed a directive for protection against the use of dangerous products in cosmetics. It regulates the composition, labeling, and packaging of cosmetic items; lists substances which these products cannot contain and substances which are permitted subject to certain restrictions, including coloring agents that cannot be used if coming into direct contact with mucous membranes.

In 1990, the Commission worked on producing a list of nonharmful substances that could be used to produce cosmetics. Because this list would contain substances proven under the laws to be safe to humans, manufacturers would not need to continue animal testing. This would create an E.C.-wide label certifying that a product has been manufactured "without being tested on animals."

See CONSUMER PROTECTION.

COST (Co-opération Européenne dans le Domaine de la Recherche Scientifique et Technique) *See* COMMITTEE ON EUROPEAN COOPERATION IN THE FIELD OF SCIENTIFIC AND TECHNICAL RESEARCH.

cost savings The potential public expenditure savings by three beneficial effects are: *static trade effect*—when public authorities buy from the cheapest suppliers; *competition effect*—leading to downward pressure on prices charged by domestic firms in previously closed sectors as they strive to compete with foreign firms entering the market; and *restructuring effect*—or the longer-run effect of economies of scale, occurring when an industry reorganizes under the pressure of new competitive conditions, with saving concentrated in certain high technology sectors.

Costa Rica *See* CENTRAL AMERICA; CENTRAL AMERICAN COMMON MARKET.

costs of non-Europe In 1986, the Commission launched a research program to judge the extent of the market fragmentation confronting European business and Community policymakers. The estimated costs, and thus the potential for gains, exceeded 200 billion ECU. The results of this program were published in the Cecchini Report.
See CECCHINI REPORT.

cotton seeds Community assistance is available per hectare harvested.

Council, The *See* COUNCIL OF EUROPE.

Council for Mutual Economic Assistance (CMEA, COMECON) An economic organization was founded in 1949 by the USSR, Bulgaria, Czechoslovakia, Hungary, Poland, and Romania to assist intra-economic development through joint coordination of efforts. Later member nations include Cuba, the German Democratic Republic, and Mongolia, with Angola, North Korea, and North Vietnam maintaining observer status. Negotiations on a trade agreement between COMECON and the Community began in 1978. By 1984, E.C. imports from COMECON amounted to 9.2 percent of total purchases outside, and exports to COMECON accounted for 6.1 percent of overall shipments to third countries. In 1986, the Community and the economic cooperation group of East European countries signed a joint declaration on the establishment of official relations. At the same time, the Community proposed to the European members of the economic bloc—Bulgaria, Czechoslovakia, the German Democratic Republic, Hungary, Poland, Romania and the Soviet Union—a normalization of bilateral diplomatic relations. By 1987, trade between the E.C. and COMECON was worth almost $50 billion. A joint declaration of mutual recognition was signed on June 25, 1988, providing a potential E.C. market of more than 400 million consumers within nations affiliated with COMECON. In 1988, Cuba became the first non-European member of COMECON to establish diplomatic relations with the Community. The bulk of E.C. imports from COMECON consists of fuel, averaging about $20 billion worth of oil and oil products each year from the Soviet Union. The events in the Eastern bloc nations since the fall of 1989 will have a significant impact on the future of COMECON.

By 1990, many economists felt that COMECON had lost its purpose. For it to survive it would have to become a different organization with its trade based on hard currencies and market prices and not on barter, nonconvertible currencies, and artificial prices. While worldwide trade rose by approximately 8.5 percent in 1989, trade among the COMECON partners was stagnant. The heads of government of the 10 members of COMECON (the Warsaw Pact countries plus Cuba, Vietnam, and Mongolia) decided during their summit in Sofia on January 9 and 10 to undertake a major reform of the organization and immediately set up a committee in charge of studying these reforms. The Soviet Prime Minister proposed replacing the transferable ruble with a free convertible currency and carrying out exchanges between COMECON countries based on global prices.
See COMPLEX PROGRAM.

Council of Europe This group was formed in 1949 as an inter-governmental organization of European nations with 10 founder members: Belgium, Denmark, France, Ireland, Italy, Luxembourg, the Netherlands, Norway, Sweden, and the United Kingdom. Eleven countries later joined: Turkey, Greece,

Iceland, the Federal Republic of Germany, Austria, Cyprus, Switzerland, Malta, Liechtenstein, Portugal, and Spain. The Council's aim is "to achieve a greater unity between its members for the purpose of safeguarding and realizing the ideas and principles which are their common heritage and facilitating their economic and social progress." It has no legislative jurisdiction over its members and should not be confused with the European Community. The Council is required to ensure coordination of member states' general economic policies. It has the power to take decisions in implementing the objectives of the Community Treaties. Member states are represented either by their foreign minister or by the minister responsible for the particular subject being dealt with at a given meeting. Each member state takes the chair of the Council for six months, in absolute alphabetical order. The heads of state or government meet two times a year as the "European Council." The European Council is described as the Council of Ministers meeting at head-of-state and government level. In November 1989, Hungary applied to join the 23-nation Council of Europe, the first Warsaw Pact member to do so.

See PERMANENT REPRESENTATIVES COMMITTEE.

Synonymous with EUROPEAN COMMUNITY SUMMIT; EUROPEAN COUNCIL.

Council of European Communities *See* COUNCIL OF MINISTERS.

Council of Ministers (Council of European Communities) This group is the final decisionmaking body of the Community under the Treaty of Rome. It was partly modified by the European Council of heads of government. Each government has one representative on the Council of Ministers. Participants at Council meetings change according to subject matter. Thus, if the theme is finance, the E.C.'s 12 finance ministers attend; when industrial policy is discussed, industry ministers participate. The "senior" Council formation is that of the foreign ministers. They deal with external relations, but can also take on particularly urgent issues in other sectors. The foreign ministers coordinate the work of other council formations and prepare the twice-yearly sessions of the European Council. The Council of Ministers is the top authority both on Community matters and on political cooperation issues. The Single European Act gave it legal recognition but did not define its powers. The presidency of the Council of Ministers (and of the European Council) rotates among the member states every six months. The Council can take decisions unanimously, by absolute majority or by qualified voting. Decisions in areas covered by the single market program can be taken by majority vote, with the exception of fiscal matters.

See COUNCIL OF MINISTERS SECRETARIAT; EUROPEAN COMMUNITY; EXTERNAL TRADE; LEGISLATIVE PREPARATION; RESEARCH.

Council of Ministers Secretariat The Secretariat services the Council of Ministers. It chooses its own staff and is divided into Directorates-General covering primary areas of Community involvement.

See COUNCIL OF MINISTERS.

Council of Mutual Economic Assistance *See* COUNCIL FOR MUTUAL ECONOMIC ASSISTANCE.

Court of Auditors This Court was established in 1975 by amendment to the Treaty of Rome. It consisted of 10 members (one from each Community nation) appointed for a six-year term by the Council of Ministers in consultation with the European Parliament. The Court may comment on the accounts for all Community institutions and can issue advisory opinions. Internal auditing however, is carried out by each institution's financial controller. Presently there are 12 members.

See FINANCE.

Court of First Instance Established by decision of the Council of Ministers in October 1988 to relieve the higher European Court of Justice from hearing certain types of cases involving natural and legal persons. Jurisdiction of the new court covers disputes between the E.C. and its civil servants; actions brought against an E.C. institution by individuals and actions relating to the implementation of the competition rules applicable to firms; and actions brought against the E.C. Commission by companies or associations of companies and actions relating to matters covered by the Treaty establishing the European Coal and Steel Community (such as levies, prices, restrictive agreements, and so on). The new court consists of 12 members, who elect their president from among their number for a three-year term, and will usually sit in chambers of three or five judges. Decisions of the Court of First Instance are appealable to the European Court of Justice. The new court occupies two new courtrooms in the Court of Justice headquarters on the Kirchberg Plateau in Luxembourg City.

In September 1989, 12 new judges were appointed to man this new junior branch of the Court of Justice. They are expected to consider about 150 lawsuits each year, which should cut the workload of the Court of Justice by about one-third.

See CHRONOLOGY (OCTOBER 1988); EUROPEAN COURT OF JUSTICE.

Court of Justice, The European *See* EUROPEAN COURT OF JUSTICE.

cranes *See* CONSTRUCTION PRODUCTS.

credit *See* CONSUMER CREDIT.

credit institutions *See* BANKING; INSURANCE.

CREST Comité de Recherche Scientifique et Technique. *See* COMMITTEE ON SCIENTIFIC AND TECHNICAL RESEARCH.

Crete, Island of *See* INTEGRATED MEDITERRANEAN PROGRAM.

Crocodile Club *See* CHRONOLOGY (JULY 7–9, 1981).

CRONOS The Community Statistical Office Computerized Economic Data Bank.

See DATABASES AND DATABANKS OF THE E.C.

cross-border mergers Before the passage of various directives and other regulations easing the way for the single market of 1992, it was difficult for companies in different member states to merge. A directive harmonizes the laws on cross-border mergers of public limited companies so as to facilitate this process. It does so by adding additional requirements to the previous directive on national mergers to cover aspects unique to cross-bor-

der mergers (due to different legal systems applying). In this way the directive will protect shareholders, creditors, and employees when all the assets and liabilities in a company are transferred to another company in another member state. E.C. cross-border mergers and acquisitions in 1989 rose to 1,314 from 847 in 1988 and their value reached $50 billion against $31.6 billion. Purchasers came from 31 countries, with the U.K.-based company purchases accounting for 53 percent of the total value in Europe.

See COMPETITION DIRECTORATE; MERGERS; PUBLIC LIMITED COMPANIES.

CSCE *See* CONFERENCE ON SECURITY AND COOPERATION IN EUROPE.

Cuba This island has been a member of the Council for Mutual Economic Assistance since 1974. In 1988, Cuba became the first non-European member of COMECON to establish diplomatic relations with the Community.

See COUNCIL FOR MUTUAL ECONOMIC ASSISTANCE.

culture The cultural sector is a political and economic necessity given the goals of completing the internal market by 1992 and progressing from a People's Europe to a closely knit European union. The Commission set a program for achieving goals by 1992 in five fields: the creation of a European cultural area, the promotion of the European audio-visual industry, access to cultural resources, training for the cultural sector, and dialogue with the rest of the world.

See INTERNAL MARKET; PEOPLE'S EUROPE; SINGLE EUROPEAN ACT.

Curaco *See* OCT.

currencies of E.C. and EFTA countries

Belgium	Belgian franc.
Denmark	krone divided into 100 ore.
France	French franc.
German Federal Republic	deutsche mark.
Greece	dracmai divided into 100 lepta.
Irish Republic	Irish pound divided in 100 pence.
Italy	lira
Luxembourg	Luxembourg franc (at parity with Belgian franc which is legl tender in Luxembourg).
Netherlands	gulden divided into 100 cents.
Portugal	escudo divided into 100 centavos.

Spain	peseta divided into 100 centimos
United Kingdom	pound sterling divided into 100 pence.
Turkey	Turkish lira divided into 100 kurus (piastres).
Austria	schilling divided into 100 groschen.
Iceland	krona.
Norway	krone divided into 100 ore.
Switzerland	Swiss franc divided into 100 Rappen/centimes.
Finland	Finnish mark divided into 100 pennis.

customs checks *See* VALUE ADDED TAX.

customs classification *See* BTN.

customs duties Since the Community is a Customs union, all imports into the Community are charged at a uniform rate whichever nation they enter. The Common Customs Tariff (CCT) averages about six percent. Customs duties are imposed on some agricultural products as well as levies. Rates also apply to fruit and vegetables. Duties can be lowered or suspended by the Council of Ministers.
See FINANCE.

customs union This is an arrangement whereby nations agreed to do away with customs barriers between themselves and to apply a common tariff to nations outside the Community so that the level of protection will be the same wherever a product enters the Community. It was formed by the six Community founder members in 1968, and extended to include newer member nations of the E.C.
See CUSTOMS DUTIES; DUTY-FREE ALLOWANCES; EUROPEAN MONETARY SYSTEM; EXTERNAL TRADE; HARMONIZATION.

CXT The Common External Tariff.
See COMMON CUSTOMS TARIFF.

cycling *See* BICYCLES.

cyclones *See* CIVIL PROTECTION.

Cyprus After the U.K.'s entry into the Community, Cyprus and the Community concluded an Association agreement in 1972 aimed at improving trade between the parties on a non-discriminatory and cooperative basis. The Community provides loans and grants to Cyprus. On October 19, 1987, the E.C. and Cyprus signed a customs union agreement to abolish all trade obstacles between them. Under the accord, the two sides would dismantle all trade barriers over the next 15 years and Cyprus would apply Community customs tariffs to non-E.C. imports. The E.C. is the island's main trading partner, accounting for 54 percent of its imports and 28 percent of its exports.

Czechoslovakia This country is a founder member of the Council for Mutual Economic Assistance (COMECON). Events of the fall of 1989 may significantly alter its relationship with the E.C. The current agreement between the E.C. and Czechoslovakia, effective April 1, 1989, is a simple trade accord. In January 1990, a Czech delegation met in Brussels with a view to examining the possibility of extending the current agreement, notably to economic cooperation, the transfer of technology, and the elimination of quantitative restrictions. In May 1990, Czechoslovakia signed a trade and economic cooperation accord with the E.C., replacing a December 1988 accord, that will give it better access to markets in the 12 nations. The E.C.'s two-way trade with Czechoslovakia was about $2.4 billion in 1989. The new 10-year accord covers trade in industrial and agricultural goods and will remove quantitative trade restrictions.
See COUNCIL FOR MUTUAL ECONOMIC ASSISTANCE, EASTERN EUROPE.

D

Dahomey *See* BENIN.

dairy products In April 1968, a common price policy for milk went into effect. At the same time a common target price was established, this being the price which it was thought producers should receive for their milk delivered to dairies, subject to market outlets being available inside and outside the Community. In March 1987, the Council of Ministers agreed on a package for reducing Community milk output and limiting the amount of dairy products farmers can sell into storage at guaranteed prices. The reforms call for a cut of 9.5 percent in dairy production over the next two years and provide for adjustment assistance. The butter mountain was dissolved resulting in the disposal of over a millions tons of butter held in E.C. cold storage. The Commission can now suspend E.C. butter purchases once a limit of 180,000 tons has been bought at intervention prices, unless the weighted average price falls below 92 percent of the intervention price.
See MILK AND MILK PRODUCTS; MOUNTAIN.

dangerous substances (packaging and labeling) A 1967 directive is aimed at guaranteeing that all Community nations adopt common standards in the packaging and labelling of poisonous or dangerous substances.
See CHEMICALS; CONSUMER PROTECTION.

Danube Commission Constituted in 1949, this Commission is based on the 1948 Belgrad Convention relating to navigation control on the river Danube. It is composed of representatives from the nations on the Danube; one each for Austria, Bulgaria, Hungary, Romania, Czechoslovakia, U.S.S.R., and Yugoslavia. It checks that the Convention provisions are carried out; establishes a uniform buoying system on all the Danube's navigable waterways and sees to the fundamental arrangement relating to navigation on the river. Since 1954, the Commission has had its headquarters in Budapest.

databases and databanks of the E.C. The E.C. offers numerous options for information users. The major ones, listed alphabetically, include:

(1) AGREP—inventory of current agricultural research projects in the E.C.
(2) BROKERSGUIDE—inventory of information brokers.
(3) CELEX—European Community legal database.
(4) COMEXT—external trade statistics of the E.C.
(5) CRONOS—European statistical database.
(6) DIANEGUIDE—online guide to European database producers, hosts, databases, and databanks.
(7) EABS—references to the published results of scientific and technical research programs.
(8) ECDIN—environmental data and information network on chemicals.
(9) ECU—daily ECU exchange rates.
(10) ENDOC—directory of environmental information and documentation centers.
(11) ENREP—directory of environmental research projects.
(12) EURISTOTE—directory of university thesis and studies on European integration.
(13) EURODICAUTOM—online terminology databank.
(14) IES—inventory of publicly funded information technology R & D projects, research sites, and electronic mail addresses.
(15) MEDREP—inventory of biomedical and health care research projects.

(16) PABLI—online monitor of E.C. development projects.

(17) REGIO—E.C. regional statistical databank.

(18) SCAD—database on documents published by the Community and periodical articles on the Community.

(19) SESAME—hydrocarbon technology and energy demonstration projects.

(20) TED—daily calls for tenders for public works and supply contracts.

(21) THESAURI—analytical inventory of structure vocabulary.

data-processing *See* COMPUTERS; TELECOMMUNICATIONS; TELEMATICS.

data-transmission *See* TELECOMMUNICATIONS.

Davignon Report At the Hague summit in 1969, a report was prepared on the best means of achieving progress towards political unification (chaired by Vicomte Etienne Davignon). A united Europe should be "based on a common heritage of respect for the liberty and rights of man and bring together democratic states with freely elected Parliaments."

dawn raids In 1989, the European Court of Justice upheld the Commission's right to raid companies for evidence of alleged price-fixing, confirming the Commission's extensive powers to enforce E.C. competition rules. Further, it boosts the drive to promote competition in the Community in advance of the single market. The court backed the right of the Commission to investigate a firm's books immediately if it suspects a violation of competition law. In addition, the Commission has the right to seek information which it cannot necessarily identify in advance. With the assistance of national authorities, it can search for information even if the targeted firm is unwilling to cooperate. Should a firm resist, the investigators must secure a search warrant according to national law, but the company exposes itself to fines until the Commission actually begins the investigation. National authorities are not permitted to determine whether an investigation is justified, but may ensure that any enforcing measures are neither arbitrary nor out of proportion with the inquiry's aim.

DDT *See* TOXIC EFFLUENT.

decisions These are Community laws. They are directly binding on those to whom the Decisions are addressed (governments, companies or individuals).

Cf. DIRECTIVES; OPINIONS; RECOMMENDATIONS; REGULATIONS.

See COMMUNITY LAW; LEGISLATIVE PREPARATION.

Dedicated Road Infrastructure for Vehicle Safety in Europe *See* DRIVE.

defective goods *See* PRODUCT LIABILITY.

deficiency payment This is a U.K. Exchequer payment to producers or agricultural marketing boards in the U.K. which is based on the difference between the guaranteed price and market prices.

Dehousse, Fernand *See* CHRONOLOGY (MAY 17, 1960).

Dekker, Wisse *See* EUROPEAN ROUND TABLE.

Delors Committee A 17-member group, chaired by Jacques Delors, President of the E.C. Commission. It has been studying since September 1988 "concrete steps toward economic and monetary union" in the 12-nation bloc. The committee consists of the 12 heads of the E.C.'s national monetary institutions and four outside experts on European monetary affairs. The creation of a European central bank and common currency were primary concerns under discussion. The Delors Report recommended rapid steps toward monetary and economic union. It proposed a first phase, beginning in July 1990, in which governments harmonize their monetary and economic policies. The second and third phases would require changes in the Treaty of Rome. The second phase would involve the creation of a regional central bank and the third would bring a single currency. In November 1989, Britain's Prime Minister Margaret Thatcher urged the E.C. not to go against market forces in its single-currency plan. Instead the Prime Minister argued that governments would have an incentive to lower national inflation rates, thereby increasing confidence in their own currencies. She argued that under the Delors plan inflation could be higher because the central banking authority would probably try to accommodate the average inflation levels within the E.C.

See CENTRAL BANK; CHRONOLOGY (APRIL 1989); MADRID MEETING.

Delors, Jacques He is nicknamed "Mr. 1992," the appointed president of the European Community's executive commission since 1985. His major efforts have been in the elimination of trade barriers within Europe by the end of 1992. He envisions Europe with a single currency and monetary policy managed by a central bank, and pursues generous social guarantees and possible employee participation in company decisionmaking. As part of his European Social Charter, he wants to mandate collective bargaining and extensive management consultation with unions. In June 1990, he was reappointed E.C. Commission President at the Dublin Summit until the beginning of 1993.

Delors Report See DELORS COMMITTEE.

DELTA (The Development of European Learning through Technological Advance) Funded by the Council of Ministers in the summer 1988 for two years with 20 million ECU, its aim is to harness information technology and telecommunications to the development of teaching methods suitable for retraining people as often as necessary during their working lives. The research program covers word and image processing, new techniques of data storage, direct broadcasting by satellite, and artificial intelligence, with special attention to European standards.

See EDUCATION.

de minimis rule This refers to agreements of minor importance within the European Community. Small and medium-sized firms have concluded many agreements that the E.C. does not consider as violating the competition rules because the economic effect involved is not significant. This rule applies to agreements between firms that meet the criteria as to market share and turnover, laid down in the Notice concerning agreements of minor importance. Generally, if the two criteria are met, then Article 85(1) of the Treaty of Rome is inapplicable and, therefore, the

Parties involved can refrain from notifying the Commission.

See COMPETITION POLICY.

dénaturation See DENATURING.

denaturing The act of making a commodity unfit for human consumption by, for example, contaminating wheat with fish oil. To encourage the use of wheat as animal feed, a denaturing premium can be granted to authorized users which makes wheat competitive with less expensive coarse grains. Sugar can also be denatured to be used for animal feed.

Denmark This nation is a former member of the European Free Trade Association. It left EFTA on signing the Treaty of Brussels in 1972 and joined the Community in January 1973. Foreign trade accounts for 40 percent of Denmark's gross national product. The 1992 internal market effort could bring Denmark at least 100,000 new jobs and a benefit of more than $5 billion. It now has a government with an undisputed mandate in key areas of foreign and domestic policies. The Danish Government hopes to create 150,000 new jobs in the private sector over the next four years, and at the same time create such a large surplus on its balance of trade that it will blot out rising interest payments on foreign debt, paving the way for repayment and resulting in a lower interest rate and more economic opportunity. Only 80 Danish industrial firms employ more than 500 people, the vast majority are by consequence quite small. On average, more than half of Danish industrial production is exported. Fortunately, most of its corporations are preparing for 1992, either planning or effecting more internationalization, or planning defenses against predators, national or international. In the financial sector, a large concentration of the many small institutions is projected, perhaps with a strong move toward financial supermarkets, that is, breaking down of the existing Danish barriers between various types of banking, insurance, real estate, and mortgage services. In the industrial sector, Denmark officials hope that E.C. predictions that the single market is of special significance to smaller firms will come true. However, smaller in operation may be a disadvantage in developing production and marketing clout. Denmark already has the highest tax rates in the world on average. Taxes on cars equal twice their price, and taxes on electronics, wines, alcohol, and tobacco have created a large border trade with Germany. The combination of a very strong krone—allied to the German mark in the European Monetary System—and the high wage increases—6 percent a year over 2 years—given by private and government employers, make life almost impossible for Danish exports. Further complicating the economy, Denmark produces little of the high-value consumer goods, and the Danish people spend 50 cents or more of every extra dollar on imports.

See FAROE ISLANDS.

dental practitioners Since 1980, regulations permit dentists and dental surgeons to practice their profession anywhere in the Community subject to minimum training requirements and mutual recognition of qualifications, except in Italy.

See WORK AND EMPLOYMENT.

deposit guarantee schemes *See* BANKING.

derogations These are exceptions that are allowed in an E.C. decision. There is a proposal for a Council directive that would abolish nearly all of the derogatives permitted to the member states in the directive relating to the Value Added Tax system. The proposed abolition is necessary in order to achieve greater neutrality of the VAT system at Community level, and because one of the sources of finance for the Community is a percentage of member state VAT revenue. The original directive excludes transactions in gold, other than gold for industrial use, and for services supplied by authors, artists and performers.

See VALUE ADDED TAX.

detergents The E.C. Commission on June 17, 1971, proposed a directive concerning Community-wide standards of biodegradability of laundry detergents. The directive ensures a level of biodegradability of at least 80 percent for four types of detergents: anionics, cationics, ampholoytes, and non-ionics. Anionic detergents alone account for about 85 percent of European synthetic detergent production.

See CHEMICALS.

developing countries *See* LESS DEVELOPED COUNTRIES.

Development Assistance Committee of the Organization for Economic Cooperation and Development (DAC) This Committee assumed the membership and functions of the former Development Assistance Group at the end of 1961. It provides a forum for consultations amongst donor nations on the subject of aid to the less developed countries.

Development Bank *See* BANK FOR EUROPE.

Development Fund (EDF) It was the first Fund, established in 1958, to provide aid funds for dependencies of the six founder Community members. It is administered by the European Commission.

Development of European Learning through Technological Advance *See* DELTA.

Development of Statistical Expert Systems *See* DOSES.

DIANE The Direct information access network for Europe.

See EURONET DIANE.

DIANEGUIDE *See* DATABASES AND DATABANKS OF THE E.C.

diesels *See* VEHICLES.

dietetic foods A 1977 Directive provides for standards and controls on the marketing and labelling of such foods with regard to their claimed nutritional value to the consumer.

See CONSUMER PROTECTION.

DIN *See* EUROPEAN STANDARDS INSTITUTE.

dioxon Following several incidents in which high levels of one of the world's most toxic substances were found in milk, the Commission is studying ways to stop the chemical from entering the food chain.

See ENVIRONMENT.

diplomas, mutual recognition of In 1964 the E.C. agreed to the freedom of movement for employed people.

See DOCTORS; LAWYERS; MUTUAL RECOGNITION.

Direct Information Access Network for Europe *See* EURONET DIANE.

directives These are Community laws, adopted by the Council of Ministers on a proposal from the European Commission. It remains with national authorities to suggest legislation for conforming with the spirit of the directive and legislation does not go into effect until this is accomplished. Directives usually establish a time limit for governments to comply, and are binding on the member states to which they are addressed as regards the results to be achieved, but leave the form and methods of achieving it to the discretion of the national authorities.

Cf. DECISIONS; OPINIONS; RECOMMENDATIONS; REGULATIONS.

See COMMUNITY LAW; CONSULTATION PROCEDURE; COOPERATION PROCEDURE; FRAMEWORK HORIZONTAL DIRECTIVES; SPECIFIC HORIZONTAL DIRECTIVES; LEGISLATIVE PREPARATION.

discrimination This consists of restrictive trade measures which favor one nation at the expense of another.

divergence indicator *See* EUROPEAN MONETARY SYSTEM.

Djibouti This nation is one of the ACP states and is a signatory to the Lomé Conventions.

doctors Beginning in 1976, doctors from Community nations, holding an appropriate diploma or degree, can practice their profession in any Community nation. The legislation does not apply to non-nationals, even those trained in a Community school. It also provides for the coordination of laws, regulations, and administrative practice in regard to the profession, and establishes minimum training rules, guaranteeing a total of at least six years' training.

See WORK AND EMPLOYMENT.

document transmission *See* APOLLO.

dogs *See* ANIMAL HEALTH AND MEAT INSPECTION.

Dominica *See* CARIBBEAN BASIN.

Dominican Republic This nation is one of the ACP states and a signatory of the Lomé Conventions.

See LATIN AMERICA.

Dooge Committee *See* CHRONOLOGY (JUNE 25 AND 26; 1984; MARCH 9; 1985).

doors The E.C. passed standards for automobile doors in 1970, specifing that they must be built to allow easy entry. If the opening is more than 700 millimeters off the ground, the vehicle must have a running board, for which standards exist. Standards are also provided for the location and construction of locks and hinges.

door-to-door selling In 1986 the Council of Ministers agreed on a Directive, first proposed in 1977, that will provide protection for consumers who purchase products from door-to-door salespeople. It provides for a seven-day period in which consumers can reconsider the wisdom of purchases they have made from doorstep sellers, whether they pay in cash or through a credit arrangement.

See CONSUMER PROTECTION.

DOSES (Development of Statistical Expert Systems) A 1989 E.C. research program to promote the use of advanced techniques for processing statistical data, in particular, the application of an expert system for the whole chain of statistical data processing.

double taxation A directive was proposed in 1988 to eliminate double taxation in connection with the adjustment of transfers of profits between associated enterprises. Some multinational firms currently suffer from double taxation because national tax authorities adjust transfer prices between subsidiaries in the group. This directive would eliminate this source of double taxation within the Community.

See TAXATION.

Downing Street Summit *See* CHRONOLOGY (MAY 7–8; 1977).

dried fodder A flat rate aid is set yearly to improve community supplies of vegetable proteins. A guide price is set annually at a level considered to be fair to producers.

Provision is given for measures to be applied in the event of market disturbances owing to imports or exports.

DRIVE (Dedicated Road Infrastructure for Vehicle Safety in Europe) A research program approved in the summer of 1988 by the Council of Ministers for making road traffic smoother and safer within the Community. Research will aim to improve analysis of traffic accident data; evaluation of road conditions and pollution; radar; traffic management, and signaling systems. Standardization to ensure compatibility of national systems in this area is another goal. DRIVE is funded for three years, receiving 60 million ECU from the Community.

See BIOTECHNOLOGY; DELTA; SCIENCE; VEHICLES.

driver's license *See* SYMBOLS.

driving hours To maintain safety and reduce accidents, the Community set regulations regarding working hours and conditions of drivers including the minimum age of drivers of commercial vehicles and the maximum driving periods (they cannot exceed 48 hours in any one week or 92 hours in any two consecutive weeks and must be interspersed with defined rest periods). In addition, the regulations forbid payments to crews in the form of bonuses and wage supplements. Commercial vehicles over a given weight and larger coaches must be fitted with a tachograph or recording instrument.

See TACHOGRAPHS; TRANSPORT; VEHICLES.

driving licenses This 1980 Directive permits the mutual recognition and exchange of driving licenses when a Community national changes residence from one member nation to another. A common-format, rose-colored Community driving license was introduced for issue to newly qualified drivers, although the license itself will be national.

See TRANSPORT.

drug trafficking The single market of 1992 may be helping this escalating problem. Europe is experiencing a widespread increase in the use of cocaine. There is a Turkish heroin connection in Germany. Spain's physical proximity to Morocco ensures it will remain a key entry point for hashish. Latin Americans use Spain as their base for an efficient cocaine network. Jamaican traffickers funnel cocaine to Great Britain, and so on. The Council of Europe's antidrug task force, known as the Pompidou Group, believes that cocaine and intravenous drug use are a massive health threat to the E.C. In May 1989, this Group formally recognized the need for an E.C. convention that would enable judges in any member nation to confiscate the assets of suspected traffickers, even if they had committed no crime in that particular state. The E.C. Council in 1989 passed resolutions to establish a Community-wide data bank on drug abuse, harmonize anti-AIDS policy, and institute single standards for urine tests. E.C. member states also agreed to sign the United Nations Convention Against Illicit Traffic in Narcotic Drugs and Psychotropic Substances. In 1989 the Trevi Group, made up of the E.C.'s justice and interior ministers, established a permanent commission aimed at broadening inter-European police cooperation, establishing a single intelligence network, and recommended legal changes to allow for pursuit across borders.

Dublin Summit *See* EUROPEAN FOUNDATION FOR THE IMPROVEMENT OF LIVING AND WORKING CONDITIONS; WINE.

dumping This is the selling of goods abroad at prices below those which the exporter charges for comparable sales in its own country, and often involves a government subsidy. A subsidy includes most financial benefits granted to overseas nations on the production or exports of good (but not rebates of custom duties, or internal sales taxes) granted when such items are exported. In 1979, the Community adopted its GATT anti-dumping legislation which set procedures for dealing with dumped imports. Responsibility rests with the European Commission, which supervises and operates the relevant Community legislation with help from member nations. Following an investigation, should the Community verify the wrongdoing, the Community can impose its antidumping or countervailing duties. Any duties imposed are applicable in all member nations, but these are waived if the foreign exporter ceases dumping or exporting the product. In February 1989, the E.C.

Commission proposed tougher import laws that are expected to lead to the imposition of a 20 percent antidumping duty. It would mark the first time the E.C. has set dumping duties on products made in the United States by Japanese companies, based on the "rules of origin" which determine where a product is made. Such duties could dissuade other Japanese manufacturers with U.S. operations from shipping to Europe.

See COMPUTERS; EXTERNAL TRADE; RECIPROCITY; SOUTH KOREA.

durum wheat This is hard-grain wheat used in making pasta. Producers must qualify for special deficiency payments to encourage them to grow more of the product which is heavily imported from non-E.C. nations.

See CEREALS.

duty-free allowances Visitors or returning residents are entitled to bring back certain goods duty- or tax-free, the amount depending on whether travel is within the Community or from third nations. Also, it is now possible to receive small parcels from abroad duty-free, including small quantities of tobacco and wine intended for private use.

See HARMONIZATION; TRANSPORT; VALUE ADDED TAX.

E

E The European Community stamp placed on products indicating that the item(s) has met with the standards established by the European Community.

EABS *See* DATABASES AND DATABANKS OF THE E.C.

EAEC (Euratom) *See* EUROPEAN ATOMIC ENERGY COMMUNITY.

EAGGF (The European Agricultural Guidance and Guarantee Fund). *See* FARM FUND.

earthquakes *See* CIVIL PROTECTION.

East African Community Kenya, Uganda, and Tanzania signed a four-year association agreement in Arusha, Tanzania, on September 24, 1969. The agreement relates mainly to reciprocal rights and obligations in trade, but also contains provisions on free movement of persons and capital, freedom to supply services, and the right of establishment of companies from and in any of the three signatory states comprising the East African Community.

See ARUSHA CONVENTION.

Eastern Europe Often referred to as Central Europe. Includes in the strictest sense five nations (East Germany, Czechoslovakia, Hungary, Poland, and Yugoslavia) having an estimated $425 billion economy, but in the broader meaning also encompasses Romania (Rumania), Bulgaria, and the Soviet Union. Eastern Europe accounts for only seven percent of the E.C.'s total trade. A major problem is the fact that no Eastern European nation has a convertible currency. Events of the fall 1989 may lead to significant changes in Eastern Europe's relationship to the European Community and to the rest of the western economies of Europe. Thus far, the E.C. has proposed a plan to aid Eastern Europe to include: easier access to Western markets by lowering tariffs, especially for farm exports; direct gifts of farm machinery and pesticides to help Polish and Hungarian agriculture; more foreign investment in Eastern Europe, encouraged by $1.1 billion in loans from the European Investment Bank over three years; professional and management training to give Poland and Hungary the skills to run a market economy; and environmental protection to help East Europeans clean up areas poisoned by years of over-industrialization and bad management. The E.C. plans to open offices in Budapest and Warsaw in 1990. In 1988, Eastern European nations' share of trade with E.C. nations were: Imports—Soviet Union, 53 percent; East Germany, 6 percent; Poland, 14 percent; Rumania, 9 percent; Czechoslovakia, 9 percent; Hungary, 9 percent; Bulgaria, 0.2 percent; and Albania, 0.3 percent. Exports—Soviet Union, 49 percent; East Germany, 6 percent; Poland, 13 percent; Rumania, 3 percent; Czechoslovakia, 10 percent; Hungary, 11 percent; Bulgaria, 7 percent; and Albania, 0.3 percent. Expectations are that these nations, other than perhaps East Germany, will first become members of the European Free Trade Association before consideration is given to membership in the E.C. On February 1, 1990, the executive body of the E.C. announced plans for bringing Eastern European nations into a closer economic and social relationship with the 12 member states by putting these nations on par with non-community members like Switzerland, Sweden, and Austria.

See BULGARIA; BANK FOR EUROPE; CZECHOSLOVAKIA; EUROPEAN FREE TRADE ASSOCIATION; GERMAN DEMOCRATIC REPUBLIC; HUNGARY, REPUBLIC OF; POLAND; ROMANIA, REPUBLIC OF; UNION OF SOVIET SOCIALIST REPUBLICS; YUGOSLAVIA.

East Germany *See* GERMAN DEMOCRATIC REPUBLIC.

EBRD (European Bank for Reconstruction and Development) *See* EUROPEAN DEVEL-OPMENT BANK.

E.C. *See* EUROPEAN COMMUNITY.

ECA The Economic Cooperation Administration, established in 1948 to administer the funds allocated for European reconstruction under the United States Foreign Assistance Act of the same year.

ECAC The European Civil Aviation Conference, established in 1955 to promote the coordination and orderly development of European air transport.

ECDIN *See* DATABASES AND DATABANKS OF THE E.C.

ECE The Economic Commission of Europe (United Nations) is a special agency formed in 1947 to study and publish periodic reports on specific economic problems of Eastern and Western Europe. It is headquartered in Geneva.

ECGD The Export Credits Guarantee Department is a governing body providing export credit insurance facilities to U.K. exporters.

ECLAIR (European Collaborative Linkage of Agriculture and Industry through Research) A 1989 E.C. research effort to promote the application of new developments in the life sciences and in biotechnology. ECLAIR's purpose is to research, adapt, and develop agricultural products for industrial use, to research and promote new industrial techniques for processing and transforming agricultural raw materials; and to research and develop environmentally less harmful industrial inputs in agriculture.

ECMA (The European Computer Manufacturers Association) It is active in the field of standardization.

Ecofin The Economics and Finance Council of the E.C.

Economic Act *See* CHRONOLOGY (NOVEMBER 6 AND 12, 1981).

Economic and Social Committee (ESC) A consultative body of 189 members that was established by the Treaty of Rome. It has functioned since 1958 with its members nominated by governments and appointed by the Council of Ministers for a four-year renewable term. ESC is divided into three groups representing employers, trade unions and general interests (e.g., professional, consumer, commercial).

See EUROPEAN COMMUNITY; LEGISLATIVE PREPARATION; REPRESENTATIVE ORGANIZATIONS; STANDING COMMITTEE ON EMPLOYMENT; TRIPARTITE CONFERENCE.

Economic Commmission of Europe *See* ECE.

Economic Cooperation Administration *See* ECA.

Economic Cooperation Agreement This E.C. agreement established a financial and loan program with Costa Rica, El Salvador, Guatemala, Honduras, Nicaragua, and Panama.

See CARIBBEAN BASIN; LOMÉ CONVENTIONS.

Economic Development Institute *See* INTERNATIONAL BANK FOR RECONSTRUCTION AND DEVELOPMENT.

Economic Research, Association of European Institutes of This organization was founded in 1957 with institutes in 10 nations. It is headquartered in Bonn, Federal Republic German.

economic union This goal was affirmed in October 1972, at the Paris summit, by the Nine (the original six E.E.C. Members, plus Denmark, Irish Republic, U.K.). They agreed to increase their collaboration in the fields of scientific research and advanced technology.

Ecrêtement This is a formula constituting a move towards tariff harmonization. It involves departing from the concept of a straight linear cut in tariffs by introducing the idea of target rates and reducing by 50 percent the difference between existing national rates and the target rates instead of the difference between existing tariff rates and nil.

E.C.S.C. *See* EUROPEAN COAL AND STEEL COMMUNITY.

ECTEL *See* EUROPEAN TELECOMMUNICATIONS AND PROFESSIONAL ELECTRONICS INDUSTRY. It was formed in 1986 from Eucatel (European Conference of Associations of Telecommunication Industries) and ECREEA (European Conference of Radio and Electronic Equipment Associations).

ECU
(1) *See* DATABASES AND DATABANKS OF THE E.C.
(2) *See* EUROPEAN CURRENCY UNIT.

Ecuador This nation has an agreement with the Community on trade in hand-made items.
See ANDEAN PACT; LAFTA; LATIN AMERICA.

ECVP *See* EUROPEAN COMMUNITY'S VISITORS PROGRAM.

ECYO (European Community Youth Orchestra) Founded by the International Youth Foundation of Great Britain, which put forward the proposal for its creation to the European Parliament in 1974. A resolution for its creation was passed in 1976. The main purpose of establishing this orchestra was to demonstrate through music the cooperation of European youth, thereby setting an example as a symbol of the European ideal—a united community of nations cooperating and working for peace, harmony, social justice, and human dignity.

EDA *See* EUROPEAN AREA OF DEVELOPMENT.

EDF The European Development Fund.
See DEVELOPMENT FUND.

education A 1976 Resolution identified the first program of educational cooperation, including educating migrant workers and their families; forming closer relations between various education systems, especially higher education; improving the teaching of foreign languages; encouraging the mobility of pupils, students, and researchers, the mutual recognition of diplomas, and periods of study in Community nations; and providing equal opportunity for all to all forms of education. The Community set up two educational institutions, the European University Institute and the European Center for the Development of Vocational Training. COMETT (Community in Education and Training for Technology), approved in July 1986, encourages cooperation between universities and industry, at the European level; promotes a European identity through student place-

ments in firms located in other member states; encourages economies of scale through the joint organization of new training programs, improves the initial training of students and the continued training of skilled personnel and executive staff; develops the level of training in response to technological and social changes; strengthens and diversifies possibilities for training at local, regional, and national levels; and exploits the opportunities offered by new information and communication technologies. The ERASMUS program, adopted on June 15, 1987, involves 3,600 higher education establishments and some 6 million students primarily to encourage students to do part of their studies in a university in another member state. YES (Youth Exchange Scheme) for Europe for students of all ages encourages youth exchanges throughout the European Community. In March 1989, education ministers agreed that technical and vocational education in all 12 countries should be divided into two cycles—one covering the last two years of high school and the other providing specialized training for two to three years beyond high school (each country already recognizes each other's high-school diplomas)—and that governments should provide public education for all students through the age of 16. (In Spain and Portugal, the age is presently 14.) Both the E.C. and the Council of Europe have set goals for foreign-student enrollments of at least 10 percent of each country's students by the mid-1990s. The challenge is daunting: how to reconcile 12 independent education systems that teach different curriculums in 9 languages.
See COMETT; EQUALITY; ERASMUS; EURYDICE; EXCHANGE VISITS; ILLITERACY.

education grants The Community offers grants for the development of joint programs of study between institutions of higher education in member nations. It provides for short study visits for education administrators to study administration systems in other nations and for administrators in secondary education and specialists in vocational training nominated by member governments to study their respective interests in other Community nations.
See EDUCATION; EXCHANGE VISITS; FI-

NANCE; GRANTS AND LOANS; RESEARCH; UNIVERSITY RESEARCH.

E.E.C. *See* EUROPEAN ECONOMIC COMMUNITY.

E.E.C. Six *Synonymous with* THE ORIGINAL SIX.
See ORIGINAL SIX, THE.

EEG (Europese Economische Gemeenschap, The European Economic Community (Dutch)).

EEIG *See* EUROPEAN ECONOMIC INTEREST GROUPING.

EES *See* EUROPEAN ECONOMIC SPACE.

EFTA *See* EUROPEAN FREE TRADE ASSOCIATION.

EGF *See* EUROPEAN GUARANTEE FUND.

eggs An E.C. regulation established standards for eggs in their shell sold for eating. It covers grading, packaging, freshness, weight, and quality. Export restitution payments are made to permit exporters to sell on world markets.
See AGRICULTURE, COMMON AGRICULTURAL POLICY; ANIMAL HEALTH AND MEAT INSPECTION; CONSUMER PROTECTION; POULTRY.

EGKS (Europaische Gemeinschaft fur Kohle und Stahl, The European Coal and Steel Community (German)).

Egypt This nation has had a cooperation agreement with the Community since 1977 and a bilateral agreement for textiles since 1978.
See MASHRAG STATES; MEDITERRANEAN POLICY; MNCS.

EIB *See* EUROPEAN INVESTMENT BANK.

ELDO (The European Launcher Development Organization) *See* EUROPEAN SPACE AGENCY.

ELEC (The European League for Economic Cooperation) This is an international nonparty organization that brings together experts in finance, economics, and industry to study problems and to suggest solutions.

electricity By 1995 the Community expects that the proportion of electricity generated from oil and gas should be reduced to less than 15 percent.
See ENERGY; GAS.

electromagnetic compatability *See* HARMONIZATION.

electronic payments *See* TECHNOLOGIES.

El Salvador This country has an agreement with the Community on certain textiles and hand-made products.
See CENTRAL AMERICA; CENTRAL AMERICAN COMMON MARKET.

EMA The European Monetary Agreement. It replaced the European Payments Union. Since 1958, EMA has provided a multilateral system of clearing foreign balances between the participating nations.
See EUROPEAN MONETARY SYSTEM; EUROPEAN PAYMENTS UNION.

EMCF *See* EUROPEAN MONETARY COOPERATION FUND.

emergency telephone A single emergency telephone number—112—will be in use in most E.C. nations by the end of 1992. To overcome language problems, the system identifies callers by country and is operated by international telephone operators.

EMP (A European Member of Parliament)

Employment, Standing Committee on This Committee was created in 1970 by the Council of Ministers. It advises the Council and Commission on employment policy. It is composed of trade union and employer representatives, appointed by the European trade union and employers' organizations, plus ministers of labor or social affairs, and the member of the Commission responsible for social affairs.
See EUROPEAN COMMUNITY; TRIPARTITE CONFERENCE.

EMS *See* EUROPEAN MONETARY SYSTEM.

EMU *See* EUROPEAN MONETARY UNION.

EMUA (The European Monetary Unit of Account) *See* UNITS OF ACCOUNT.

EMUG (The European MAP Users' Group).
It coordinates European interests in the MAP
(Manufacturing Automation Protocol) activity.

ENDOC *See* DATABASES AND DATABANKS OF
THE E.C.

energy A resolution in 1980 outlined a broad
framework from which an overall energy policy would emerge. By 1990, the Community
seeks to "decouple" energy and growth by
lowering the average Community ratio of energy consumption to growth of the gross domestic product to 0.7 or less; to reduce oil
consumption to approximately 40 percent
overall of energy consumption; to meet 70–
75 percent of electricity production by means
of solid fuels (coal) and nuclear energy; to
make greater use of renewable energy sources
(solar, geothermal); and to adopt an energy
pricing policy conducive to encouraging the
rational use of energy. Horizontal objectives
include completion of the internal market,
common pricing principles for energy consumption, improved security of supply, development of external relations, protection of
the environment, regional development, and
promotion of technological innovation. The
Commission, in conjunction with the European Coal and Steel Community and the European Atomic Energy Committee, sponsors
a wide range of energy research programs.
The Council's 1986 resolution on new Community energy objectives for 1995 called on
the Commission to monitor progress towards
these objectives: concentrating on pricing
policies, assessing demonstration projects and
oil and gas technology programs; monitoring
the solid fuel sector and the refining industry,
imports of refinery products, and the energy
efficiency program, with particular reference
to electricity and renewable energy sources.
The objectives for 1995 are: (1) natural gas—
to maintain the share of natural gas in the
energy balance (with a policy aimed at ensuring stable and diversified supplies), and
continuing and possibly increasing natural gas
exploration and production within the Community; (2) solid fuel—to promote the consumption of solid fuel and improve the
competitiveness of solid-fuel production capacities in the Community. The share of solid
fuel in energy consumption should be increased; (3) electricity—to continue with, and
increase, the measures taken to reduce the
share of oil and gas in the production of electricity as much as possible. The proportion of
electricity generated from oil and gas should
be reduced to less than 15 percent by 1995.
Taking into account the substantial part played
by nuclear energy, it has also been agreed by
the Council of Ministers that appropriate
measures be taken to ensure that all aspects
of design, construction, and operation of nuclear installations fulfill optimum safety conditions; (4) new energy sources—to increase
substantially the contribution of new and renewable energy sources to the replacement
of traditional fuels, so that these energy sources
can play a significant role in the total energy
balance. In addition, the E.C. believes that
billions of ECUs could be saved by a single
market in gas and electricity. In 1989, it proposed facilitating intra-E.C. trade in gas and
electricity, clarifying energy pricing, and coordinating future investments in the energy
sector. By July 1990, E.C. states will guarantee energy transit rights, to be followed by
their coordination of investment in energy
production and transport, and, finally, by
providing transit rights for electricity sold by
a company in one E.C. nation to one in another.

See ELECTRICITY; GAS; JOINT EUROPEAN
TORUS; JOINT RESEARCH CENTER; NUCLEAR
ENERGY; OIL; SCIENCE AND TECHNOLOGICAL
COMMITTEE; SOLID FUEL; THERMIE; THIRD-
PARTY FINANCING.

energy service company financing *Synonymous with* THIRD-PARTY FINANCING.

enforcement of competition law *See* POWERS OF INVESTIGATION.

engineers The Commission proposal of May
13, 1969, enables persons engaged in "research, creation, consultation, and application in the technical field" to open offices and
offer their services anywhere in the Community. Engineers are the largest professional group affected. The Commission
abolished legal restrictions preventing Community nationals engaged in these professions
from practicing in any member country; established transitional arrangements to secure

mutual recognition of the many different types of diplomas awarded in this field; provided for member states which do not now make a distinction between engineering study and other kinds of technical training to enact the necessary laws to make this distinction. This remains a proposal and has not yet become a directive.

England *See* UNITED KINGDOM.

ENREP *See* DATABASES AND DATABANKS OF THE E.C.

environment In 1972, the head of government recognized the need for a Community environment policy. The Council of Ministers on November 22, 1973, adopted its first Environment Action Program. It is designed to improve the quality of life and living conditions of the Community with programs to reduce or prevent pollution and to take positive action to improve the environment. By 1970, more than 50 directives or recommendations had been adopted.

March 1987 to March 1988 was the European Year of the Environment (EYE). The Community's environmental action program covering the period to 1992 makes environmental protection an essential element of all economic and social policies.

On March 2, 1989, the E.C. countries agreed to eliminate by the end of the century their production and use of chemicals that harm the atmosphere's shield destroying the ozone layer, with an 85 percent cut as soon as possible. The chemicals are chlorofluorocarbons (CFCs), which are widely used as coolants in refrigerators and air-conditioners, as propellants in aerosol spray cans, in foam insulation, and as solvents. An agreement also freezes the use of halons, used in fire extinguishing systems, at 1986 levels after 1992, but does not include carbon tetrachloride or methyl chloroform, also used in industrial processes. The 12 member nations of the EC and the United States account for 75 percent of annual production and 60 percent of worldwide chlorofluorocarbon consumption of about two billion pounds a year. In December 1989, the European Council, meeting in Strasbourg, agreed to establish a European environment agency. The Commission decided on January 17, 1990, that CFCs should be eliminated in the E.C. by 1997, or three years before the date generally agreed on worldwide. The Community currently produce 450,000 tons of CFCs out of the world production of 1.1 million tons.

See AIR POLLUTION; BEACHES; EUROPEAN AGENCY; EUROPEAN FOUNDATION FOR THE IMPROVEMENT OF LIVING AND WORKING CONDITIONS; LEADED GASOLINE; MARINE POLLUTION; NOISE; PCBs; PILOTS; TANKERS; TOXIC EFFLUENT; VEHICLES; WASTE; WASTE OILS; WATER; WILDLIFE.

environmental protection *See* ENVIRONMENT.

EOF The Europaeiske Okonomiske Faelleskab, The European Economic Community (Danish).

EP *See* EUROPEAN PARLIAMENT.

EPC *See* EUROPEAN POLITICAL COOPERATION.

EPO (The European Patents Office.) *See* EUROPEAN PATENT CONVENTION.

EPOCH (European Program on Climatology and Natural Hazards) A 1989 E.C. research program to provide scientific and technical support for the environmental policy of the Community. Its purpose is to improve productivity of Community environmental research efforts by coordinating national programs and to promote the scientific and technical quality of environmental research. *See* ENVIRONMENT.

EPS *See* EUROPEAN POLITICAL COOPERATION.

epsilon symbol *See* AEROSOL.

EPU *See* EUROPEAN PAYMENTS UNION.

equality A 1975 directive forbids discrimination based on sex. It provides for legal appeal for those who allege discrimination and protects workers who complain. A 1976 directive requires equal treatment in vocational training, working conditions, and promotional possibilities for working men and women. A 1979 directive requires "progressive implementation of the principle of equal treatment for men and women in matters of social security."

See POVERTY; SOCIAL POLICY; WOMEN.

equal pay *See* EQUALITY; POVERTY; WOMEN.

Equatorial Guinea This nation is one of the ACP states and a signatory to the Lomé Convention of 1988.

ERASMUS (European Action Scheme for the Mobility of University Students) This program was designed to enable university students to spend a year of their university studies in another member state. As a first step in the free exchange of scholarly credentials, the ERASMUS program in 1987 sent 16,000 students from both universities and technical colleges to schools in other member countries for up to six months. To qualify for an ERASMUS grant, which ranges from approximately $280 to $700 a year, students must enroll in one of the more than 1,000 ERASMUS-approved university programs. The grants are designed to cover travel expenses and any differences in the cost of attending school abroad instead of at home. None of the participating universities charge tuition fees. Of 32,000 applicants in 1989, ERASMUS expects to finance 28,000 students and teachers. During the 1989 academic year, 4,046 university teachers will visit a university in another E.C. state. In addition, the Commission granted more than 470,000 ECU to European university and student associations enabling over 20,000 young Europeans to study in another Community state during the 1989–1990 academic year. The goal is to sponsor 160,000 people by 1992.

See COMETT; EDUCATION; YOUTH FOR EUROPE.

ERDF (The European Regional Development Fund.)
See REGIONAL FUND.

ERM *See* EXCHANGE-RATE MECHANISM.

ERMES *See* EUREOPEAN RADIO MESSAGING SYSTEM.

ERP (The European Recovery Program) It encompassed large-scale American financial aid in the form of grants and loans to the European nations following World War II.
Synonymous with MARSHALL PLAN.

ERT *See* EUROPEAN ROUND TABLE.

ESA
(1) *See* EURATOM SUPPLY AGENCY.
(2) *See* EUROPEAN SPACE AGENCY.

ESC *See* ECONOMIC AND SOCIAL COMMITTEE.

ESF (The European Social Fund.)
See SOCIAL FUND.

ESLAB (The European Space Laboratory.)

ESPRIT (The European Strategic Program for Research and Development in Information Technology) It was officially launched in February 1984, involving work on mini-supercomputers, on improving industrial production by getting computers to communicate with each other; and on computer systems that will be able to control equipment and appliances in private homes. It also involves work on establishing Europe-wide software certification procedures and developing computerized work stations that simultaneously use voice, writing, data, and charts. ESPRIT II, approved in 1988, had 158 contracts funded with 3.2 billion ECU of which half will be provided by the E.C. and the other half by the participants in the scheme. Computer-aided design standards for Very Large Scale Integration (VLSI), the Portable Common Tool Environment (PCTE) interfaces, the Communication Network for Manufacturing Applications (CNMA), and the Office Document Architecture (ODA) are notable examples of international standards being established through ESPRIT projects. For 1990–1993 ESPRIT had 450 projects with $5 billion allocated by the E.C. and industry.
See INFORMATION TECHNOLOGY.

Esquipulas II This is an agreement to establish stable and lasting peace in Central America. Communiques were signed by the E.C. and the Central American countries in Managua during the summer of 1988 when the E.C. increased aid for refugees and displaced persons in those countries.
See CENTRAL AMERICA.

ESRO (The European Space Research Organization.)

establishment, right of This concept includes the right to engage in nonwage earning activities and to own and operate enterprises. It is meant to eliminate restrictions on the freedom of establishment of nationals of a member nation in the territory of another member nation as proposed by the Treaty of Rome.

ESTI
(1) The European Solar Testing Installation.
(2) The European Space Technology Institute.

Ethiopia This nation is one of the ACP states and a signatory to the Lomé Convention of 1988.

ETSI (The European Telecommunications Standards Institute) It is an organization which takes over CEPT's (Conference of Postal and Telecommunications Administrations) specification-making role. It is located in Sophia Antipolis (near Nice), France.
See EUROPEAN TELECOMMUNICATIONS STANDARDS.

ETUC *See* EUROPEAN TRADE UNION CONFEDERATION.

ETUI *See* EUROPEAN TRADE UNION INSTITUTE.

EUA The European Unit of Account.
See UNITS OF ACCOUNT.

Eudised (The Automated Multilingual Thesaurus of Eurydice.)
See EURYDICE.

EUR The Unit of Account of the E.E.C. used by the Statistical Office of the European Community.

EURAM *See* BRITE.

EUR-6 The original members of the E.E.C. in 1952.

EUR-9 The nine members of the E.C. in 1973.

EUR-10 The ten members of the E.C. in 1981.

EUR-12 The twelve members of the E.C. in 1986.

EURATOM (EAEC) *See* EUROPEAN ATOMIC ENERGY COMMUNITY.

EURATOM Supply Agency (ESA) This agency was established in 1958 by the Treaty of Rome with capital from the Community and member nations. It has a right of option on ores, source materials, and certain fissile materials produced within the Community, and an exclusive right to conclude contracts on nuclear materials coming from inside or outside the Community.
See ENERGY; NUCLEAR ENERGY.

EUREKA In 1988, this E.C. program sponsored 213 nondefense joint projects among 18 countries, at a cost in excess of $4 billion, to produce electronic systems and goods ranging from high-definition television to robots to computer chips. EUREKA encourages high-tech firms to pool their projects and resources. In return, governments do their utmost to facilitate collaboration by giving financial backing to projects.

Eureka-A, a later project, is a 19-nation program involving 302 joint research projects in which 1,600 companies cooperate (99 percent of them European) to develop, for example, high-definition standards and external automobile guidance systems. Governments provide up to 40 percent of the funds for some projects at a cost of $10.3 billion, including $4 billion for the JESSI semiconductor program. The EUREKA/EUROROBOT program plans to transfer the most advanced application of robotics to the factory floor.
See JESSI.

EURET (Recherche dans le Transport en Europe). A 1989 research program of the E.C. for the development of a Community transport system capable of responding to the expected increase in demand for all types of transport (except trucks)—both quantitatively and qualitatively—resulting from the completion of the internal market.
See TRANSPORT.

EURISTOTE *See* DATABASES AND DATABANKS OF THE E.C.

EURO- A prefix applied to existing or proposed European projects, such as Euro-patents, Eurovision.

Euro-ads Advertisements that, except for the language, are similar in message and often identical or nearly identical in execution.
See EUROBRANDS.

Euro-Arab dialogue Negotiations on economic, financial, and other types of cooperation between the E.C. and the Arab League, resulting from the Copenhagen summit of December 1973.

Euro-barometer (Euro Barometre) *See* PUBLIC OPINION POLLS.

Eurobrands Products having a single brand name that are sold throughout most or all of Europe.
See EURO-ADS.

Eurochecking (Eurochequing) In 1983, the E.C. waived its antitrust rules to permit E.C. banks to continue applying a single set of terms for clearing international currency transactions made through the Eurocheque system. Eurocheque is an international payment system set up in 1968 by European financial institutions. Its members include banks and other credit institutions in some 40 European and Mediterranean countries, including the members states of the E.C. These checks may be cashed by bank customers at any of the system's member banks. They are often accepted as payment for hotel and restaurant bills and for purchases at shops and gas stations. Eurocheque customers are issued plastic "guarantee cards" which assure merchants and others who accept Eurocheques that the check will be honored by the bank it is drawn on. The primary advantage of the international use of Eurochequing is convenience to the checkwriter. Within the E.C., the rate of commission charged by Eurocheque clearing centers ranges from 1.25 percent in Luxembourg and the Netherlands to 2.25 percent in Belgium. There is no clearing charge in some participating countries.
See MADRID MEETING.

Eurocheque *See* EUROCHECKING.

Euro-coins In April 1987, Belgium symbolically underscored the growing importance of the ECU by launching an issue of ECU-denominated coins. Euro-coins are considered legal tender in Belgium and possibly elsewhere in the Community. Two coin values were issued, one in gold worth 50 ECU ($57.50) and another in silver denominated at 5 ECU ($5.75).
See EUROPEAN CURRENCY UNIT.

Euro-Control The European Organization for the Safety of Air Navigation was created in 1963, to strengthen cooperation among member nations in matters of air navigation, and specifically to provide for the common organization of air traffic services in the upper airspace.

EUROCO-OP The European Community of Consumers' Cooperatives.

Eurocrat A European Civil Servant.

Euro-currency *See* EURO-DOLLARS.

EURODICAUTOM *See* DATABASES AND DATABANKS OF THE E.C.

Euro-dollars These are dollar balances held by private persons or firms in European banks. They provide a stock of international currency not appearing in governmental returns. The system came into being during the Suez crisis of 1957. Traffic is not confined to dollars. It is also a fund of international short-term capital which usually flows to those nations offering highest interest rates.

EuroFed In March 1990, the E.C. Commission proposed that the 12 member states gradually fold their national currencies into the ECU and also form a new institution—the EuroFed—to coordinate E.C. monetary policy. Essentially, EuroFed would be the new European Central Bank. It would direct a common E.C.-wide monetary policy and would be legally committed to price stability. It would be an independent institution subject to democratic scrutiny. A ruling Council consisting of the 12 governors of the national central banks would set overall policy, and a small board of directors, appointed for relatively long terms, would run day-to-day monetary operations.

Eurofer *See* STEEL.

Eurofighter a production program in which British, German, Italian, and Spanish companies are set to build 800 new fighter aircraft at a cost of more than $30 billion.

Euro-Info *See* EURO-INFO CENTERS.

Euro-Info Centers The Commission established European information centers for businesses to keep track of amendments to legislation and help small and medium-sized firms become aware of opportunities. They are multi-purpose information offices, situated in specified areas and intended to assist the companies in those areas. The offices are linked to a central task force having access to E.C. data banks, and managing a two-way flow of information. The task force provides logistical support to existing structures (chambers of commerce, business consultants, administrative centers) selected for this purpose as part of a pilot phase. The first center was inaugurated in October 1987 with 39 centers expected to be distributed throughout the Community. Since December 1985 the Commission has published a monthly bulletin called Euro-Info, providing the business community with information on the E.C. initiatives that might have an impact on small and medium-sized companies.

Euro-investing *See* EUROLIST.

Euro-Jim *See* CANCER.

Euro-license Community citizens are eligible for an optional European driving license valid throughout the Community as approved by the European Parliament in 1976.
See DRIVING HOURS; VEHICLES.

Eurolist To promote Euro-investing, heads of major stock exchanges planned in the spring of 1990 to create a single European equities market, which, with a combined capitalization of close to $2 trillion, would rival the U.S. market. Projected for 1991 is Eurolist, a pool of up to 300 of the Continent's largest stocks as measured by market capitalization. These stocks will be traded on exchanges throughout the E.C., denominated in each bourse's local currency.
See SECURITIES.

Euro-loaf *See* BREAD.

Euro-lottery A lottery that would serve to finance projects in the field of E.C. culture.

The draw and the announcement of results would be public and would be televised throughout the Community with the results expressed eventually in ECUs.

EUROMART (The European Cooperative Measures for Aeronautical Research and Technology). A study financed by the E.C. and released in October 1988 pointed to the need for a cooperation program based on 10 key issues. This program started with a two-year pilot phase (1989–1990) covering aerodynamics, materials, acoustics, calculations, systems and on-board equipment, conception and manufacturing technologies, and propulsion. It includes a total of 50 projects.

Euromissile A French-German consortium to build antitank and antiaircraft missiles.

Euronet Eurydice, The European Information Network.
See EURONET DIANE; EURYDICE.

Euronet Diane (Direct Information Access Network for Europe) This network was created in 1980 as an information service with a special transmission network (Euronet) linking London, Paris, Rome, Frankfurt, Dublin, Brussels, Amsterdam, Luxembourg, and Copenhagen. It is Europe's first high-speed, computerized, information retrieval system. It is composed of independent European computerized information services that can give access to databases and data banks on numerous subjects. Initially, 40 host computers gave access to over 300 data banks covering a wide variety of scientific, technical, social, and economic information. Over 2,300 organizations use DIANE, with a number of countries outside the E.C. using the system. It was first conceived on June 24, 1971, when the Council of Ministers adopted a resolution recommending coordination of activities in the field of scientific and technical information.
See RESEARCH.

Euro-Nord Northern Europe, Denmark, Sweden, Norway, Finland, and Iceland.

EURONORM These are European standards accepted by the 12 member nations of the E.C.

Europabus A network of road services, tours, and excursions run under the administration of the European railways both inside France and beyond its frontiers.

Europa Nostra Begun in Paris in 1964, it became the first federation of the major nongovernmental organizations in Western Europe concerned with the preservation of historic buildings and their sites. Europa Nostra links some two dozen federated societies in 10 nations, and about a dozen associate organizations.

Europe Is composed of 23 Eastern (often called Central) and Western European nations with a population of 520 million and a gross national product of nearly $5 trillion, compared to, the $4 trillion economy of the United States and Japan's $2 trillion.
    See EASTERN EUROPE; EUROPEAN COMMUNITY; EUROPEAN FREE TRADE ASSOCIATION.

European Action Scheme for the Mobility of University Students *See* ERASMUS.

European Agricultural Guidance and Guarantee Fund (EAGGF) (FEOGA) *See* FARM FUND.

European Area of Development (EDA) The European Area of Development is a crossborder industrial zone on 1,200 acres within one hour's drive of Luxembourg's international airport. The plan for creating the European industrial zone was approved by the E.C. in December 1986. It enjoys financial support from the E.C. and a package of advantageous conditions including direct grants and reimbursements, help in hiring and training staff, and tax breaks.

European Assembly *See* EUROPEAN PARLIAMENT.

European Atomic Energy Community (Euratom) (EAEC) EAEC was created in 1958 by the Treaty of Rome to encourage the development of a civil nuclear industry in Europe. Its principal concerns are the promotion of technical, environmental, and safety aspects within the industry. It has responsibility for ensuring that Community nuclear industries are regularly supplied with fuels and ores, and that nuclear items are not used for other than civil purposes. It has provided, since 1977, loans for investment in electricity-producing nuclear power stations and industrial fuel cycle plants.
    See ENERGY; EUROPEAN COMMUNITY; EURATOM SUPPLY AGENCY; JOINT EUROPEAN TORUS; JOINT RESEARCH CENTER; RESEARCH.

European Audio-Visual Space *See* AUDIO-VISUAL POLICY.

European Bank for Reconstruction and Development *See* EUROPEAN DEVELOPMENT BANK.

European Center for the Development of Vocational Training (CEDEFOP) This Center was opened in Berlin in 1977 to assist the European Commission in encouraging, at the Community level, the promotion and development of vocational and further educational training. Vocational training accounts for 90 percent of E.C. social fund expenditure.
    See EDUCATION; EDUCATION GRANTS; EUROPEAN FOUNDATION FOR THE IMPROVEMENT OF LIVING AND WORKING CONDITIONS; EUROPEAN UNIVERSITY INSTITUTE; IRIS; STANDING COMMITTEE ON EMPLOYMENT.

European Center for Vocational Training *See* EUROPEAN CENTER FOR THE DEVELOPMENT OF VOCATIONAL TRAINING.

European Central Bank *See* CENTRAL BANK.

European Charter *See* COMMON DECLARATION OF EUROPEAN BUSINESSES.

European Cinema and Television Year *See* AUDIO-VISUAL POLICY.

European civil servants *See* EUROCRAT.

European Coal and Steel Community (E.C.S.C.) This is the first European Community created by the Treaty of Paris in April 1951 through an agreement signed by the six founder members (Belgium, France, Germany, Italy, Luxembourg, and the Netherlands). Its goal was to transfer control of the basic materials of war (coal and steel) away from each national government to common institutions, and to plan for economic expansion, rational distribution, and production, and to safeguard employment within the industry. The Treaty sought to abolish duties and quantitative restrictions on trade in coal and steel between member nations and to eliminate restrictive practices such as cartels. Grants are supplemented by the Community.

See COAL AND STEEL, CONSULTATIVE COMMITTEE FOR; COURT OF FIRST INSTANCE; ENERGY; EUROPEAN COMMUNITY.

European Coal and Steel Community Consultative Committee *See* COAL AND STEEL, CONSULTATIVE COMMITTEE FOR.

European Code Against Cancer *See* CANCER.

European Collaborative of Agriculture and Industry through Research *See* ECLAIR.

European Commission This Commission was established by the Treaty of Rome as one of the principal Community organizations. It has three major responsibilities: initiation of policy; implementation of policy; and "conscience" of the Community to ensure that Community obligations are carried out. The total number of the bureaucracy of the European Commission in Brussels is 9,100, responsible for 320 million people.

See ANNUAL REPORT; BUDGET; COMMITTEE OF PERMANENT REPRESENTATIVES; ECONOMIC AND SOCIAL COMMITTEE; EUROPEAN COMMUNITY; EUROPEAN COURT OF JUSTICE; EUROPEAN PARLIAMENT; EXTERNAL TRADE; HARMONIZATION; LEGISLATIVE PREPARATION; MANAGEMENT COMMITTEES; POWERS OF INVESTIGATION; RESEARCH.

European Committee for Electrotechnical Standardization (CENELEC) (Comité Européen de Normalisation Electrotechnique) CENELEC has a membership composed of the standards institutions of the Community and the nations of the European Free Trade Assocation. Standards are adopted by majority voting.

See EUROPEAN COMMITTEE FOR STANDARDIZATION; HARMONIZATION.

European Committee for Standardization (CEN) (Comité Européen de Normalisation) Its membership consists of the standards institutions of the Community and the nations of the European Free Trade Association. Standards are adopted by majority voting.

See EUROPEAN COMMITTEE FOR ELECTROTECHNICAL STANDARDIZATION; HARMONIZATION.

European Communities Act The legislation enacted in 1972 in the United Kingdom as a result of signing the Treaty of Accession.

European Community (E.C.) The three European communities, created by the Treaty of Paris and the Treaty of Rome—European Coal and Steel Community, European Atomic Energy Community, and the European Economic Community—merged in 1965 to form the E.C. In 1973, the six founder members (Belgium, France, Italy, Luxembourg, Germany and the Netherlands) were joined by Denmark, the Irish Republic and the United Kingdom. Greece became a full member on January 1, 1981 with Portugal and Spain joining in 1986. Austria applied for membership in July 1989, with Turkey expected to follow. Its aims are to break down trade barriers within a common market and create a political union among the peoples of Europe. It has its own budget raised from its own resources, e.g., customs duties, agricultural levies, a proportion of Value Added Tax; offers loans, subsidies, or grants through a variety of financial instruments including the European Investment Bank, the Farm Fund, Regional Fund, and Social Fund, and European monetary system. Collectively these 12 nations have a unified market and a $3.8 trillion economy.

See ENVIRONMENT; DATABASES AND DATABANKS OF THE E.C.; EUROPEAN COMMUNITY, STATISTICS; EUROPEAN FREE TRADE ASSOCIATION; FINANCE; OBJECTIVES OF THE E.C.; REGIONAL FUND; TRANSPORT.

European Community, databases and databanks *See* DATABASES AND DATABANKS OF THE E.C.

European Community, legislation *See* LEGISLATION PREPARATION.

European Community, statistics (1988)

		Area ('000 km)	Popula-tion ('000)	(GDP) Per Head $
B	Belgium	30.5	9,855.3	10,603
DK	Denmark	43.1	5,111.6	14,946
D	Germany	248.7	61,175.1	13,509
GR	Greece	132.0	9,895.8	4,325
E	Spain	504.8	38,386.8	5,632
F	France	544.0	54,947.1	12,280
IRL	Ireland	68.9	3,535.0	6,817
I	Italy	301.3	57,004.9	8,297
L	Luxem-bourg	2.6	365.9	12,876
NL	Netherlands	41.2	14,424.2	11,460
P	Portugal	92.1	10,089.3	2,705
UK	United Kingdom	244.1	56,487.8	10,533
EC12		2,253.3	321,278.8	113,983

Source: Eurostat
(GDP) = Gross Domestic Product

European Community Study Organization of the United States On October 29, 1987, a group of 35 academics meeting in Washington, D.C., agreed to form a new national organization to promote E.C. studies in the United States. The organization publishes a newsletter, sponsors an annual conference, organizes panels at national conferences and encourages links between Americans and Europeans working on the Community.

European Community Summit *Synonymous with* EUROPEAN COUNCIL.
See COUNCIL OF EUROPE.

European Community Youth Orchestra *See* ECYO.

European Community's Visitors Program (ECVP) Established in 1974 by the Commission and European Parliament to enable young leaders from the United States, Canada, Latin American nations, Australia, New Zealand, and Japan to visit Europe as guests of the E.C. The ECVP sends a total of 50 visitors to Europe each year, of which about 20 are Americans.

European Company Statute A statute providing an optional system of company (corporate) law, as an alternative to national law, for European firms operating in two or more member states. It was designed to stimulate cooperation among business people and bring progress on the social front by providing a mechanism for worker participation along various lines.

The proposal had its origins in the White Paper, published by the Commission in 1985. It is intended to encourage the formation of European companies capable of meeting American or Japanese competition. In preparing for 1992, this statute will allow companies incorporated in different member states to merge, to form a holding company or a joint subsidiary without coming under the jurisdiction of conflicting national laws. Use of the European Company Statute is voluntary. Its objective is to overcome the present legal difficulties inherent in associations or mergers between companies from different member states.

See COMPANY LAW; CROSS-BORDER MERGERS; EUROPEAN ECONOMIC INTEREST GROUPING.

European Conference of Associations of Telecommunications Industries *See* ECTEL.

European Conference of Postal and Telecommunications Administrations *See* CEPT.

European Conference of Radio and Electronic Equipment Associations *See* ECTEL.

European Convention of Human Rights *See* COUNCIL OF EUROPE.

European Cooperation on Scientific and Technical Research *See* COMMITTEE ON SCIENTIFIC AND TECHNICAL RESEARCH.

European Cooperative Measures for Aeronautical Research and Technology *See* EUROMART.

European Council *Synonymous with* EUROPEAN COMMUNITY SUMMIT.
See COUNCIL OF EUROPE.

European Court of Auditors *See* COURT OF AUDITORS.

European Court of Human Rights This court was established by the Council of Europe in 1950 to decide cases concerning possible violation of human rights. It may only deal with a case where the European Commission of Human Rights has failed to find a settlement, and where signatory governments have accepted its compulsory jurisdiction or, failing that, with governmental consent. In questions of jurisdiction, the matter is settled by decision of the court, the judgment being final.

European Court of First Instance *See* COURT OF FIRST INSTANCE.

European Court of Justice One of the Community's four major institutions. The court has the responsibility of ensuring that the interpretation and application of Community law is observed. The court's judgments are final and cannot be referred to any other court. The European Community's judiciary branch is based in Luxembourg. It operates in nine languages, with 13 judges (to make sure there are no tie votes) coming from 12 nations—with the 5 largest member nations taking turns having 2 judges at once—and 6 advocates-general. The independence of the judges is guaranteed by statute and is expressed in rules of procedure. Their deliberations are secret, the judges are irremovable, they are immune from legal proceedings, and their immunity can be waived only by a unanimous decision of the court itself, the person concerned being excluded from the deliberations. The court sits in plenary session requiring a quorum of seven judges to assure that deliberations are valid. It exercises jurisdiction over civil matters including trade, antitrust, individual rights, and environmental law. It does not hear international law cases from outside Europe and often strikes down laws of member nations because Community law supersedes national law when there are conflicts. By virtue of the Single European Act signed in January 1986, at the request of the Court of Justice, the Council may attach to the court a Court of First Instance, with jurisdiction to hear certain classes of action brought by natural or legal persons. (This was done in 1988.) The activities of the court reach beyond their main task of securing the attainment of the customs union to common rules on numerous matters from agriculture and transport to freedom of establishment and freedom of competition. By early 1990 there were 43 outstanding cases of a government ignoring a court ruling on the nonimplementation of a directive, or on an abuse of the single market. Italy had ignored 23 judgments, followed by Greece (eight), Belgium (six) and Germany (five).

See COURT OF FIRST INSTANCE; EUROPEAN COMMUNITY; HARMONIZATION; LEGISLATIVE PREPARATION; POWERS OF INVESTIGATION; SINGLE EUROPEAN ACT.

European cultural area *See* CULTURE.

European Currency Unit (ECU) On March 13, 1979, the EUA (European Units of Account) was renamed the ECU, and is now the Community's sole unit of account. The ECU is a composite monetary unit consisting of a basket of Community currencies (that is, the 12 national components) equivalent to the European Unit of Account.

In mid-1985, the Community central banks agreed to the first improvements in the function of the ECU by raising the rate of interest on the ECU, relaxing the rule whereby the amount a debtor central bank could settle in ECUs was limited to 50 percent of the claim being settled, and introducing a new mobilization mechanism enabling EMS central banks requiring intervention funds to mobilize through the European Monetary Cooperation Fund their net ECU creditor positions and a proportion of the ECUs allocated to them by the Fund in return for the deposit of 20 percent of their gold and dollar reserves. In 1986, the revised Treaty (Single European Act) related the ECU directly to economic and monetary union, as a force by 1992 in the field of financial services and it has been projected as a currency that could be used freely in all the European nations alongside national currencies. In 1987, the Belgians minted the first silver coins denominated in 50 ECU and 5 ECU.

Since 1987 the Statistical Office has published a special brochure giving the main statistics relating to the various uses of the ECU, e.g., the most recent Lomé Convention covering the period to 1990 provides for a total volume of 8.5 billion ECU. The amount of bonds denominated in ECU between January 1981 and October 1988 totaled 46.2 billion ECU ($51.3 billion). Loans granted between January 1983 and June 1988 amounted to 15.5 billion ECU ($17.2 billion). ECU futures and options traded at the FINEX in New York and the Philadelphia Board of Trade between January 1987 and June 1988 were valued at over $5.5 billion. By mid-1988, the value of the 45 investment funds in ECU denomination had reached almost 1.7 billion ECU ($1.9 billion). The ECU has fluctuated slightly over the years when compared to the U.S. dollar. In 1986 the average exchange rate was 1 ECU = $0.98. Towards the end of 1989, 1 ECU was approximately equal to 1.2 U.S. dollars.

In September 1989 the "new" ECU included the Spanish peseta and the Portuguese escudo, with revisions for the new weights of all component currencies. The new currency weights were divided as follows:

German mark	30.1 percent
French franc	19.0 percent
Pound sterling	13.0 percent
Italian lira	10.15 percent
Dutch guilder	9.4 percent
Belgian franc	7.6 percent
Luxembourg franc	0.3 percent
Spanish peseta	5.3 percent
Danish krone	2.45 percent
Irish pound	1.1 percent
Greek drachma	0.8 percent
Portuguese escudo	0.8 percent

By the fall of 1989 the ECU had become one of the top five currencies most widely used in international transactions. People can now buy travelers checks denominated in ECU, keep bank accounts in the currency, buy ECU-based unit trust shares, take out ECU loans and mortgages, and have credit card companies bill accounts in this currency. In the fall 1989, Luxembourg became the first of the 12 member states to encourage ECU use in daily life. Throughout November 1989, all shops, cafes, restaurants, and hotels in the City of Luxembourg displayed their prices in both Luxembourg francs and ECU. Residents are encouraged to pay their monthly rent, electricity, and heating bills with ECU checks, and some companies are paying their employees in ECUs.

See CENTRAL BANK; CHRONOLOGY (SEPTEMBER 20, 1989); EURO-COINS; EUROPEAN CURRENCY UNIT BONDS; EUROPEAN CURRENCY UNIT FUTURES AND OPTIONS; EUROPEAN MONETARY SYSTEM; FINANCE; MADRID MEETING; MARJOLIN STUDY; UNITS OF ACCOUNT.

European Currency Unit bonds The major ECU bonds are as follows:

(1) *Fixed rate bonds* with average maturities between three and 15 years and comparable interest rates. They account for about 88 percent of the total market.

(2) *Adjustable rate bonds* with interest adjustments every 3 to 6 years at the investor's or issuer's option or according to bilateral agreement.

(3) *Zero coupon bonds* with fixed interest payments at maturity.

(4) *Floating rate notes* issued mainly by state-guaranteed banks and sovereign states, with interest-rate adjustments every 3 to 6 months to reflect market movements.

(5) *Convertible bonds* that permit conversion into bonds or shares. These are well suited to counterbalance exchange-rate risks.

(6) *Cum warrant issues* that entitle the holder to purchase additional bonds or the issuer's shares.

See EUROPEAN CURRENCY UNIT; EUROPEAN CURRENCY UNIT FUTURES AND OPTIONS.

European Currency Unit futures and options Under an ECU futures contract, the buyer (or seller) has the right and not the obligation to buy (or sell) at a specified future date a fixed amount of ECUs at a price agreed when the contract was concluded. Under an ECU options contract, the buyer has the right, but not the obligation, to buy (call) or sell (put) a fixed amount of ECUs at a specified future date. ECU options have been traded on the Philadelphia Stock Exchange since February 1986, while ECU futures have been traded on the Financial Instrument Exchange forming part of the New York Cotton Exchange and on the Chicago Mercantile Exchange since January 1986. The Chicago Mercantile Exchange introduced a special incentive system in May 1986, resulting in a surge in the number of futures contracts traded in Chicago.

European Development Bank The 12 member states met in Paris on January 15–16, 1990, to discuss the creation of the EBRD. (European Bank for Reconstruction and Development). The Bank's purpose is to help rebuild the former Soviet-bloc economies. The Bank was formerly estabished at a treaty ceremony on May 30, 1990. The bank had an initial capital of $12 billion (10 billion ECU) and will make its first loans to Eastern European nations by early 1991. Sixty percent or more of the credits from the bank will be channeled into Eastern Europe's emerging private sector. Only 40 percent of the funds may be granted directly to governments. The bank has 42 shareholders. The United States has 10 percent of the bank's capital, while the Soviet Union will have 6 percent. Moscow agreed, for a period of three years (until 1993) to borrow no more than its paid-in capital contribution. The E.C. as a whole, will control 51 percent of the capital. Operations will begin in April 1991, and the bank will be headed by a Frenchman, Jacques Attali. The 42 members of the new bank picked London as the bank's headquarters.

See CHRONOLOGY (NOVEMBER 18, 1989; MAY 30, 1990).

European Development Fund *See* DEVELOPMENT FUND.

European Development of Science and Technology (CODEST) The body which advises the Commission on new trends in science.

European Development Pole In November 1986, the Commission approved a bid by the Belgian, French, and Luxembourg governments to set up a three-frontiers European development pole (a measure of the nation's boundaries) that would give a boost to regional development and contribute to European integration.

European Diary a weekly radio report on major developments in the E.C. that is broadcast at the close of business each Friday by Business Radio Network and selected independent radio stations across the United States.

European District A concept where Luxembourg would represent for Europe what the District of Columbia represents to the United States, a politically neutral territory where all the E.C. institutions are located and all the political, administrative, and regulatory business is done.

European Economic Community (E.E.C.) One of the three European communities established in 1958 under the Treaty of Rome by the 6 founder members (Belgium, France, Germany, Italy, Luxembourg, and the Netherlands), with goals to lay the foundations for a closer union among the peoples of Europe; to form a common market by eliminating trade barriers; and to work for the constant improvement of living and working conditions. It is coordinated by the European Commission, the Council of Ministers, the European Parliament, and the European Court of Justice. In 1965, the E.E.C. merged with the European Coal and Steel Community and the European Atomic Energy Community forming the European Community.

See EUROPEAN COMMUNITY; MERGER TREATY.

European Economic Interest Grouping (EEIG) Legislation was passed, effective July 1, 1989, creating a new instrument facilitating cross-frontier cooperation for firms within the Community engaging in certain joint activities such as research and development, purchasing, production and selling, operation of specialized services, quality control of substances, computerized data processing, and the formation of multidisciplinary consortia in the construction industry to tender for public or private contracts. EEIG establishes rules, applicable to all members, on the structure and method of operation, particularly small and medium-sized companies, with a framework for retaining their economic and legal independence within a structure enjoying full legal capacity. By regulation EEIG members are given a large amount of freedom in organizing their internal relations and in the choice of the grouping's method of operation. The regulation sets mandatory and supplemental measures to protect third parties, and to a certain extent, the members themselves. EEIG has two organs—the members acting collectively and the manager or managers. Groupings need not be formed with capital and members are free to choose ways of financing the grouping, making EEIG a completely flexible instrument of cooperation. EEIG's encourage cross-border cooperation and benefit businesses which do not wish to merge or form joint subsidiaries, but wish to carry out certain activities in common. By the end of 1989 five E.C. states had modified their national legislation to permit registration of EEIGs.

See COMPANY LAW.

European Economic Space (EES) A group formed by the E.C. and the European Free Trade Association (EFTA) to deal with the implications of 1992 for the Continent's other trading bloc, ie., Eastern and Soviet Europe. All 18 nations unanimously declared their political support for cooperation between the groups.

See EUROPEAN FREE TRADE ASSOCIATION; EUROPEAN FREE TRADE ZONE; EUROPEAN ROUND TABLE.

European Economic Unity In April 1989, Jacques Delors, president of the European Commission, announced his Community plan for economic unification. It entails the following three stages:

Stage one: The 12 European Community nations would strengthen the coordination of their economic and monetary policies. Britain and other community nations not belonging to the eight-nation linked exchange rate system would join.

Stage Two: A framework would be established to set key economic objective and budget deficit limits for member nations. The Community would monitor performance if major deviations occurred. A European system of central banks, similar to the Federal Reserve System, would be set up to establish a common monetary policy.

Stage three: Exchange rates would be irrevocably locked. Rules on macroeconomic and budgetary policy would become binding. The single central bank would be responsible for making the community's monetary policy, intervening in the currency markets, and holding reserves. A single currency would be adopted.

See CENTRAL BANK; EUROFED; EUROPEAN MONETARY SYSTEM.

European Energy Agency Dutch Prime Minister Lubbers in 1990 suggested the establishment of the European Energy Agency that could help the Soviet Union to better exploit its enegy resources by supplying much needed capital and high technology.

European Environment Agency In January 1989, in a speech to the European parliament, E.C. President Jacques Delors launched the idea of a European environmental measurement and verification network. In June 1989, the E.C. Commission proposed the creation of the European Environment Agency, having as its main objective to assist the Community, its member states, and interested non-E.C. countries to improve methods of environmental protection. Its activities would include the collection of data, the scientific assessment of environmental damage, and risk forecasting. The proposed agency would be the center of a network providing objective information necessary to formulate and implement effective environmental policies. It would provide technical, scientific, and economic information for Commission assessment of the implementation and results of environmental action and legislation. The agency would develop environmental modeling and forecasting techniques for appropriate preventive action. Atmospheric emissions, water quality, pollutants, the state of soil and vegetation, and land cover and use will be particularly important in determining the quality and sensitivity of the environment and the pressures on it. In December 1989, the European Council, meeting in Strasbourg, agreed to establish this environmental agency. In January 1990, the Danish members of the European Parliament agreed to have the future European Environment Agency headquarters in Copenhagen. The Irish proposed scattering some 20 specialized environmental centers around the E.C.

See ENVIRONMENT; POLLUTION.

European financial area On October 28, 1987, the E.C. Commission adopted proposals for the final stage of a plan to liberalize capital movements within the Community. The proposals consist of three legal texts aimed at establishing the principle that capital movements are totally free, and containing safeguard clauses designed to deal with serious short-term disturbances that may occur, and allowing for transition periods for the application of the new law to certain member states, for example, Spain, Portugal, Greece and Ireland.

See CAPITAL, FREE MOVEMENT OF.

European Foundation This foundation was proposed by the European Council in December 1977 to improve "mutual understanding among the people of the Community; to promote understanding of Europe's cultural heritage; and to assist European intergration."

See EDUCATION.

European Foundation for the Improvement of Living and Working Conditions This foundation was created in Dublin in 1975 to seek ways of improving living and working conditions in the Community. Work is done by contract through universities or other appropriate organizations.

See EUROPEAN FOUNDATION; FINANCE.

European Free Trade Agreement *See* EUROPEAN FREE TRADE ASSOCIATION.

European Free Trade Association (European Free Trade Agreement) (EFTA) EFTA was created in 1959 under the Stockholm Treaty as a counter-institution to the European Economic Community. Its three goals are: (1) to achieve free trade in industrial items among the member nations; (2) to assist in the creation of a single market embracing the nations of Western Europe; and (3) to contribute to the expansion of world trade in general. EFTA members are Norway, Sweden, Finland, Austria, Switzerland, and Iceland. They have a $640 billion economy compared to the E.C.'s $3.8 trillion economy.

Since July 1, 1977, there has been an almost complete free trade area in industrial goods in 18 Western European nations. Tariff concessions apply to industrial items of EFTA origin; agricultural products do not come under the provisions of free trade.

There is no common customs tariff within EFTA. Members impose their own rates of duty on products entering from outside the EFTA area. Trade between EFTA and the Community represents 24.5 percent of all Community trade (a little more than E.C.-U.S. trade) and between 40 and 64 percent of EFTA's imports and exports. The value of E.C. trade with EFTA in 1988 was $220 billion, or $56 billion more than trade between the Community and the United States. In March 1989, EFTA agreed to open negotiations with the E.C. for a special and improved trading relationship "to strengthen links between the trading groups ahead of the 1992 market unification."

In late 1989, EFTA officials in Geneva stated that Hungary, Poland, Yugoslavia, and the Soviet Union have contacted them about the possibility of joining, with Hungary probably being the first to reach an agreement. Formal negotiations began on June 20, 1990, between EFTA and the E.C. to establish a common economic zone, the so-called European Economic Space.

See CHRONOLOGY (DECEMBER 14–15, 1987); CUSTOMS UNION; EASTERN EUROPE; EUROPEAN ECONOMIC SPACE; EUROPEAN FREE TRADE ZONE; EXTERNAL TRADE.

European Free Trade Zone Effective January 1, 1984, the last of the industrial trade barriers between the E.C. and the members of the European Free Trade Association (EFTA) were abolished. It marked the culmination of a series of free trade agreements signed between the E.C. and the individual EFTA countries in the early 1970s. Initially, these agreements eliminated import quotas on industrial products traded between E.C. and EFTA countries. Import duties on the bulk of these products were eliminated by 1977. For a second group of industrial products—mainly textiles and nonferrous metals—tariffs were phased out gradually over a longer period. For the most economically sensitive products, such as paper, the timetable for dismantling E.C.-EFTA tariffs was extended until the beginning of 1984. On December 7, 1989, the Community, meeting in Strasbourg reached a broad agreement to create an enlarged free-trade zone that would include the six members of EFTA. The pact was signed on December 19, 1989, in Brussels at a meeting of foreign and trade ministers from the 18 nations of EFTA and the E.C. thus creating a European Economic Space.

See EUROPEAN ECONOMIC SPACE; EUROPEAN FREE TRADE ASSOCIATION.

European Guarantee Fund (EGF) A Spanish proposal that would attempt to raise funds for reducing Third World debt with the backing of government funding. The EGF, whose creation would depend on three conditions (that debtor countries agree on economic adjustment programs with the International Monetary Fund, that commercial banks shoulder their share of the burden, and that creditor countries not belonging to the European fund make an equivalent contribution), aims to strengthen the multilateral approach to solving the debt problem.

European Information Centers *See* EURO-INFO CENTERS.

European Information Market Observatory *See* EUROPEAN INFORMATION SERVICES.

European Information on Cancer Year *See* CANCER.

European Information Services A 1988 Council of Ministers approved program, with 36 million ECU in funding over a two-year period. These services are used to cofinance pilot projects aimed at developing advanced information systems in collaboration with companies across Europe, with priority given to road transport information, tourism information, image banks and standards information, as well as intelligent interfaces to electronic information services. It will also establish a European Information Market Observatory, which will track trends in the information market, improve the quality of market data and provide better decision-making tools. It supports wider exploitation of publicly held information by the private sector by overcoming legal, administrative, and technical barriers, and by simplifying information access methods and support for users of such services.

European Investment Bank (EIB) Established by the Treaty of Rome in 1958 to help implement specific economic policy objectives of the European Economic Community. EIB is still committed to serving the E.C.'s mission as a market partner. It is an independent body with capital contributed by Community nations. Its goal is to contribute via investment loans in projects to "the balanced and steady development of the common market in the interest of the Community" in regions qualifying for national aid schemes. Activities involve modernization, conversion, or the creation of new activities in areas of high unemployment that are of interest to several nations or the Community as a whole, such as improved road and rail communications or protection of the environment. It can assist finance projects outside the Community as under the Lomé Conventions and certain cooperation agreements. It can lend to private and public enterprises, to states and financially autonomous public authorities, and to financial institutions, for the purpose of assisting small investors through global loans. It provides loans based on money raised on capital markets by the Commission, which also decides on the eligibility of projects. Advanced loans can also be provided to relieve the balance-of-payments problems of member states, subject to certain conditions. During the fiscal year 1987, financing was provided by the EIB from its own resources for projects within or of direct interest to each of the 12 member states totalling 7.0 million ECU, reflecting an increase of 4.9 percent over the previous year's figure of 6.7 million. Aggregate financing within the Community climbed from 7.1 million in 1986 to 7.5 million in 1987, or by 5.4 percent at current prices and by 4.2 percent in real terms. The EIB hit a new high in lending activity in 1989, creating more than 40,000 new jobs and increasing green investments by 40 percent. The E.C.'s own bank lent 12.2 billion ECU ($14.8 billion) in 1989, a 56 percent rise over the 1988 figure of 10.2 billion ECU ($12.2 billion).

See EUROPEAN COMMUNITY; FINANCE; INDUSTRIAL POLICY; REGIONAL FUND; SMALL BUSINESSES.

European Launcher Development Organization *See* EUROPEAN SPACE AGENCY.

European League for Economic Cooperation *See* ELEC.

European MAP Users' Group *See* EMUG.

European Monetary Cooperation Fund (EMCF) This fund was established as the nucleus of a reserve system of the central banks, and has operational responsibility in the field of a Community currency exchange system. The Fund governors are from member states' central banks. It uses the Bank for International Settlements as its agent, and intervenes on the foreign exchange markets at the request of member nations. EMCF acts as a banker for the Communities in certain circumstances.

See MADRID MEETING; BANK FOR INTER-NATIONAL SETTLEMENTS (BIS).

European Monetary System (EMS) Officially introduced on March 13, 1979, EMS's goal is to create a zone of monetary stability in Europe, through the implementation of certain exchange rates, credit, and resource transfer policies to ensure that monetary instability does not interfere with the process of genuine integration with the Community. Assistance is conditional, a borrower nation must agree to certain economic and monetary conditions.

Spain joined the exchange rate mechanism in June 1989, one year ahead of schedule, leaving only Britain among the main E.C. countries as a holdout against full participation in the monetary bloc. Britain is a partial EMS member, with the pound of the ECU monetary basket, but it hasn't yet joined the exchange-rate mechanism that forces member currencies to stay within certain ranges. In June 1989, the 12 member nations, meeting in Madrid, agreed that by July 1, 1990, they would broaden the EMS to coincide with an end to exchange controls and obstacles to community-wide banking, securities, and insurance operations. In September 1989, British officials attempted to derail a movement to establish a European central bank and a single European currency. Their alternate proposal called for "competing currencies" in which all community currencies would become legal tender in every member state of the E.C., arguing that it would help foster currency stability, without involving the sacrifice of sovereignty implicit in a single central bank. The U.K. joined the EMS in October 1990.

See EMA; EUROPEAN ECONOMIC UNITY; EUROPEAN MONETARY UNION; EXCHANGE-RATE MECHANISM; FINANCE; MADRID MEETING.

European Monetary Union (EMU) The Basle Agreement of April 24, 1972, established an exchange rate scheme to limit the margins of fluctuation between Community currencies (the Snake) to a permissible margin of fluctuation against the dollar (the Tunnel). The first stage of EMU, as agreed at the European Summit in Madrid in June 1989, began on July 1, 1990. The emphasis during this stage was on enhancing economic and monetary coherence among E.C. members, strengthening policy coordination within the existing institutional framework, implementing the internal market program, and reforming E.C. structural funds.

See EUROPEAN MONETARY SYSTEM; FINANCE; MADRID MEETING.

European Nature Conservation Year The year 1970 was set aside for promoting the conservation of the countryside, winning the battle against air and water pollution, and ensuring the adequacy of natural resources to meet the rising demands of a growing population. Once completed, the campaign was proclaimed a great success in getting people to be more aware of the beauty and limits of nature.

European Organization for the Safety of Air Navigation *See* EURO-CONTROL.

European Parliament It is one of the four major institutions of the European Community. Established under the Treaty of Rome as the European Assembly, the European Parliament is composed of 518 seats, directly elected every five years in accordance with a uniform procedure in all member nations. It has 15 specialized committees and it meets in Strasbourg, France. Most proposed legislation cannot be formally adopted by the Council until it has received the Parliament's opinion. The European Parliament can dismiss the European Commission (a power it has never used) and the E.C.'s annual budget cannot be adopted without Parliament's agreement. The Single European Act increased its legislative role by giving it the right to a second reading of proposed legislation and more latitude in amending legislation before it is formally adopted. The Parliament must give its assent to important agreements the E.C. enters into, such as cooperation agreements with third countries, or the accession of new members. Thus, it has full power to ratify.

See BUDGET; EUROPEAN COMMUNITY; EUROPEAN PARLIAMENT, COMMITTEES;

EUROPEAN PARLIAMENT, POWERS; LEGISLA-
TIVE PREPARATION.

European Parliament, Committees There
are numerous specialized standing committees dealing with specific areas of Community
interest: Political Affairs; Agriculture; Budgets; Economic and Monetary Affairs; Energy
and Research; External Economic Relations;
Legal Affairs; Social Affairs and Employment;
Regional Policy and Regional Planning;
Transport; Environment; Public Health and
Consumer Protection; Youth, Culture, Education, Information, and Sport; Development and Cooperation; Budgetary Control;
and Rules of Procedure and Petitions.

European Parliament, powers Its formal
legislative powers are limited to the right to
be consulted on Commission proposals before
these are adopted by the Council of Ministers. It may suggest amendments, but apart
from the special conditions attaching to the
Community budget, nothing in the Treaties
obliges either of the other institutions to accept them. The 1975 Treaty of Rome gave
Parliament extensive control over the budget, including not only the power to amend,
but, in some circumstances, to reject the budget. It has the responsibility to check whether
the budget, once approved, has been put into
effect.
See EUROPEAN COMMUNITY.

European Patent Convention The European Patent Convention was endorsed in
Munich in the fall of 1983. Under its terms,
a single application may be filed with European Patent Office for a European patent.
This application must be endorsed with the
names of the European countries for which
the patent is required. When granted, the
European patent takes the form of a national
patent in all the countries designated by the
applicant except the Community countries.
A Community patent rather than a national
patent will be granted in the 12 E.C. member
states, even if only a single Community country is designated. The European Patent is
available to all persons worldwide.
See PATENT LAW.

European Payments Union (EPU) The Union
is a regional, multilateral payments system
established in 1950 to encourage multilateral
trade and payments among the Western European countries. All nations in Western Europe except Finland and Spain were members.
In 1958, EPU was dissolved and replaced by
the European Monetary Agreement.
See EMA; EUROPEAN MONETARY SYSTEM;
MADRID MEETING.

European People's Party *See* CHRISTIAN
DEMOCRATIC PARTIES, FEDERATION OF.

European Political Cooperation (EPC) Under the Luxembourg Report of 1970, procedures were set to encourage political
cooperation among Community member nations. The EPC is involved in the process of
information gathering, consultation, and
common action among the 12 E.C. member
states in the field of foreign policy. Ad-hoc
working units deal with special areas of policy. The Community's aim is to maximize its
influence in international affairs through a
single coherent European approach. The Single European Act put the EPC on a treaty
basis for the first time, although it remains
distinct from the structures and procedures
of the E.C. Its key features are a commitment
to consult and cooperate on foreign policy
issues and to work towards coordinated positions and joint actions; a commitment to decisionmaking by consensus among
governments, as well as the confidentiality of
consultations; and a commitment to direct
contacts between foreign ministries, allowing
speed and flexibility.
The EPC process works at the following
levels:
European Council—comprised of the heads
of state or government of the E.C. member
states, their foreign ministers and the E.C.
Commission, Presidency;
Foreign Minister Meetings—ministers hold
at least two EPC meetings per presidency as
well as one informal weekend;
The Political Committee—comprised of
senior Foreign Ministry officials of the member states, it manages the day-to-day business
of the EPC and serves as a clearinghouse for
routine decisions; it also prepares for the ministers' discussions;

Group of European Correspondents—consists of one official from each member state's Foreign Ministry to monitor the smooth functioning of the EPC; and

Working Groups—comprised of some 15 to 20 groups of experts that hold regular meetings two or three times per presidency.

European Port Data Processing Association (EVHA) EVHA was created in 1979. It is financed jointly by the Community and the ports themselves. This computer system initially linked the ports of Glasgow, Copenhagen, Hamburg, Bremen, Bremerhaven, Rotterdam, Antwerp, Le Havre, and Genoa. The system is aimed at lowering costs, reducing the risk of pollution, and increasing safety and efficiency in the shipping sector.

European Program on Climatology and Natural Hazards *See* EPOCH.

European Radio Messaging System (ERMES) After 1992, the 12 member states will commence ERMES, allowing bleeper communications across national borders. In addition, the system could encompass neighboring countries outside the E.C. (e.g., EFTA nations), although they would not be bound to the timetable agreed by the E.C. telecommunication ministers.
See TELECOMMUNICATIONS.

European Reconstruction and Development Bank *See* EUROPEAN DEVELOPMENT BANK.

European Recovery Program *See* ERP.

European Regional Council (ERC) The ERC was created in the summer of 1985, bringing together the regions of the E.C. member states to handle regional relations with the E.C. and the Council of Europe. Initially nearly 80 regional and 50 inter-regional associations joined the new body, which is based in Strasbourg, France.

European Regional Development Fund *See* REGIONAL POLICY, REGIONAL FUND.

European Research and Technology Community *See* RESEARCH AND TECHNOLOGICAL DEVELOPMENT POLICY.

European Research in Advanced Materials (EURAM) *See* BRITE.

European Road Safety Year More than 50,000 people are killed on Community roads each year. For this reason, 1986 was chosen as the year to tackle the main causes of accidents, including poor maintenance of vital parts of vehicles, bad weather, high speed, and driver inattention. The Commission proposed lower speed limits, stricter standards for carriage of dangerous goods on public roads, and harmonization of requirements for drivers licenses.

European Round Table (ERT) This is a 40-member organization of European industrialists that have combined sales of $400 billion a year and more than three million workers on their payrolls. The Chairman of ERT Wisse Dekker, chief executive officer of Netherland's Philips Gloeilampenfabrieken NV presented the advantages of eliminating internal trading barriers in his "Agenda for Action—Europe 1990" this paved the way for the E.C.'s 1985 White Paper on the single market. ERT strongly supports Europe's integration and the development of a greater European Economic Space.
See EUROPEAN ECONOMIC SPACE.

European schools This program commenced in 1957 for children of parents working for the Community, with schools in Brussels, Luxembourg, Varese (Italy), Karlsruhe (Germany), Mons, Mol (Belgium), Munich, and Culham (U.K.).
See EDUCATION.

European Science Foundation The Foundation began operation in 1975. It links the national research programs of 16 nations and promotes collaboration in research though increased mobility among research workers, exchange of information and ideas among participating nations, and harmonization of research activities and programs.

European Security Community (ESC) Proposed by England's Sir Leon Britttan in 1990, ESC would become the European pillar of NATO. It would not have the same members as the E.C., since Ireland (and later perhaps Austria) might not want to join while Turkey, Norway, and Iceland (NATO members not in the E.C.) would participate.

European Social Charters *See* DELORS, JACQUES.

European Social Fund (ESF) *See* SOCIAL FUND.

European Space Agency (ESA) ESA, headquartered in Paris, replaced the European Launcher Development Organization and the European Space Research Organization (which launched Skylark, the first European space probe, in 1964). An agreement was signed in Paris on May 30, 1975, by the 10 member nations establishing ESA. ESA's 13-nation program has built 28 satellites for weather, telecommunications, and research and is building the $4.8 billion Hermès space shuttle and part of the planned International Space Station. Ariane (officially titled Arianespace) has been the most visible sign of European commitment in the space sector. Hermès, the second component of Europe's space future, will be a smaller version of the American space shuttle. Columbus, the last element of the triad, is a habitable module for space research. Man Tended Free Flyer (MTFF) will be a reduced version of Columbus, which can be put in orbit by Ariane and requires no human presence on board. The year 1992 has been designated as the International Year of Space.
See APOLLO; INTERNATIONAL SPACE UNIVERSITY.

European Space Research Organization *See* EUROPEAN SPACE AGENCY.

European standard A standard approved by the European Committee for Standardization (CEN) or by the European Committee for Electrotechnical Standardization (Cenelec) as a European Standard (EN) or Harmonization Document (HD) according to the Common Rules of those organizations.
See EUROPEAN TECHNICAL APPROVAL; PUBLIC PROCUREMENT.

European Standards Institute The creation of a standards organization to accelerate standards and technical specifications, and to ease certification was proposed under legislation known as the Green Paper. This effort would attempt to harmonize private national standardization bodies like DIN in Germany, BSI in Britain, and AFNOR in France.
See GREEN PAPER; TELECOMMUNICATIONS.

European Strategic Program for Research and Development in Information Technology *See* ESPRIT.

European technical approval A favorable technical assessment of a product's fitness for use for a particular purpose, based on its meeting the specific requirements.
See EUROPEAN STANDARD; PUBLIC PROCUREMENT.
Cf. COMMON TECHNICAL SPECIFICATION.

European technologies for Energy Management *See* THERMIE.

European Telecommunications Standards Created to improve standardization in telecommunications. Community measures toward standardizations include; (1) completing the initial stage leading to mutual recognition of type approvals for telecommunications terminal equipment, adoption of common standards for direct satellite TV broadcasting, allocation of frequencies for public pan-European digital mobile communications, and help for the less-advanced Community regions; and (2) completing agreements (such as recommendations) demonstrating the political will of the E.C. countries to move ahead voluntarily, to open up access to public telecommunications contracts, to set the scene for the joint development of advanced telecommunications technologies in intergovernmental applications, and to promote European standards and their common application. In evolving a free market for terminal equipment, the Community has adopted a directive on mutual recognition of conformance tests for terminals.
See GREEN PAPER; TELECOMMUNICATIONS.

European Telecommunications Standards Institute *See* ETSI.

European Trade Union Confederation (ETUC) ETUC is a confederation of 32 trade union organizations in 18 Western European nations. It was formed in 1952. Its goal is to influence European policies in the interests of working people and their families throughout the European Community, the European

Free Trade Association, and the Council of Europe. In a rally organized by the ETUC, an estimated 10,000 trade unionists from E.C. states gathered in Brussels in October 1989 to demand guaranteed workers' rights when the Community completes its single market.

See EUROPEAN COMMUNITY; EUROPEAN TRADE UNION INSTITUTE; REPRESENTATIVE ORGANIZATIONS.

European Trade Union Institute (ETUI) ETUI was established in 1978, as the research, information/documentation, and educational arm of the European trade union movement. It deals with European aspects of economic, social, and political developments of importance to the workers and the union.

European Unit of Account (EUA) *See* EUROPEAN CURRENCY UNIT; UNITS OF ACCOUNT.

European University Institute An Institute was first proposed at the Conference of Messina in 1955. Over 20 years later, in 1976, the Institute was inaugurated in Florence to help outstanding research students in preparing doctoral theses or in doing advanced research in many fields. The Institute also cooperates with other centers of learning in fostering knowledge and understanding of current problems with special meaning to the Community. Scholarships are provided. It maintains four departments: law, economics, history and civilization, and political and social sciences. Most work is conducted through seminars and research teams. Those who attended the Institute for at least two years and complete an original research study obtain the title of Doctor of the European University Institute.

See EDUCATION; EDUCATION GRANTS; RESEARCH; UNIVERSITY RESEARCH.

European Venture Capital Association *See* VENTURE CONSORT.

European Wildlife and Natural Habitat *See* WILDLIFE.

European Workshop for Open Systems *See* EWOS.

European Year of the Environment *See* ENVIRONMENT.

Europe day *See* SYMBOLS.

Europe without frontiers According to the European Parliament's estimates, barriers that prevent the formation of a grand European area without internal frontiers costs Community citizens tens of billions of ECUs each year. The Commission's White Paper of 1985 provides for the gradual dismantling, by 1992, of all the physical, technical and fiscal barriers that still obstruct the free circulation of persons, goods, services, and capital between the nations of the Community. To abolish physical frontiers, starting January 1, 1988, there will be a single document replacing the 70 national forms previously used for bringing goods across frontiers. To abolish technical frontiers, a system will be put in place to eliminate barriers that still inhibit the free circulation of persons, goods, services and capital. To eliminate fiscal frontiers, a mechanism will be created for compensation between member states, as well as substanttial measures to approximate indirect taxes, so that the remaining disparities will be insufficient to divert traffic or distort trade. This last mechanism is needed because, although all member nations of the Community have the same system of value-added tax, there remain differences from country to country in the number and level of VAT rates.

See FRONTIER BARRIERS; WHITE PAPER..

Euroregions Formed in several frontier regions in Europe, they are concerned with co-operation and contact in many areas, ranging from economic and social affairs to transportation coordination efforts in the multinational area making up the region.

EUROROBOT *See* EUREKA.

Eurostamp This stamp depicts a map of the E.C. on the right, with the stamp's value in ECUs (together with the conversion rate to the currency of the issuing country) on the left.

EUROSTAT This is the Statistical office of the European Communities. It is located in Luxembourg and is one of the Directorates-General of the E.C. Commission. Its task is to collect and process statistical data in the E.C. member states and their main trading partners to serve as a basis for the policy decisions taken at Community level. EU-ROSTAT harmonizes and aggregates these data via approximately 100 publications and computer networks. Its data banks can be directly accessed from all countries of Europe, the United States, Japan, and Australia.

See DATABASES AND DATABANKS OF THE E.C., NIMEXE.

Euro-sterling Sterling deposits accepted and employed by banks outside the United Kingdom. The market in such sterling is centered in Paris and is smaller than the Euro-dollar market.

Eurosyndicat Index This is an index number for European stock exchange securities.

EUROTECNET This is a June 1983 approved Community program aimed at developing vocational training in the new technologies. It provides for a European network to strengthen links between the member states, and has 135 demonstration projects noted for their innovative approaches to training. It provides for transnational cooperation promoting the exchange of information on project objectives, methods, and results, and the development of joint projects.

EUROTOX The European Standing Committee for the Protection of Populations against the Long-Term Risks of Intoxication.

EUROTRA (Programme Européen de Traduction automatique de conception avancée). A 1989 E.C. research program to develop a machine capable of translating all official languages of the Community.

Eurydice The Community's educational information network began operations in September 1980 as the official educational organ in each member state and in E.C. Commission offices. Its services are available to educational policymakers to aid in the coordination and information gathering processes. The system was authorized in 1976 as a means of improving the exchange of ideas and information between the different specialized authorities in the member states. Later the system became accessible through the Euronet electronic data bank.

See EDUCATION; EURONET DIANE.

EVG (Europäische Verteidigungsgemeinschaft) The European Defense Community (German).

EVHA *See* EUROPEAN PORT DATA PROCESSING ASSOCIATION.

EWG (Europäische Wirtschaftliche Gemeinschaft) The European Economic Community (German).

EWOS (The European Workshop for Open Systems) A body concerned with the development of the Open Systems Interconnection (OSI), a communications/computer standard network. It was formally established in December 1987.

See OSI.

Exchange-Rate Mechanism (ERM) A part of the European Monetary System scheme that restricts the movements of E.C. currencies against each other.

See EUROPEAN MONETARY SYSTEM.

Exchange visits Under the Treaty of Rome, member nations are required, within the framework of a joint program, to encourage the exchange of young workers.

See EDUCATION GRANTS; FINANCE; WORK AND EMPLOYMENT.

Excise duties Taxes imposed on certain commodities varied by country, inhibiting trade. Proposals were made in 1972 and 1973 for harmonization of the duties on manufactured goods, tobacco, spirits, wine, beer, and mineral oils. In 1985 similar proposals dealt with alcoholic beverages, and to some extent, cigarettes. The White Paper of 1985 set a 1992 deadline for achieving the following objectives: bringing the rates closer together, abolishing or reducing other excise duties to the extent that they involve border formalities, and linking the bonded warehouses of the different member states. Rates series proposals deal with taxation on alcoholic beverages, cigarettes, tobacco, and mineral oils.

See CONTROL OF GOODS; CONTROL OF INDIVIDUALS; HARMONIZATION; VALUE ADDED TAX.

Exclusive dealing agreements Agreements by which producers grant absolute territorial protection to specified distributors, by guaranteeing to the holder of the concession the exclusive right to secure supplies from the producer and the exclusive right to distribute the product in the specified territory. This exclusive right is usually reinforced by prohibiting all resellers in other areas from exporting into the area allocated to the concession holder.

Exhaust systems *See* VEHICLES.

Export credit insurance A directive was proposed in 1977 for the adoption of uniform Community principles for medium and long-term transactions with public and private buyers. It set minimum percentages for down-payments, maximum repayment periods and minimum interest rates. The directive set guidelines on local costs and identified procedures for the working mechanism of the arrangement.

Export Credits Guarantee Department *See* ECGD.

Export refunds *See* RESTITUTION PAYMENTS.

Export restitution payments *See* RESTITUTION PAYMENTS.

External dimensions These are the conditions which the E.C. seeks to negotiate with its foreign trade partners for right of access to the single European market envisioned by the Community's 1992 legislative program.
See EXTERNAL TRADE.

External trade The Community commercial trade policy is based on uniformly set principles dealing with tariff and trade agreements, liberalization, export policy, and protective measures, including dumping and subsidies. There are uniform regulations governing imports and exports throughout the Community. Since January 1, 1975, all external trade negotiations are conducted by the Commission, subject to approval by the Council of Ministers, and not bilaterally by member nations. The Community has created a network of trading agreements with nations of all continents in the form of association agreements, free trade agreements, trade or economic cooperation agreements and the Lomé Conventions. External trade accounts on average for nearly 27 percent of the gross domestic product of the Community countries. The nations most reliant on trade are the Belgo-Luxembourg Economic Union (where an average of imports and exports comes to 65 percent of GDP), Ireland, and the Netherlands. At the other end of the scale, trade as a proportion of GDP is 20 percent for France and 15 percent for Spain. The Community imports nearly 45 percent of its energy needs and about three-quarters of other vital raw materials. Therefore to maintain its standard of living, it must export finished goods. Fifty-five percent of the Community's trade is carried out with other industrialized free-economy nations and about 36 percent with the countries of the Third World.
See COMPETITION POLICY; COUNCIL FOR MUTUAL ECONOMIC ASSISTANCE; DUMPING; FINANCE; FOOTWEAR; GENERAL AGREEMENT ON TARIFFS AND TRADE; GENERALIZED SYSTEM OF PREFERENCES; STEEL.

EYE (The European Year of the Environment) *See* ENVIRONMENT.

EZU (Europäische Zahlungs-union) The European Payments Union (German).

F

fairs *See* TRADE FAIRS.

Falkland Islands These islands are a dependent territory of the U.K., covered by the Lomé Conventions. *See* OCT.

FAR *See* FISH; FISHERIES AND AQUACULTURE RESEARCH.

farm fraud *See* FRAUD.

Farm Fund (European Agricultural Guidance and Guarantee Fund) (EAGGF) (Fond Europeen d'Orientation et de Garantie Agricole (FEOGA) A fund that finances the Common Agricultural Policy and accounts for up to 70 percent of the Community budget. The Fund can contribute up to 50 percent of the cost of eligible projects based on specific criteria. The Guarantee Section of the Fund guarantees the intervention price or support price system of the CAP and provides grants. *See* AGRICULTURE, COMMON AGRICULTURAL POLICY; AGRICULTURE, PROCESSING AND MARKETING; AGRICULTURE, PRODUCTION GROUPING; FARM INFORMATION AND TRAINING SERVICES; FARMING MARGINAL TERRAIN; FARM MODERNIZATION; FARM RETIREMENT; FORESTRY; SILK WORMS.

farm information and training services The Farm Fund reimburses 25 percent of national government expenditure on farm guidance and information services to assist farmers. It is used also for training programs for farmers. *See* AGRICULTURE, COMMON AGRICULTURAL POLICY; FINANCE; SOCIAL FUND.

Farming *See* AGRICULTURE.

farming marginal terrain Direct payments, depending on the scale of the farm, are available to hill farmers and others in difficult climatic regions or terrain. The Farm Fund reimburses national governments 25–35 percent of eligible national expenditure.

See AGRICULTURE, COMMON AGRICULTURAL POLICY; FARM MODERNIZATION; FINANCE.

farm modernization Assistance for farming from the Farm Fund is made in the form of grants for low-income farms capable of improvement within a national development program, or as cash incentives to encourage beef and lamb production. Grants also are made to assist farmers to keep better accounts, for the general improvement of land and irrigation, and so forth. The Farm Fund reimburses 25 percent or more of national government eligible expenditure based on the regional economic climate.
See AGRICULTURE, COMMON AGRICULTURAL POLICY; FINANCE.

farm retirement The Farm Fund assists olders farmers and farm employees to retire early. Legislation provides for an annual payment to farmers aged between 55 and 65 who cease farming so that their land can be leased or sold to other farmers, or used, as in many cases, for other purposes.
See AGRICULTURE, COMMON AGRICULTURAL POLICY; FINANCE.

Faroe Islands The E.C. established a special import system for 95 percent of Faroese exports, mainly fish and fish byproducts. A Danish dependency located between Iceland and Britain, it received special concessions on all other E.C. markets in return for autonomous concessions granted by the Faroe Islands on some imports of E.C. products.

FAST *See* FORECASTING AND ASSESSMENT IN THE FIELD OF SCIENCE AND TECHNOLOGY.

Father of Europe *See* MONNET, JEAN.

fats, oils, and oilseeds These items were brought under Common Market regulation in 1966 to minimize undercutting olive oil output. Customs duties are imposed on some lower-priced imports.

See AGRICULTURE, COMMON AGRICULTURAL POLICY; GENERAL AGREEMENT ON TARIFFS AND TRADE; OLIVE OIL.

federalism A political concept for a more rapid approach to integration by which supranational political institutions are superimposed over national authorities.

federalization The process of combination between sovereign or independent states for the purpose of establishing a common central governmental agency.

Federal Republic of Germany *See* GERMANY, FEDERAL REPUBLIC OF.

Federal Trust for Education and Research A U.K.-based research organization specializing in European affairs.

federation The collective administration of formerly independent states by a single government in charge of all common policies vis-a-vis the outside world.

Federation of Christian Democractic Parties *See* CHRISTIAN DEMOCRATIC PARTIES, FEDERATION OF.

Federation of the Twelve In January 1990, Jacques Delors, president of the European Commission, outlined the goal of the E.C. as a Federation of the Twelve—a "profoundly original" construction and which would be executed "in transparency and in the clear definition of who does what."

feedingstuffs In 1970, Community techniques of sampling and analysis for the official control of animal feedingstuffs was introduced. It fixed the maximum permissible levels for harmful substances and products, and presented methods for marketing of feedingstuffs and additives.

See AGRICULTURE, COMMON AGRICULTURAL POLICY; PLANT HEALTH CONTROLS.

FEOGA (Fond Européen d'Orientation et de Garantie Agricole) The European Agricultural Guidance and Guarantee Fund.

See FARM FUND.

fertilizers In 1976, legislation was introduced harmonizing the laws of Community countries regarding the composition, labeling, packaging, and denomination of simple and compound fertilizers.

See CHEMICALS; CONSUMER PROTECTION.

Fiji This nation is one of the ACP states and a signatory to the Lomé Convention in 1988. A Protocol annexed to the Convention guarantees Fiji sugar exports to the Community.

See SUGAR.

film *See* AUDIO-VISUAL POLICY.

finance The Community instrument affecting finance is the European Monetary System. Its purpose is to stabilize fluctuations in exchange rates among participating nations and to support the less prosperous participating states; to set tax policies to encourage trade and capital investments; to establish investment policies for the free movement of capital, the protection of investors and Community investment itself; and to set the income and expenditure associated with the European Community's budget. Community revenues derives from the common customs tariff, levies, and up to one percent of the Value Added Tax.

See FINANCIAL SERVICES; GRANTS AND LOANS; MADRID MEETING.

financial integration Preparing for the single European market in 1992, the process of financial integration is to be speeded up to allow the Community to play its full part in the internationalization and modernization of the financial system and to create an open, competitive, and stable European financial area, which is a prerequisite for a frontier-free Europe.

See CAPITAL, FREE MOVEMENT OF.

financial mechanism In response to British concerns about future U.K. contributions to the Community budget, a mechanism was adopted by the the Dublin European Council in 1975 and became Community legislation in 1976. It involved a formula relating to the gross contribution of member nations to the budget. Amended in 1980, it enabled Britain to benefit from higher budgetary reimbursements as a means of lowering its net contribution to the Community budget.

See BUDGET; FINANCE; FINANCIAL SERVICES.

financial services In terms of output, financial services account for about 7 percent of gross domestic product for the Community, varying from 14 percent in Luxembourg to 4.5 percent in France. About three million jobs are in the financial services sector, or about 3.5 percent of total Community employment. A first banking coordination directive, adopted in 1977, established common standards for the granting of banking licenses and introduced the basic principle of home country control.

The general method of achieving full freedom of establishment and free trade in financial services by 1992 required a total of 22 proposals. These proposals require (1) the harmonization of essential prudence standards for financial institutions and for the protection of investors, depositors, and consumers; and (2) the mutual recognition of the competence of the supervisory bodies and standards of each member state; and, (3) based on the first two points, home country control and supervision of financial institutions that wish to operate in other member states.

By 1992, a bank will be able to offer the full range of its services throughout the entire Community and set up branches in another member state as easily as in its own, where insurance can be bought on the most reasonable terms and be valid throughout the Community, and where the market for securities and capital is of a size sufficient to meet the financing needs of European industry and attract investors from all over the world.

See BANKING; FINANCE; SECURITES.

Finet Foundation (The Paul Finet Foundation) *See* ORPHANS.

Finland This nation signed a cooperation agreement with the Council for Mutual Economic Assistance in 1973. Finland is an associate member of the European Free Trade Association, joining on March 27, 1961.

fire safety In 1984, the E.C. recommended that member states adopt equivalent national fire safety standards to protect guests and employees at the 175,000 hotels and inns within the E.C. borders. The recommendation calls for uniformity in fire codes, with minimium standards for compliance by hotel keepers to ensure tourists and business travelers an equivalent degree of fire protection throughout the E.C. The recommendation also requires protected fire escape routes, appropriate alarm systems, and emergency lighting, as well as a display of each hotel's floor plan at appropriate places on the premises.

fiscal controls The introduction over the years since 1967 of a common Value Added Tax (VAT) system, in place of the widely varying national turnover taxes, has been one of the Community's success stories. As part of the 1992 agenda, the next major step is to align the number and level of VAT rates in the member states. Alignment of rates will remove all need for VAT controls at internal frontiers when taken in conjunction with the following measures: the treatment of VAT on intra-Community imports and exports in the same way as VAT on sales and purchases within a member state, and the establishment of a clearinghouse mechanism to ensure that VAT revenue is allocated to the member state of consumption. The 1985 White Paper also gave impetus to the process by programming proposals for harmonization of rates and for linkage of the bonded warehouse system (which member states currently use for controlling movement of excise goods).

See EXCISE DUTIES; VALUE ADDED TAX.

fiscal federalism The economics of multilevel government finance.

fish A joint declaration, adopted in May 1980 by the Council of Ministers, stated the need to adopt a new Common Fisheries Policy (CFP). On January 25, 1983, the 10 member states agreed to the CFP. The new measures replaced the provisions of a 1971 fisheries policy adopted by the six original E.C. members prior to Britain entering the Community. CFP's goals are: to implement a rational and nondiscriminatory Community policy for managing resources; to ensure a fair distribution of catches, paying special attention to the needs of regions highly dependent on fishing and to losses from third-country waters; to establish effective controls on the conditions applying to fisheries; to adopt structural measures, including Community financial help; and to promote long-term fisheries agreements with third countries. Two hundred-mile exclusive fishery zones and water quality standards for shellfish breeding were created, along with short-term technical measures to conserve stocks. The CFP is to run until December 31, 1992. The European Commission will prepare a report assessing the CFP's success prior to deciding whether any changes should be made before beginning a further 10-year term. The E.C. minister in charge of fisheries in May 1987 agreed to grant about $11.2 million to help modernize fishing fleets throughout the 12 E.C. member states.

See AGRICULTURE, COMMON AGRICULTURAL POLICY; CHRONOLOGY (OCTOBER 30, 1976; JANUARY 25, 1983) IN APPENDIX; FAR; FINANCE.

Fish, Fisheries and Aquaculture Research (FAR) A 1989 E.C. research program to promote interdisciplinary initiatives for rational and scientific research on resources; to develop aquaculture; and to explore new methods and procedures for exploiting little-researched resources.
See FISH.

fishery policy *See* FISH.

FITCE (Fédération des Ingénieurs des Télécommunications de la Communauté Européenne, The Federation of Telecommunications Engineers in the European Community.)
See TELECOMMUNICATIONS.

flag *See* CHRONOLOGY (MAY 29, 1986); SYMBOLS.

flag discrimination These are practices designed to secure preferential treatment for ships of a particular nationality, mainly in the assignment of cargo.

FLAIR (Food Linked Agro-Industrial Research Program) A 1989 research program to contribute to Europe's competitiveness in the food industry, to improve food safety and quality for the consumer, and to strengthen food science and technology.
See FOOD.

flat-rate aids It is a method used for supporting producers of flax and hemp, hop, silkworms, and silk. These are special products which, taken together, account for a very small percentage of total Community agricultural production. Aid is granted by the hectare or by quantity produced.
See AGRICULTURE, COMMON AGRICULTURAL POLICY.

flax, hemp, and linseed The production and sale of these items are regulated by common market legislation. Assistance comes from the Farm Fund and varies according to whether production is for seed or for fibres.
See AGRICULTURE, COMMON AGRICULTURAL POLICY.

floods *See* CIVIL PROTECTION.

fluorocarbons In 1977 the E.C. recommended a directive concerning fluorocarbons used by the aerosol industry as a propellant. It urged member states to intensify research on a Community basis into the effects of fluorocarbons, to encourage industry to find alternatives, to encourage industry and users to eliminate leakage, and to prevent any increase in the production capacity of fluorocarbons.

Fond Européen d'Orientation et de Guarantie Agricole (FEOGA) The European Agricultural Guidance and Guarantee Fund.
See FARM FUND.

Fontainebleau summit *See* BUDGET; CHRONOLOGY (JUNE 25–26, 1984).

food The White Paper of 1985 recognized that a genuine common market for food could not be achieved by 1992 if the Community relied exclusively on past methods. It recommended a new strategy that combines sufficient harmonization of national regulations and standards to protect public health, provides consumers with clear labeling and protection in matters other than health, ensures fair trading, and provides for the necessary public controls. Measures mentioned in the White Paper include: additives, contact materials, labeling, food for particular nutritional uses, official inspection of food-stuffs, irradiation, quick-frozen food, and labeling for nutritional purposes.

See DAIRY PRODUCTS; EGGS; MILK AND MILK PRODUCTS; RICE.

food additives To standardize the safety of such items throughout the Community, five "horizontal" directives were issued affecting anti-oxidants, emulsifiers, stabilizers, thickeners, gelling agents and preservatives and fixing maximum levels in oil and fats of erucic acid.

See CONSUMER PROTECTION; FRAMEWORK HORIZONTAL DIRECTIVES.

food aid Funds are donated directly to needy nations through international organizations. These are two categories: emergency aid reserved for famines following natural catastrophes; and normal aid, when food is supplied free of charge to Community ports, but where the recipient nation covers the cost of transport and distribution. In August 1989, the Commission convened a 23-nation meeting to work out a two-year program of food aid to Poland and Hungary.

See FINANCE; INTERNATIONAL WHEAT AGREEMENT.

food labels In the spring of 1990, E.C. internal market ministers agreed to rules governing the nutritional information on food labels. The directive's detailed rules only become compulsory where food product manufacturers make a nutritional claim. But if claims are made, the legislation sets out two groups of nutrients for identification. The first group includes the calorie content of the product and the amounts of protein, carbohydrate, and fat it contains; the second consists of the first group's items plus sugars, saturates, dietary fiber, and sodium. For the second group, more nutritional information may be given on such things as vitamin and mineral content and cholesterol. In addition, the legislation specifies strict rules for expressing and presenting the information on packages.

Food Linked Agro-Industrial Research program *See* FLAIR.

footloose industry A manufacturing industry that is not based upon resource constraints such as coalfields, but has the ability to choose a wide range of locations.

foodstuffs—labeling A 1979 directive attempts to tighten laws in member nations on the labeling, presentation, and promotion of foodstuffs to provide greater protection against misleading descriptions and to provide consumers with more information. Manufacturers must provide detailed labels listing ingredients and giving the date from which the food in question is no longer to be consumed. The directive applies to all foods, whether prepackaged or not.

See CONSUMER PROTECTION; FOOD.

foot and mouth disease *See* ANIMAL HEALTH AND MEAT INSPECTION.

footwear In October 1977, the European Commission established a Joint Committee for the Footwear Industry, to study social and economic problems arising in the industry, and to advise on Community action. Since 1978 the Commission has employed a surveillance system of shoe imports into the Community.

See COMPETITION POLICY; INDUSTRIAL POLICY.

Foratom (Forum atomique Européen) The European Atomic Forum.

Forecasting and Assessment in the field of Science and Technology (FAST) FAST was adopted in 1978, and is a Community research program to define long-term research and development priorities for new Community research programs. FAST is a shared-cost research program involving research and forecasting centers in the Community with activities focusing on the relations between technology, work and employment, the transformation of the service industry, the communication function, the future of the food system, and the integrated development of renewable natural resources.

See RESEARCH.

foreign workers Within the E.C., foreign workers do not have the same rights as migrant Community nationals. The Treaty of

Rome confers on its nationals freedom of movement and the right to nondiscrimination in employment, remuneration, and social securitiy benefits. Member nations, under the Council of Ministers, agreed to gradually eliminate all forms of discrimination.

See MIGRANT WORKERS; SOCIAL POLICY; WORK AND EMPLOYMENT.

forestry To aid agricultural peoples in Italy and France, a five-year forestry program was launched in 1979 to replant or improve forests, construct roads, provide terracing and fire protection. In addition, studies and experiments were to be carried out. The Farm Fund contributes up to 50 percent of capital costs, subject to a minimum national contribution of 40 percent, and, except in special circumstances, a minimum five percent contribution from land owners. In 1989, the E.C. adopted a four-year program designed to protect and increase the Community's forests. These currently cover 20 percent of E.C. territory and employ, indirectly or directly, more than 2 million workers. The main aspects of this program are forest protection, the return of agricultural land to woodland, the encouragement of wood-based industries, and forest development. To stimulate domestic timber production, the E.C. extended the aid mechanisms for the processing and sale of agricultural products to articles made from cork and wood. Consequently, firms that carry out all the operations prior to the industrial sawing of logs will be entitled to subsidies. In addition, the E.C. is considering imposing a special tax on fossil fuels, such as oil and coal, to help fund efforts to save rainforests.

See AGRICULTURE, COMMON AGRICULTURAL POLICY; FINANCE.

Fortress Europe *See* RHODES SUMMIT.

Fouchet Plan *See* CHRONOLOGY (NOVEMBER 2, 1961; JANUARY 18, 1962).

four Refers to the nations which signed the Treaty of Accession (Denmark, the Irish Republic, Norway, and the United Kingdom) but because Norway did not ratify the Treaty, the Four became the Three.

Fourchette The higher and lower price levels between which member nations must op-

erate their agricultural prices. It was first introduced for cereals.

Four institutions, the They are: the European Parliament, the Council, the Commission, and the Court of Justice, with the support of the Court of Auditors. *See* INTRODUCTION.

fourth world *See* POVERTY.

framework horizontal directives Directives which lay down the philosophy and controls for a particular area, e.g., additives.
Cf. SPECIFIC HORIZONTAL DIRECTIVES.
See DIRECTIVES.

France This nation signed the Treaty of Paris in 1951, the Treaty of Rome in 1957, and the Treaty of Brussels in 1972. It is a founder member of the European Coal and Steel Community, the E.E.C. and the European Atomic Energy Commission. France looks to 1992 to represent a more solid platform for projecting its national influence and increasing its prosperity. However, there are weaknesses in France's economy, for example, the relatively small size of French companies, their lack of working capital, the absence of industrial strategy, and insufficient internationalization. The underdeveloped state of French distribution networks could lead to cheap imports from other E.C. states that could cause further joblessness at a time when the economy is weak. France's gross domestic production growth was 2.3 percent in 1987 and 2 percent in 1988. Unemployment rose to 11.5 percent from 10.75 percent in 1988, a record level.

franchisers The E.C. exempted franchisers in 1989 from most of the strict antitrust provisions of the Treaty of Rome. This reversed a 1986 decision by a West German court which ruled that the Treaty prohibited various activities that are common in most U.S. and European franchising agreements. That ruling would have limited franchisers' rights to exercise territorial or advertising control over their franchisees and would have made it harder to impose noncompetitive agreements. The new ruling exempts franchisers from that rule, and, for example, opens up the European market to U.S. franchisers. European franchisers have been growing at better than 10 percent a year since the late 1970s. In 1987, approximately 1,900 chains accounted for sales of 33 billion ECU (about $40 billion)—a little more than 10 percent of total retail sales.

fraud The E.C. is concerned about fraud in the $30 billion farm budget that accounts for about two-thirds of E.C. spending. An estimated 10 percent of E.C. funds are diverted through fraud. The E.C. Agriculture Commissioner plans to spend about $75 million in 1990 to tighten checks on commercial documents, select firms for inspection, set up a special fraud squad in the member nations, and improve cooperation among them.

In 1990, the E.C. decided to provide 10 million ECU ($12 million) a year for five years for a crackdown on agricultural fraud in its 12 member states. The 10 million ECUs will pay for training, equipment, private detective work, specialist laboratory analyses, and inspectors to check that cargoes are what their papers say they are.

freedom of movement for workers See FOR-EIGN WORKERS; MIGRANT WORKERS; RESI-DENCE RIGHTS.

free movement of capital See CAPITAL, FREE MOVEMENT OF.

free trade area This is a group of two or more customs territories in which duties and other restrictions on trade are eliminated on most of the trade between the member nations. Unlike the Customs Union, however, free trade area territories do not pursue a common external trade policy and do not therefore have any Common External Tariff.

frontier barriers The Commission's objective, as required by the Single European Act, is to coordinate policy and integrate national legislation to eliminate completely by 1992 the barriers and controls in connection with crossing the Community's internal frontiers. Community citizens should not have to produce documents of identity and nationality and obtain customs clearance of goods in their baggage when passing from one member state to another. The Commission's White Paper envisages a two-stage process for removing

frontier control of persons. In the first stage, frontier formalities will be made more flexible and less systematic. In the second stage, when the strengthening of the Community's external frontiers and cooperation between the relevant national authorities has reached appropriate levels, the frontier controls will be abolished.

See CONTROL OF GOODS; CONTROL OF IN-DIVIDUALS; EUROPE WITHOUT FRONTIERS; EX-CISE DUTIES; VALUE ADDED TAX.

fruit and vegetables Community policy attempts to stabilize fluctuating markets for these perishable goods through a system of purchasing (buying-in) certain produce when market prices fall for three successive days to 40–70 percent below the basic price set by the Council of Ministers. The Farm Fund reimburses producer cooperatives or member governments for buying-in costs, but only for goods reaching Community qualitative standards. A regulation provides for disposal of bought-in produce through free distribution to charities or schools, for animal feed, or for industrial purposes and distilling, but not for destruction. It also sets common graded quality standards, other than for local use, for products to be eaten fresh. Imports are controlled by imposing a countervailing duty when the price of imports falls below the references price for two successive days. This reference price is primarily a minimum import price based on the cost of production and marketing.

See AGRICULTURE, COMMON AGRICUL-TURAL POLICY; PLANT HEALTH CONTROLS; PROCESSED FRUITS AND VEGETABLES; SEEDS, COMMON CATALOGUE.

fruit jams, jellies, marmalade, and chestnut puree These items can be marketed in the Community provided they conform to the definitions and regulations in a Directive detailing the minimum amount of fruit that they must contain. Ultimately, the E.C. is concerned with the health and safety of these products, more than composition.

See CONSUMER PROTECTION.

fruit juices (soft drinks) An amended 1975 directive abolished barriers to trade and offered protection to the consumer from misleading products. The directive defines various items and provides a positive list of the substances and quantities admitted in the production and processing of fruit juices. Substances not found on the list are not to be manufactured.

See CONSUMER PROTECTION.

functionalism The step-by-step approach to integration, through agreements in economic sectors such as agriculture, tariffs, transport, etc.

fusion *See* JOINT EUROPEAN TORUS; NUCLEAR FUSION.

G

G-24 *Synonymous with* Group of 24.

Gabon This nation is one of the ACP states and a signatory to the Yaounde Conventions of 1963 and 1969 and the Lomé Convention of 1988.

Gambia This nation is one of the ACP states and a signatory to the Lomé Convention of 1988.

game meat *See* ANIMAL HEALTH AND MEAT INSPECTION.

gas To counter the decline of natural gas supplies, the European Commission recommended three lines of action: (1) technological development to enable isolated gas fields in the North Sea or beyond and difficult geological formations to be exploited; (2) diversification of external suppliers plus extended contracts with Norway; and (3) development of natural gas substitutes through liquified petroleum gas and coal gasification. By 1995, the Community objective is to maintain the present share of natural gas in the Community's energy balance. In July 1989, the Commission adopted three proposals to open up E.C. wholesale markets in natural gas and electricity. These measures would establish wider access to energy networks in E.C. countries and would require greater disclosure of pricing data and the exchange of information on energy investment projects.
See ENERGY.

gaseous emission *See* VEHICLES.

gasoline *See* LEADED GASOLINE.

GATT *See* GENERAL AGREEMENT ON TARIFFS AND TRADE.

GCC *See* GULF COOPERATION COUNCIL.

GDP *See* GROSS DOMESTIC PRODUCT.

GDR *See* GERMAN DEMOCRATIC REPUBLIC.

General Agreement on Tariffs and Trade (GATT) On January 1, 1948, a multilateral trade treaty was signed embodying reciprocal commercial rights and obligations as a means of expanding and liberalizing world trade. It established common regulations and obligations concerning international trading arrangements and the framework for the negotiation of agreements to liberalize world trade. It was accepted by over 80 fully participating nations, with nearly 30 others signing under special arrangements. These nations account for almost 80 percent of world trade. The European Commission negotiates on behalf of the Community in the Multilateral Trade Negotiations under GATT.

In April 1989, GATT adopted measures to strengthen its credibility and fend off protectionism by member nations by imposing time limits on each stage of the negotiating procedure. For example, once three trade officials are chosen for a dispute panel, they must reach a decision within six months—three months if the complaint is particularly urgent, involving, for example, perishable goods. The new measures also establish a mechanism to monitor countries' compliance with adverse rulings. The GATT trade rounds were:

1947	Geneva Round creating GATT
1949	Annecy Round
1950–51	Torkay Round
1955–56	Geneva Round
1960–61	Dillon Round
1964–67	Kennedy Round
1973–79	Tokyo Round
1986–90	Uruguay Round

See ARTICLE XXXV; EXTERNAL TRADE;

KENNEDY ROUND; MONTREAL ROUND; TOKYO ROUND; URUGUAY ROUND.

General Agreement to Borrow. *See* GROUP OF TEN.

Generalized System of Preferences (GSP) GSP was adopted by the Community on July 1, 1971. It is a set of tariff preferences for developing countries to encourage diversification of their economies. Tariff preferences are generalized—that is, normally granted by the majority of industrialized nations without discrimination, or unilateral—that is, they are not the result of negotiations with the beneficiary nations. Preferences are not reciprocal in that the beneficiary nations are not required to grant corresponding duty exemption on imports. The Community submits its annual offer of reduced duty or duty-free imports on a large number of processed goods originating from developing nations, within the limits of certain quantities. Once that limit is reached, the customs duties established in the Common customs tariff can again be applied. By 1980, 13 nations, mainly from Asia and Latin America, accounted for 70 percent of preferential imports. The Community offered generalized preferences to all the member countries of the Group of 77 (all those designated as developing countries by the United Nations) as well as certain territories or countries dependent on Community nations, such as Hong Kong, Macao, and French Polynesia. In all, the Community scheme now applies to 128 independent nations and more than 20 dependent territories.

The Community's current policy differentiates among the beneficiaries. By diminishing or increasing the preferential advantage for beneficiary nations that have lesser or greater need of it, the Community can intensify its efforts to open up its markets to the neediest countries. In the summer of 1988, the Commission increased the amounts of exports under the system by nine percent, providing relief from almost one billion ECU of customs duties. The GSP now provides for duty-free access for all manufactured products from developing countries that do not receive preference on a contractual basis (as do, for example, the 66 African, Caribbean, and Pacific members of the Lomé Conven-

tion) and includes sensitive industrial sectors such as footwear, textiles, steel, and petrochemical products. Under the 1989 proposal, preferential amounts for each product and country in textiles would be equivalent to 0.2 percent of total 1985 E.C. imports for dominant textile suppliers, or state-trading countries, and one percent of such imports in the case of other suppliers.

In agriculture, the E.C. has accorded reductions of import duties on nearly 400 products. For 1989, the Commission proposed reducing the GSP duty rates for certain products, such as processed tobacco products, mushrooms, okra, pawpaw, chutney and lime juice. For the least developed countries, the GSP duty rate would be zero on pineapples, dried figs, grapes, and frozen strawberries. Ending a stalemate, negotiators from the Cairns Group (the 14 GATT members including Canada, Australia, Brazil, and New Zealand) in April 1989 agreed in principle to curb government farm subsidies and agricultural import barriers, calling for a freeze on subsidies and import barriers at current levels and unspecified reductions in 1990.

See EXTERNAL TRADE; FINANCE; LOMÉ CONVENTIONS.

General Treaty of Central American Economic Integration *See* CENTRAL AMERICAN COMMON MARKET.

Geneva Round *See* GENERAL AGREEMENT ON TARIFFS AND TRADE.

geographical inertia This is the tendency of older industrial regions to survive by the contraction and adaptation of old, heavy industries, and by the development of new light industry.

geothermal energy The Community contributes to research on the exploitation of the heat from the earth's depths.

See ENERGY; FINANCE; RESEARCH; SOLAR ENERGY.

German Democratic Republic (GDR) This nation—commonly called East Germany—has been a member of the Council for Mutual Economic Assistance since 1950. East Germany's 16.6 million population, with a GNP of $207.2 billion and $30.7 billion in exports, makes it the most economically advanced state of Eastern Europe. Since November 1989, rapid changes have come to East Germany.

Under current E.C. rules, imports from East to West Germany are considered internal German transactions, and are free to enter E.C. channels, according these imports special status. Some regions in the E.C. are concerned almost competition from East Germany's workers. For example, low-paid workers in Spain and Italy would face formidable competition. Should Spain and Italy fear loss of jobs they might well push even harder for protectionist barriers. Even West Germany's own two million unemployed workers are justifiably wary. In the meantime, East Germany seeks greater economic ties with West Germany. On December 9, 1989, the leaders of the European Council meeting in Strasbourg stated, "We seek the strengthening of the state of peace in Europe in which the German people will regain its unity through free self-determination." The E.C. backs the idea of one Germany as long as it does not bring instability to Europe. On December 19, 1989, the E.C. disclosed proposals for a wide-ranging trade and economic pact with East Germany.

In March 1990, the E.C. and East Germany initiated an agreement to expand and strengthen trade and economic cooperation over the next five years, calling for greater cooperation in a range of fields including the environment, agriculture, and tourism. It also set out a five-year timetable for gradually dismantling quotas and tariffs on a variety of industrial and agricultural products. East Germany will allow as of July 1, 1990, a free flow of goods from nations in the E.C. Following its economic and monetary union with West Germany, East Germany adopted E.C. trading and customs rules. During this period of uncertainty, East Germany will continue to honor all existing trade agreements with East bloc nations and that trade with them will remain free of tariffs until the end of 1990.

See CHRONOLOGY (DECEMBER 8–9, 1989); COUNCIL FOR MUTUAL ECONOMIC ASSISTANCE; EASTERN EUROPE; GERMANY, FEDERAL REPUBLIC OF.

Germany, Federal Republic of This nation, commonly called West Germany—became a founder member of the European Coal and Steel Community in 1951, and the European Economic and Atomic Energy Communities in 1972. Though the world's fourth largest economy (behind the United States, the Soviet Union, and Japan), Germany is the world's largest exporter and had a trade surplus in 1989 of $75.3 billion. West Germany has a population of 61 million with a GNP of $870 billion, exports of $323 billion, and a $72.8 billion trade balance. Unionized workers in West Germany enjoy the highest pay and shortest working hours in the E.C. They worry that the plan for a single market would send jobs to southern Europe, where labor is cheaper and less demanding. "Social Dumping" would result and manufacturing jobs would go to Spain, Portugal, and Greece.

In 1988, Germany had a rise in exports of about 4 percent and an increase in consumer spending by around 3.5 percent. In 1989, it registered surpluses of 10.2 billion marks with Britain (compared with 8 billion marks in 1988), 9 billion marks with France (7.9 billion in 1988), 5.4 billion marks with Italy (3.8 billion marks in 1988), 2 billion marks with the Netherlands (400 million marks in 1988), and 5.5 billion marks with Belgium and Luxembourg (4.8 billion in 1988). In 1988, U.S. citizens bought goods from Germany worth 50 billion marks (about $28 billion). In the same period, Germany made purchases from the United States worth 25 billion marks. The United States ranked sixth among nations importing German goods.

Nearly half of West Germany's exports consisted of automobiles. Machinery and chemical products remain critical exports. The United States is the most important foreign investment area for the German economy, accounting for 30 percent of German direct investment. With a four percent growth in 1989, West Germany is left with a record current-account surplus of over 100 billion German Marks ($54 billion) compared with 85 billion marks ($46 billion) in 1988. For 1990, West Germany is expected to have a 160 billion Mark ($87 billion) trade surplus. In addition, the influx of over 600,000 German immigrants—ethnic Germans from Poland and the Soviet Union—and the influx of East Germans will pick up the slack resulting from an aging population and the falling birth rate of the past two decades. It is expected that the boost to the labor force will generate an additional one percent real annual growth in the early 1990s. Events of the fall 1989 in East Germany and Eastern Europe are certain to increase the role of West Germany in the evolution of the single market of 1992 and trade eastward. Economic unification with East Germany occured in July 1990, with political unification in early October 1990.

See CHRONOLOGY (DECEMBER 8–9, 1989); EASTERN EUROPE; GERMAN DEMOCRATIC REPUBLIC.

Ghana This nation is one of the ACP states and a signatory to the Lomé Convention of 1988.

Gibraltar As a colony of the United Kingdom at the time, Gibraltar was included when the U.K. joined the E.C. in 1973.

Gilbert Islands *See* KIRIBATI.

glass A 1988 proposed Council directive seeks to introduce a single Community standard for motor vehicle safety glass, to promote the single market for motor vehicles and to replace the various national standards now in effect. The use of laminated glass would be mandatory, rather than the less safe toughened glass.

See VEHICLES.

GNP *See* GROSS NATIONAL PRODUCT.

golden triangle The area of the E.E.C. bounded by Paris, the Ruhr, and Milan, containing the areas of economic growth.

goods *See* CONTROL OF GOODS.

government contracts The annual value of government procurement in the E.C. is estimated at about $550 billion, of which roughly 20 percent is subject to open tendering and only two percent awarded to non-national firms. The Commission aims to substantially open E.C. procurement practices by the end of 1992 and to extend competition into the telecommunications, water, energy, and transport sectors. It also has proposed to improve the remedies open to suppliers who believe that the contracting authority has violated their Community right to bid. An E.C. content rule of origin will be the likely vehicle used for limiting third-country competition.

According to the U.S. Department of Commerce, the U.S. government will continue to press the E.C. to open up procurement to U.S. companies, both in bilateral discussions and in the multilateral trade negotiations taking place under the General Agreement on Tariffs and Trade (GATT).

See PUBLIC PROCUREMENT; PUBLIC WORKS CONTRACTS.

grain sector The first phase of policy reform was introduced in the 1986–87 marketing year, involving price cuts for feed wheat and barley, and continuing for the third year a price freeze for bread wheat. In addition the Commission approved a cutting back of the period during which farmers could sell their grain to public authorities and the tightening of quality standards when they did so, together with the introduction of a corresponsibility levy (a producer tax) on every ton of grain sold off the farm. These measures taken together effectively reduced price support by between 10 and 15 percent, depending on the type of grain involved.

See DURUM WHEAT.

grants and loans The financial instruments of the E.C. are the Guidance Section of the European Agricultural Guidance and Guarantee Fund, the European Social Fund, the European Regional Development Fund, the European Coal and Steel Community grants and loans, the European Investment Bank, the New Community borrowing and lending Instrument, the Euratom loans, and the specific measures for certain sectors (energy, transport, environment, research, and innovation). Financial aid can be categorized as assistance for investment, covering productive investment, infrastructure investment, and energy; assistance for facilitating occupational and geographical mobility and employment subsidies; assistance for exploiting potential for internally generated development; and assistance for research and the dissemination of knowledge.

See FINANCE.

Greece Greece signed an Association agreement with the E.C. on July 9, 1961, and joined as its tenth member on January 1, 1981. Greece's balance of payments have ceased to be an urgent problem and its total foreign debt has been stabilized at around $20 billion, equivalent to approximately 35 percent of its gross national product. Greece's inflation rate, although four or five times the E.C. average, has dropped from 25 percent to between 12 and 14 percent. Investment of domestic and foreign capital is rising and unemployment is down to 7.4 percent in 1988. A nonloan capital inflow for 1989 of $1.8 billion enabled the deficit to be covered and official reserves climbed to above $5 billion. Problems remaining include the gap represented by per capita gross national product barely 40 percent of the E.C. average, exports equivalent to less than 20 percent of gross national product against a Community figure of 31 percent, productivity at less than half the E.C. average, and an unacceptably low educational level. Greece hopes with the coming of 1992 to become the strategic center for extending investments to markets in the Middle East, Eastern Europe, and Africa.

green currencies Common support prices under the Common Agricultural Policy are fixed annually in Units of Accounts, but farmers actually receive money in their own currencies from the Farm Fund, calculated at special exchange rates called green currencies.

See AGRICULTURE, COMMON AGRICULTURAL POLICY; MONETARY COMPENSATORY AMOUNTS.

Cf. GREEN POUND.

greenhouse effect The E.C. joined with the United States, Canada, and 15 other countries in signing the 1985 Vienna Convention on the Protection of the Ozone Layer and the Montreal Protocol. The agreements call for nearly complete elimination of chlorofluorocarbons (CFCs), methane, nitrous oxide, and halons.

Greenland Greenland, a Danish dependency, became part of the E.C. when Denmark joined in 1973. After its local government won semi-autonomy under Denmark's Home Rule Act in 1979, it expressed its wish to leave the E.C. and did so as of January 1, 1985. Greenland retains close ties with the E.C. under a draft agreement.

See OCT; WHALE PRODUCTS.

green paper This legislation was passed by the European Commission in June 1987. Its broad lines cover:

(1) Completing the phased opening up of the computer terminal equipment market to competition.
(2) Opening up the telecommunications service market, excluding at this stage a number of basic services considered essential to meet current public service goals and objectives.
(3) Establishing the right for services to operate across member states' national borders.
(4) Continuing the exclusivity or special rights for telecommunications administrations (public and private carriers) to supply and operate the network infrastructure; and a recognition of their central role in establishing future generations of infrastructures.
(5) Separating regulatory and operational functions of telecommunications administrations.
(6) Opening up of the market for satellite ground stations to the extent that the equipment is associated with telecommunications terminals rather than infrastructure.
(7) Recognizing that telecommunication tariffs should be responsive to cost trends.
(8) Developing a consensus from both sides of industry in order to smooth the transition and to maximize the opportunities presented by the new networks and services to create employment.
(9) Using telecommunications to accelerate economic development and reduce the isolation of outlying regions of the Community.
(10) Establishing common European positions within the various international bodies.
(11) Creation of a European Standards Institute.

See EUROPEAN STANDARDS INSTITUTE; TELECOMMUNICATIONS.

green pound It represents the rate at which the prices fixed under the Common Agricultural Policy translated into sterling. These prices are fixed in Units of Account originally based on the United States dollar.

Cf. GREEN CURRENCIES.

Grenada This nation is one of the ACP states and a signatory to the Lomé Convention of 1988.

See CARIBBEAN BASIN.

Gross Domestic Product (GDP) The total of goods and services produced in a nation over a given time period, usually a year.

Gross National Product (GNP) The gross domestic product plus income from abroad less income paid abroad. It is equal to gross national income—the total of incomes of the residents of a nation from all sources.

groupes de travail These are E.C. working groups.

See COMMITTES.

Group of Ten This is a reference to the ten principal industrial nations (the United States, the Netherlands, the United Kingdom, Sweden, France, Japan, Germany, Italy, Belgium, and Canada, with Switzerland as an unofficial member), signatory to the 1962 General Agreement to Borrow. The agreement allows the International Monetary Fund, when supplementary funds are needed, to use the Groups' currencies up to specified amounts.

See GENERAL AGREEMENT ON TARIFFS AND TRADE.

Group of 24 The 24 industrialized nations of the world. Most recently they have coordinated their efforts toward the economic recovery of the Eastern European countries by facilitating market access in the markets of the 24 nations, facilitating investment in Central and Eastern Europe, and assisting in cleaning up the environment.

Synonymous with G-24.

See PHARE PROGRAM.

Group of 77 *See* GENERALIZED SYSTEM OF PREFERENCES.

GSP *See* GENERALIZED SYSTEM OF PREFERENCES.

GSTP (The Generalized System of Tariff Preferences.)

See GENERALIZED SYSTEM OF PREFERENCES.

Guarantee cards *See* EUROCHECKING.

guaranteed price This is the price determined at the U.K.'s Annual Price Review, held in accordance with the Agricultural Acts of 1947 and 1957, as being the prices which farmers, as a whole, should receive for specified agricultural commodities.

guaranteed waiver *See* TRANSIT PROCEDURE.

Guatemala Since 1978 this Central American nation has had a bilateral agreement on textiles.

See CENTRAL AMERICA, CENTRAL AMERICAN COMMON MARKET.

GUD Gestion de l'Union Douaniére. It is a part of the EEC Commission, with responsibility for administration of the Customs Union.

guide price This is the equivalent of a target price for beef and veal. It serves both as a target price and as the gauge for basing import control and intervention buying. Within the Community a single rate applies.

See AGRICULTURE, COMMON AGRICULTURAL POLICY; INTERVENTION PRICE.

Synonymous with RECOMMENDED PRICE.

Guinea This nation is one of the ACP states and a signatory to the Lomé Convention of 1988.

Guinea-Bissau This nation is one of the ACP states and a signatory to the Lomé Convention of 1988.

Gulf Cooperation Council (GCC) For the GCC (Saudi Arabia, Kuwait, Qatar, the United Arab Emirates, Oman, and Bahrain) the Community represents its principal trading partner and the largest developed region within a short range of the Gulf. In 1983 and 1984, for the first time in 10 years, the Community recorded a surplus on its trade balance. In 1984, the Community's imports from the Gulf states represented 4.5 percent of its total imports. Exports to the Gulf states represented 6.4 percent of E.C. total exports. Community agricultural exports account for roughly 20 percent of the Gulf market. In 1984, the Community imported roughly 20 percent of its crude oil and 9 percent of its refined products. On March 24, 1988, the E.C. and the GCC reached a trade and cooperation agreement providing that both sides will continue to grant to each other Most Favored Nation status and will not introduce any new tariffs or trade restrictions.

gun ownership In the fall of 1989, the Commission proposed a set of minimum standards for gun ownership, recommending that the right to own most firearms be restricted to people over 18 years of age whom national authorities do not regard as a threat to public order. Private citizens would be barred from owning some categories of weapons altogether. Gun owners from the 12 member states would have to apply for a European firearms certificate, which would identify the gun's legal owner while permitting hunters and sports participants to take legally acquired weapons from one E.C. state to another. No national laws restricting the right to carry weapons are affected by the E.C. proposal.

Guyana This nation is one of the ACP states and a signatory to the Lomé Convention of 1988. A protocol annexed to the Convention guarantees its sugar exports to the Community.

See CARIBBEAN BASIN; SUGAR.

gypsies *See* POVERTY.

H

hairdressers To ensure the mutual recognition of qualifications for hairdressers, a European Commission proposal was placed before the Council of Ministers in 1972. It permits hairdressers to practice their profession anywhere in the Community. By January 1984 hairdressers could establish themselves freely in any E.C. member state which regulates their trade.

See WORK AND EMPLOYMENT.

Haiti This nation has a bilateral agreement with the Community on textiles. Haiti joined the Lomé IV convention in 1989.

See LATIN AMERICA.

halons *See* ENVIRONMENT.

handicapped people Community help concentrates on stimulating "the employment and geographical and professional mobility" of handicapped individuals through vocational and other training aided by the Social Fund, which can contribute up to 50 percent (60 percent in high unemployment areas) to government approved or aided training programs. The European Commission established a network of Community-sponsored rehabilitation and training centers. In April 1988, the E.C. launched a program to help the more than 30 million handicapped people within its 12 countries. A four-year program, called Helios, costing about 19 million ECU (about $23.6 million) will be aimed at helping the handicapped to lead independent lives; to make certain that they are consulted before projects concerning them are implemented, and to publicize their contribution made to society.

See FINANCE; SOCIAL POLICY.

Hanover meeting *See* INTERNAL MARKET.

Harmonization (Internal Community trade) Harmonization is a broad description of the program to abolish tariffs and other barriers to a single European market. Customs duties (tariffs) were abolished among the six founder members of the Community in 1968, and among the Nine (the original six plus Denmark, Irish Republic, and the U.K.) in 1977. The Council of Ministers periodically announces new directives for the approximation (harmonization) of national laws or of administrative regulations that affect the proper operation of the common market, For nontechnical barriers, sometimes applied for health or environmental reasons, the Commission seeks informal harmonization rather than by directive. For technical barriers, the 1979 GATT Agreement on Technical Barriers to Trade is designed to check, at international levels, the proliferation of national divergent technical standards and regulations by signatory nations. In 1983, the Community adopted a directive requiring member states to notify the Commission of new regulations and standards for certain products prior to their enactment, with the Commission having the power to freeze introduction of these member states' regulations for up to a year. In 1987, the Council adopted a directive on pressure vessels. Other directives deal with toys, machine safety, and electromagnetic compatibility.

See COMMON CUSTOMS TARIFF; COMPANY LAW; COMPETITION POLICY; CUSTOMS UNION; ENVIRONMENT; GENERAL AGREEMENT ON TARIFFS AND TRADE; GLASS; INDUSTRIAL POLICY; INDUSTRIAL STANDARDS; MUTUAL RECOGNITION; NOISE; NON-TARIFF BARRIERS TO TRADE; RULERS; SIMPLE PRESSURE VESSELS; SINGLE CUSTOMS DOCUMENT; STANDARDIZATION; TRANSPORT; WORK AND EMPLOYMENT.

Havana Charter *Synonymous with* INTERNATIONAL TRADE ORGANIZATION.

HDTV *See* HIGH-DEFINITION TELEVISION.

health and safety The Council of Ministers adopted a Resolution in 1978 to increase the protection of workers against occupational risks "by improving conditions of work, knowledge and human attitudes." The goal is to achieve common statistical means of assessing the gravity and causes of work place accidents; the harmonization of exposure limits for certain dangerous substances that are known carcinogens and other harmful substances; the improvement of machine safety through the design, construction, and use of plant; the limitation of noise levels; and the development of common methods of monitoring pollutants and environmental conditions at work.

See ANIMAL HEALTH AND MEAT INSPECTION; CANCER; ENVIRONMENT; PLANT HEALTH CONTROLS; SOCIAL POLICY; TOXIC EFFLUENT; WORK AND EMPLOYMENT.

helios *See* HANDICAPPED PEOPLE.

hermes *See* EUROPEAN SPACE AGENCY.

High-Definition Television (HDTV) The E.C. seeks U.S. support for its standard of high-definition television as the world norm. HDTV provides television with wide, crisp, cinematic-quality pictures and compact-disk-quality digital sound. In June 1990, a group of 14 broadcasting and telecommunications concerns from five E.C. states launched a consortium to promote HDTV. The consortium, called Vision 1250, will develop fixed and mobile HDTV facilities to be introduced commercially in the E.C. beginning in 1992.

history *See* APPENDIX.

Holland *See* NETHERLANDS, THE.

home authorization *See* BANKING.

home safety The Commission recommended establishing in each Community nation a network of monitoring centers, particularly hospitals and clinics, to maintain detailed records of accidents occurring within the home. These centers would highlight major safety risks in the home caused by specific consumer items.

See CONSUMER PROTECTION.

Honduras This nation has an agreement with the Community on trade in certain textiles and hand-made items.

See CENTRAL AMERICA; CENTRAL AMERICAN COMMON MARKET.

honey In any of its forms, only genuine honey can be sold in the Community. A 1974 directive defines honey and the rules regarding composition, description, and labeling.

See CONSUMER PROTECTION.

Hong Kong This U.K. dependent territory has had an agreement with the Community on textiles since 1978.

See PACIFIC RIM.

hops Hops can only be sold within the Community if they conform to qualitative and other standards set down in a 1977 E.C. regulation. The regulation provides for subsidies to encourage producers to plant better varieties, with half the cost to be absorbed by the Farm Fund.

See AGRICULTURE, COMMON AGRICULTURAL POLICY; AGRICULTURE, PRODUCTION GROUPING; FINANCE.

hormones *See* ANIMAL HEALTH AND MEAT INSPECTION; CHRONOLOGY (FEBRUARY 17–18, 1989).

horns In 1970, technical standards for automotive horns, applicable throughout the E.C., were passed. The horn directive prescribes Community-wide standards for construction and installation as well as acceptance tests. The noise level must be between 105 and 118 decibels. The horn must function for at least 50,000 one-second beeps. Horns meeting Community standards do not have to undergo any other tests in the member states if they bear the E.C. seal of approval, meaning that they have met the construction and performance standards specified in the directive.

See NOISE.

horses *See* ANIMAL HEALTH AND MEAT INSPECTION.

hotel safety *See* CONSTRUCTION PRODUCTS; FIRE SAFETY; HEALTH AND SAFETY.

Hot Money
(1) A term pertaining to capital movements, usually of a short-term character, which take place either for

speculative reasons or in response to interest rate differentials.

(2) These are overseas funds placed in a nation at short-term that are liable to rapid withdrawal should confidence in a currency be shaken or if interest differentials swing against the nation where the funds are deposited.

See CAPITAL, FREE MOVEMENT OF.

Hungary, Republic of This country is a founder member of the Council for Mutual Economic Assistance. The Community has a bilateral agreement with Hungary regarding textiles. Hungary signed a trade agreement with the E.C. in September 1988 that removed many restrictions on Hungarian imports and established diplomatic relations. Hungary was the first Soviet-bloc country to sign a nonpreferential trade agreement with the E.C., which provides for the gradual removal of all discriminatory quantitative restrictions by 1995, and covers all industrial and agricultural products except those for which sectoral agreements already exist, such as textiles and some agricultural products. In September 1989, the E.C. proposed more than $650 million in new aid for 1990 to help Hungary and Poland reform their ailing economies. It would include supplying machinery and pesticides. Exports from the two nations would ultimately have lower tariffs and fewer trade restrictions. The two nations would be eligible for secured loans from the European Investment Bank and other E.C. institutions. By the fall of 1989 the newly renamed Republic of Hungary began to anticipate applying for associate membership with the E.C. In addition, in November 1989, Hungary applied to join the 23-nation Council of Europe, the first Warsaw Pact member to do so.

See COUNCIL FOR MUTUAL ECONOMIC ASSISTANCE; EASTERN EUROPE.

I

IBRD *See* INTERNATIONAL BANK FOR RE-CONSTRUCTION AND DEVELOPMENT.

Iceland This island joined the European Free Trade Association in March 1970, and signed a preferential trade agreement setting up an industrial free trade area in 1973.

ICFC The Industrial and Commercial Finance Corporation was formed under the auspices of the Bank of England and other institutions to provide financing for industrial development. It also administered a block loan from the European Investment Bank.

ICFTU *See* INTERNATIONAL CONFEDERATION OF FREE TRADE UNIONS.

IDA (The International Development Association of the United Nations.)
See INTERNATIONAL BANK FOR RECONSTRUCTION AND DEVELOPMENT.

identical treatment Some E.C. officials want firms operating abroad to receive the identical treatment and rights that the E.C. would extend to foreign firms. For instance, in banking the E.C. might seek an exemption from U.S. restrictions on bank activities. The United States would argue strongly that nations have differing regulatory views on how best to serve and protect the public, and U.S. firms should not be excluded from other markets because of such differences.
Cf. NATIONAL TREATMENT.
See RECIPROCITY.

identity *See* SYMBOLS.

IDIS *See* INTERBOURSE DATA INFORMATION SYSTEM.

IES *See* DATABASES AND DATABANKS OF THE E.C.

IFC *See* INTERNATIONAL FINANCE CORPORATION OF THE UNITED NATIONS.

illiteracy In May 1987, E.C. Education Ministers began a two-year program to fight illiteracy in the E.C. It calls for more intensified exchanges of information among national experts. A research program was begun in a number of pilot schools to test measures that might be used at different levels of education.
See EDUCATION.

ILO *See* INTERNATIONAL LABOR ORGANIZATION.

IMCO (The Intergovernmental Maritime Consultative Organization) This specialized agency of the United Nations was established in 1959 to facilitate cooperation between governments on technical issues affecting international shipping, such as navigation, safety, and pollution control.

IMF *See* INTERNATIONAL MONETARY FUND.

immigrants *See* MIGRANT WORKERS.

IMP *See* INTEGRATED MEDITERRANEAN PROGRAM.

IMPACT (Information Market Policy Actions). A 1988 research program to establish a single market in information services before 1992. IMPACT aims to stimulate and strengthen the competitiveness of European sellers, promote the use of advanced information services, and support joint efforts to coordinate the policies of the individual member states.

income tax *See* LABOR.

incorporation measures In an effort to generate economic activity and create jobs, the E.C. Commission proposed a directive that would make self-employment more attractive and facilitate the start-up, expansion, and transfer of small businesses in Europe. The directive requires all E.C. member states to offer sole traders the possibility of limited liability by incorporation as a single-member company. While ensuring adequate protection for third parties dealing with businesses, the resulting ability to separate the assets of the business from the private assets of the entrepreneur should encourage more self-employment.

incoterms These are international rules for the interpretation of terms used in foreign trade contracts.

India In December 1973 India signed a commercial cooperation agreement with the Community to develop and diversify trade between the two. On June 23, 1981, a five-year agreement on nonpreferential commercial and economic cooperation was signed providing for new forms of joint action in trade, industry, science, energy, and development. In 1985, E.C. imports from India reached 2.6 million ECU, while E.C. exports to India were 5.5 million ECU. A June 1987 cooperation program with the E.C. involved a number of initiatives in the areas of industrial and telecommunications standards, quality assurance and conformity testing, computer software, data banks, energy, steel, engineering, and several other areas.

See OPERATION FLOOD.

indicator price system Is an agricultural price support system used in the United Kingdom. A deficiency payment is made to U.K. producers based on the difference between a guaranteed price and an indicator (or market) price. It represents a price which producers might reasonably be expected to secure under normal market conditions

See DEFICIENCY PAYMENT.

indirect taxation *See* DOUBLE TAXATION; SECURITIES; TAXATION.

Indonesia This nation has agreements with Community on hand-made products and textiles. It is a member of the Association of South East Asian Nations with whom the Community concluded a cooperation agreement in December 1979.

See ASSOCIATION OF SOUTH EAST ASIAN NATIONS; PACIFIC RIM.

industrial cooperation The Single European Act, by eliminating internal frontiers, creates opportunities and incentives for cooperation between businesses in different member states, and strengthens the position of European businesses when competing on world markets. Company mergers across frontiers involve the application of differing national laws and often have tax implications that can act as a severe disincentive. When businesses wish to pursue jointly a single activity, there is no appropriate and administratively straightforward corporate form for doing so. To remedy this situation legislation will create an environment of industrial cooperation across national frontiers.

See COMPANY LAW; INTELLECTUAL PROPERTY; TAXATION.

industrial policy This policy derives primarily from the Treaty of Paris, which established measures of intervention in the coal and steel industries. Member nations cooperate on a limited scale in joint Community action to help safeguard some industries against third-country imports, and to encourage reorganization and conversion to meet increasing external competition.

See COMPANY LAW; COMPETITION POLICY; ENERGY; FINANCE; HARMONIZATION; INDUSTRIAL COOPERATION; INDUSTRY-STATE AIDS; NON-TARIFF BARRIERS TO TRADE.

industrial property This is a generic classification for patents, trademarks, copyright, 'know-how' and related agreements.

industrial standards Although each E.C. state has its own set of industrial standards, the list of product categories covered by harmonization and mutual recognition is growing. The E.C.'s new approach will mandate minimum standards and then require member countries to recognize other E.C. countries' standards. As an example, France was forced to accept German Edam cheese for sale, despite the fact that the cheese did not meet minimum French fat content. German beer purity laws also were found in violation of the mutual recognition concept.

See BEER; HARMONIZATION; STANDARDS.

industry and services Within the Community, manufacturing industry contributed 36.5 percent of GNP and the service industry 60.1 percent in 1986. Manufacturing employed 40 million people and the service industry 75.9 million. In 1987, Community exports represented 20.4 percent of world exports compared with the United States' 13.2 percent and Japan's 12.1 percent, making the Community the world's leading trader.

industry-state aids The European Commission does not want to prevent national governments from giving state aid to ailing industries as long as they do not contravene Community rules on fair competition. The Community approves such assistance when it is needed to correct severe regional imbalances, to help encourage industrial growth or change, to allow specific industries to contract without undue social distress, or to neutralize, at least temporarily, distortions of competition resulting from outside forces. The Commission does not discourage state aid in such fields as data processing, electronics, telematics, and aerospace.
See HARMONIZATION; INDUSTRIAL POLICY.

inflation This is the increase in the price level creating a decrease in the purchasing power of the monetary unit. The inflation rate is the rate of change in prices, determined on an annual, monthly, or other basis. The E.C.'s inflation rate rose to 4.4 percent in 1988 from 2.6 percent the previous year. The 1988 rate equaled the United States inflation rate and significantly exceeded Japan's rate of nine-tenths of a percent. In 1989, inflation was highest in Greece, at 14.25 percent, and Portugal, at 13 percent, and the lowest in West Germany was 3 percent. Overall, E.C. inflation was 4.8 percent in 1989, with 1990 projected to be 4.5 percent.
See CONSUMER PRICE INDEX.

INFO 92 An E.C. data base available in Danish, Dutch, English, French, German, Italian, Portuguese, and Spanish. With a personal computer hooked up to a telephone and a password the user can determine, at any time, the state of Europe 1992 and incorporation of Community directives into the national legislation of E.C. member states. The charge for consulting the data base is 10 ECU

($12) per hour. A document containing the same information is published twice a year by the Office for Official Publications of the European Communities based in Luxembourg.

Information and Documentation on Minority Languages *See* MERCATOR.

information services *See* TECHNOLOGIES.

Information Technology (IT) IT is one of the fastest developing areas of industrial activity, with annual growth rates in IT markets expected to continue at 15–25 percent into the 1990s. In world trade, electronic equipment will overtake the automotive sector in the 1990s. With worldwide research and development spending on information technologies rising from $35 billion in 1986 to some $90 billion in 1990, IT will remain one of the dominant sources of technolgical advance until the end of the century. Standards in IT have become critical. The sheer growth in the number of IT systems inevitably brings about an increase in the amount of contact between systems, in the need for compatibility, and creates a demand for IT specialists. The Community standardization policy for IT is to secure the needs of the IT-using sectors, now that effective deployment of IT is one of the keys to maintaining competitiveness on world markets; to remove barriers to trade in IT, with special reference to the internal European market; to ensure the viability of the European IT industry; and to contribute to the creation of a competitive environment.
See CERTIFICATION; CONFORMANCE TESTING; ESPRIT.

initiation of policy This is one of the principal tasks of the Commission. After exhaustive preliminary discussions, a policy is "initiated" when it is laid before the Council for action.

Initiative 1964 This successful effort set a timetable for achieving the Community customs union. Although modified several times, it sought to dismantle intra-Community tariffs to achieve a customs union by July 1, 1967—two and one half years ahead of the Rome Treaty date.
See CHRONOLOGY (OCTOBER 1, 1964).

inland waterway *See* TRANSPORT.

insider trading In 1989, the Council of Ministers adopted a directive making insider trading illegal for "primary" insiders (those who acquire privileged information in the course of their profession) and for "secondary" insiders (those who trade on the basis of confidential information from primary sources). "Insider information" is defined as anything not yet made public which, if widely known, would have a significant effect on a share's price. The directive also provides for cooperation between the member states' competent authorities and contains rules regarding professional secrecy vis-a-vis these authorities. The deadline for member implementation is June 1, 1992.

See SECURITIES.

INSIS *See* INTER-INSTITUTIONAL INTEGRATED SERVICES INFORMATION SYSTEM.

inspection *See* ANIMAL HEALTH AND MEAT INSPECTION; FOOD.

Institutions of the Community They are the Council of Ministers, the Commission, the European Parliament, and the Court of Justice. *See* INTRODUCTION.

insurance Insurance rates presently differ significantly in the 12 member states. In France, a basic life insurance policy costs about two-thirds more than in relatively free-wheeling Britain. In Portugal, insurance is priced at 10 times higher than in Britain. The European insurance markets tend to be very fragmented with local rules governing premiums and policy terms and discouraging cross-border competition. A 1973 directive sought to coordinate the laws, regulations, and administrative provisions "relating to the pursuit of the business of direct insurance other than life insurance." By 1992, for an insurance company established in one member state be able to cover risks situated in other member states will require harmonization of essential standards for supervision; mutual recognition by the national supervisory authorities of the controls operated by each other; and home country control. Through coordination of national supervisory activities, home country control will mean that any insurance company operating in several

member states will be controlled by the authorities in its home base, except for consumer protection purposes in specified cases. In December 1989, the E.C. ministers agreed to permit cross-border shopping by consumers for life insurance starting in 1992 thus allowing individuals, whether directly or through an insurance broker, to take out life-insurance contracts in an E.C. member nation other than the one in which they reside. Firms establishing group life-insurance plans on behalf of their workers will also be permitted to shop abroad. Insurance companies will not be permitted to market life insurance directly, or through an agent in another member state, if there is no bilateral accord between the two nations allowing them to do so. This restriction, however, will not apply to group insurance. Early in 1990, the E.C. commissioner for financial services proposed framework directives on life and non-life insurance, enabling companies to operate throughout the E.C. on a single insurance license.

See FINANCIAL SERVICES; MADRID MEETING.

Integrated Mediterranean Program (IMP) IMP was launched in September 1986 with the beneficiary being the Greek island of Crete. About $470 million in aid over a seven-year period is aimed at helping the E.C.'s southernmost region to develop faster. Crete, which is among the Community's most disadvantaged regions, where agriculture accounts for much of its income and employment, will use these funds for industry and for developing the island's facilities.

Integrated Services Digital Network *See* ISDN.

integration This is the process of bringing together in a closer relationship the separate E.C. states.

See INTERNAL MARKET.

intellectual property Differences between member states' trademark, copyright, and patent laws have an adverse impact on intra-Community trade and on the ability of firms to treat the common market as a single environment for their activities. With trademarks, the existence of the distinct national systems (and the combined Benelux system) creates obstacles to Community-wide marketing, in addition to cumbersome and costly administrative and legal burdens. A single European market requires a single Community trademark system. In April 1990, the E.C. submitted a detailed proposal to trade negotiators for new international rules to protect rights to intellectual property such as patents, copyrights, and trademarks. The draft would protect patents for 20 years, copyrights for 25 to 50 years, and the initial registration of a trademark would be valid for 10 years under the proposal.

See TAXATION; TRADEMARKS.

InterAmerican Bank *See* ALLIANCE FOR PROGRESS.

interbank agreements In 1989, the Commission called for an end to interbank agreements on interest rates, contending that such agreements are similar to price cartels in restricting competition.

Interbourse Data Information System (IDIS) IDIS commenced in May 1984. It permits each E.C. stock exchange to quote the prices at which a given corporation's shares are being traded in other E.C. financial centers. The system's goal is to reduce the compartmentalization of securities exchanges in the E.C. The network provides the stock-price information needed to enable a broker to trade shares for clients on whatever stock market offers the most advantageous terms at any given moment.

See SECURITIES.

Intergovernmental Conference *See* CHRONOLOGY (SEPTEMBER 9, 1985).

Intergovernmental Maritime Consultative Organization *See* IMCO.

Inter-Institutional Integrated Services Information System (INSIS) INSIS was formally launched by a decision of the E.C. Council of Ministers in December 1982. It is a user-driven program and is scheduled to become operational in 1990 to provide link-ups of electronic mail, videotext, and videoconferencing between Brussels, Strasbourg, and Luxembourg—the three centers of E.C. in-

stitutional activity. It will save time and money in the exchange of information.

See RACE; STAR; TELECOMMUNICATIONS.

internal commerce and trade *See* HARMONIZATION; INTERNAL MARKET.

internal community trade *See* HARMONIZATION.

internal market These are trade activities within the 12 member states. The Commission's White Paper urged the completion of the internal market as a prerequisite for an efficient, modern Europe that can provide industry and commerce with a structural framework in which they can be fully competitive. Directives, decisions, and recommendations are required for dealing with three primary barriers: (1) physical; (2) technical, (including barriers to public contracts, free movement of workers and members of the professions, capital movements and the services market, and to industrial cooperation); and (3) tax. In all, 279 directives are being debated, down from the 300 originally proposed. By the end of 1989, the number of texts having undergone final adoption by the Council had risen to 142; there were 10 partial adoptions and six common positions. The Council had thus achieved nearly 60 percent of the program contained in the White Paper for the establishment of a single market.

See CECCHINI REPORT; EUROPE WITHOUT FRONTIERS; SINGLE EUROPEAN ACT; WHITE PAPER.

International Bank for Reconstruction and Development It commenced operation in June 1946 to provide funds and technical assistance to facilitate economic development in its poorer member countries. Funds come from capital subscribed by member nations, sales of its own securities, sales of parts of its loans, repayments, and net earnings.

Synonymous with the WORLD BANK.

See BRETTON WOODS.

International Carriage of Dangerous Goods by Road *See* ADR.

International Confederation of Free Trade Unions (ICFTU) Provides for cooperation with the United Nations and the International Labor Organization and for regional organizations to promote free trade unionism, especially in underdeveloped nations. Its first congress was held in London in December 1949.

International Development Association of the United Nations Established in 1960 as a United Nations Specialized Agency. It is an affiliate of the World Bank, having the same management and staff, but is a separate legal entity with separate funds. It was established to meet the problem of a growing number of less developed nations whose need for outside capital is greater than their ability to service conventional loans.

International Labor Organization This organization was established under the Treaty of Versailles in 1919. It became affiliated with the United Nations in 1946. Its aims are the improvement of working conditions throughout the world, the spread of social security, and the maintenance of standards of social justice. It gives technical assistance, especially for training, to developing nations.

International Monetary Fund This Fund was established on December 27, 1945, as an independent international organization of the United Nations. It is authorized to supplement its resources by borrowing. Its purpose is to promote international monetary cooperation by expanding international trade and exchange stability; to assist in the removal of exchange restrictions and in the establishment of a multilateral system of payments; and to alleviate any serious disequilibrium in members' international balance of payments by making the resources of the Fund available to them under adequate safeguards.
See BRETTON WOODS.

International Organization for Standardization *See* ISO.

International Space University (ISU) a loosely formed group of multinational scientists and innovators who plan to create an international group of space explorers.

International Standard Industrial Classification (ISIC) This is a categorization of economic activity used in compiling and presenting official statistics issued by the United Nations.

International Sugar Agreement This agreement has been in force since 1969. It attempts to maintain stable and remunerative export prices by means of export quotas for that part of the international market (about half) not covered by the U.S. Sugar Act, the Commonwealth Sugar Agreement, and Soviet-Cuban purchase arrangements. The European Community is not a member.

International Telegraph and Telephone Consultative Committee *See* CCITT.

International Trade Federations *See* TRADE UNIONS.

International Trade Organization (ITO) Drawn up in March 1948, it has been replaced by GATT.
Synonymous with HAVANA CHARTER.

International Trade Secretariats *See* TRADE UNIONS.

International Wheat Agreement This 1971 agreement consists of two legal instruments—The Wheat Trade Conventions, concerned with international cooperation in wheat matters, and the Food Aid Convention, concerned with apportioning cereal contributions as food aid to developing nations.
See CEREALS; FOOD AID.

intervention agency Each Community government is required to have an intervention agency responsible to the European Commission for administering aspects of the Common Agricultural Policy, in particular providing for the buying-in of certain farm products at the intervention price.
See AGRICULTURE, COMMON AGRICULTURAL POLICY; INTERVENTION PRICE.

intervention price The fixed price established under the CAP price support system for agricultural commodities. The intervention agency of each member nation has the responsibility of buying farm products when market prices fall below a certain established intervention price, e.g., cereals, between 12–30 percent below the target price.
See AGRICULTURE, COMMON AGRICULTURAL POLICY; BASE PRICE OR BASIC FINANCE; INTERVENTION AGENCY; TARGET PRICE.

investment The European Commission is empowered to borrow funds from the capital market under the "New Community Instrument for Borrowing or Lending" (NCI). Funds are to be used for encouraging E.C. investment in cooperation with the European Investment Bank. The funds cover a higher proportion of the fixed investment cost of an approved project than loans drawn solely from the Bank's own resources.

See CAPITAL, FREE MOVEMENT OF; EURO-LIST; FINANCE; FINANCIAL SERVICES; NEW COMMUNITY INSTRUMENT; SECURITIES.

Investment Bank, European *See* EUROPEAN INVESTMENT BANK.

Iran Since 1971, this nation has had an agreement with the Community on hand-made items.

Iraq This country signed a cooperation agreement with the Council for Mutual Economic Assistance.

See COUNCIL FOR MUTUAL ECONOMIC ASSISTANCE.

Ireland This nation joined the European Community on January 1, 1973.

There has been a dramatic recovery in the public finances of Ireland.

Government borrowing, which had been a 13 percent of gross national product fell to about 6 percent in 1988. Interest rates have been falling by a total of 6 percentage points since 1986 and are now close to most E.C. states' rates. Ireland's balance of payments changed from deficit to surplus. Inflation fell to 2 percent in 1988, the lowest rate in 30 years. Manufacturing output continues to grow by 10 percent per annum, and exports move ahead by 11 percent per annum in volume terms. In spite of such growth, the labor market remains volatile. Ireland has an unemployment rate of 18 percent and emigration continues at 30,000 per year. About one-third of foreign firms set up operations in the Shannon Duty Free Zone. Today, about 100 international companies have operations there, half of them from the United States. Ireland's future rests heavily on its attraction as a center for high-technology research. From its 23 electronic firms in 1972, the electronics sector has since grown to over 350 firms that export $3.64 billion worth of goods in Europe. In the Autumn of 1989 an Irish Government report indicated that the completion of the single market will not close the 50 percent gap between Irish living standards and the Community average, but that the gap may actually widen. The report found that Ireland's performance in many economic sectors was better than the E.C. average between 1973–1980, but "much worse" between 1980–1986. An average of the two periods showed that Ireland had converged little toward average E.C. income levels. The government has cut corporate income taxes to 10 percent from 43 percent for finance-industry companies operating internationally. It is giving tax rebates on rental leases and real-estate investment that can make locating in Dublin almost a no-tax proposition.

See NORTHERN IRELAND.

IRIS IRIS is the European network of vocational training for women. It is meant to open all types and levels of training programs to women. The E.C. program will continue until 1992 as a complement to the November 1987 Commission Recommendation on Vocational Training for Women. Its goal is the achievement of equal treatment for men and women in regard to employment, vocational training, promotions and working conditions.

See EUROPEAN CENTER FOR THE DEVELOPMENT OF VOCATIONAL TRAINING.

Irish Republic *See* IRELAND.

ISDN (The Integrated Services Digital Network) A concept in which all forms of information to be transmitted (voice, data, image) are translated into digital bitstreams and can be handled within a common network infrastructure.

ISIC *See* INTERNATIONAL STANDARD INDUSTRIAL CLASSIFICATION.

Isle of Man *See* CHANNEL ISLANDS; MAN, ISLE OF.

ISO The International Organization for Standardization. This organization sets worldwide standards for any subject not covered by a specialist agency.

Israel Since 1975, this country has had an agreement with the Community establishing an area of free trade and cooperation, including industrial, technical, and financial cooperation. In 1989 Israel ran a $3.5 billion trade deficit with the Community.

See MEDITERRANEAN POLICY, MNCs.

ISU *See* INTERNATIONAL SPACE UNIVERSITY.

IT *See* INFORMATION TECHNOLOGY.

Italy This nation became a founder member of the European Coal and Steel Community, in 1951, the European Economic Community, and the European Atomic Energy Community in 1957. The Italian economy is expanding at a rate of three percent per year which is better than any of its European partners. The performance of the major State-owned sectors of Italian industry and banking has been tremendously improved. Italy's main worry remains the persistent imbalance in the national budget. The deficit is equal to 12 percent of gross national product, involving a great waste of resources. Italy's standard of living has jumped 23.9 percent resulting in the highest consumer spending of any people in the E.C. states. On January 6, 1990, the Italian government announced it would bring lira trading into line with other major currencies in the European Monetary System, allowing it to trade within a 2.25 percent fluctuation band in the currency grid, instead of the wider 6 percent band. This action became a further positive step toward the E.C. monetary union.

See SAN MARINO, REPUBLIC OF.

ITO *See* INTERNATIONAL TRADE ORGANIZATION.

ITS (The International Trade Secretariats) *See* TRADE UNIONS.

ITU The International Telecommunication Union.
See CCITT.

ivory In June 1989 the E.C. banned ivory imports from Africa, where the number of African elephants declined to fewer than 500,000 from 1.5 million in 1978.

Ivory Coast This nation is one of the ACP states and a signatory to the Lomé Convention of 1988.

J

Jamaica This nation is one of the ACP states and a signatory to the Lomé Convention of 1988. A Protocol annexed to the Convention guarantees the nation's sugar exports to the Community.

See CARIBBEAN BASIN; SUGAR.

jams *See* FOOD.

Japan Japan, like other non-E.C. members, fears that the E.C. will erect higher walls against imports as it proceeds with plans to remove internal trade barriers by 1992. Japanese investment in the E.C. member states jumped to $6.6 billion in the year ending March 31, 1988, from $3.5 billion the fiscal year prior. Japanese firms poured nearly $9 billion in direct investment into Europe in the fiscal year ending March 31, 1989.

More than 400 Japanese firms operate in Europe, up from 157 in 1983. For the first time since 1988, Japanese firms have sought European takeover targets, especially in the consumer goods and high-technology industries.

The E.C. has proposed measures to freeze Japanese car imports' share at about 10 percent, and may require a 70 percent local-content level, gradually rising to 80 percent, for cars built by Japanese firms in Europe or in other markets outside Europe.

Japanese manufacturers, fearing further import restrictions in 1992, are gearing up for major production facilities within the E.C. Since the E.C. isn't likely to block the Japanese investments through exchange controls or other direct means, member states are pushing for revising the E.C. import policies. In addition, further pressure is building on Tokyo to admit Europeans to Japan's market, which until recently has been minimal. European unity in 1992 will mean that the 12 member states will soon have to compete in their own countries with the very Japanese

industrial giants they were trying to keep away. The Community's $28 billion deficit with Japan is expected to widen into the 1990s, despite an increase in E.C. exports to Japan.

E.C. Trade with Japan (in billion dollars)*

	Exports	Imports	Trade Balance
1984	7.4	20.3	−12.9
1985	8.0	21.8	−13.8
1986	11.2	32.7	−21.5
1987	15.5	39.5	−24.0
1988	20.0	48.4	−28.4

*Source: Eurostat

The E.C. says that it will grant no more trade concessions in the General Agreement on Tariffs and Trade Uruguay Round without a "fundamental change in Japan's propensity to import manufactured and processed agricultural products," while Japan's main concern is its access to the E.C.'s larger and more dynamic market. Tokyo fears that certain E.C. states, notably France and Italy, will push through a more protectionist arrangement than those already in effect. The E.C. feeling is that Japanese investment should involve a transfer of new technologies, managerial know-how, and labor skills that will help make European business more competitive. In addition, to encourage the European semiconductor industry, which trails its Japanese and American competitors, the Community has imposed high tariffs and tough regulations of origin. Under these conditions, semiconductors that Japanese firms assemble in Europe will be considered Japanese unless the capital-intensive heart of the process—etching the silicon wafer—is carried out in Europe, not in sophisticated Japanese factories.

In May 1990, the E.C. and Japan held high-level talks for the first time in three and a half years, to deal primarily with the issue of the Community's persistent trade deficit with Japan. In the first nine months of 1989, the

E.C.'s exports to Japan amounted to just 44.9 percent of its imports. Japan's investment in the E.C. at the end of March 1989 was $30.2 billion against only $3.0 billion for the community in Japan.

See CAR INDUSTRY; COMPUTERS; DUMPING; FINANCE; PACIFIC RIM.

JDI The Joint Declaration of Intent is annexed to the Treaty of Accession and states that the E.C. states will examine with Bangladesh, India, Malaysia, Singapore, and Sri Lanka any trade problems that arise from the Treaty's implementation, and will attempt to find appropriate solutions.

JESSI The Joint European Submicron Silicon. It is a $5 billion program to develop new generations of semiconductors and the machines to manufacture them. Four billion dollars come from the EUREKA project.

See COMPUTERS; EUREKA.

JET *See* JOINT EUROPEAN TORUS.

Job information (Système Européen de Diffusion des Offres et des demandes d'emploi enregistrees en Compensation internationale) (SEDOC) The Treaty of Rome encourages member nations to establish proper mechanisms "to bring offers of employment into touch with applications for employment" as part of the principle of freedom of movement for Community workers.

See MIGRANT WORKERS; WORK AND EMPLOYMENT.

JOCE (Journal Officiel des Communautés Européenees) The Official Journal of the European Communities.

Joint Declaration of Intent *See* JDI.

Joint European Submicron Silicon (JESSI) *See* COMPUTERS.

Joint European Torus (JET) JET begun in 1978 is a doughnut-shaped vacuum vessel for creating inexpensive, clean energy by the fusion of hydrogen atoms. The objective is to construct such an experimental vessel large enough to study a plasma in conditions simulating those in a thermo-nuclear reactor. JET is the major activity of the Community Fusion Program and is operated jointly by the European Atomic Energy Commission and

member institutions. Fourteen nations are participants. It is located in Culham, England. JET will be phased out when NET (Next European Torus) is completed.

See ENERGY; EUROPEAN SCHOOLS; JOINT RESEARCH CENTER; NUCLEAR ENERGY; NUCLEAR FUSION; RESEARCH; SCIENCE AND TECHNOLOGICAL COMMITTEE.

Joint Opportunities for Unconventional or Long term Energy supply *See* JOULE.

Joint Research Center (JRC) JRC deals with research on nuclear energy, solar energy, and related matters. It was created by the European Atomic Energy Community in 1957.

See ENERGY; FINANCE; JOINT EUROPEAN TORUS; NUCLEAR ENERGY; RESEARCH; SCIENCE AND TECHNOLOGICAL COMMITTEE; SOLAR ENERGY.

Jordan This nation entered into a cooperation agreement with the Community in 1977, allowing for free access to the Community market for industrial goods and preferential treatment for agricultural items.

See MASHRAG STATES; MEDITERRANEAN POLICY; MNCs.

JOULE (Joint Opportunities for Unconventional or Long term Energy supply). A 1989 research program to develop energy technology that takes account of new and renewable energy sources. Its goal is to increase security of supply and reduce energy imports and to contribute to environmental protection.

See ENERGY.

JRC *See* JOINT RESEARCH CENTER (EURATOM).

juices *See* FOOD.

jurists A professional identification card was adopted by the Community's legal profession signaling that group's readiness to practice freely throughout the Community. The right to free movement for jurists was approved in March 1978 and became official in the spring of 1979. The new document identifies the bearer as a professional practitioner and enables him or her to practice in any member country, in many cases with the help of local colleagues.

See LAWYERS.

K

Kennedy Round This economic meeting was made possible by the U.S. Trade Expansion Act of 1962, which achieved substantial cuts in industrial, but not in agricultural, tariffs. The three elements covered by the Kennedy Round were agreed to by the GATT ministers meeting in May 1963 and put into effect on May 4, 1964. The program was completed on June 30, 1967. The three elements were: a reduction, by an average of 35–40 percent in tariffs and other barriers to trade; improvement in access to world markets for agricultural products; and expansion of outlets for the exports of less developed nations. The term is sometimes used to cover only the tariff element in these negotiations. One example of the reduction is that the Community tariff on cars dropped from 22 percent to 11 percent.

See CHRONOLOGY (APRIL 15, 1964; JUNE 30, 1967) IN APPENDIX; MONTREAL ROUND; TOKYO ROUND.

Kenya This nation signed the Arusha Convention in 1968. It is one of the ACP states and a signatory to the Lomé Convention of 1988. A Protocol annexed to the Convention guarantees the nation's sugar exports to the Community.

See ARUSHA CONVENTION; SUGAR.

Kiribati (formerly Gilbert Islands) This nation is one of the ACP states and a signatory to the Lomé Convention of 1988.

know-how licensing These are agreements through which one firm possessing technical information not covered by patents authorizes another to use it to produce goods or services. Such agreements were exempted by the Commission in 1989 from the E.C.'s competition rules. This measure was enacted in recognition of the increasing economic importance of non-patented technical information such as descriptions of manufacturing processes, recipes, formulas, and drawings. Like patent licenses, know-how agreements are procompetitive in that they facilitate the transfer of technology and boost innovation, but they may, in particular circumstances, inhibit competition by imposing territorial restrictions. Given that the transfer of know-how is frequently irreversible, the Commission felt that it was necessary to provide greater legal certainty for undertakings as regards the compatibility of such agreements with the competition rules.

See PATENT LAW.

konzern A German term, this is the aggregate of enterprises bound together by one enterprise exercising control of the others by holding shares in them or in other similar ways.

Korea, Republic of Since 1978 the Community has had a bilateral textile agreement with South Korea. The Community concluded a bilateral arrangement with South Korea on certain steel products allowing South Korean steel producers to sell their products at delivered prices and to allow a certain penetration rebate in order to ensure the competitiveness of the imported products. Community imports from South Korea doubled between 1978 and 1985 rising from 1.4 million ECU to 3.3 million ECU. During the same period Community exports to Korea also more than doubled, from 1.0 million ECU to 2.7 million ECU. In 1984, Germany and the U.K. accounted for 61 percent of the Community's imports from Korea, while exports from these countries made up 53 percent of the Community total.

Kuwait *See* GULF COOPERATION COUNCIL.

L

labeling *See* FOOD; FOOD LABELS; FOOD-STUFFS-LABELING.

labor Two general obstacles to free movement of labor must be removed by 1992 if the single market in goods and services is to be matched by a single market for labor and the professions. The White Paper program proposes an income tax for workers who live and work in different member states to supersede national taxes. Proposals also deal with the administrative problems faced by unemployed workers residing in another member state.

LAFTA (The Latin American Free Trade Association) Formed in 1961 by Argentina, Brazil, Chile, Mexico, Paraguay, Peru, and Uruguay. Colombia, Ecuador, and Venezuela joined later. Its aim is an eventual Latin American Common Market. LAFTA's permanent secretariat is at Montevideo, Uruguay.

languages French is the primary working language of the European Communities, though the seven official languages (Danish, Dutch, English, French, German, Italian, Spanish) all have equal status. Most official acts, resolutions, directives, and decisions must be published in all seven languages. No language takes precedence over another.
  See MERCATOR.

Laos Since 1975 Laos has had an agreement with the Community dealing with certain textiles and hand-made items.

large exposures *See* BANKING.

Latin America Economic and trade cooperation agreements were concluded with Mexico in 1975, with Brazil in 1980, and with the nations of the Andean Pact (Bolivia, Colombia, Ecuador, Peru, and Venezuela) in 1983. A trade agreement with Uruguay was concluded in 1974. In 1985, a cooperation agreement with the countries of the Central American isthmus (Costa Rica, Guatemala, Honduras, Nicaragua, Panama, and El Salvador) has been concluded. Total European Community financial and technical assistance from 1979 to 1984 to all Latin American countries and the Island of Hispaniola, including national and regional projects, was 254 million ECU. West Germany is both Latin America's largest buyer and largest supplier, followed by Italy and France. On June 13, 1985, three resolutions were adopted by the European Parliament—one approving the Commission's proposal for a cooperation agreement with Central America, and the other two supporting economic relations with Latin America and Community cooperation for development.
  See ANDEAN PACT; CENTRAL AMERICA; ESQUIPULAS II.

Latin American Economic System (SELA) SELA was established in 1975. It comprises all the Latin American countries and a number of the Caribbean countries. It has a two-fold objective: to promote regional cooperation and integration and to encourage consultation between member countries to coordinate positions in international forums and in dealings with other countries. The E.C. Commission has had official contacts with SELA's Permanent Secretariat in Caracas, Venezuela.

Latin American Free Trade Association *See* LAFTA.

lawyers After March 1979, lawyers have been permitted to provide services in any member nation in the European Community. They do not, however, have a right of establishment and a right to practice anywhere in the Community. They are exempt from residence and registration requirements of the host member nation, but must practice under the same conditions as locally registered lawyers.

See JURISTS; WORK AND EMPLOYMENT.

LDCs *See* LESS DEVELOPED COUNTRIES.

lead *See* TOXIC EFFLUENT.

leaded gasoline A proposed E.C. standard would require all new cars sold in the E.C. from 1991 on to burn unleaded gasoline and would reduce the permissible levels of other pollutants in automobile exhaust. The proposal requires lead-free gasoline to be available at all gas stations and garages in the E.C. beginning in 1989. All 1989 car models would have to be designed to run on unleaded fuel only. Automobile manufacturers would have until the 1991 model year to modify the engine designs of existing models to the unleaded-fuel-only formula.

See ENVIRONMENT; POLLUTION.

leasing In the fall 1989, the E.C. began consideration of a single license for leasing companies that would permit them to operate throughout the 12 member states once they have home country authorization. Similar to the Second Banking Directive guidelines already established for banks, the proposals would involve establishing minimum capital and supervisory rules for all leasing institutions. The growth of leasing as a financial vehicle in the E.C. has created anomalies because, in some member states, leasing is regarded as a banking activity, while in others it is not. Banks already engaged in leasing stand to benefit from the market opening created by the Second Banking Directive, but other firms in the leasing industry may be at a disadvantage in terms of market access.

See BANKING.

Lebanon Since 1977, this country has had a cooperation agreement with the Community providing free access to Community markets for industrial items and preferential treatment for agricultural goods. In 1989, the E.C.'s member state governments decided to give Lebanon's civil war victims over $9 million in emergency humanitarian aid, including $5.6 million worth of food assistance.

See MASHRAG STATES; MEDITERRANEAN POLICY; MNCs.

legal expenses insurance *See* INSURANCE.

legal status The Community can be a party to a contract and can defend its interest in law, free of intervention on the part of the member nations. The Community has the capacity to conclude agreements with third states, unions of states, and international organizations.

legislative preparation This is the lengthy drafting stage for a European Commission proposal before it reaches the Council of Ministers. Beginning with a working paper, the Commission then approves the proposal and sends it forward to appropriate expert committees. After Committee review, the Commission, following formal approval, sends the proposal to the Council of Ministers. It must be referred to the European Parliament and to the Economic and Social Committee for comment. Should the proposal finally arrive before the Council, it can only be amended by unanimous agreement. Should there be agreement, the proposal can be adopted by a (weighted) majority before becoming law.

See COUNCIL OF MINISTERS.

leisure industry *See* TOURISM.

Lesotho This nation is one of the ACP states and a signatory to the Lomé Convention of 1988.

Less Developed Countries (LDCs) These are poor nations with low per capita income, little industrial development, and limited economic and social infrastructure.

See THIRD WORLD.

leucosis *See* ANIMAL HEALTH AND MEAT INSPECTION.

levies These are varying duties applied to imports of agricultural items into the Community. Their purpose is to bring the imports' prices up to the threshold price as fixed under the Common Agricultural Policy.

See AGRICULTURE, COMMON AGRICULTURAL POLICY; BUDGET; FINANCE.

levy subsidy There is a subsidy to producers or suppliers of a commodity financed by a levy on sales of that commodity. The subsidy can be payable to domestic producers or to specific overseas suppliers. The levy can be raised on all sales or simply on imports.

Liberal and Democratic Parties within the E.C. Fourteen Liberal parties from eight E.C. nations met in March 1976 in Stuttgart and agreed to form a "Federation of Liberal and Democratic Parties within the E.C." to prepare for the direct election to the European Parliament.

Liberia This nation is one of the ACP states and a signatory to the Lomé Convention of 1988.

Libya *See* MEDITERRANEAN POLICY; MNCs.

Liechtenstein Although not a Community member, Liechtenstein is subject to Community rules regarding imports from third (non-Community) nations.

linear tariff cuts This is a uniform reduction in tariffs that is determined by their relation to the different sectors of a national tariff.

LINGUA Adopted on July 28, 1989, the objective of the LINGUA program is to promote a quantitative and qualitative improvement in foreign language competence among Community citizens. The program consists of a series of measures to be implemented by the Commission in order to support and complement the policies of the member states in this field.

local content The proportion of an item manufactured in an E.C. nation to that proportion manufactured in a non-E.C. nation. For example, in the production of cars, the Treaty of Rome states that member states may not impose quotas against each others' goods. However, should a significant proportion of the item be manufactured in a non-E.C. state, quotas may still be fixed.

Lomé Conventions The first Convention was signed at Lomé, Togo, (Lomé I) on February 28, 1975. It became effective on April 1, 1976, and expired on February 28, 1980. Lomé II, came into force on March 1, 1980, and expired on March 1, 1985. It was designed to provide a "balanced response" to the varying needs of developing nations that are signatories to the Convention. Under Lomé I, 99.5 percent of ACP agricultural exports entered

the Community market duty-free and Community Funds were authorized to help finance projects. In Lomé II, signed by 58 ACP nations, later extended to 60, the duty-free arrangements affecting agricultural items were extended allowing in ACP exports of tomatoes, carrots, onions, and asparagus, and preferential arrangements for beef and veal were consolidated. In December 1984, 66 African, Caribbean, and Pacific countries signed a new convention with the Community, to run to 1990. Lomé III freed the signatories from all customs duties on 99.5 percent of their exports to the Community, with no reciprocal concessions required on their part.

In 1985, the Community decided to strengthen cooperation in a range of sectors—rural development, energy, industry, fisheries, social, and cultural problems. The Community provides technical and financial aid, amounting to 8.5 billion ECU (about $9.9 billion) for the period ending in 1990, with grants, loans, and risk capital transactions. In October 1988, negotiations began on the fourth Lomé Convention. Discussions included a demand that countries receiving funds to compensate them for lost export earnings due to lower commodity prices should no longer have to repay some of the money when commodity prices increase, and a request for further trade concessions for ACP exports.

The Lomé IV Agreement was ratified in December 1989. Lomé IV will run for 10 years, compared with five years for previous Conventions.

The total amount of aid that the E.C. will make available to these countries during the first five years will be 12 billion ECU. Implementation of the Conventions is governed by the Council of Ministers, the European Commission and a member of each of the ACP nation governments.

Two new members, Haiti and the Dominican Republic, joined the existing 66 ACP countries, followed by Namibia (after its independence) to bring the number of ACP states to 69.

See ACP (STATES); AID TO DEVELOPING COUNTRIES; CARIBBEAN BASIN; DEVELOPMENT FUND; EXTERNAL TRADE; FINANCE; FOOD AID; GENERALIZED SYSTEM OF PREFERENCES; STABILIZATION OF EXPORT EARNINGS; THIRD WORLD.

Luxembourg This nation became a founder member of the European Coal and Steel Community in 1951, the European Economic Community and the European Atomic Energy Community in 1957 and the Treaty of Brussels in 1972. Although the E.C.'s Parliament is formally housed in Luxembourg, it has not sat there for several years. Other E.C. institutions, including the rapidly growing European Court of Justice, the European Investment Bank, and the computer and statistical services of the Commission, remain firmly rooted in the Grand Duchy. The Grand Duchy's sound economy moved along at an annual growth rate of 3.4 percent for the past 15 years, rising to 3.9 percent in 1984 while maintaining a stable inflation rate at around 1.5 percent. A strong banking structure makes Luxembourg a powerfully attractive source of foreign investment. It has enjoyed a remarkable growth of over 40 percent in bank deposits. Its practice of paying out to savers every penny of interest earned has openly attracted deposits from Belgium and Britain, and, more circumspectly, from France and Germany. These deposits have helped to facilitate the growth of a retail banking center that has, to a large extent, compensated for the drop in Euro-dollar lending, the activity on which the Grand Duchy's bankers initially thrived. Should the E.C. be successful in imposing a withholding tax on Luxembourg (the withholding tax is also opposed by Britain and West Germany) the impact on this small country will be minimal. Probably, the rate of the tax will be dropped to 10 percent, or less. The more direct threat to Luxembourg comes with the E.C.'s move to harmonize all indirect taxes, including excise duties. Luxembourg has very low excise duty rates on tobacco, beer, and spirits, and thereby enjoys considerable custom from neighboring nations where the rates are significantly higher. Should all E.C. excise duties be harmonized, there would be a considerable loss of trade to the Grand Duchy. At present, a case of wine bought in Luxembourg can be 30 percent cheaper than the identical wine bought in Belgium, France, or West Germany. The same ratio applies for cigarettes. Fortunately, the Grand Duchy has been attracting a huge rush of investment money into European Unit Trusts for 1992 enterprises. Its cherished banking activity continues to attract foreign monies. Concentrating on Euro-dollar lending in the 1970s, Luxembourg has now switched to the growing sector of personal portfolio management. Its potential for being a magnet of European and overseas investment is certain to continue.

Luxembourg (Agreement) Compromise The agreement settled a dispute that arose from a Commission opinion that the new budget procedure would be a step towards full budgetary powers for the European Parliament. France, in rejecting the proposal in 1965 walked out of the Community's proceedings. All sides compromised, and by January 29, 1966, France agreed to resume participation with the E.C.

See CHRONOLOGY (JANUARY 28–29, 1966).

M

machine safety *See* HARMONIZATION.

Madagascar (Malagasy Republic) This nation is one of the ACP states and a signatory to the Yaoundé Conventions of 1963 and 1969 and the Lomé Convention of 1988. A Protocol annexed to the Convention guarantees the country's sugar exports to the Community.
See SUGAR.

Madrid meeting In June 1989, the 12 nations of the E.C. agreed to go ahead with the first steps toward monetary union. The first phase, which took effect on July 1, 1990, would require an end to exchange controls and obstacles to European-wide banking, securities, and insurance services. The final two phases would involve the adoption of a common currency and the creation of a regional central bank.

Maghreb Agreement A trade agreement was signed with Algeria, Morocco, and Tunisia in April 1976 to take effect July 1, 1976. For each nation it meant that there would be duty free entry of industrial items into the Nine E.E.C. nations except for certain petroleum items and cork. Some tariff concessions were also given on agricultural goods.

mail In 1989, the Commission proposed curbing national postal monopolies to give the E.C.'s single market cheaper and more efficient mail services, but stopped short of opening normal mail deliveries to outside firms. This is part of the E.C.'s drive to deal with divergences in postal service standards and the different national regulations governing them. The Commission proposed that a core of essential postal services, such as letters, postcards, and small packages, remain a monopoly, but that other services be opened to free competition, with common E.C. standards to guarantee confidentiality and other minimum requirements. Providers of core services would be allowed to compete in those areas as long as they did not subsidize one activity with another.

major accident hazards The E.C. policy for the prevention of major accident hazards was established by the Council directive of June 24, 1982. The policy objectives are to establish Community legislation on the prevention and management of industrial hazards, and to harmonize the obligations of manufacturers in the different member states to avoid distorting competition within the Community. The directive identified ways to prevent major accidents at the design stage, through quality control and maintenance, compliance with standards and selection of equipment. It also recommended recordkeeping, stricter operating rules, and training for operating personnel. The directive does not apply to: (1) nuclear installations and plants for the processing of radioactive substances and material; (2) military installations; (3) installations for the manufacture and separate storage of explosives, gunpowder, and munitions; and (4) extraction and other mining operations. It also does not apply to installations used for the disposal of toxic and dangerous waste covered by other Community Acts that encompass the prevention of major accidents.

Malagasy Republic *See* MADAGASCAR.

Malawi This nation is one of the ACP states and a signatory to the Lomé Convention of 1988. A Protocol annexed to the Convention guarantees the country's sugar exports to the Community.
See SUGAR.

Malaysia This nation is a member of the Association of South East Asian Nations (ASEAN). In December 1979, the Community concluded a cooperation agreement seeking "to consolidate, deepen and diversify" commercial relations. A bilateral agreement limiting textile exports to the Community has been in operation since 1978.

See ASSOCIATION OF SOUTH EAST ASIAN NATIONS; PACIFIC RIM; TEXTILES.

Mali This nation is one of the ACP states and a signatory to the Yaoundé Conventions of 1963 and 1969 and to the Lomé Convention of 1988.

Malta Since 1979 this island has had an association agreement with the Community. It provides for the creation of a Customs Union. Malta begins a formal application process to join the E.C. in July 1990.

Man, Isle of Free trade in agriculture and industrial items was agreed upon with the Isle of Man under the Treaty of Accession. The island is exempt from other E.C. regulations, including VAT, the free movement of labor, freedom of establishment, and the competition policy.

management committees The Council of Ministers delegated power to the European Commission to discharge Council decisions and to administer the day-to-day operations of the Community. It accomplishes this delegation through various committees. Unlike Council decisions, however, the E.C. Committees' opinions are not binding on the Commission. The committees may bring disagreements before the Council which can, within one month, reverse the Commission's decision.

See AGRICULTURE, COMMON AGRICULTURAL POLICY; COMMITTEES; EUROPEAN COMMUNITY; LEGISLATIVE PREPARATION.

Cf. ADVISORY COMMITTEE; REGULATORY COMMITTEE.

Manioc *See* THAILAND.

Mansholt Plan A Commission plan for agricultural reform was presented to the Council of Ministers in December 1968. Formulated by Dr. S. Mansholt, Vice President of the Commission, it proposed a restructuring of agriculture in the E.C. with the objective of raising the living standards of farmers and workers and of ceasing the persistent increase in the common agricultural policy's costs. The plan envisaged the creation of large agricultural units.

Synonymous with AGRICULTURE 1980.

See CHRONOLOGY (DECEMBER 18, 1968) IN APPENDIX; MONTANT DE SOUTIEN.

Man Tended Free Flyer (MTFF) *See* EUROPEAN SPACE AGENCY.

manufacturing equipment *See* ADVANCED MANUFACTURING EQUIPMENT.

marine pollution In 1978, the Community adopted two directives for reducing the risk of pollution through accident. The first sets the boundaries required by deep sea pilots operating in the Channel and the North Sea. The second identifies the safety standards applicable to tankers that use any of the ports of Community nations.

See ENVIRONMENT; MAST; PILOTS; TANKERS; TOXIC EFFLUENT; TRANSPORT.

Marine Science and Technology *See* MAST.

maritime transport *See* TRANSPORT.

Marjolin study This major inquiry on the Community's economic and monetary union of 1975 was headed by former E.C. Commission Vice President Robert Marjolin. This study was instrumental in the evolution of the European Currency Unit.

market integration In preparation for the single market of 1992, the E.C. proposed nearly 300 directives, later reduced to 279, for removing nontariff barriers of three types: *physical barriers*—e.g., border controls causing transport delays and administrative requirements causing excessive paperwork; *technical barriers*—e.g., divergent product and process standards inhibiting production and marketing; protection in public procurement markets; and divergent company tax and business laws; and *fiscal barriers*—e.g., differing rates of indirect taxation.

market organization This organization was set up under the Common Agricultural Policy for most agricultural products of the E.C. It supports the price farmers receive for their produce primarily by the buying up of output by public authorities to reduce quantities on markets and so raise prices. It has a system of minimum prices for imports, which prevents them from undercutting and so lowering Community prices.

marriage bureau *Synonymous with* BUSINESS COOPERATION CENTER.

marriage contract This informal agreement permits the 12 members of the European Community to live and prosper together, promising economic and social cohesion, the further strengthening of their zone of monetary stability, scientific and technological cooperation, as well as the development of a European social dimension (to maintain individual cultures and languages) and coordinated action to protect the environment.

Marshall Plan *See* ERP.

Mashrag states Composed of Egypt, Jordan, Lebanon, and Syria, they signed trade and cooperative agreements in January and February 1977 and thus completed the E.C. Mediterranean Policy.
See CHRONOLOGY (JANUARY 18, 1977); MEDITERRANEAN POLICY.

MAST (Marine Science and Technology) A 1989 E.C. research program to improve knowledge of the marine environment; to promote new exploration technologies for the protection and exploitation of marine resources; to coordinate national R&D programs.
See MARINE POLLUTION.

Mauritania This nation is one of the ACP states and a signatory to Yaoundé Conventions of 1963 and 1969 and the Lomé Convention of 1988.

Mauritius This nation is one of the ACP states and a signatory to the Lomé Convention of 1988.
See ASSOCIABLE.

May 9 This was declared Europe Day, to commemorate the day in 1950 that Robert Schuman, then France's Minister for Foreign Affairs, made the famous speech which led, a year later, to the creation of the first European Community, the European Coal and Steel Community.

MCAs *See* MONETARY COMPENSATORY AMOUNTS.

MDP EUROPE This is an E.C. project to develop a multilingual description of goods to ease dealings between sellers and potential buyers.

ME (Mouvement Européen) The European Movement.

Measures to Encourage the Development of the Community Audiovisual Industry *See* MEDIA.

meat inspection *See* ANIMAL HEALTH AND MEAT INSPECTION.

MEC (Mercato Comune Europeo) The European Common Market (Italian).

MEDIA (Measures to Encourage the Development of the Community Audiovisual Industry) was launched in 1987. It was planned with the help of more than 1,000 companies and organizations in the European audiovisual industry. It is designed to work as a catalyst and provide start-up capital for audiovisual projects in the areas of production, distribution, financing and training. The E.C. contributes 50 percent of funds needed for each project, while industry, national administrations, or patrons of the arts provide the rest. In 1988, 11 projects and pilot experiments were selected, including a European Cinema Club, a European Film Distribution Office, a European Fund for Broadcasting Across the Barriers of European Language, the European Organization for an Independent Market, and the SCRIPT Fund which promotes cultural creativity in the audiovisual industry by providing aid for screenplays at the writing, development, and preproduction stages.
See AUDIO-VISUAL POLICY.

medical and public health research Research is carried out indirectly on behalf of the Community by approved national research institutions in accordance with guidelines set by a Janary 1974 resolution on scientific and technological research. The Commission coordinates the research. Other programs include research designed to update basic standards for protection against health hazards from ionizing radiation, and to evaluate the biological and ecological consequences of nuclear activities and the use of nuclear energy and ionizing radiation. Also proposed is the creation of a Community organ bank for matching human organs and blood.

See ENERGY, FINANCE, RESEARCH, SCIENCE AND TECHNOLOGICAL COMMITTEE.

medical practice This 1986 directive on specific training in general medical practice was passed, allowing mutual recognition of medical qualifications throughout the member states.

medicinal products See PHARMACEUTICALS.

Mediterranean global approach See MEDITERRANEAN POLICY.

Mediterranean Non-Candidates See MNCS.

Mediterranean Policy In 1972, the Community announced a "Mediterranean global approach" to relations with the nations of the Mediterranean basin (Algeria, Morocco, Tunisia, Egypt, Jordan, Libya, Syria, and Israel). The Mediterranean countries are granted duty-free access to the Community for their industrial products, various customs concessions for agricultural produce, and European Investment Bank loans and grants which totalled 1.6 million ECU for the period 1987–1990. The Mediterranean countries constitute the E.C.'s third-largest customer and its fourth-largest supplier. The Mediterranean countries' 1987 trade deficit was about $16 billion.

See MASHRAG STATES, MNCS, THIRD WORLD.

medium-sized companies See SMALL AND MEDIUM-SIZED ENTERPRISES.

Medium-Term Economic Policy Committee of the E.C. This committee was created in 1964. It examines the probable development of the Community's economies over the medium-term.

MEDREP See DATABASES AND DATABANKS OF THE E.C.

memory chips See COMPUTERS.

MEP A Member of the European Parliament.

MERCATOR An E.C. computerized project designed to link European ports and test the feasibility of exchanges of data between parties involved in international trade.

On January 16, 1990, the Commission created an information and documentation network allowing greater exchange of information on minority languages and cultures with regard to third parties, as well as between minorities themselves. The pilot program with four centers will lay down the bases of a computerized data bank and will study how all bodies, public and private, from the different regional or minority linguistic communities, can be involved in this initiative. MERCATOR will provide reliable information that is processed in such a way as to attain different sectors of the public: political and administrative decision makers, researchers, teachers, journalists, and young people.

mercury See TOXIC EFFLUENT.

mergers A number of directives and regulations on Company law deal with the harmonization of national regulations dealing with domestic mergers of public limited liability firms where one firm acquires all the assets and liabilities of another, and the latter is dissolved without liquidation. The overall goal is to coordinate the procedures for, and effects of, mergers and similar activities to arrive at an equivalent degree of protection throughout the Community for the members, creditors, and workers of firms involved.

The cross-border merger was seen as a technique for simplifying the procedures for forming or restructuring complex economic entities. To facilitate mergers of companies from different member states, a regulation allows two or more companies to merge by forming a new type of Community company; another regulation allows a firm from one member state to be acquired by a company from another. On December 22, 1988, the Community proposed a directive to harmonize the widely differing rules on corporate takeovers in its 12 member nations. Under the legislation, a firm offering to purchase more than a third of another firm's shares must offer to buy all shares. A firm initiating a takeover would also have to state its intentions about the target company's future activities, the fate of its work force, and its indebtedness. The proposed legislation was impelled by an unprecedented wave of mergers by European firms within the E.C., fueling monopoly fears. The Commission claimed that there were 383 mergers within the Community in 1988, a 26 percent jump from 1987, and 111 joint-venture agreements, a 23 percent rise. Business specialists claim the speed of expansion is far greater than E.C. estimates. In 1988 alone, they claim, there were close to 500 mergers and acquisitions within Europe, with the value of intra-European deals soaring to $81.5 billion, up from $11.1 billion in 1985. Cross-border mergers and acquisitions accounted for 42.4 percent of all intra-European deals in 1988, up from 13.8 percent in 1985. Continued concentration of industry at this pace could create serious problems for the planned barrier-free market. Mergers and acquisitions are most common in companies in similar or related businesses that are strengthening their domestic market positions, firms that are moving to link proven and related companies throughout Europe into a centrally managed one, and businesses that are buying minority shares in European counterparts to position themselves for possible takeovers. Most of the activity in mergers and acquisitions is in the middle market—deals valued at less than $50 million. The industries sought and purchased are concentrated in consumer goods, foods, drink, and tobacco, with banking, insurance, and business service transactions following. Corporate restructuring in Europe falls mainly along the Italian-Swiss-French-English axis; there is a hesitancy to pursue joint ventures in which like firms remain independent but combine development of products and services. E.C. deals by European firms are still small in comparison to European acquisitions in North America.

In late September 1989, the 12 E.C. governments reached broad agreement on the size of corporate mergers that would be subject to approval. The regulation gives the Commission power to review and block large transborder mergers, as opposed to an earlier regulation where the Commission could intervene only after the merger had taken place and if a complaint was filed under the Treaty of Rome's antitrust rules. Now the Commission can review mergers of companies with global combined revenue of more than five billion ECUs ($5.27 billion). That threshold would be reduced to two billion ECUs by the end of 1992. If two-thirds of the combined revenue is in a single E.C. state, the nation would retain its regulatory powers over the merger. In the fall of 1989, two new directives were proposed—on merger control and on the regulation of takeover bids. The merger control proposal empowers the Commission to review mergers in advance and, should it choose, the Commission could block or order the restructuring of mergers that appear to interfere with goals of the Community. Concentrations would be evaluated for their compatibility with the common market and could be disallowed if they impeded maintenance or development of effective competition. The Commission has one month from the date of notification to decide whether to initiate a formal investigation. In addition, the Commission could empower those member nations directly concerned by the merger to apply their national legislation to guarantee effective competition in their respective local markets. On December 21, 1989, E.C. ministers agreed to give the Commission the power to block larger mergers on antitrust grounds. The Commission is expected to examine 40 to 50 mergers a year after the plan takes effect on September 21, 1990.

See COMPANY LAW; COMPETITION DIRECTORATE; HARMONIZATION; MERGERS; EMPLOYEE PROTECTION; TAKEOVER REGULATIONS; WORK AND EMPLOYMENT.

mergers, employee protection Under a directive applying to the transfer of any undertaking, in whole or in part, to another employer, workers must be informed of the reasons and implications of the transfer. Their rights must be safeguarded, including those under collective agreements and pension rights, until termination or retirement.

See COMPANY LAW; MERGERS; SOCIAL POLICY; WORK AND EMPLOYMENT.

Merger Treaty This Treaty revised the treaties creating the European Communities and Acts relating to the Communities, and merged the institutions of the three Communities: the

European Coal and Steel Community, the European Economic Community, and the European Atomic Energy Community, first created under the Treaty of Paris in 1951 and the Treaty of Rome in 1957. On July 1, 1967, the major institutions of the European Community became the European Commission, the Council of Ministers, the European Parliament, and the European Court of Justice. It also created a single Economic and Social Committee.

See PERMANENT REPRESENTATIVE COMMITTEE.

Messina Conference The foreign ministers of the six member nations of the E.C.S.C. met at Messina, Italy, on June 2–4, 1955, to discuss proposals for further European integration made by the three Benelux nations. The ministers, in the Messina Resolution, adopted the objectives of the Benelux program but identified different procedures for, and a more gradual approach to, their implementation.

See MESSINA RESOLUTION.

Messina Resolution "The Governments of Belgium, France, German Federal Republic, Italy, Luxembourg, and the Netherlands considered in 1955 that the moment has arrived to initiate a new phase on the path of constructing Europe. They believe that this has to be done principally in the economic sphere, and regard it as necessary to continue the creation of a United Europe through an expansion of joint institutions, the gradual fusion of national economies, the creation of a common market, and the gradual coordination of social policies. Such a policy seems to them indispensable to preserve for Europe its place in the world, to restore its influence, and to improve steadily the living standards of its population." This June 4, 1955, Resolution was signed by the six foreign ministers. The aims included the joint development of large-scale communications facilities, the development of exchanges of gas and electric power and its cost reduction, the creation of a joint organization to coordinate these activities and for the development of atomic energy for peaceful purposes.

See MESSINA CONFERENCE.

metric system This system of weights and measures was introduced in France in 1799 and is widely used by most countries of the world, including members of the E.C.

Mexico This nation has had a nonpreferential agreement on commercial and economic cooperation with the Community since 1975, and a bilateral agreement on textiles since 1978.

See CENTRAL AMERICA; LAFTA.

MFA *See* MULTIFIBRE ARRANGEMENTS.

MFN *See* MOST-FAVORED NATION.

midwives Since January 1983, midwives can practice their profession anywhere in the Community, subject to the minimum training requirements and mutual recognition of qualifications set out in directives that specify a minimum range of activities permitted a midwife within each member nation. Three years of training for direct entrants is required. In the case of a registered general nurse or equivalent, 18 months training is required followed by one year's clinical practice for those wishing to take advantage of free movement to other states.

See WORK AND EMPLOYMENT.

migrant workers For Community nationals the Treaty of Rome confers the right of free movement within the Community without discrimination in employment, remuneration, and other conditions of work, except for employment in the public services and certain restrictions regarding the rights of establishment. It includes the right of covered workers to have and retain social security benefits—a right extended in 1981 to the self-employed. In 1976 the Council adopted a resolution on a program for migrant workers and members of their families on the basis of a proposal from the Commission. The Commission is active in three areas: development of Community legislation for migrants who are citizens of member states; consultation between member states and the Commission on problems faced by migrants and introduction of Community guidelines to deal with such problems; and access to information for migrants to make them aware of their rights. Since 1981, the children of migrant workers receive special intensive language training in the language of their country of residence as well as in their native language.

See EXCHANGE VISITS; FOREIGN WORKERS; MIGRATION; SELF-EMPLOYED; SOCIAL POLICY; WORK AND EMPLOYMENT.

migration With the legislative actions leading to 1992, E.C. officials expect a large scale migration, precipitated by the new freedom to travel. Perhaps 15 percent of Europe's population, nearly 50 million people, will move from one country to another over the next few decades. After 1992, the same right to free movement must apply throughout the E.C. Unfortunately, the E.C. has not yet agreed on a common policy on migrants, such as their entry into the Community or the conditions for their remaining. What has been agreed upon is a policy on refugees stating that they should seek asylum in the nation of first arrival.

See MIGRANT WORKERS; RESIDENCE RIGHTS.

milk and milk products A 1968 regulation of the Common Agricultural Policy established a common annual target price for milk. Because only about a quarter of the production goes for liquid consumption, most price management is concerned with milk items, for which there are intervention prices for butter and skim milk and, in Italy only, for cheese. Threshold prices were set for 12 pilot products which influence the threshold prices of others. The importer pays a levy to cover the difference between the imported landed price and the threshold price. Legislation also regulates the fat content of milk sold for human consumption.

In December 1986, E.C. farm ministers decided to cut milk production by 9.5 percent over the next two years and abolished the automatic right of producers to sell surplus production to public authorities and to make it available on only a very restricted basis.

See AGRICULTURE, COMMON AGRICULTURAL POLICY; CONSUMER PROTECTION; DAIRY PRODUCTS; FINANCE; NEW ZEALAND; OPERATION FLOOD.

milk, condensed and dried Community regulations set the rules for the composition, description, and labeling of condensed milk and dried milk products intended for human consumption.

See AGRICULTURE, COMMON AGRICULTURAL POLICY; CONSUMER PROTECTION.

minced meat *See* ANIMAL HEALTH AND MEAT INSPECTION.

mineral oils *See* EXCISE DUTIES.

mineral water The E.C. implemented new regulations that set forth the properties bottled drinking water must exhibit in order to be advertised as mineral water. The rules, adopted in 1980, came into force on July 17, 1984. They not only define the properties and characteristics of a true mineral water, but also establish quality control standards for mineral-water bottlers. A product can now only be labeled or advertised as "natural mineral water" if it is free of harmful bacteria and originates from an underground source or rock stratum supplied by one or more natural springs. In addition to its natural purity, such water also must contain a recognizably higher content of minerals and trace elements than found in ordinary drinking water. The regulations also prohibit mineral water from being mechanically or chemically processed for purposes other than separating unstable elements such as iron and sulfur or for the removal or addition of carbon dioxide. In addition, mineral water must be sold exclusively in sealed containers as a means of discouraging fraud. There is a ban on misleading advertising. For example, bottlers will no longer be able to claim that their products possess special powers for curing or preventing disease.

See WATER.

Mines Safety and Health Commission This Commission was formed in 1957 by Council recommendation. In 1974, the Council extended its competence to cover extractive industries, mining or nonmining.

MNCs (The Mediterranean Non-Candidates) These are countries with which the Community has preferential agreements. They are: Algeria, Cyprus, Egypt, Israel, Jordan, Lebanon, Malta, Morocco, Syria, Tunisia, Turkey, and Yugoslavia. Albania and Lybia have no agreements with the European Community, while Portugal and Spain are new E.C. members. By 1984, generally all MNCs had free entry to Community markets for their manufactured goods, without limits of the kind that exist in the Generalized System of Preferences.

See GENERAL AGREEMENT ON TARIFFS AND TRADE; MEDITERRANEAN POLICY.

mobile telephone *See* TECHNOLOGIES.

Monaco This nation is an autonomous principality with intimate Treaty links with France. Since 1963 there has been a complete Customs Union between the two nations, although Monaco retains independent responsibility for external affairs, including adherence to treaties. It is not a member of the European Community, although in practice Monaco receives full benefits as a result of the Customs Union with France.

Monetary Committee Created by the Treaty of Rome, this consultative body was established to promote the coordination of the policies of the member states in the monetary field to the full extent needed for the functioning of the Common Market.

Monetary Compensatory Amounts (MCAs) Common support prices for items under the Common Agricultural Policy are paid in green currencies at special exchange rates. Thereby the prices farmers receive vary among nations when measured in normal exchange rate terms. Common pricing becomes more difficult when exchange rates fluctuate. To offset such fluctuations, MCAs were introduced in 1971. This is a system of border subsidies or levies that are applied to adjust up or down the national price when farm goods move from one Community nation to another state. In January 1990, MCAs still applied in the Community were partially dismantled given the monetary realignment. MCAs were dismantled by 30 percent.

See AGRICULTURE, COMMON AGRICULTURAL POLICY; FINANCE; GREEN CURRENCY.

Mongolia This nation has been a member of the Council for Mutual Economic Assistance since 1962.

See COUNCIL FOR MUTUAL ECONOMIC ASSISTANCE.

MONITOR A 1989 E.C. research program of strategic analysis, forecasting and evaluation in matters of research and technology. It attempts to identify new directions and priorities for Community research and development policy; to help show more clearly the relationships between R&D and other Community policies; and to improve the evaluation of R&D programs.

Monnet, Jean Born at Cognac, France, in 1888. He was the initiator of the Schuman Plan which launched the European Communities and of the "relaunching of Europe" in 1955 which led to the Common Market and Euratom. He was the first President of the ECSC High Authority. At a meeting of the Western Heads of State in Luxembourg in April 1976, it was decided to confer the title "Honorary Citizen of Europe" on Jean Monnet for his work as a founder of the European Community. He died in 1979.

Monnet Committee *See* ACTION COMMITTEE FOR UNITED STATES OF EUROPE.

monopolies *See* TELECOMMUNICATIONS.

montant de soutien (amount of support) One of the Mansholt proposals for dealing with agriculture in the 1967 Kennedy Round was the binding of the amount of price support for any given commodity. It involves agreeing to a world price or reference price which is taken as the norm (ceiling price) for international commercial transactions. Each country that deals with a specific commodity submits to GATT the total remuneration received by its producers for that item. The world or reference price is then subtracted from the total remuneration and the difference constitutes the "amount of support" which would be the remaining stable-price for three years.

See MANSHOLT PLAN

montant forfaitaire (amount of forfeiture) These are sums by which the levy on imports from one member nation to another are reduced, giving E.C. suppliers preferential treatment over outside suppliers. This sum is to be increased by stages so that at the end of the negotiated transitional period the levies on trade between member states will be eliminated.

Synonymous with ABATTEMENT FORFAITAIRE.

Montreal Round In December 1988, a 96-nation trade meeting was called under GATT to give political momentum to the four-year round of world trade talks (the Uruguay Round) that began in 1986. Resolved were: liberalizing trade in services, swifter settlement of trade disputes, freer trade in tropical products, reducing tariffs by 30 percent, easing nontariff barriers, easing some investment restrictions, and monitoring countries' trade policies. The meeting agreed on immediate steps to bring down import barriers for tropical products such as coffee, rubber, and bananas. A central objective of the E.C. was to give strong impetus particularly to the process of writing multilateral rules for trade in services. Four issues were deadlocked: liberalizing trade in agriculture, new protections for intellectual property, textile trade reforms, and rules for safeguards against imports. In February 1989, the United States decided to abandon its insistence that Europe commit itself in advance to seeking the elimination of all trade-distorting farm subsidies by some specified date after the year 2000. The United States urged a "ratchet down" approach to farm subsidies over many years.

See KENNEDY ROUND; MADRID MEETING; TOKYO ROUND; URUGUAY ROUND.

Montserrat A U.K. overseas territory, covered by the Lomé Convention.

Morocco This nation, since 1976, has had a cooperation agreement which provides free access to the Community market for industrial items and preferential treatment for agricultural goods. Morocco is part of the E.C. Mediterranean Policy.

See MAGREB AGREEMENT; MEDITERRANEAN POLICY; MNCs.

mortgages *See* BANKING.

Most Favored Nation (MFN) A concept, embodied in the GATT, of granting to other nations any advantage, favor, privilege, or immunity which is granted to the trade of a nation receiving the most favorable treatment. An exception to this is made in the GATT for preferential tariff margins existing at the inception of the GATT.

motorcycle A directive relating to the permissible noise levels of exhaust systems of motorcycles was proposed in 1988. There is an existing directive that regulates the permissible noise levels of motorcycle exhaust systems. A proposed amendment aims to bring existing national type approval for motorcycle exhaust systems closer together and include replacement exhaust systems within its scope.

See NOISE.

motor vehicle industry *See* HARMONIZATION; VEHICLES.

mountain This term refers to the high prices set for some agricultural items that resulted in over-production leading to Community intervention to support prices, with the result that stocks or mountains in the intervention stores have risen. Attempts to lower the mountains run into difficulties because they either reduce agricultural incomes or are obviously illogical—such as using milk-powder as cattle food or selling butter at low prices to non-E.C. buyers.

See DAIRY PRODUCT.

movies *See* AUDIO-VISUAL POLICY.

MTFF (Man Tended Free Flyer.)
See EUROPEAN SPACE AGENCY.

MTNs (Multinational Trade Negotiations.)

MultiFibre Arrangements (MFA) This is a system of limits, under GATT, on imports of textiles and clothing from less developed countries. The MFAs generally do not affect MNCs (Mediterranean countries with preferential agreements with the E.C.), whose exports of textiles and clothing are subject to voluntary export restrictions.

See INDIA; TEXTILES.

Multinational Disclosure Rules A Commission directive under the Treaty of Rome ensures that multinational firms situated within the Community publish comparable information drawn up on uniform lines to provide a minimum degree of protection for shareholders, employees, and third parties. To ensure proper comparisons it was proposed that items incorporated in group accounts be valued using identical methods, although a degree of flexibility would be permitted in applying these principles as there may be practical difficulties in exceptional cases. It prescribed a special valuation method for group accounts in respect of holdings of group undertakings in the capital of other firms not belonging to the group, but where, by virtue of the holdings, a substantial influence is exerted on the running of the firms, as in a joint venture. Certain information is to be given in the notes to group accounts, to disclose the structure of the group, the identity of the group undertakings and the relationship between them.

mutton and lamb *See* SHEEPMEAT.

mutual recognition The Court of Justice developed this principle in its case law, notably in the Cassis de Dijon judgment. It signifies acceptance by all member states of products lawfully and fairly manufactured and sold in any other member state, even if such products are manufactured on the basis of technical specifications different from those laid down by national laws in force in so far as the products in question protect in an equivalent fashion the legitimate interests involved.

See CASSIS DE DIJON CASE; HARMONIZATION; INDUSTRIAL STANDARDS.

N

NACE (Nomenclature Générale des Activités Economoques des Communautés) It was used by the original Six for the classification of economic activities. It is an alternative to the International Standard Industrial Classification.

Namibia After 75 years under South African control, Namibia achieved independence on March 21, 1990.
See LOMÉ CONVENTIONS.

National Referendum Campaign (NRC) An anti-Common Market organization active in the United Kingdom during the debate on the referendum.

national trademark *See* TRADEMARKS.

national treatment The United States accords national treatment (granting reciprocal rights unilaterally) in nearly every sector (excluding banking) and believes that it should be granted unconditionally. However, the E.C. may make national treatment and the right to do business conditional on receiving the same treatment for E.C. firms in the foreign country.
Cf. IDENTICAL TREATMENT.
See RECIPROCITY.

natural disasters *See* CIVIL PROTECTION.

natural gas *See* ENERGY.

natural mineral water *See* MINERAL WATER.

NCI *See* NEW COMMUNITY INSTRUMENT.

Nepal This nation established diplomatic relations with the E.C. in 1975. In 1985, E.C. exports were 47 million ECUs and E.C. imports were 36 million ECUs, of which 10 million ECUs (or just over 25 percent) entered duty-free under the Community's normal tariff regime.

NET (Next European Torus) *See* NUCLEAR FUSION.

Netherlands, the This country became a founder member of the European Coal and Steel Community in 1951, the European Economic Community and the European Atomic Energy Community in 1957 and signatory to the Treaty of Brussels in 1972. The Dutch are presently the second-largest investors in the United States. By sector of business activity, 53 percent of Dutch firms operating in the United States derive 20 percent or more of their revenues from manufacturing; 29 percent from finance, insurance, and real estate; 28 percent from wholesale trade; 10 percent from transportation, communications, utilities, and sanitation; 8 percent from services; 8 percent from mining, construction, agriculture, forestry, and fishing; and 6 percent from retailing. Although the Netherlands has the third-highest wage costs in the E.C., they are justified by the skill and training levels of its workers.

By international standards, the Dutch government's budget deficit remains high, with growing pressures from environmental clean-up projects. Joblessness remains high, and days lost to sickness are among the highest in Europe. About 800,000 people draw disability benefits—twice the number of unemployed or about 16 percent of the adult population. Consequently, as a result of the numbers of disabled, unemployed, and retired, and women who are not in the work force, only 52 percent of the adult population works. The Dutch gross domestic product is projected to slow from 3.2 percent in 1989 to 2.2 percent in 1990, while the E.C. average continues to move along at about 3.0 percent.

NETT (Network for Environmental Technology Transfer) A research program to promote cooperation between industrial enterprises and users in the field of clean technologies. Consultancy services are associated with the network, which was established by the E.C. Commission in 1988 as an independent association. NETT supplies information on markets, technical options open to industry, current or prospective environmental standards and regulations, exisitng programs of support, and financial and technical support by the E.C. and national governments.

See ENVIRONMENT.

Network for Environmental Technology Transfer *See* NETT.

New Caledonia *See* OCT.

New Community Instrument (NCI) NCI was launched in 1978 as a Community borrowing and lending scheme. It is administered jointly by the Commission and the European Investment Bank. Loans go towards projects meeting Community objectives, primarily to help finance investments in energy, industry (especially small businesses), and facilities. January 17, 1990, marked the beginning of the end of the NCI with several states being opposed to its renewal. The NCI will continue its operations with the funds it still has, then it will disappear. The basis for the action was that the NCI was doing the same job as the European Investment Bank and was able to diversify its intervention mechanisms and cover all loan requirements. The European Commission, on the other hand, felt that it was vital that the NCI has a specific fund, primarily to finance small and medium-sized enterprises, and to safeguard rural areas via the financing of projects aimed at promoting diversification of rural economies. The Commision proposed to make the NCI permanent, by transforming it into a revolving fund.

See INVESTMENT.

New ECU *See* CHRONOLOGY (SEPTEMBER 20, 1989); EUROPEAN CURRENCY UNIT.

new poor *See* POVERTY.

New Zealand Butter imports are subject to levies at Community ports to ensure that they will not undercut Community butter prices. Exports are restricted to certain levels in return for a tariff concession of a 20 percent reduction of the Community duty on imports. New Zealand's earnings from exports to the Community derive from wool, butter, sheepmeat, as well as hides, skins, and leather. The Community's principal imports from New Zealand consist of wool, mutton and lamb, and dairy items.

See AUSTRALIA; BUTTER; PACIFIC RIM; SHEEPMEAT.

Next European Torus *See* NUCLEAR FUSION.

Nicaragua *See* CENTRAL AMERICA; CENTRAL AMERICAN COMMON MARKET.

Niger This nation is one of the ACP states and a signatory of the Yaoundé Conventions of 1963 and 1969 and of the Lomé Convention of 1988.

Nigeria This nation is one of the ACP states and a signatory to the Lomé Convention of 1988.

NIMEXE This is the Nomenclature for the External Trade Statistics of the Community and statistics of trade between member nations.

nine It consists of the original Six E.E.C. members (Belgium, France, Federal German Republic, Italy, Luxembourg, and the Netherlands) and the Three (Denmark, the Irish Republic, and the United Kingdom).

noise Noise is considered a pollutant by the Community program should it interfere with sleep, speech, cause annoyance, affect the performance of work, or cause damage to hearing. Directives include the range of permissible noise levels for cars, trucks, and motorcycle exhaust systems. A 1980 directive attempts to lower noise from subsonic aircraft.

See CONSTRUCTION PRODUCTS; ENVIRONMENT; HARMONIZATION; TRANSPORT.

nonassociated states Those nations not covered by the Lomé Conventions. Since 1976, the community has allocated a small amount of financial assistance to the poorest of these nations.

See DEVELOPMENT FUND; EXTERNAL TRADE; FINANCE.

noncompulsory expenditure *See* BUDGET.

Non-Europe *See* COSTS OF NON-EUROPE.

nonlife insurance *See* INSURANCE.

nonquota sector *See* REGIONAL FUND.

Non-Tariff Barriers (NTBs) to Trade The Treaty of Rome instructs the Council of Ministers to seek to harmonize or approximate regulations to ensure the free movement of items throughout the Community.
See HARMONIZATION.

Nordek Treaty On February 4, 1970, the Norwegian, Swedish, Danish, and Finnish Governments approved this treaty strengthening their economic cooperation. It provided for a Customs Union and Common External Tariff with alignments in two steps, the first was on January 1, 1972, and the other on January 1, 1974. The Common External Tariff was based on the four countries' average current tariffs and became the same general level as the E.C.'s tariff.

Nordic Council A Treaty between the Nordic nations was signed in Helsinki in 1953, going into effect in 1962. Its goal is to develop cooperation in the fields of legislation, cultural, social and economic policies and in transport and communications. The Treaty was revised in 1971.

Northern Ireland Foreign investment is at a record level in Northern Ireland. Development agreements of $664 million were concluded in 1989, the best showing in its history, resulting in more than 5,600 new jobs. Reasons include a skilled work force, an advanced infrastructure, flexible incentive packages, and its E.C. status. One hundred and fifty international companies now employ 37,000 workers in Northern Ireland, accounting for more than one third of the total manufacturing employment. More than 25 major American corporations, employing more than 13,000 local people, have facilities in Northern Ireland. Its Industrial Development Board provides financial support with selective grants for plants, machinery, and equipment, plus assistance toward start-up costs, including employment and training grants.
See IRELAND, UNITED KINGDOM.

North Korea *See* COUNCIL FOR MUTUAL ECONOMIC ASSISTANCE.

North Vietnam *See* COUNCIL FOR MUTUAL ECONOMIC ASSISTANCE.

North Yemen *See* YEMEN ARAB REPUBLIC.

Norway This nation became a founder member of the European Free Trade Association in 1960. In 1972, it applied for membership into the Common Market, but then withdrew.
See CHRONOLOGY (SEPTEMBER 25, 1972) IN APPENDIX, COMMITTEE ON EUROPEAN COOPERATION IN THE FIELD OF SCIENTIFIC AND TECHNICAL RESEARCH, ENERGY; TEN, THE.

NRC *See* NATIONAL REFERENDUM CAMPAIGN.

NTBs *See* NON-TARIFFS BARRIERS TO TRADE.

nuclear energy The Treaty of Rome established the European Atomic Energy Community for promoting research in the field of nuclear energy. It established uniform safety standards to protect the health of workers and of the general public, facilitated investment in the development of nuclear energy, and ensured safeguards against diversion of nuclear materials. Under the Community's technological research and development effort for 1984–87, more than half its total budget was allocated to nuclear fission and reactor safety projects where research was devoted to accident prevention, especially to the study of the behavior of nuclear plant operating staff in various situations and to man-machine interaction. In February 1980, the Council of Ministers adopted a Commission proposal for the management and storage of radioactive waste covering the period to 1992. The Commission is working to apply the experience gained in safeguarding against ionizing radiation to protection against other forms of radiation, such as microwaves and laser beams, and to other areas as well.

In 1986, nuclear energy—which provided 13 percent of the energy and 33 percent of the electricity produced in the Community—enabled the Community to save the equivalent of more than 130 million tons of oil, which is nearly the Community's present overall production. It is anticipated that the proportion of electricity generated by nuclear energy will rise from 35 to 40 percent between 1990 and 1995.

On April 26, 1986, a serious accident occurred in reactor No. 4 at the Chernobyl nuclear site in the Soviet Union. As a result, the E.C. adopted new approaches to nuclear safety to protect against contaminated food, improve information systems and set up networks for protection and mutual assistance in the event of a nuclear accident or radiation emergency and public information programs on nuclear dangers and protection from them. In October 1987, the first meeting of the Standing Conference on Health and Safety in the Nuclear Age was held to provide the public, through the media, with as much objective information as possible about the potential hazards of ionizing radiation from all sources. The Commission publishes regular reports on the levels of radioactivity in the environment. It established the REM (Radioactivity Environmental Monitoring) computerized databank, under the responsibility of the Joint Research Center at Ispra, for the collection of environmental radioactive contamination data in the Community. The AORS (Abnormal Occurrence Reporting System) involves the exchange of information on operational incidents at nuclear power plants with a view to analyzing cause and effect.

The Terme source project was established to achieve a consensus among European scientists on the parameters for evaluating the quantity of radioactive material released after a nuclear accident.

See ENERGY; EURATOM SUPPLY AGENCY; FINANCE; NUCLEAR FUSION; PLUTONIUM.

nuclear fusion The developmental path towards a fusion reactor able to produce energy has led to the successor to Joint European Torus (JET) begun in 1978, the Next European Torus (NET). In 1989–90 the detailed design of NET was developed. The ultimate goal of the Community fusion program is the construction of a demonstration reactor.

See JOINT EUROPEAN TORUS, NUCLEAR ENERGY, TELEMAN.

nuclear safety *See* NUCLEAR ENERGY, TELEMAN.

nurses Since 1979 qualified nurses are free to practice their profession anywhere in the Community, subject to the minimum training requirments and mutual recognition of qualifications set out in directives.

See MIDWIVES, WORK AND EMPLOYMENT.

nutritional information *See* FOOD LABELS.

O

Objectives of the E.C. Upon merger of the European Coal and Steel Community, the European Atomic Energy Community, and the European Economic Community in 1965, the following objectives were identified by the newly formed European Community.

(1) To establish the basis for a closer union among European nations;

(2) To further the economic and social progress of the member countries by jointly eliminating barriers dividing them;

(3) To further the improvement of working and living conditions within the Community;

(4) To act together to promote steady expansion, balanced trade, and fair competition;

(5) To strengthen the unity of member countries' economies by bringing the various regions into line with each other, and assisting developing areas;

(6) To abolish restrictions on international trade by means of a common commercial policy;

(7) To strengthen the bonds between Europe and countries overseas; and

(8) To combine resources to promote peace and freedom. A series of measures to achieve these goals were drawn up. The major areas are:

   (1) the elimination of customs duties and trade restrictions between member countries;

   (2) The establishment of a uniform external customs tariff and a common commercial policy towards nonmember countries;

   (3) The removal of restrictions on the freedom of movement of labor, capital, and services;

   (4) The establishment of a common transport policy;

   (5) The establishment of a common agricultural policy;

   (6) The setting up of a system to prevent distortion of competition within the Community;

   (7) The coordination of member countries' economic policies;

   (8) The modification of national laws to bring them into line with each other, in cases where such laws have an effect on the establishment or functioning of the Common Market;

   (9) The establishment of a European Social Fund to improve employment possibilities for workers and to help raise the standard of living;

   (10) The creation of a European Investment Bank to further economic expansion within the Community; and

   (11) The association of nonmember countries with the Community in order to expand trade and assist economic and social development, both within the Community and abroad.

See EUROPEAN COMMUNITY.

OCDE (Organisation de Coopération et de Développement Économiques.) *See* ORGANIZATION FOR ECONOMIC COOPERATION AND DEVELOPMENT.

Ockrent Report This is the E.E.C.'s statement on the establishment of a Free Trade Area running parallel with the E.E.C. It was denounced by the French Government in 1958 when negotiations among E.E.C. members terminated.

OCT The Overseas Countries and Territories, of member states of the E.C., associated under Part IV of the Treaty of Rome. The territories concerned include British possessions such as the Falkland Islands, the Cayman Islands, and the British Antarctic Territory, as well as New Caledonia and French Polynesia, and the Netherlands Curacao. Greenland is also an OCT member since leaving the E.C. in 1985, but is subject to a special arrangement. In all, the territories involve a total population of over 700,000 people. The overseas territories have been part of a cooperative regime with the Community since 1981, paralleling the Lomé Convention.

See GREENLAND.

OECD *See* ORGANIZATION FOR ECONOMIC COOPERATION AND DEVELOPMENT, FORMERLY OEEC.

OECE (Organisation Européenne de Coopération Économique) The Organization for European Economic Cooperation.

OEEC (The Organization for European Economic Cooperation, now OECD) *See* ORGANIZATION FOR ECONOMIC COOPERATION AND DEVELOPMENT.

OERS (Organisation Européenne de Recherches Spatiales) The European Space Research Organization.

Official Journal of the European Communities (OJ) (OJEC) A daily Community publication, published in all of the official languages. It comes in three parts: Legislation (regulations, directives, decisions); Communications and Information (drafts legislation, the European Parliament proceedings, business of the European Court of Justice, Community recruiting notices, opinions of the Economic and Social Committee); Supplement (notices and public supply contracts).

See LEGISLATIVE PREPARATION; PUBLIC WORKS CONTRACTS.

oil In December 1979, the Council of Ministers agreed on import ceilings with the goal of keeping total import levels to the 1978 level of 472 million tons. As an objective, the Community expects to keep oil down to around 40 percent of energy consumption while net oil imports are to be maintained at less than one-third of total energy consumption.

See ENERGY; MARINE POLLUTION; TANKERS; WASTE OILS.

OJ (OJEC) *See* OFFICIAL JOURNAL OF THE EUROPEAN COMMUNITIES.

olive oil This product has been regulated by the E.C. since 1966. Regulation affects primarily Italian and French producers. Their imports are subject to variable levies covering the difference between the Community guide price and the landed import price. When market prices fall below the guide price, set by the Council of Ministers, producers are paid bridging or deficiency payments to bring them up to the guide price. The Farm Fund assists producers to maintain a register of their olive groves.

See AGRICULTURE, COMMON AGRICULTURAL POLICY; FATS, OIL, AND OILSEEDS; FINANCE.

Oman *See* GULF COOPERATION COUNCIL.

112 *See* EMERGENCY TELEPHONE.

On the table *See* CONSULTATION PROCEDURE; COOPERATION PROCEDURE.

ONP *See* OPEN NETWORK PROVISION.

OPEC (The Organization of Petroleum Exporting Countries). It represents the interests of Venezuela, Indonesia, and Middle Eastern and North African oil-exporting nations vis-à-vis the international oil companies. It pursues the twin goals of securing a greater share of revenues for its members and of achieving greater control by its members over the ownership and management of their oil resources, as regards both production and marketing (participation issue). Its first major success was the Teheran Agreement of 1971. In October 1989, the E.C. and OPEC agreed to cooperate on environmental and technical issues. These talks were the first between the two institutions since the oil cartel was established.

Open Network Provision (ONP) In March 1990, the 12 member states adopted a common position on the Open Network Provision Directive, which facilitates access to public telecommunications networks and services by private companies. The ONP directive is designed to prevent the PTTs from fixing unfair access conditions for new, competing telecommunications services. The directive's purpose is to eliminate obstacles through the harmonization of technical conditions so that networks can connect with each other properly; through harmonized service conditions so that users know they can get a basic standard of service in each member state; and through harmonized tariff principles so that users will be able to calculate how much Pan-European services will cost. The Council agreed to an ONP program to provide specific directives in certain ONP areas (e.g., leased lines and voice telephony) and the option for mandatory legislation should access problems persist.

See TELECOMMUNICATIONS.

Open Systems Interconnection *See* OSI.

Operation Flood This project was started in 1970 as a way of both leading India toward self-sufficiency in milk production and increasing social integration in disadvantaged rural areas. Rather than simply adopting a short-term approach of shipping milk to India, the Community developed a strategy of using food aid as a source of investment. Powdered milk, butter, and vegetable oils were provided to local communities, and farmers and their families were organized so that unnecessary links in the distribution chain could be eliminated. The E.C. contributed about 62 percent of the supplies for Operation Flood. In 1986, the E.C. completed its evaluation of Operation Flood finding that its program had resulted in the creation of modern, nationwide facilities for the collection, processing, and distribution of milk, and had improved milk supplies while keeping prices at an acceptable level.

opinions These are written statements by the Council(s) or Commission(s) of considerable guidance value, but without binding force.

Cf. DECISIONS, DIRECTIVES, RECOMMENDATIONS, REGULATIONS.

ORE (Organisation Régionale Européenne de la Confédération internationale des syndicats libres) The European Regional Organization of the International Confederation of Free Trade Unions.

Organization for Economic Cooperation and Development (OECD) (Organisation de coopération et de développement économiques (OCDE) This organization was created by the Paris Convention of 1960 by 20 founder states (Austria, Belgium, Denmark, France, Germany, Greece, Iceland, Ireland, Italy, Luxembourg, the Netherlands, Norway, Portugal, Spain, Sweden, Switzerland, Turkey, the United Kingdom, the United States, and Canada). It was later joined by Japan, Finland, Australia, and New Zealand. Yugoslavia is an associate member under special statute. Its objectives are to promote economic and social welfare throughout the OECD area by assisting member governments in the formulation and coordination of policies; to stimulate and harmonize members' aid efforts in favor of developing nations; and to contribute to the expansion of world trade.

See BIAC; EUROPEAN COMMUNITY; ORGANIZATION FOR EUROPEAN ECONOMIC COOPERATION.

Organization for European Economic Cooperation (OEEC) On June 5, 1947, U.S. Secretary of State George Marshall proposed that America assist in Europe's economic recovery, with understanding that the European nations would reach some agreement about their requirements and the part they would play in the plan. In July, 16 nations met in Paris and created the Committee of European Economic Cooperation (CEEC). They signed a report formulating an economic recovery program. On March 15, 1948, a report recommended the need for a permanent coordinating body. Its functions were to develop economic cooperation between member nations and to assist the United States government in carrying out its program of aid to Europe. It was replaced by the Organization for Economic Cooperation and Development in 1961.

See ORGANIZATION FOR ECONOMIC COOPERATION AND DEVELOPMENT.

Organization of Petroleum Exporting Countries *See* OPEC.

Original Six, The They are Belgium, the Netherlands, Luxembourg, West Germany, France, and Italy. *Synonymous with* E.E.C. SIX.

orphans In 1965, the European Coal and Steel Community through the Paul Finet Foundation provided financial assistance to orphans of those workers in the coal, iron, and steel industries who died since June 1965 from industrial accidents or occupational illnesses.

See EDUCATION; FINANCE; INDUSTRIAL POLICY.

Ortoli Facility A Community loan program that began in 1980, named after Commissioner François-Xavier Ortoli, that was designed to channel large-scale investment financing for major projects of importance to the Community.

OSI (The Open Systems Interconnection) It is a large and growing set of standards concerned with communication and interworking between computer systems of all types from any suppliers.

See EWOS.

OTC (The Organization for Trade Cooperation of GATT).

overall balance of concessions The E.C. may adopt some measure of overall reciprocity based on the degree of market access provided E.C. firms in specific foreign markets or the magnitude of the concessions offered by individual foreign countries in the current multilateral trade negotiations under the GATT.

See RECIPROCITY.

Overseas Countries and Territories *See* OCT.

own funds *See* BANKING.

own resources The Community in 1970 passed a decision to finance its budget. Revenue is collected by governments and automatically passed on to the European Commission in the form of customs duties from the Common Customs Tariff, from agricultural levies, and up to one percent of Value Added Tax on a common harmonized base of goods and services.

See BUDGET, FINANCE, VALUE ADDED TAX.

ozone layer *See* ENVIRONMENT.

P

PABLI *See* DATABASES AND DATABANKS OF THE E.C.

Pacific Rim This extensive area extends from Japan and South Korea through the South China Sea, surrounded by Taiwan, China, Hong Kong, the Philippines, Malaysia, Singapore, Thailand, and Indonesia, then on to Australia and New Zealand, covering an area twice as vast as Europe and the United States combined. Rim imports by E.C. member states have grown by about 14 percent from the mid-1970s to the mid-1980s and comprise a third of the E.C.'s imports. In 1984, Rim imports by the E.C. were one-quarter agricultural, two-fifths raw materials and one-third manufactured goods.

packaging *See* PLASTIC PACKAGING.

Packet-Switched Public Data Networks (PSPDNs) *See* GREEN PAPER, TELECOMMUNICATIONS.

Pakistan This nation has had agreements since 1976 with the Community dealing with textiles and hand-made items. The E.C. is its main trading partner with some 20 percent of Pakistan's foreign trade with the Community. The E.C. helped to develop its exports of such items as leather, light engineering goods, and jewelry. Pakistan receives project aid and direct food aid. A new E.C./Pakistan commercial, economic, and development cooperation agreement was put into force on May 1, 1986. It provides for intensified support for Pakistan's development programs.

Panama Since 1976 Panama has had an agreement with the Community on hand-made items.
See CENTRAL AMERICA.

Panel of Wise Men *See* TAX BARRIER.

Pan-European Mobile Communications These are recommendations and directives aimed at making full use of the technological opportunity provided by the improved definition of the second- generation common mobile systems in Europe; creating a European-wide mobile communications system; and ending the unacceptable incompatibility of systems (both public and private), thus eliminating the breakdown of mobile communications at frontiers.
See RACE, TELECOMMUNICATIONS.

Pan-European television *See* TELEVISION.

Papua New Guinea This country is one of the ACP states and a signatory to the Lomé Convention in 1988.

Paraguay Since 1976, Paraguay has had an agreement with the Community on trade in hand-made items.
See LAFTA, LATIN AMERICA.

parallel imports This exists where, in addition to the official route by which goods are imported by an exclusive distributor into a given territory, there is also a second parallel route, used by another trader in the territory who has obtained the goods from a third party outside the territory. The parallel importer is a source of competition for the exclusive distributor.

Paris, Treaty of *See* TREATY OF PARIS.

Parliament, European *See* EUROPEAN PARLIAMENT.

passports In 1974, a Passport Union working committee was created. In 1978, the European Council agreed on the introduction of a uniform passport (with a deep lilac color) so as to avoid all passport checks at Community borders.

See HARMONIZATION; PEOPLE'S EUROPE; TRANSPORT.

pasta war On October 27, 1986, the E.C. endorsed an agreement with the United States to end a long-running dispute over pasta and citrus fruit. In the agreement, the United States recognized the E.C.'s right to grant special and unreciprocated trade concessions to Third World countries. The United States had challenged preferential trade agreements with non-E.C. Mediterranean states on the grounds that such agreements discriminated against its own exports of citrus fruit to Europe. The agreement also traded greater access for American citrus exports to the E.C. for greater access for E.C. exports of olives, olive oil, and cheese to the United States, and also ended U.S. restrictions on pasta imports, mainly from Italy, imposed in retaliation for the alleged discrimination on U.S. citrus imports.

Patent-Cooperation Treaty *See* PATENT LAW.

Patent law The Community Patent Convention (CPC) signed in December 1975 in Luxembourg, together with the European Patent Convention (EPC), offers a complete body of European Patent Law and procedure. It provides a choice between acquiring a national patent governed by national law and a Community patent. The Patent-Cooperation Treaty became effective in 1978. On May 23, 1990, the Commission held its first European congress dealing with patent and innovation matters in Madrid, entitled Patinnova 90. It dealt with the protection of innovation—improving the environment of Europe's competitiveness. Its overall objective is to improve general awareness of the economic and marketing importance of the patent system, including issues of protection and filing policies for technical innovation, the role of patent attorneys and other patent consultants in filing and protection strategies, the patent-assisted marketing of inventions from university and research institutions, the impact of patent-assisted marketing of licences on the competitiveness of industry in the single-market, strategies for avoiding and solving patent disputes and litigation, and requirements to be met in the future by the system of industrial property rights and by the patent system in particular.

See EUROPEAN PATENT CONVENTION; HARMONIZATION; KNOW-HOW LICENSING.

Patinnova 90 *See* PATENT LAW.

Paul Finet Foundation *See* ORPHANS.

PCBs (PolyChlorinated Biphenyls) In 1985, the E.C. Commission proposed a Europe-wide ban on the production and sale of PCBs, claiming that less severe measures had failed to reduce the amounts of this carcinogen found in the environment. In 1976, the E.C. adopted two directives restricting PCB use. The first established rules for the safe disposal of waste PCBs. The second barred most uses of PCBs, except in mining equipment and in closed system devices such as transformers, inductors, and condensers. The 1985 proposal prohibited these remaining uses, but did not require the disposal of existing PCBs-containing equipment on the grounds that forced disposal could create a bigger environmental hazard than the equipment's continued use.

See ENVIRONMENT.

PCIJ The Permanent Court of International Justice.

pensioners *See* RESIDENCE RIGHTS.

Pentagonal Initiative Founded in Budapest in November 1989 as a new regional alliance to encourage political and economic cooperation among its members—Italy, Czechoslovakia, Austria, Hungary, and Yugoslavia. The alliance is expected to bring East Europe closer to the E.C. The bulk of the existing accords involve projects for improving transportation links between the countries of the alliance.

People's Europe The European Council considered it essential that the Community should respond to the expectations of the people of Europe by adopting measures to strengthen and promote Community identity and image both for its citizens and for the rest of the world. To this end, the Council approved the creation of a European passport available to member states' nationals by January 1, 1985, a single document for the movement of goods, the abolition of all police and customs formalities for people crossing intra-Community frontiers, and a general system for ensuring the equivalence of university diplomas, in order to bring about the effective freedom of establishment within the Community. The Committee examined symbols of the Community's existence, such as a flag and an anthem; the formation of European sports teams; the streamlining of procedures at frontier posts; and the minting of a European coinage, namely the ECU.

See CIVIL PROTECTION; CULTURE; PUBLIC OPINION POLLS; VOTING RIGHTS.

People's Republic of China *See* CHINA.

permanent abandonment premium *See* WINE.

Permanent Representatives Committee The Council is assisted by a large number of working parties and a permanent Committee. This Committee, created in 1958, comprises the Permanent Representatives (ambassadors) of the member states to the Communities. The Merger Treaty of July 1, 1967 institutionalized it and confirmed its role, which is primarily to prepare the ground for Council meetings.

See COUNCIL OF EUROPE, MERGER TREATY.

Personal Protective Equipment (PPE) PPE includes any device or appliance designed to be worn or held by an individual for protection against one or more safety and health hazards in the execution of his or her activities. A June 14, 1989, directive was proposed with an effective date of July 1, 1992. The directive covers combined PPE and interchangeable components essential to its satisfactory functioning. PPE must preserve the health and ensure the safety of users without prejudice to the health and safety of other individuals, domestic animals or goods, when properly maintained and used for its intended purpose.

Peru This nation has had agreements with the Community on trade in textiles and handmade items since 1983.

See ANDEAN PACT; LAFTA; LATIN AMERICA.

pesticides A 1976 directive sets maximum levels of pesticide residues that are permitted in produce for human consumption.

See AGRICULTURE, COMMON AGRICULTURAL POLICY; PLANT HEALTH CONTROLS.

PETRA A Council decision of December 1987 established the five-year PETRA program. Its purpose is to help member states with vocational training for young adults. PETRA's goals are to reensure that all young people who so wish receive one or more years' vocational training upon completion of their compulsory education; raise the standard and quality of initial training and improve the preparation of young people for adult and working life, and for continuing training; diversify training so as to make it suitable for all young people and ensure that it leads to recognized qualifications; enhance the capacity of training systems to adapt to economic, social and technological change; and develop European standards in initial vocational training.

See EUROPEAN CENTER FOR DEVELOPMENT OF VOCATIONAL TRAINING.

Phare program (Poland, Hungary: Assistance for Economic Restructuring) An E.C. 1990 aide program for Poland and Hungary, with eventual extension of comparable assistance to other East European nations.

See GROUP OF 24.

pharmaceuticals (proprietary medicinal items) The Community has long attempted to abolish barriers to the free movement of medicinal items, subject to public health safeguards for their conception and production. On January 1, 1967, a directive was passed requiring that the placing of a proprietary medicinal item on the market of a member nation must be subject to the authorization of the competent authority of that nation. Two 1975 directives regulated content and proof of the results of tests carried out with proprietary medicinal products that were the subject of applications for marketing authorization. They identified the necessary qualifications for persons preparing documents, the particulars concerning control methods and test results, and application procedures for marketing authorizations. Since publication of the 1985 White Paper, five proposals have been adopted by the Council. Among them are new Community rules on the marketing and development of medicines produced by biotechnology and the protection of highly innovative pharmaceutical products, and the pricing of pharmaceutical products and reimbursement by national social security schemes. Other proposals include rules covering vaccines, products derived from human blood, radiopharmaceuticals used for diagnostic purposes, and generic medicines. Still other proposals are concerned with the elimination of the remaining obstacles to free circulation of pharmaceutical products within the Community, the harmonization of the conditions of distribution of pharmaceutical products to patients, and the provision of information to doctors and patients. At present, companies must seek clearance for a new drug separately in each of the 12 E.C. member states. By July 1989, an E.C. working group considered two proposals for harmonizing drug approval. The first would set up a single European agency that would be responsible for reviewing and passing judgment on all applications. Alternatively, drug companies would be allowed to seek approval from only one of the 12 existing national regulatory agencies. Once that approval is granted, the drug could be sold throughout the E.C. In September 1989, Commission Ministers discussed proposals that would give pharmaceutical makers the option to add 10 years to the 20-year patents on new drugs. Adding 10 years would lengthen effective protection to about 18 years, in line with effective protection of 15 to 16 years in the United States and Japan.

In January 1990, the Council proposed three directives on the wholesale distribution of medicinal products for human use. They concern the legal status for the supply of medicinal products for human use, the labeling of medicinal products for human use, and packaging leaflets.

pharmacists A 1985 directive concerns the coordination of laws, regulations, or administrative actions in respect of certain activities in the field of pharmacy. It defines the minimum range of activities that formally qualified pharmacists may pursue in all member states and facilitates the right to set up practice as a pharmacist in any member state.

Philippines, the This nation is a member of the Association of South East Asian Nations (ASEAN) with whom the Community concluded a cooperation agreement in December 1979 seeking to "consolidate, deepen and diversify" commercial relations. A 1978 bilateral agreement restricts textile exports to the Community.

See ASSOCIATION OF SOUTH EAST ASIAN NATIONS; PACIFIC RIM; TEXTILES.

pigmeat *See* SLUICE GATE PRICE.

pilots A Community directive, effective January 1, 1980, requires all member nations, in the interests of safety, to guarantee that vessels choosing to use the services of pilots in the North Sea and the English Channel should be able to call on adequately qualified deep sea pilots.

See ENVIRONMENT; TANKERS; TRANSPORT.

Pitcairn Island This island is an overseas U.K. territory which is included in the Lomé Conventions.

plant health controls Harmonization of national laws and regulations on essential arable plant health requirements will be needed by 1992. The harmonization must reach the point where it is possible for plants and plant products, destined for export across the Community's internal frontiers, to be controlled and certified at the point of departure. The resulting certification then needs only to be checked at the point of import into the other member states. Within practical limits, a similar system should apply to imports from non-E.C. countries. Legislation has been adopted on a plant protection product, ethylene oxide, pesticide residues and additives. Another proposal, on protective measures against organisms harmful to plants, has been partially adopted. Other draft proposals include plant protection products ethoxyquin and diphenylamine. To meet the 1992 timetable, other plant protection legislation includes proposals for a community plant health inspectorate, for measures protecting against the introduction of organisms harmful to plants or plant products, for controls on pesticide residues on fruit and vegetables, for certification of seedlings and reproductive materials of fruit plants and decorative plants; and for plant health certificates. Legislation on liability in respect to plant health, alignment of plant health standards, and the creation of a European law on plant breeders' rights are also needed.

See ANIMAL HEALTH AND MEAT INSPECTION.

plastic packaging The Commission in the spring 1990 adopted a directive establishing E.C. standards for plastic matter that comes into contact with foodstuffs. As of January 1, 1993, it will be illegal to bring foodstuffs into contact with plastic materials that do not meet the criteria set out in the directive. This applies not only to plastic packaging (e.g., bottles for beverages and films for wrapping food) but also to plastic kitchen utensils and to machines and instruments for the production of foodstuffs (e.g., conveyer belts and siphons).

plutonium An E.C. research program on the plutonium cycle and its safety aspects was adopted by the Commission in March 1979. Its primary concern is the safe use of plutonium used as a nuclear fuel. It includes studies on the radiological impact of the plutonium cycle; research on safety in fabricating and transporting plutonium compounds; and the safety of light-water reactors.
See NUCLEAR ENERGY.

poison pill In the spring of 1990, the Commission endorsed a plan to limit poison pill takeover defenses, asserting the rights of individual shareholders. It intends to facilitate cross-border takeovers, thereby helping European companies attain the economies of scale necessary to compete globally. The proposal would amend a Company Law Directive to limit the power of directors in a target company to buy thier own stocks; another Company Law Directive which already limits the situations in which large companies can issue nonvoting shares would be strengthened; and still another Company Law Directive would be changed to restrict the ability of a subsidiary to buy shares in its parents as a defensive tactic.
See COMPANY LAW.

Poland, Republic of This country is a founder member of the Council for Mutual Economic Assistance. In October 1989, the E.C. provided food aid to Poland, including 10,000 tons of beef and 5,000 tons of olive oil, a further indication of Community interest in Eastern Europe. Toward the end of 1989, Poland anticipated applying for associate membership with the E.C. Events of the fall of 1989 may significantly alter Poland's relationship with the E.C.
See COUNCIL FOR MUTUAL ECONOMIC ASSISTANCE; EASTERN EUROPE; HUNGARY, REPUBLIC OF.

polling *See* PUBLIC OPINION POLLS.

polluting products Guidelines issued in September 1989 will require that washing powders and household cleaning products sold in the E.C. must carry standard labels allowing consumers to choose the safest and least polluting brands.

pollution In December 1989, the European Council, meeting in Strasbourg, agreed to establish a European environmental agency.
See BEACHES; CAR POLLUTION; ENVIRONMENT; EUROPEAN ENVIRONMENT AGENCY; EUROPEAN FOUNDATION FOR THE IMPROVEMENT OF LIVING AND WORKING CONDITIONS; GREENHOUSE EFFECT; LEADED GASOLINE; MARINE POLLUTION; NOISE; PILOTS; RECYCLING—PAPER; TIRES AND DRINK CONTAINERS; RHINE; TANKERS; TOXIC EFFLUENT; VEHICLES; WASTE; WASTE OILS; WATER; WILDLIFE.

PolyChlorinated Biphenyls *See* PCBs.

Polynesia *See* OCT.

Pompidou Group *See* DRUG TRAFFICKING.

poor *See* POVERTY.

ports *See* MERCATOR.

Portugal This nation joined the European Free Trade Association in 1960. Portugal signed a basic trade agreement with the Community on July 22, 1972. In 1975, the E.C. granted Portugal emergency financial aid and, since that time, various protocols covering the industrial and agricultural fields and labor and industrial cooperation have been negotiated. In 1977, Portugal applied for admission as a member state and substantive negotiations commenced in 1981. Portugal joined the Community in 1986, subject to a minimum five year transition period. With E.C. membership, Portugal received over 600 million ECU (about $660 million) in 1988 and one billion ECU in 1989 (about $1.1 billion), plus long-term European Investment Bank loans. Portugal has an inflation rate of 12.7 percent, second only to Greece. In one year, Portugal received nearly $700 million from new direct foreign investment. This represents an all-time annual record, and more in one year than the entire total of direct foreign investment in 50 pre-E.C. years. Foreign money poured in during 1987, including $430 million in productive investment (152 percent more than in 1986) over $3 billion in emigrant's remittances; and over $1.5 billion in tourist revenues. This offset the trade deficit and kept the balance of payments about $700 million in the black. Portugal's program of privatization of state run firms, which began in April 1989, will continue for six years. Eventually, it will free companies from bureaucratic control, and with time, will assist in repaying a national debt that now consumes 81 percent of gross domestic product.

postal fees *See* CONTROL OF GOODS.

postal services *See* MAIL.

potatoes This farm product is not covered by the Common Agricultural Policy. However, the marketing of seed potatoes is subject to Common Market regulations.

See AGRICULTURE, COMMON AGRICULTURAL POLICY.

poultry Poultry for consumption is tightly controlled by Community legislation on hygiene and water content. Directives specify standards in slaughterhouses, cutting-up premises and stores, and inspection procedures. A 1976 regulation deals with the water content in frozen poultry.

See AGRICULTURE, COMMON AGRICULTURAL POLICY; ANIMAL HEALTH AND MEAT INSPECTION; CONSUMER PROTECTION; EGGS.

poverty In 1974, a social policy program was adopted by the Community to combat poverty. Its purpose is to identify the causes and to suggest new ways to fight poverty. In 1984, Community ministers stated that "the poor shall be taken to mean persons, families and groups of persons whose resources (material, cultural and social) are so limited as to exclude them from the minimum acceptable way of life in the Member State in which they live." "New poverty" describes the plight of the average person who has insufficient resources

to cope with misfortune such as unemployment or sickness. On December 19, 1984, the Council of Ministers adopted a second program to combat poverty, allocating 29 million ECU for the period 1985–1988. The program will reach the disadvantaged urban districts, impoverished rural areas, the long-term unemployed and the young unemployed, the elderly, single parent families, refugees, returning migrants, and marginals (minorities such as gypsies, nomads, travellers, tramps, the homeless, drop-outs, and others who lives outside the social security net).

See FINANCE.

powers of investigation One of the major responsibilities of the E.C. Commission is to combat practices that interfere with free competition in the Community market. The Commission keeps markets under constant observation and has the power to investigate a firm's conduct directly. Legislation establishes uniform rules of competition. All firms must be able to compete freely in the larger barrier-free market, and big companies must be prevented from abusing a dominant position. On the basis of assembled facts, the Commission assesses whether the firms investigated have or have not infringed on the Community laws. It may then declare the restrictive practice prohibited, or issue a negative clearance (granting immunity from antitrust law), or grant an exemption. All decisions are subject to review by the Court of Justice of the E.C.

PPE *See* PERSONAL PROTECTIVE EQUIPMENT.

predation In the spring of 1990 the Commission sought powers to act faster against airlines engaged in anticompetitive activities. A proposed amendment to the 1987 air transport package would allow the Commission to order airlines to suspend "predatory" fares or other unfair practices, pending a subsequent review by Commission experts. At present, it takes the Commission an average of three months to act in such cases. The four major predatory practices of airlines are: providing excessive capacity or frequency on a given route to keep other airlines out of the market; charging fares considerably lower than the airline's costs; granting override commission to travel agents; and granting excessive loyalty benefits (e.g., frequency flyer points) to passengers. The amendment would advance the goal of a liberalized, single market in air transport in which competition is maintained and the consumer benefits.

See AIRLINE SECTOR.

preference A favor granted to the trade of a nation or group of nations. It may be in terms of preferential tariff treatment or other charges, or other trade rules or formalities, e.g., import or export licensing.

prélevement *See* LEVIES.

pressure vessels *See* HARMONIZATION.

PREST (The Party on Scientific and Technical Research Policy).

price index The Community publishes a monthly Consumer Price Index, summarizing and comparing movement in the index prices in Community nations.

See CONSUMER PROTECTION.

price support *See* GRAIN SECTOR.

primary product This represents any product of a farm, forest, or fishery, or any mineral, in its natural form or processed, marketed in substantial volume in international trade.

Principles of the Treaty of Rome *See* TREATY OF ROME.

Priority foreign countries *See* SUPER 301.

prix de base *See* BASIC PRICE.

prix d'écluse *See* SLUICE GATE PRICES.

prix de réference *See* REFERENCE PRICE.

prix de seuil *See* THRESHOLD PRICE.

prix d'intervention *See* INTERVENTION PRICE.

prix d'orientation *See* GUIDE PRICE.

prix indicatif *See* TARGET PRICE.

processed fruits and vegetables A 1979 regulation provides financial aid for listed processed fruit and vegetables based on the difference between production prices in the E.C. and non-E.C. nations.

See AGRICULTURE, COMMON AGRICUL-TURAL POLICY; FRUIT AND VEGETABLES; PASTA WAR.

producer tax *See* GRAIN SECTOR.

product liability To remove the burden of proof from the consumer, the Commission proposes placing liability on the manufacturer or importer of defective items, irrespective of fault.

See CONSUMER PROTECTION.

product testing The Commission proposed in July 1989 a community-wide system for testing and certifying products, calling for the mutual recognition of testing and certification so that a product approved by authorities in one E.C. country could be marketed anywhere elsewhere in the Community.

professions The Commission's White Paper identified obstacles specific to certain regulated professions, as they relate to the recognition of foreign qualifications. The Community proposed the harmonization of professional training comparable to that which exists in the medical professions, and a general system of mutual recognition by the member states of each other's higher education diplomas. This harmonization already exists for a number of professions.

See ACCOUNTANTS; ARCHITECTS; AUDITORS; DENTAL PRACTITIONERS; DOCTORS; HAIRDRESSERS; MIDWIVES; NURSES; PHARMACISTS; VETERINARY SURGEONS.

Programme Européen de Traduction automatique de conception avancee *See* EUROTRA.

proposals Items for action sent by the European Commission to the Council of Ministers. Before making a final decision, the Council seeks opinions from the European Parliament, the Economic and Social Committee, and the Committee of Permanent Representatives. Ultimately, a proposal can be adopted as a decision, a directive or a regulation.

See EUROPEAN COMMUNITY; HARMONIZATION; LEGISLATIVE PREPARATION; OFFICIAL JOURNAL OF THE EUROPEAN COMMUNITIES.

proprietary products *See* PHARMACEUTICALS.

protectionism *See* GENERAL AGREEMENT ON TARIFFS AND TRADE.

protective measures Measures which may be taken by a member nation when a sudden balance of payments crisis occurs and where the Council has not given immediate assistance.

PTOM (Pays et Territoires d'Outre-Mer, Overseas Countries and Territories). *See* OCT.

public authorities The State, regional, or local authorities, bodies governed by public law, or association formed by one or several of such authorities or bodies governed by public law.
See PUBLIC PROCUREMENT.

public contracting entities Public authorities and public undertakings.
See PUBLIC AUTHORITIES; PUBLIC PROCUREMENT.

public health *See* ANIMAL HEALTH AND MEAT INSPECTION; PLANT HEALTH CONTROLS.

public limited companies A directive under the Merger Treaty concerns the structure of public limited companies and the powers and obligations of their organs. The directive's purpose is to ensure that by 1992 managers of these firms are effectively supervised on behalf of shareholders, and to ensure employee participation in the management of such companies, with the holding of an Annual General Meeting. Member states must assure that such companies are organized according to either a two-tier board structure (management body and supervisory body) or a one-tier system (administrative body in which the actions of the executive members are reviewed by the non-executive members. These bodies will be responsible for the closure or transfer of the whole or part of the undertaking, substantial extension or reduction in the activities of the undertaking, important organizational changes, and the establishment or ending of long term cooperation with other firms.
See CROSS-BORDER MERGERS.

Public opinion polls—(Eurobarometer) (Euro-Barometer) (Euro-Barometre) These E.C. polls have been conducted on behalf of the European Commission each spring and autumn since September 1973 with Eurobarometer. These polls deal with attitudes to unifying Western Europe, membership, integration. Results are sent to different representative samples of the population in each of the Community nations. Eurobarometer's main function is to provide the citizens of the member states and of the Community with information on their attitudes to one another, their perceptions of the problems facing them and the vision of the future capable of inspiring their support. Preparing for the decade into the 1990s a poll indicated that Community people are increasingly indifferent. "The European mood is less one of wanting to construct Europe than to get on with living in it. Their hopes and fears for the future are principally economic and social. They think much less in political terms. But Europeans are still prepared to make an active stand for the great causes which most closely affect their lives—such as that of peace." As the single market program gains momentum, more people in Europe have focused on the E.C.'s decision-making process and have concluded that the mechanism is not sufficiently democratic. Despite majority support for the process of economic integration, polls indicate three out of four E.C. citizens favor a referendum in which the question of European union would be decided by the public. A majority favor giving the Parliament full legislative power. Proponents of more openness in the E.C. use these poll results to demonstrate a growing backlash against the "democratic deficit" of the present process.
See PEOPLE'S EUROPE.

public procurement Public procurement as a whole amounted to some 15 percent of GDP or 550 billion ECU, about $630 billion for the 12 member states in 1987. Public undertakings account for 63 percent of public procurement in Belgium, and between 35–40 percent in France, Germany, and Italy. Because of a lack of open and effective competition, only two percent of public procurement contracts in the Community are awarded to firms from a member state other than the member state advertising the tender. Directives dealing with public supply contracts and public works have proven unsuccessful. New proposals will overcome shortcomings of these directives by limiting exclusions, reducing excessiveness, and introducing new procedures. Another proposal deals with implementing effective remedies in cases of national or other discrimination in awarding contracts. The value of the E.C. public-procurement sector—that is, purchases and works by government, regional, or local authorities—together with contracts by public-sector enterprises amounts annually to around 400 billion ECU, about $460 billion. Opening of public procurement is a keystone to the completion of the internal market by 1992. The Commission approved the introduction of a monitoring system to ensure that competitive tendering for public-sector contracts is observed. It involves preventive measures to inform recipients of E.C. funding of the obligations they thereby assume. Should public procurement rules be breached, the Commission can consider suspending further payment of funds or ordering past payments to be returned.

See GOVERNMENT CONTRACTS; INDUSTRIAL COOPERATION; INTELLECTUAL PROPERTY; PUBLIC WORKS CONTRACTS.

public supply contracts *See* PUBLIC PROCUREMENT.

public undertakings Any undertaking over which public authorities may exercise control, either directly or indirectly, or by virtue of ownership, financial participation, or by operation of law.

See PUBLIC PROCUREMENT.

public works contracts A 1972 directive requires common procedures for advertising and awarding public sector construction contracts for which the estimated cost is one million ECUs or higher. Contracts must be awarded either to the lowest bidder (usually the most economic tender), taking into account price, period of completion, technical merit, and so forth. In mid-October 1988 the E.C. Council of Ministers unanimously agreed on a proposed directive on public works contracts that would amend the directive that has been in force since 1972, making procedures for awarding public works contracts more open, giving entrepreneurs a chance to compete in all member states on an equal footing. In addition, public authorities must specify standards and technical specifications agreed to at the European level, and these specifications must be met by the companies executing the contract. Prior notice of forthcoming contracts and their specifications must be published in the E.C.'s Official Journal to aid firms to prepare their tenders correctly, and notice of contracts awarded must be published. In February 1990, E.C. ministers agreed that public contracts in telecommunications, energy, transport, and water industries will be opened to E.C.-wide competition in 1993. As part of the agreement, the clause "Buy Europe" was included which allows contractors to dismiss bids with less than 50 percent E.C. content. Should they decide to permit a non-E.C. bid to compete, it would have to be at least three percent cheaper than the lowest E.C. bid. The ministers agreed that this Buy Europe clause would be dropped if negotiators at the GATT succeeded in eliminating preferential buying rules world-wide.

See COMPETITION POLICY; OFFICIAL JOURNAL OF THE EUROPEAN COMMUNITIES; PUBLIC PROCUREMENT.

Punta des Este *See* ALLIANCE FOR PROGRESS; CHRONOLOGY (SEPTEMBER 15–20, 1986) IN APPENDIX; URUGUAY ROUND.

Q

Qatar *See* GULF COOPERATION COUNCIL.

quadrilaterals In 1981, and each year since, the Community meets with the United States, Canada and Japan to discuss trade problems.

qualified majority *See* ARTICLE 100A.

quick-frozen foods *See* FOOD.

quota This is a restricted volume of imports or exports, or of imports admitted at a particular tariff rate. The establishment of the E.C. required the abolition of quantitative restrictions between member states. No detailed provisions regarding quotas is made in the Treaty of Rome with respect to third countries, but its Article 3 required that member states unify their lists of liberalized products as far as possible. The Council of Ministers allocates the share of quotas then they are applicable. By setting quotas, the Community does not fix quantitative restrictions as such but permits a certain quantity of a produce to enter the Community duty-free, or with a reduced tariff. Quotas may be adopted either in the framework of preferential agreements or to meet the need of certain sectors within the Community.

See RECIPROCITY.

R

RACE (Research and Development in Advanced Communications for Europe) The Community established this program in 1986 as part of an overall strategy to promote the rational development of the various telecommunication systems and services that are emerging in Europe. Its specific objective is to allow the gradual evolution towards a Community integrated broadband communications system, early next century. RACE's full goals are:

(1) To promote the European Community's telecommunications industry, so as to ensure that it maintains a strong position at European and world levels in a context of rapid technological change.

(2) To enable European network operators to confront the technological and service challenges with which they will be faced.

(3) To offer opportunities to service providers to improve cost performance and introduce new or enhanced telecommunication and information services which will both earn revenue in their own right and give indispensable support to other productive sectors of the Community.

(4) To make available to end users, at minimum cost and with minimum delay, the telecommunication services which will sustain the competitiveness of the European economy over the next decades and contribute to maintaining and creating employment in the Community.

(5) To contribute to the formation of a Community internal market for telecommunications equipment and services, as the basis for sustained strength on world markets.

(6) To contribute to regional development within the Community by supporting the development of common functional specifications for equipment and services permitting the less prosperous regions to benefit fully from the introduction of advanced telecommunications in the Community.

The E.C. has budgeted $580 million through June 1992 for this program.
See STAR; TELECOMMUNICATIONS.

radiation protection program *See* MEDICAL AND PUBLIC HEALTH RESERACH; NUCLEAR ENERGY.

Radioactivity Environmental Monitoring (REM) *See* NUCLEAR ENERGY.

radio messaging: In November 1989, the E.C. nations agreed to commence a European radio messaging system after 1992 to enable business executives and other users of bleepers to page each other across national borders.

raids *See* DAWN RAIDS.

railways In an effort to upgrade rail services after 1992, the E.C. Commission proposed in November 1989 that the European railway sector be opened to private enterprise. The railways would remain state monopolies, but private firms would be permitted to ship goods in competition with the rail companies. In January 1990, a Council directive was presented on the development of the Community Railways, along with an amending directive on the establishment of common rules for certain types of combined carriage of goods between member states. A proposal was also introduced by the Council amending a regulation concerning the obligations inherent in the concept of a public service in transports by rail, road, and inland waterway. A decision was made on the Community's high speed rail links to be developed within a European network that will guarantee to its users a high quality service. These lines consist of those railways which permit speeds of more than 200 km per hour on new lines and of more than 160 km per hour on existing lines that have been improved.

RAPID An E.C. database containing the daily releases of the Commission's Spokesman's Service.

R & TD *See* RESEARCH AND TECHNOLOGICAL DEVELOPMENT POLICY.

ratchet down *See* MONTREAL ROUND.

rate bracket system In 1968, the Council approved a regulation on an obligatory bracket system of rates for transport of merchandise by road. The spread between the highest and lowest rates cannot exceed 23 percent of the highest rate. Each rate was based on a base price established in relation to a number of specific criteria and could only be modified by agreement of the member states directly involved, with the Commission participating in the negotiations in a consultative capacity. Prices can be freely set within the limits of the rates.

Recherche dans le transport en Europe *See* EURET.

reciprocity The Commission's intent is to provide a guarantee of similar or at least non-discriminatory opportunities for E.C. enterprises to operate in foreign markets on the same basis as local firms. The United States, Japan, and other nations question whether the E.C. will respect its international obligations. In general terms the Commission is not asking for mandatory reciprocity, just the power to seek it where appropriate. Not all E.C. trading partners, according to the Commission, would be asked to make the same concessions, nor would the Community insist on concessions from all its partners. Many developing countries would be excluded. The E.C. will seek reciprocity in testing and certification procedures. There will also be bilateral accords for transport, telecommunications, and information data base services. Should the 12 states agree on common rules for takeover bids, the Commission has said it

would want to negotiate reciprocity for foreign states. Before allowing foreign firms to take over an E.C. company, the Commission would want to be assured of the right of an E.C. company to do the reverse in that foreign company's home territory.

See GENERAL AGREEMENT ON TARIFFS AND TRADE; IDENTICAL TREATMENT; NATIONAL TREATMENT; OVERALL BALANCE OF CONCESSIONS; RHODES SUMMIT.

recommendations Under the Paris Treaty the Commission can adopt recommendations which are binding as to the ends but not as to the means.

Cf. DECISIONS; DIRECTIVES; OPINIONS; REGULATIONS.

recommended price *Synonymous with* GUIDE PRICE.

Reconstruction and Development Bank *See* BANK FOR EUROPE.

recycling, paper, tires, and drink containers Member states, in 1978, suggested a three-year research and development program for recycling paper and cardboard to lower pollution and conserve national resources. In December 1980, the Council of Ministers urged greater use of recycled paper and cardboard and the development of new technologies to improve the quality of recycled items. Other recommendations are being considered for the use of returnable drink containers and improved durability and recycling for the rubber content of used tires.

See ENVIRONMENT; FINANCE; RECYCLING, TENDERS; RESEARCH; SCIENCE AND TECHNOLOGICAL COMMITTEE.

recycling, tenders On November 1, 1979, the Council began a research and development program concerned with the recycling of urban and industrial wastes. The first call for tenders is open to individuals, institutions, or an association of individuals or companies operating with the Community.

See ENVIRONMENT; FINANCE; RECYCLING, PAPER, TIRES AND DRINK CONTAINERS; RESEARCH; WASTE.

reference price Similar to the threshold price, the Common Agricultural Policy reference price deals with food and vegetable imports. When such imports enter Community ports priced lower than the reference price, levies are charged to bring them up to that price. In addition, customs duties can also be charged. It is also used to describe weighted Community average prices for cattle and representative prices for pigs and pigmeat.

See AGRICULTURE, COMMON AGRICULTURAL POLICY; BEEF AND VEAL.

refugees *See* MIGRATION.

REGIO *See* DATABASES AND DATABANKS OF THE E.C.

regional policy The E.C. regional policy has three facets. First, it attempts to coordinate the regional policies of member states. Second, it introduces a regional dimension to other policies of the Community, and third, it provides a wide range of financial aid for development activity to benefit the less-favored regions of the Community.

It functions through the European Regional Development Fund (ERDF). The fund is assisted by a Committee created by the Council to aid the Commission in the operation of the Regional Fund. The primary task of the Committee is to examine applications for assistance, particularly in respect to large development projects. It also studies regional development programs and annual information submitted by governments.

See REGIONAL FUND; REGIONAL FUND COMMITTEE.

Regional Policy, Regional Fund (European Regional Development Fund) (ERDF) ERDF's purpose is to correct regional economic imbalances within the Community. "Quota" sector regions benefiting from the Fund are limited to those that are assisted by national governments through their development aid schemes. Grants from the Fund are for supplementing, not replacing, national assistance. "Non-quota" sector regions are allotted five percent of the Fund's appropriations from the Community budget. Grants, determined by ERDF executives, are used for projects outside nationally aided regions, to help finance specific development measures arising from new regional problems

caused by economic crisis or the Community's own policies.

See EUROPEAN COAL AND STEEL COMMUNITY; EUROPEAN INVESTMENT BANK; FARM FUND; FINANCE; INDUSTRIAL POLICY; REGIONAL FUND COMMITTEE; SOCIAL POLICY

Regional Policy, Regional Fund Committee This Committee was created by a 1975 Council decision to assist the European Commission in examining applications for regional assistance and in making allocations from the Regional Fund.

See REGIONAL FUND; REGIONAL POLICY.

regions These are areas of the member nations which, for reasons of national economic change, have obsolete, obsolescent, or declining industries, and suffer from lack of investment and high unemployment.

regulations These are Community laws, adopted by the Council of Ministers on a proposal from the European Commission, that are binding on governments of member states, and thereby on all of its citizens and organizations. They are the equivalent of a national statute or Act of Parliament and take effect without reference to any national legislation, to which they are superior.

Cf. DECISIONS; DIRECTIVES; OPINIONS; RECOMMENDATIONS.

See HARMONIZATION; LEGISLATIVE PREPARATION.

regulatory committee A committee set up by the Council in which a management style formula is applied to other fields. It was used initially in the management of the Common Customs Tariff, then for the management and adaptation of common standards (food, veterinary and plant health regulations, for instance), environmental legislation, and so on. The procedure is similar to that followed in the management committees, but with greater scope for appeals to the Council.

Cf. ADVISORY COMMITTEE; MANAGEMENT COMMITTEES.

REM (Radioactivity Environmental Monitoring) *See* NUCLEAR ENERGY.

remembrement The French policy of rationalization and enlargement of land-holdings to establish a more efficient farming system.

Repetitive Strain Injury (RSI) With the increased use of computers, people are suffering from RSI, symptoms of which include great pain in hands and arms. The E.C. passed a law, to go into effect January 1, 1993, making it mandatory for employers to supply workers with keyboards unattached to the screen, and making both keyboard and screen moveable. Also included are standards for seating, desks, and lighting.

representative organizations Special lobby groups, separate from official consultative bodies, monitor and when possible influence, Community policy decisions. They are used to communicate the views and demands of their members to governments and the European Commission and to explore and respond to initiatives and proposals for Community legislation. Examples include the Committee of Agricultural Organizations in the European Community, the Confederation of Industries of the European Community, the European Trade Union Confederation.
See LEGISLATIVE PREPARATION.

Republic of Hungary *See* HUNGARY, REPUBLIC OF.

Republic of Korea *See* KOREA, REPUBLIC OF.

resale price maintenance This is the practice by a supplier of prescribing, and taking action to enforce, retail or wholesale prices for the resale of items.

research In January 1974 the Council of Ministers adopted four resolutions identifying the guidelines for a coherent policy of scientific and technological research. The Committee on Scientific and Technical Research was created to coordinate national research and development policies and to advise the Council of Ministers and the European Commission. Independent scientific experts work out of the Committee for European Research and Development and the Research and Development Interservice Committee, composed of Community and other European non-Community members. The eight principal objectives of Community cooperation on research are:

(1) Promoting agricultural competitiveness (and that of fisheries);
(2) Promoting industrial competitiveness;
(3) Improving the management of raw materials;
(4) Improving the management of energy resources;
(5) Stepping up development aid;
(6) Improving living and working conditions;
(7) Improving the effectiveness of the Community's scientific and technical potential; and
(8) improving the flow of scientific information.

A Joint Research Center (JRC) with its four research establishments at Ispra in Italy, Karlsruhe in the Federal Republic of Germany, Geel in Belgium, and Petten in the Netherlands was founded by the European Atomic Energy Community. In 1989 the E.C. proposed an additional $8.4 billion on scientific research over the next five years. In addition, to better coordinate research activities, it was suggested that the 37 existing funded programs be reduced to six basic areas: information technology and telecommunications, industrial technology, the environment, biotechnology, energy, and human resources. From 1989 to 1995 the Commission, governments, and firms will have at their disposal as much as $16 billion to develop new technologies.
See AIRCRAFT INDUSTRY; COAL AND STEEL, CONSULTATIVE COMMITTEE FOR; COMMUNITY BUREAU OF REFERENCE; ENERGY; EURONET DIANE; FINANCE; FORECASTING AND ASSESSMENT IN THE FIELD OF SCIENCE AND TECHNOLOGY; JOINT EUROPEAN TORUS; JOINT RESEARCH CENTER; NUCLEAR ENERGY; RESEARCH AND TECHNOLOGICAL DEVELOPMENT POLICY; SCIENCE AND TECHNOLOGICAL COMMITTEE.

Research and Development in Advanced Communications for Europe *See* RACE.

Research and Development Interservice Committee (CIRD) CIRD was created in 1975. It is composed of representatives of the different Directorates-General and Services of the European Commission and of the Joint Research Center. It guarantees the flexible and effective coordination of scientific and technical research undertaken by the Commission's various units.

See COMMITTEE ON SCIENTIFIC AND TECHNICAL RESEARCH; RESEARCH; RESEARCH AND TECHNOLOGICAL DEVELOPMENT POLICY; SCIENCE AND TECHNOLOGICAL COMMITTEE.

Research and Technological Development (R & TD) policy The Single European Act of 1987 contains provisions designed to speed up European integration by completing a vast single market by 1992. It established a European Research and Technology Community, giving the Community specific powers in the field of scientific and technical cooperation, and established a framework for a program of research and technological development through 1991. Its eight primary areas of action are:

(1) Quality of life, including health care (emphasizing cancer and AIDS research), radiation protection, and the environment;
(2) Information technology and telecommunications;
(3) Industrial technologies of manufacturing, advanced materials, raw materials, technical standards, and reference materials;
(4) Biological resources, including biotechnology;
(5) Energy, including thermonuclear fusion, radioactive waste management and storage, and the decommissioning and dismantling of nuclear facilities;
(6) Science and technology for development;
(7) Marine resources; and
(8) European scientific and technical cooperation.

The European Research and Technology Community will become a vital component of the single European market which the Commission is striving to achieve by 1992.

research into European integration See UNIVERSITY RESEARCH.

residence rights Agreement was reached in 1989 by the Council of Ministers on an approach to allow E.C. students, pensioners, and people of independent means to live in any of the 12 member states as long as they can support themselves. For students, formal proof of income will not be required as long as the student can show that he or she has the means to live in the host country. Retirees and people of independent means will be required to prove they have sufficient funds to pay their way in a nation other than their country of origin. For pensioners settling in a more expensive state, this might require both a basic state pension from the home nation and additional income.

residues See ANIMAL HEALTH AND MEAT INSPECTION.

resolutions Adopted by the Council of Ministers on recommendations from the European Commission, resolutions indicate agreement on a principle or intent. They possess legislative or binding force. Resolutions from the European Parliament take two forms, opinions of the Parliament when called on to consider issues presented to it by the Commission or the Council, and requests for action from the Parliament addressed to the Council or the Commission.

See DECISIONS; DIRECTIVES; LEGISLATIVE PREPARATION; REGULATIONS.

restitution payments These are payments on exports by E.C. member nations to make up the difference between the world price and the higher domestic price in the exporting nation. Payments are gradually charged to the E.C.'s Agriculture Guidance and Guarantee Fund so that by the end of the transitional period (stages for implementation, usually longer for newest members) all exports of agricultural produce from the Community will be financed out of this central fund.

Synonymous with COMPENSATION PAYMENTS; EXPORT REFUNDS.

restrictive practices See COMPETITION POLICY.

restructuring effect *See* COST SAVINGS.

retaliation list *See* SUPER 301.

retirees *See* RESIDENCE RIGHTS.

Rhine A Community decision established the International Commission for the Protection of the Rhine Against Pollution. Its major goal is to develop common research on the origins of Rhine pollution, to suggest approaches by which the river can be protected, and to establish common protection arrangements. A Technical Secretariat sits in Koblenz.

See ENVIRONMENT; POLLUTION.

Rhodes Summit The December 2–3, 1988, meeting of E.C. leaders marked their 40th gathering. It represented the halfway point in reaching the goals of 1992. As stated in its closing report, the single market "will be of benefit to Community and non-Community countries alike and . . . will not close in on itself. Post-1992 Europe will be a partner and not a fortress." The internal market "will be a decisive factor contributing to greater liberalization in international trade on the basis of the GATT principles of reciprocal and mutually advantageous arrangements."

rice The Council of Ministers each year sets a target price for husked rice and intervention prices for paddy rice. These prices are derived from the target price but take into account conversion rates, manufacturing costs, and the value of their byproducts. Imports are subject to threshold prices, import licences, and levies, and advance fixing can be suspended for a given time period. An export levy can be introduced if there is a shortage within the Community.

See AGRICULTURE, COMMON AGRICULTURAL POLICY; INTERVENTION PRICE; TARGET PRICE.

right of establishment *See* ACCOUNTANTS; AGRICULTURE, RIGHT OF ESTABLISHMENT; AIRLINE SECTOR; ARCHITECTS; AUDITORS; DENTAL PRACTITIONERS; DOCTORS; HAIRDRESSERS; LAWYERS; MIDWIVES; NURSES; SELF-EMPLOYED; VETERINARY SURGEONS; WORK AND EMPLOYMENT.

rights In the spring of 1977 the Commission, the Council, and the European Parliament signed in Luxembourg a joint declaration on fundamental rights emphasizing that the E.C. is determined to secure and enhance individual freedom and liberty under the law. Today, Community Europeans have a new citizenship, which brings with it a whole range of rights guaranteed by the Community, with uniformity of interpretation maintained by the European Court of Justice. These rights include equal pay for men and women, the right to work in the country of one's choice and to receive equal pay with workers native to that country, the right to buy and sell without being hindered by frontiers and with the guarantees that Community legislation offers to consumers, the right to benefit from fair prices based on free competition and, finally, the right to legal redress across Community borders, in disputes concerning the environment or any other issue.

See FREEDOM OF MOVEMENT; RESIDENCE RIGHTS.

rim *See* PACIFIC RIM.

road transport *See* TRANSPORT.

robotics *See* TELEMAN.

Romania (Rumania) This country is a founder member of the Council for Mutual Economic Assistance. It has concluded trade agreements with the Community on textiles, steel, and other industrial items. Romania benefits from tariff concessions under the Community Generalized System of Preferences. In 1976 it was the first State-trading country to negotiate a textile trade agreement with the Community. Romania subsequently agreed to arrangements on trade in steel and agricultural products and, in 1980, concluded a long-term agreement on industrial trade and an agreement setting up a joint committee. Events of the fall 1989 may well alter its future relationship with the E.C.

See COUNCIL FOR MUTUAL ECONOMIC ASSISTANCE; EASTERN EUROPE.

Rome Treaty *See* TREATY OF ROME.

RSI *See* REPETITIVE STRAIN INJURY.

rulers In 1971, the E.C. Commission proposed to harmonize laws on rulers used professionally, for example in surveying, measuring the depth of liquids, or garment-making. Technical specifications for manufacturing and calibrating rulers had varied in different parts of the Community.

See HARMONIZATION.

Rules of Competition These rules are contained in the Treaty of Rome and its implementing regulations. They encompass the field of restrictive trade practices, types of trade agreement prohibited and permitted, monopolies, and mergers.

See DAWN RAIDS.

rules of origin *See* DUMPING.

Rumania *See* ROMANIA.

Rwanda This nation is one of the ACP states and a signatory to the Yaoundé Conventions of 1963 and 1969 and the Lomé Convention of 1988.

S

St. Christopher and Nevis These islands are signatories to the Lomé Convention of 1988.
Synonymous with ST. KITTS-NEVIS.
See CARIBBEAN BASIN.

St. Helena St. Helena is a U.K. dependency included in the Lomé Convention of 1988.
See CARIBBEAN BASIN.

St. Kitts-Nevis *Synonymous with* ST. CHRISTOPHER AND NEVIS.

St. Lucia St. Lucia is one of the ACP states and a signatory to the Lomé Convention of 1988.
See CARIBBEAN BASIN.

St. Vincent and Grenadine They are one of the ACP states and a signatory to the Lomé Convention of 1988.
See CARIBBEAN BASIN.

saccharin In 1978, the Commission suggested that member states act immediately to ban saccharin in food for children. It suggested its presence should be disclosed on labels, and warnings should be included on saccharin sold in tablets, as a measure to ensure daily consumption of the substance does not exceed 2.5 milligrams per kilogram of body weight.

SAD *See* SINGLE ADMINISTRATIVE DOCUMENT.

safety *See* FIRE SAFETY; GLASS; HARMONIZATION; HEALTH AND SAFETY; SIMPLE PRESSURE VESSELS.

Safety, Hygiene and Health Protection at Work, Advisory Committee on This is a Commission committee on social policy. It was created by the Council in 1974.

safety, sales practices This 1978 directive was designed to safeguard the consumer from sales away from business premises that are liable to press customers into purchasing items that they do not want. It excludes sales initiated by the consumer, those affecting immovable property, contracts for a value of less than 15 ECU, and foodstuffs and drinks delivered by regular roundsmen.
See CONSUMER PROTECTION.

sales practices safety *See* SAFETY, SALES PRACTICES.

San Marino, Republic of Though independent, this Republic is closely linked with Italy through a long-dating treaty of cooperation and friendship, including a Customs Union. It is not a European Community member, but indirectly benefits through the Customs Union. In May 1983, diplomatic relations between the E.C. and San Marino were established. In 1985, the E.C. opened relations to resolve the issue that the Republic is neither part of Italy nor a European territory and is thereby considered a third country, despite the fact that it has been included in the Community's customs territory since 1968. Goods travel freely between San Marino and the E.C. and customs duties paid on goods from third countries destined for San Marino, but imported through an E.C. member state, are retained by the E.C. Italy makes annual payments to San Marino to compensate for duties and levies not collected by San Marino itself.

Saò Tomé and Principe They are one of the ACP states and a signatory to the Lomé Convention of 1988.

Saudia Arabia *See* GULF COOPERATION COUNCIL.

SCAD *See* DATABASES AND DATABANKS OF THE E.C.

Schengen agreement Originally conceived in 1985, five nations (West Germany, France, Belgium, the Netherlands, and Luxembourg) meeting in Schengen, Luxembourg, were to have signed an agreement on December 14, 1989, removing all border controls and allowing people to travel freely within the five-country area. Negotiations collapsed over the issue of controlling the East Germany borders.

On June 19, 1990, these five states agreed to allow the free movement of people across their borders. Once ratified by the five Parliaments it is expected to come into effect in early 1992. Under the pact, border checks will be lifted to permit free movement within the five-nation zone, thus providing a blueprint for the entire Community. The five governments plan to tighten immigration and police controls on those entering the area.

Schengenland *See* SCHENGEN AGREEMENT

school milk In May 1977, the Community's subsidy scheme was introduced. The Community contributes from the Farm Fund to the financing of national government programs for supplying milk and certain milk items to school children at lowered prices.

See FINANCE; MILK AND MILK PRODUCTS; OPERATION FLOOD.

Schuman Plan This plan was proposed by French Foreign Minister Robert Schuman on May 9, 1950. It called for a conference to discuss the pooling of the coal and steel resources of Western Europe. It led the way towards the establishment of the European Coal and Steel Community in April 1951.

SCIENCE (Stimulation of the International Cooperation and Interchange Need by European Research Scientists) SCIENCE promotes the exchange of research workers within the E.C. through grants, and finances research projects, including twin laboratories in different member states. SCIENCE was adopted in summer 1988, and will run until 1993. It funds research into superconductivity.

See BIOTECHNOLOGY; DELTA; DRIVE.

Science and technological committee This E.C. committee's activities include working toward eliminating duplication of effort, reducing the cost of national and Community projects, improving their effectiveness, and gradually harmonizing procedures for formulating and implementing scientific policies within the Community. It created the Committee on Scientific and Technical Research to advise the Council and the European Commission.

See COMMITTEE ON EUROPEAN COOPERATION IN THE FIELD OF SCIENTIFIC AND TECHNICAL RESEARCH; COMMUNITY BUREAU OF REFERENCE; FINANCE; RESEARCH.

Science and Technology for Development *See* STD.

Science and Technology for Environmental Protection *See* STEP.

Science and Technology for Regional Innovation and Development in Europe. *See* STRIDE.

Scientific Committee for Food This committee made up of qualified experts was established in 1974. Its primary purpose is to advise the Commission on all issues dealing with the protection of human life and health as they relate to food items. In addition, it deals with the composition of foodstuffs, the application of additives, the existence of contamination, and other related issues.

See CONSUMER PROTECTION.

scrap and build policy *See* SHIPBUILDING.

SDRs *See* SPECIAL DRAWING RIGHTS.

seals *See* WILDLIFE.

Second Banking Coordination Directive *See* BANKING.

Second reading *See* EUROPEAN PARLIAMENT.

securities By 1992 a European securities market system has to be created to meet the needs of both investors and companies who go to the markets for capital and borrowings. Financial intermediaries authorized in one member state will be able to operate throughout the Community on the basis of a single license given in their home member states. The Community has coordinated the conditions for admission of securities to official stock exchange listing, the contents, scrutiny, and method of publication of the listing particulars, and the publication of information by quoted companies. This has taken place in parallel with the achievements in the field of liberalization of capital movements. By 1992 there will be collective investment undertakings for transferable securities, known as UCITS (Collective Investment undertakings or Collective investment in transferable securities). This classification includes open ended mutual funds such as unit trusts, information on the acquisition and disposal of major holdings in listed companies, prospectuses issued when securities are offered for subscription or sale, mutual recognition of the listing particulars published for the admission of securities to official stock exchange listing, and investment services. Effective October 1, 1989, an E.C. directive came into force, allowing fund managers to operate freely throughout the 12 E.C. countries on the basis of a single authorization from one member government. At the Madrid meeting in June 1989, the 12 agreed that by July 1, 1990, they would broaden the European Monetary System to coincide with an end to exchange controls and obstacles to community-wide banking, securities and insurance operations. In the spring of 1990, the Commission set minimum capital-adequacy rules for securities firms to apply across the E.C. In combination with other pending legislation, it will allow any investment services firm established anywhere in the E.C. to do business throughout the trading bloc.

See CAPITAL, FREE MOVEMENT OF; EUROLIST; FINANCIAL SERVICES; INDIRECT TAXATION; INSIDER TRADING; INTERBOURSE DATA INFORMATION SYSTEM; MADRID MEETING; TAXATION.

SEDOC (**Système Européen de Diffusion des Offres et des demandes d'emploi enregistrees en Compensation internationale.**) The European system for the international clearing of job vacancies.

See JOB INFORMATION.

seeds Legislation passed in June 1966 attempted to upgrade the quality of marketed seeds and seedlings and assist in their free circulation within the Community, provided they conformed to the rules on labeling and packaging. Certification procedures were set down in several directives. Gene banks have been formed to preserve varieties that may

have disappeared from commercial usage. The European Commission is involved in research to assess and exploit natural variability for the production of new types of plants. Effective July 1, 1972, common rules were set covering dry husked vegetables, hybrid corn, oil seeds, and fruit, and other seeds for sowing. To help Community farmers, the regulation provided for production grants in the form of a lump sum per quintal of seeds produced. The regulation established a single system of trade at the Community frontier, with the application of the Common Customs Tariff as the only measure for protection for these seeds—excluding hybrid corn, for which there is a system of reference prices with compensating charges.

See AGRICULTURE, COMMON AGRICULTURAL POLICY; SEEDS, COMMON CATALOG.

seeds, common catalog An amended directive applies to vegetable seeds. It brings together in a common catalog the various national catalogs of vegetable varieties. Only those in the common catalog can be sold. Seeds must have national certification involving field trials prior to inclusion within the catalog.

See AGRICULTURE, COMMON AGRICULTURAL POLICY; FRUIT AND VEGETABLES.

SELA *See* LATIN AMERICAN ECONOMIC SYSTEM.

self-employed The Treaty of Rome provides for the free movement of workers throughout the Community. In November 1980, the Council of Ministers passed legislation to include the self-employed in amended regulations enabling these people to benefit from equality of treatment with nationals regarding the internal legislation of the Community nation in which they are employed. The amended regulations also provide for entitlement to social security benefits such as those for sickness, disability, old age, maternity benefits, death, and, in some situations, unemployment compensation.

See WORK AND EMPLOYMENT.

semiconductors In December 1986, an E.C. directive was passed on the legal protection of topographies of semiconductor products to harmonize member state legislation regarding the protection of such products. The directive not only provides protection for the creator of the design, it also allows for the free movement of semiconductors within the Community.

Senegal One of the ACP states, Senegal was signatory to the Yaoundé Agreements of 1963 and 1969, and is now a signatory to the Lomé Convention of 1988.

Senior Council *See* COUNCIL OF EUROPE.

services The proposals for 1992 for financial, telecommunications, and transport services and for free movement of labor are intended to increase competition, efficiency, and the choice available to individuals and business users in a single European market.
See FINANCIAL SERVICES; INDUSTRY AND SERVICES; TELECOMMUNICATIONS; TRANSPORT.

SESAME *See* DATABASES AND DATABANKS OF THE E.C.

Seychelles This nation is one of the ACP states and a signatory to the Lomé Convention of 1988.

sheepmeat In the 1970s, sheepmeat was one of the few agricultural products for which there was no common market organization. Mutton and lamb were included in the Common Agricultural Policy effective October 20, 1980. The policy consists of measures for guaranteeing producers' incomes through a combination of direct payments and intervention to sustain market prices. Basic income support for producers is provided through an annual premium set to compensate for the decrease of income when the market falls below a reference price.
See AGRICULTURE, COMMON AGRICULTURAL POLICY; NEW ZEALAND.

shellfish *See* ANIMAL HEALTH AND MEAT INSPECTION.

shipbuilding A 1978 directive urged coordination of assistance to the shipbuilding industry within a medium-term strategy of regulated contraction, including sufficient social provisions and the creation of new jobs for those negatively affected by technological change. Externally, the Community sought cooperation from third-country shipbuilders in lowering production and sharing orders in a regulated fashion. The Commission proposed in 1979 a "scrap and build" policy to assist both the shipbuilding and shipping industry. Under this program, an established ship owner would be eligible for grant assistance if, when placing an order for an ocean-going ship, the ship owner sent ships to be scrapped representing twice the tonnage to be built. The proposal was never passed.
See COMPETITION POLICY; FINANCE; INDUSTRIAL POLICY; INDUSTRY, STATE AIDS; REGIONAL FUND; SOCIAL FUND; TRANSPORT.

shipping *See* TRANSIT PROCEDURE; TRANSPORT.

shipping register The Commissioner responsible for transport policy proposed in the summer 1989 to set up a Community shipping register, under which vessels flying the E.C. flag would qualify for a series of advantages designed to lower their operating costs and boost their competitiveness on the world market. The Community register, which would operate alongside national registers, stipulates that the vessel flying the E.C. flag must be owned by an E.C. citizen, and that all its officers and at least one-half of its crew must be E.C. nationals.

shoes *See* FOOTWEAR.

Sierra Leone This nation is one of the ACP states and a signatory to the Lomé Convention of 1988.

silk worms Legislation of 1972 attempts to encourage silk worm rearing through the creation of producer institutions that would encourage producers to support the rules regarding output and marketing. The Farm Fund reimburses national governments 50 percent of eligible expenditure.
See AGRICULTURE, COMMON AGRICULTURAL POLICY; AGRICULTURE, PRODUCTION GROUPING; FINANCE.

simple pressure vessels A June 1987 directive ensures a minimum level of safety throughout the Community for pressure vessels. The harmonization of safety standards will also aid the free movement of such products. In addition, a universally recognized testing procedure and mark of conformity will prevent wasteful checks being carried out in each member state.

See HARMONIZATION.

Singapore Singapore concluded an agreement with the Community on trade in textiles in December 1977. It is a member of the Association of South East Asian Nations (ASEAN), which concluded a cooperation agreement with the Community in 1979.

See ASSOCIATION OF SOUTH EAST ASIAN NATIONS; PACIFIC RIM.

Single Act *Synonymous with* SINGLE EUROPEAN ACT.

Single Administrative Document (SAD) To replace the sheaf of some 70 different forms used in trade across the E.C.'s internal borders, the Single Document, effective in 1988, attempts to harmonize and simplify trade procedures and alleviate the long delays at Europe's frontier crossings. Less data has to be reported than was required in the past. The document will be adapted to the planned computerization of customs administration and, with some modifications, used in trade with third countries.

See CACTUS; CADDIA; HARMONIZED COMMODITY DESCRIPTION; CODING SYSTEM.

Single (Banking) Community License *See* BANKING, CHRONOLOGY (JANUARY 13, 1988).

single currency plan *See* DELORS COMMITTEE.

Single Customs Document *See* SINGLE ADMINISTRATIVE DOCUMENT.

Single European Act This is a major amendment to the Treaty of Rome. It is designed to facilitate the adoption of the White Paper measures within its timeframe of December 31, 1992. It changed the Community's procedures for decision making, and increased the scope for a type of majority (as opposed to unanimous) voting in the Council of Ministers. Effective July 1, 1987, it was ratified by the Parliaments of all member states to improve significantly the institutional system and set new objectives for the Community, notably the completion of the internal market—"an area without internal frontiers in which the free movement of goods, persons, services and capital is ensured in accordance with provisions of this Treaty"—by 1992 and the strengthening of economic and social cohesion, without internal frontiers. Conditions for success require a common economic area, more vigorous growth, greater effectiveness on the part of the institutions, strengthened bugetary discipline, and a common and strong external economic policy. Reforms needed include a Common Agricultural Policy adapted to the world context; Community policies with real economic impact; sufficient, stable, and guaranteed financial resources; ways to strengthen budgetary discipline; and new rules for managing the budget. In all, nearly 300 directives were proposed in the White Paper that will have significant impact on more than 320 million Europeans and others around the world.

Synonymous with SINGLE ACT.

See CHRONOLOGY (DECEMBER 2–3, 1985; JANUARY 17 AND 28, 1986); INTERNAL MARKET; WHITE PAPER.

single market *See* SINGLE EUROPEAN ACT.

SITC *See* STANDARD INTERNATIONAL TRADE CLASSIFICATION.

Six, the These are the original member nations that signed the Treaty of Rome on March 25, 1957, establishing the E.E.C. Between July and December 1957 the Treaty was ratified by the Parliaments of all the six member nations—Italy, the Federal German Republic, Belgium, France, Luxembourg, and the Netherlands—thereby bringing into being the E.E.C. on January 1, 1958.

Skylark *See* EUROPEAN SPACE AGENCY.

sluice gate price The sluice gate price is similar to the threshold price. It applies to pigmeat, eggs, and poultry. Imports of these items below the sluice gate price have levies imposed upon them to bring these goods up to that price.

See AGRICULTURE, COMMON AGRICULTURAL POLICY; REFERENCE PRICE.

Small and Medium-sized Enterprises (SMEs) They represent more than 95 percent of companies within the Community and provide more than two-thirds of European employment. The E.C. is endeavoring to institute

147

measures to enable mergers to be controlled. The idea of cooperation is to seek out opportunities for economic agents to come together and create synergies in technology and commerce and to obtain capital needed for development and for carrying out innovative plans and joint technological and commercial initiatives. In December 1988, the Commission authorized a program of experimental training initiatives to prepare these enterprises for the single market of January 1, 1993. SME managers receive about 18 days of training spread over several months.

See DE MINIMIS RULE; SMALL BUSINESSES.

small businesses The Treaty of Rome forbids all agreements or concerted practices between companies that result in the restriction or distortion of competition within the Common Market. Since January 1978, the largest aggregate market share that can be retained by firms qualifying for exemption as a small business is 15 percent and the maximum qualifying turnover is 300 million ECU. If they meet required criteria, small companies are eligble for loan assistance from the European Investment Bank and the European Coal and Steel Community through global loans. The European Commission also aids small and medium-sized firms to cooperate to their mutual profit across Community boundaries. The Single European Act provides for assessing the impact on competitiveness and employment of all proposed and existing legislation on competition to the Council and Parliament; making proposals on company law and taxation; promoting the spirit of enterprise; preparing legislative and technical manuals on subcontracting; creating Community Information Centers; initiating proposals on the development of continuous training in small businesses; and initiatives on the financing and expansion of the Business Cooperation Center.

See BUSINESS COOPERATION CENTER; COMPETITION POLICY; DE MINIMIS RULE; FINANCE; INDUSTRIAL POLICY; INTERNAL MARKET; SINGLE EUROPEAN ACT; VENTURE CONSORT; WHITE PAPER.

SMEs *See* SMALL AND MEDIUM-SIZED ENTERPRISES.

Smithsonian Agreement A December 1971 agreement by the Group of Ten setting new par values for the dollar (10 percent devaluation). It raises permissible margins of exchange rate fluctuations from plus or minus 1 percent to plus or minus 2.25 percent. The Agreement reassessed the value of foreign currencies in relation to the dollar.

See SNAKE.

snake An international agreement between Belgium, the Netherlands, Luxembourg, Denmark, Sweden, Norway and West Germany, linking the currencies of these countries together in an exchange rate system. The signatories have agreed to limit fluctuations in exchange rates among their currencies to 2.25 percent above or below set median rates as set with the signing of the Smithsonian Agreement. The snake was designed to be the first stage in forming a uniform Common Market currency. Members maintain fairly even exchange rates among themselves by buying or selling their currencies when the rates threaten to drop or rise beyond 2.25 percent limits specified. The snake in the tunnel is seen by many economists who support it as a step towards economic and monetary union, because stabilized exchange rates would make possible the introduction of a European Currency, and because stable exchange rates can only exist between states whose respective economies are advancing at the same rate.

See CHRONOLOGY (MARCH 21, 1972) EUROPEAN MONETARY UNION; SMITHSONIAN AGREEMENT.

snowstorms *See* CIVIL PROTECTION

soap *See* DETERGENTS.

social dumping The relocation of industry to less developed E.C. countries where labor is cheaper, resulting in unemployment in the more developed countries.

See GERMANY, FEDERAL REPUBLIC OF.

social charter To reassure workers, the Commission in 1989 proposed a Charter of Basic Social Rights to create minimum standards for working hours, pension guarantees, and other matters. As drafted, the charter consists of broadly defined rights. Specific requirements are for countries to require annual paid vacations and a minimum working age of 16. It also calls for some worker participation in corporate decisions. One of its aims is to protect E.C. citizens against temporary job losses due to the inevitable industrial and economic restructuring that will take place in the early days of the internal market. Once the barriers to free movement are down, the Charter would offer workers protection from social dumping—company relocation to areas where working conditions, such as wages, are lower. Other rights include a commitment to improve living and working conditions, including the setting of a maximum work week for all workers, the right to the free movement of workers, the harmonization of the right of residence in all member states, and the right to social protection under conditions equivalent to those existing in the worker's country of origin. Another right is that payment should be taken for granted for all types of work. The Commission wants a reference wage (a type of minimum wage) for workers not covered by labor contracts. Other rights include vocational training, equality of the sexes, the provision of worker information and participation, and health and safety protection in the workplace. Many E.C. employers fear that the social charter is a danger to industrial competitiveness. Union officials also argue that the social charter allows Brussels to set conditions for workers, which they oppose. The British government argues that labor relations are best left to be regulated at the national level. It is believed that enforcement of an E.C. Social Charter would put poorer E.C. nations, such as Spain, Portugal, and Greece at a disadvantage, by forcing these states to introduce minimum standards for pay and working hours, and provide for collective bargaining and worker participation in major corporate decisions. The Social Charter cannot be compulsory under European law. On December 9, 1989, the European Council meeting in Strasbourg, approved by a vote of 11 to 1 the decision to create a Charter of Social Rights for the Community. Mrs. Thatcher of Britain opposed the Charter. Britain will still have the opportunity to veto any legislation that emerges over the next few years on such matters.

See CHRONOLOGY (DECEMBER 8–9, 1989).

Social Fund (The European Social Fund) (ESF) This Fund was created by the Treaty of Rome. It was first amended in 1971 by the Council of Ministers. ESF operates under two major budgets designed to assist with training, retraining, or resettlement schemes. The Council of Ministers identifies categories of workers particularly affected by unemployment or underemployment who qualify for assistance from the Fund. Other categories include handicapped people who require assistance to return to work in the open labor market, older workers (usually over 50 years) who require retraining to find a new position, women over 35 years of age who are seeking a job for the first time, young people under 25 years of age who are unemployed because of the lack of qualifications or whose qualifications are no longer required, workers who need further technical training because of obsolescence, and employees in certain groups of enterprises who are facing severe difficulty.

See SOCIAL FUND ADVISORY COMMITTEE; HANDICAPPED PEOPLE.

Social Fund Advisory Committee This Committee advises the European Commission on the administration of the Social Fund.

See SOCIAL FUND; SOCIAL POLICY.

social policy A policy for improving workers' conditions and living standards was established by the Treaty of Rome. A Social Action Program approved by the Council of Ministers in 1974 agreed to equal pay and equal treatment for men and women in securing employment, training, and working conditions; guaranteeing the rights of workers when businesses change ownership; upgrading conditions for migrant workers whether moving within the Community or from outside; and assisting the handicapped. Until 1993 it was agreed to double the program's funds and pursue five major objectives:

(1) development of structurally backward regions,
(2) redevelopment of regions in industrial decline,
(3) fighting long-term unemployment,
(4) assistance for the recruitment of young people, and
(5) adaptation of agricultural structures. Directives have been proposed dealing

with problems posed by the need to increase employment and improve the quality of working life, the need to reexamine the means employed to ensure the future of systems of protection, i.e., social security, and the social implications of the completion of the internal market.

See EDUCATION; HEALTH AND SAFETY; INTERNAL MARKET; SINGLE EUROPEAN ACT; SOCIAL FUND; SOCIAL FUND ADVISORY COMMITTEE; WHITE PAPER; WORK AND EMPLOYMENT.

social rights *See* SOCIAL CHARTER.

SOEC The Statistical Office of European Communities.

soft terms Financial aid when it is made available at less than the cost of its provision by the donor nation.

solar energy In 1973, the Community started research programs dedicated to solar and related energy sources undertaken by the Joint Research Center at Ispra, or with shared contracts arranged between the European Commission and industry, research centers, and universities of member nations. The Community also contributes financially to the cost of projects dedicated to study liquefaction and gasification of solid fuels.

See ENERGY; FINANCE; RESERACH; SCIENCE AND TECHNOLOGICAL COMMITTEE.

Solemn Declaration on European Union *See* CHRONOLOGY (JUNE 17–19, 1983) IN APPENDIX.

Solid fuel An objective of the E.C. energy program is that the share of solid fuels (coal) in energy consumption should be increased by 1995 and that the competitiveness of production capacities should be improved.

See ENERGY.

Solomon Islands These islands are one of the ACP states and a signatory to the Lomé Convention of 1988.

solvency ratio of credit institutions *See* BANKING.

Somalia This nation is one of the ACP states and a signatory to the Yaoundé Conventions of 1963 and 1969 and of the Lomé Convention of 1988.

South Africa On September 20, 1977, the Community passed a Code of Conduct for Community companies outlining the necessity to recognize and negotiate directly with black trade unions and guarantee that rates of pay were above the poverty line within South Africa. It urged firms to provide African workers fringe benefits such as pension programs, unemployment benefits, and medical insurance and to attempt to abolish segregation in canteens and workplaces. In recent years the E.C. has condemned the practice of apartheid.

South Asian Delegation The E.C. has a small delegation in New Delhi to cover trade arrangements with India, Sri Lanka, Bangladesh, and Nepal.

See ASSOCIATION OF SOUTHEAST ASIAN NATIONS.

South Korea South Korea agreed to voluntarily limit its 1989 steel exports by not shipping more than 180,000 tons of steel to the E.C., about 74 percent of the year's basic quota but an increase of six percent over 1988 actual exports. In October 1989, the E.C. imposed provisional anti-dumping duties from 10.2 to 19.6 percent on imports of South Korean small-screen color-television sets arguing that a surge in low-priced imports had damaged E.C. producers' profits and led to job losses.

See PACIFIC RIM.

Soviet Union *See* UNION OF SOVIET SOCIALIST REPUBLICS.

soybeans In 1989, soybeans, a major U.S. export to the E.C., became the center of a trade battle. The U.S. won a 20-year fight with the E.C. over European soybean subsidies. Under the settlement, the E.C. agreed on December 20, 1989, to pass legislation before 1991 that would eliminate soybean and other oil seed subsidies.

space *See* EUROPEAN SPACE AGENCY.

Spain In 1961, Spain applied for an association agreement with the Community. This led to an industrial free trade agreement limited to the original six founder members. Spain submitted an application for full Community membership on July 28, 1977, becoming a full member on January 1, 1986. Spain sells 50 percent of its total exports to the European Community. The Royal Decree-Law 1265 enacted in June 1986 opened up opportunities for foreign investment in Spain. Direct investments are liberalized if the foreign participation does not exceed 50 percent of the firm's assets. Portfolio investments are those executed by the purchase of shares or participation in Spanish companies, not considered direct investments. Real estate investments are liberalized for nonbusiness purposes. Other forms of investment require prior administrative authorization. In all cases, investors have full rights of foreign transfer with no quantitative ceilings and may repatriate dividends, interests, and capital gains, as well as the capital originally invested, provided that the initial investment is properly registered. Spain's industrial promotion policy is directed at a series of basic objectives, such as development and expansion of industrial sectors, regions, small and medium size firms, as well as research and development, technology, and the creation of new employment. Both domestic and foreign investors can benefit from the incentives offered under these programs. Available government assistance is classified in two ways: financial—includes direct incentives (subsidies, loans, and financial participation in venture capital) and indirect incentives (tax benefits, credits, exemptions, and deductions); and non-financial—ranging from a series of services such as technical, management, and financial advice, to other diverse incentives such as special hiring advantages, help in acquiring land for industrial use, schemes for company mergers, and so on.

Spain's unemployment was officially put at over 22 percent of the available population in 1985, more than anywhere else in Western Europe. In 1989 it was 17 percent, still the E.C.'s highest. In 1987 341,000 new jobs were created, and in 1988 320,000 new jobs were added. Inflation has been falling on an annual basis from 12 percent to 4.6 percent at the end of 1988. The government's goal is to bring down the differential with Spain's major trading partners in the Community. The Spanish economy has gathered momentum, with gross capital formation in 1988, and high interest rates unable to deter firms with good businsss prospects from further borrowing. Spain's gold and foreign currency reserves are at all-time high of $33 billion, a figure that exceeds the total public and private debt, and the peseta has appreciated against all major currencies. Spanish banks are preparing for 1992 by merging and liberalizing their interest rates. The Big Seven banks held 77 percent of all deposits in Spain and 66 percent of outstanding loans.

Since joining the Community, Spain has enjoyed the region's fastest economic growth rate. In the process, with the middle class spending as never before, more than 1.5 million new jobs have been created. Foreign investment exceeding $10 billion a year has been pouring in. Spain's growth rate rose from 2.5 percent in 1985 to 4.0 percent in 1986, 5.5 percent in 1987, and 5.3 percent in 1988, in each case 1.5 to 2.0 percentage points higher than the E.C. average. Spain's two present dilemmas are a ballooning trade deficit (it was around $28 billion in 1989), and the need of the economy to grow at a faster rate than the E.C. average to make a dent on the high level of unemployment without choking off sustained expansion in the future.

Special Drawing Rights (SDRs) SDRs are a low-interest-bearing issue of reserve assets originated in 1969 by the International Monetary Fund. The creation of artificial (but gold-backed) international liquidity is intended to make a global money supply independent of the size of the U.S. balance-of-payments deficit and international gold production.

Special Telecommunications Action for Regional Development *See* STAR.

specific horizontal directives These are directives detailing how requirements are to be applied to specific segments of a wide area, e.g., flavoring as a category of additives.
Cf. FRAMEWORK HORIZONTAL DIRECTIVES.
See DIRECTIVES.

SPES *See* STIMULATION PROGRAM FOR ECO-
NOMIC SCIENCES.

Spierenburg Report *See* COMMUNITY RE-
FORM.

sports *See* SYMBOLS.

**SPRINT (Strategic Program for Innovation
and Technology Transfer)** SPRINT was
adopted in the summer of 1988 with a 90
million ECU budget for the period of 1989–
1993. It is aimed at promoting the dissemination of new technologies and innovations
by integrating national innovation infrastructures into a European network, by promoting specific projects which are of particular
demonstration value for innovative technologies, by coordinating national innovation
promotion policies, and, in association with
this, carrying out innovation monitoring. The
program is aimed at public and private consultancy bodies that, together with partners
from other E.C. member states and on behalf
of small and medium-sized enterprises, research and set up cross-border, technology-
oriented structures for cooperation.
See TECHNOLOGIES.

Sri Lanka This nation has had trade agreements since 1975 with the Community regarding textiles and hand-made items. The
E.C. represents a growing market for its exports of both agricultural products and manufactured goods. Its garment industry has
found a promising market in the Community,
while its traditional trade in precious stones
has been stimulated by the cutting and pol-
ishing of diamonds for the E.C. market. There
was a 14 percent increase in its Generalized
System of Preferences exports of coir and other
products in 1986. A textile agreement running until 1990 reflects Sri Lanka's position
as a low-income developing country, by providing its exporters additional export opportunities.
See NON-ASSOCIATED STATES.

STABEX *See* STABILIZATION OF EXPORT
EARNINGS.

Stabilization of Export Earnings (STABEX)
STABEX was introduced in the Lomé I Convention. It attempts to counter some of the
effects on ACP states' economies and pro-

ducers' incomes of sudden drops in earnings
caused either by fluctuations in world prices
or by sharp variations in production resulting
from climatic or other conditions. Under Lomé
II the scheme was extended financially. It also
lowered the thresholds of dependence on
previous exports and relations to earnings over
the previous four years, with special concessions to the least developed, landlocked and
island countries. The Community compen-
sates ACP countries for earnings losses from
exports on a range of primary commodities.
The transfers (i.e., the payments made under
STABEX) are used to finance the interests of
diversification, in other sectors of the ACP
states' economies. Under the Lomé II Convention there are rigid regulations and administrative actions dealing with monitoring
allocation of transfers and how they are to be
applied. Transfers made to ACP states that
are not classed as least developed countries
may, in certain circumstances, be reimburs-
able. Virtually all the agricultural commodities exported by the ACP states are now
secured, with the exceptions of sugar and meat,
for which there are special protocols. Under
the third Lomé Convention 925 million ECU
was allocated to cover STABEX commit-
ments. This is divided into equal annual in-
stallments.
A similar system, SYSMIN (System for
Mineral Products), provides financing to help
ACP countries maintain their mineral export
potential.
See FINANCE.

stabilizers These are farm spending controls
as adopted by the E.C.

**Standard International Trade Classification
(SITC)** SITC was adopted by the United Nations in 1950 as a basis for reporting commodity detail in foreign trade statistics, and
member nations were urged to make use of
it. It was revised in 1960.

standardization *See* EUROPEAN STANDARDS
INSTITUTE; INFORMATION TECHNOLOGY;
STANDARDS; TECHNOLOGIES; TELECOM-
MUNICAITONS.

standards The removal of technical barriers
to trade, irrespective of whether these involve technical rules, standards, tests, or cer-

tificates, are accomplished by harmonization or by mutual recognition. Any product that is introduced on Community territory, as long as it satisfies the legislation of the importing country, and is admitted on its markets, is entitled, as a matter of principle, to the benefit of free circulation throughout the Community. In the case of harmonization, European standards bodies (European Committee for Standardization (CEN), European Committee for Electrotechnical Standardization (CENELEC), etc.) operate systematically on the basis of work done at the international level. For tests and certification, the Community negotiates mutual recognition agreements where needed. In June 1989, the United States and the E.C. announced an agreement intended to make it easier for American companies to comment as European companies set new standards on industrial products.

See CHEMICALS; CONSTRUCTION PRODUCTS; FOOD; HARMONIZATION; INDUSTRIAL STANDARDS; PHARMACEUTICALS; STANDARDIZATION; TRACTORS AND AGRICULTURAL MACHINERY; VEHICLES.

standby These are arrangements made in advance of need. They are used by the IMF as arrangements under which members can negotiate a drawing with the Fund in advance and then make the drawing immediately on demand without additional consultation or Fund examination of their policies.

Standing Committee on Employment *See* EMPLOYMENT, STANDING COMMITTEE ON.

Standing Conference on Health and Safety in the Nuclear Age *See* NUCLEAR ENERGY.

STAR (Special Telecommunications Action for Regional Development) STAR is a five-year Community telecommuncations program begun in 1987 to eliminate disparities in present and future infrastructures. The management of the differentiation of services is the main challenge facing telecommunications administrations and decision-makers world-wide. STAR is active in seven member states: France, Greece, Ireland, Italy, Spain, Portugal, and the United Kingdom. It helps set up the kind of telecommunication network necessary to provide advanced services to

business users in the less favored regions, and supports measures designed to stimulate demand and encourage use of the telecommunications structure in the less favored regions.

See RACE; TELECOMMUNICATIONS.

starch Regulations provide for production refunds to be granted for certain agricultural items needed for the production of starch, potato starch, and glucose.

See AGRICULTURE, COMMON AGRICULTURAL POLICY.

static trade effect *See* COST SAVINGS.

STD (Science and Technology for Development) A 1987 research program to promote scientific cooperation between the E.C. and developing nations to their mutual benefit. Research emphasis is on agriculture, medicine, health, and nutrition in tropical and subtropical areas.

steel In December 1978, the Council of Ministers approved a plan for the industry seeking to prohibit national subsidies that increased unwanted production, to increase Community financial assistance for modernization and diversification, and to examine ways of work sharing through reducing the retirement age, reorganizing shift work, lowering the length of the working week, and restricting overtime. The plan failed, leading the Council of Ministers to enforce production quotas, anti-dumping legislation, and import levies. In 1987, European Community steelmakers abandoned efforts to close plants voluntarily as a way of cutting 20 million tons of excess capacity by 1990. The plan of the industry's lobby group Eurofer was to liberalize the E.C. steel market by scrapping a seven-year old production quota system that currently covers about 60 percent of E.C. steel output. For 1988 output was, at about 135 million tons, 8 percent higher than in 1987. Total production of crude steel for the third quarter of 1988 was about 32.6 million tons, and represented an increase of 11.1 percent over the corresponding period in 1987. The Commission forecast crude steel production at around 34 million tons for the first quarter of 1989, and consumption (6.8 million tons of exports and 2.4 million tons of imports) at around 29.6 million tons. The United States limits steel imports from a total of 29 nations, including the E.C., and wants to limit all significant categories of imported steel to 18.4 percent of its market. In October 1989, the E.C. agreed to limit its steel exports to the United States for a further two and a half years and made it clear that it won't agree to extend the quotas again after March 1992. In return, the Commission obtained U.S. concessions, including an agreement by the United States to increase the E.C.'s quota slightly, to 7 percent from 6.7 percent of the U.S. steel market.

See COAL AND STEEL, CONSULTATIVE COMMITTEE FOR; FINANCE; INDUSTRIAL POLICY; SOUTH KOREA.

STEP (Science and Technology for Environmental Protection) A 1989 research program to provide scientific and technical support for the environmental policy of the Community; to improve the productivity of the overall research effort in the Community by coordinating national programs in the field of environmental research; to promote the scientific and technical quality of environmental research.

See ENVIRONMENT.

Stimulation of the International Cooperation and Interchange Need by European Research Scientists *See* SCIENCE.

Stimulation Program for Economic Sciences (SPES) SPES was proposed in March 1988 by the Commission. It is designed to encourage cooperation among European economists on research in areas of Community concern. Apart from establishing networks among European research institutions, the plan is aimed at making professors and researchers more mobile, thus encouraging them to work in other European institutions on a temporary basis. Financial support for the plan, which will amount to 6 million ECU (about $7.2 million) for the first phase from 1989 to 1992, will take the form of study and mobility grants, subsidies for seminars or workshops, and financial assistance for research on themes of Community interest.

stock exchange, listing particulars A company law directive adopted by the Council of Ministers in March 1980 attempts to equalize

guarantees offered to investors in the member nations and to give them more protection. It set the minimum content of official stock exchange listing particulars. It covers all securities except shares issued by undertakings that are not close-ended, and securities issued by the member nations and regional and local authorities. Listing particulars must be approved by an authorized agency and must be broadly circulated to the public. The directive because of anticipated increased competition should result in the quotation of the same shares on several Community stock exchanges. A 1979 directive set the conditions for the admission of securities to these listings.

See COMPANY LAW; FINANCIAL SERVICES.

stockholders *See* CORPORATE BREAKUP RULES.

Stockholm Convention (Treaty) The Convention established the European Free Trade Association on May 3, 1960.

See EUROPEAN FREE TRADE ASSOCIATION.

stocks *See* CORPORATE BREAKUP RULES; FINANCIAL SERVICES; STOCK EXCHANGE, LISTING PARTICULARS.

Strasbourg This city located in the eastern part of France is the headquarters of the European Parliament.

Strategic Program for Innovation and Technology Transfer *See* SPRINT.

Stresa conference In July 1958, the E.E.C. brought together the signatories to the Treaty of Rome, and the representatives of farmers' federations in the six countries. The initial guiding principles of the future Common Agricultural Policy emerged from a comparison of the existing national policies and of common resources and requirements. The conference added some details to the objectives set out in the Treaty. The structure of European agriculture was to be reformed to make it more competitive, but without undermining the family character of the farm unit. Agricultural prices were gradually to be brought to a uniform level in all member states. Because production costs in the Community were higher than in the other major producing countries, prices had to be above the world market level, but should not encourage overproduction.

The aim of the Common Agricultural Policy is not total self-sufficiency. Instead, the Community wishes to participate in a balanced manner in world trade, and to protect the internal market from distortions arising from competition from outside the Community. This is the basis on which the Commission submitted proposals in June 1960; in December the Council adopted these principles creating the Common Agricultural Policy.

See AGRICULTURE, COMMON AGRICULTURAL POLICY; CHRONOLOGY (JULY 3–11, 1958; JUNE 30, 1960).

STRIDE (Science and Technology for Regional Innovation and Development in Europe) A proposed research program of the E.C. to support operational programs of the member states to promote regional capacities in the field of research and technological development, with financial contribution through the Community's structural funds.

structural funds *See* SINGLE EUROPEAN ACT.

student handbook The European Commission publishes a handbook for students in higher education to aid them in continuing their studies in another Community state. The handbook contains information on programs and grants available to all E.C. students pursuing college or university training.

See EDUCATION; EDUCATION GRANTS; EUROPEAN UNIVERSITY INSTITUTE; UNIVERSITY RESEARCH.

Stuttgart compromise *See* BUDGET.

subsidies By 1992, the Commission intends to eliminate billions of dollars in state subsidies. Between 1983 and June 1989, it had ordered $1.14 billion in paybacks in 26 cases. E.C. nations annually pump out industrial aid valued at about three percent of gross national product. The assistance ranges from major subsidies for auto makers and steel companies to lesser financing for start-up firms, for research, and for product launchings on export markets. The E.C. in preparing for 1992 is scrutinizing not only new proposals for national subsidies but it is reviewing existing subsidies that may cause unfair competition among Community companies. The United

States in its opposition to continued European subsidies of farms and businesses estimated that the E.C. spent nearly $120 billion in 1988 to support agriculture, compared with about $75 billion in the United States. An additional $50 billion in subsidies went to European steelmakers, shipbuilders, and manufacturers. In October 1989, the United States submitted to GATT a plan that proposed curbing price support subsidies within 10 years and eliminating export subsidies within five years. E.C. officials argued that the proposal's main aim was to destroy the Common Agricultural Policy. On December 20, 1989, the E.C. announced a proposal for the gradual reduction of farm subsidies, not their abolition, with countries receving credit for subsidy cuts made since 1986.

See SOYBEANS.

Sudan This nation is one of the ACP states and a signatory to the Lomé Convention of 1988.

sugar Common Market rules were passed in 1968 applying to sugar beet production and refineries within the Community. Limited support price quotas and penalties for overproduction were set. Each year the Council fixes a target price and an intervention price for sugar, and if market prices drop to the intervention level, refiners can sell to the intervention agencies at the full intervention price. The Council also fixed a "maximum quantity" for sugar production and refining which is about 27.5 percent of the basic quantity and additional to it. A 1979 directive sets out uniform procedures for analysis and testing.

See AGRICULTURE, COMMON AGRICULTURAL POLICY; CONSUMER PROTECTION; INTERNATIONAL SUGAR AGREEMENT.

super 301 A provision of the 1988 U.S. Trade Act, the U.S. Trade Representative must identify "priority" foreign countries whose trading practices are thought to curb American exports unfairly. Such identification starts a 36-month negotiating clock, at the end of which there is either agreement to lift the barriers or possible American retaliation. In May 1989, the United States singled out Japan, India, and Brazil for priority action under the law.

superzone *See* EUROPEAN FREE TRADE AS-
SOCIATION.

**Suppression of Terrorism, European Con-
vention on** *See* TERRORISM.

Supranational A body placed above the national governments of the member-states or
their departments, or to measures emanating
from such bodies.

suretyship insurance *See* INSURANCE.

Surinam One of the ACP states and a sig-
natory to the Lomé Convention of 1988. A
Protocol annexed to the Convention guar-
antees the country's sugar exports to the
Community.
See CARIBBEAN BASIN; SUGAR.

Swaziland This nation is one of the ACP
states and a signatory to the Lomé Convention of 1988. A Protocol annexed to the Convention guarantees the country's sugar exports
to the Community.
See SUGAR.

Sweden This nation is a founder member of
the European Free Trade Association which
came into force in 1960.
See COMMITTEE ON EUROPEAN COOPERA-
TION IN THE FIELD OF SCIENTIFIC AND TECH-
NICAL RESEARCH; EURONET DIANE.

swine fever *See* ANIMAL HEALTH AND MEAT
INSPECTION.

Switzerland This country is a founder member of the European Free Trade Association.
It is not presently a member of the E.C. There
is growing concern over the future of this
nation when the 12 member states of the E.C.
impact on its banking and commercial operations. One of three francs earned in Switzerland comes from ties with the E.C. In 1987,
Switzerland was the third largest supplier of
the E.C. (26.7 billion ECU) after the United
States and Japan, and its second largest customer (32.8 billion ECU) after the United
States. Out of 2.4 billion Swiss francs invested
directly by Switzerland in 1987 in E.C. states,
822 million Swiss francs went to industry and
1.5 billion SFR to the service sector (as against
only 473 million in 1986). On December 20,

1989, the E.C. and Switzerland signed an
agreement applying to traffic between the E.C.
and Switzerland with provisions similar to those
applicable within the Community. It covers
easing border controls and formalities for the
transport of goods, thereby limiting the waiting period at borders and decreasing the costs
of economic operations. The agreement is effective July 1, 1991.

symbols They represent the Community's
identity. Symbols involve adopting a European flag and anthem, celebrating a "Europe
Day," issuing a European passport, and supporting European sporting activity, and European weeks. The new flag of the Community
is a crown of 12 gold five-pointed stars on an
azure background. The European anthem is
the prelude of "Ode to Joy" from Beethoven's
Ninth Symphony, and Europe Day is May
9th—the day in 1950 that French Foreign
Minister Robert Schuman made the speech
preparing the way for the creation of the first
European Community. A European passport
was introduced in 1978 and a Community
driving license has been in existence since
1983.

synchronization German Minister for Foreign Affairs Gerhard Schroeder proposed in
1963 that the Community adopt this policy
as a means of breaking the deadlock within
the E.C. following suspension of the Com-
munity-British negotiations. The policy would
mandate the equalization, or sharing, of the
effects of Community actions in the individual
member countries.

Syria This country has had a cooperation
agreement (1977) with the Community with
provisions including free access to the Community market for industrial items and preferential treatment for agricultural items.
See GULF COOPERATION COUNCIL; MASH-
RAG STATES; MEDITERRANEAN POLICY; MNCs.

SYSMIN (The System for Mineral Products)
See STABILIZATION OF EXPORT EARNINGS.

**Système Européen de Diffusion des Offres
et des demandes d'emploi enregistrées en
Compensation internationale (SEDOC)**
See JOB INFORMATION.

T

tachographs This is a combined speedometer and mileage counter containing a device to record driving time, speed, and traveled distance. A 1977 regulation requires its installation and use in cargo and large passenger vehicles. As an accident prevention measure, Community legislation attempts to ensure effective and impartial enforcement of driving hours.

See DRIVING HOURS; TRANSPORT.

Taiwan This nation, though not a member of the MultiFibre Arrangement (MFA), has an autonomous agreement with the Community regarding restrictions on trade in textiles.

See FOOTWEAR; MULTIFIBRE AGREEMENT; PACIFIC RIM.

takeover regulations On December 22, 1988, the Commission released its proposed directive on "Company Law Concerning Takeover and Other General Bids." The directive seeks to establish harmonized regulations governing takeover bids throughout the E.C. Under the proposal which applies to large, public limited companies within the E.C. (excludes companies not quoted on the stock exchange, having less than $6.5 million in assets, turnover of no more than $15 million, and fewer than 250 employees), the offeror would be required to make a public bid for all the shares of a target firm after it acquired or controlled a certain percentage of the firm's shares. This percentage, which may not exceed one-third, would be determined by member nations. Also, the bidder would have to treat all shareholders holding a particular class of stock equally. Each member state is required to create a national authority to supervise compliance. The target firm must be given an acceptance period of not less than four weeks and not more than 10 weeks and, with certain exceptions, an offer cannot be withdrawn once it has been published. Lastly, offerors must revise bids upward to pay all shareholders equally if shares are bought from any shareholder at a higher price than that specified in the offer brochure. The Commission set only minimum rules, allowing national authorities to enact stricter regulations should they so wish. Approval of the directive may be in question since takeover rules in the member states presently vary widely. The Commission plans to propose early in 1990 measures intended to ease corporate takeovers in Europe.

See MERGERS.

tankers A 1978 directive set minimum requirements for certain tankers entering or departing from Community ports. To reduce marine pollution, it states that all tankers of more than 1600 gross registered tons must contact the appropriate authorities of the member nation concerned regarding cargo content. In addition, they must fill in a check list, use the services of a radar and radio station, and report any incident which may impact on safety at sea.

See ENVIRONMENT; PILOTS; TRANSPORT.

Tanzania This nation is one of the ACP states and a signatory to the Lomé Convention of 1988. A protocol annexed to the Convention guarantees the country's sugar exports to the Community.

See ARUSHA CONVENTION; SUGAR.

target price This is the basic Common Agricultural Policy price for each commodity as fixed each year by the Council of Ministers. Community policies of price support for farmers are tied directly to these target prices.

See AGRICULTURE, COMMON AGRICULTURAL POLICY; BASIC PRICE; GUIDE PRICE; INTERVENTION PRICE; REFERENCE PRICE; SLUICE GATE PRICE; THRESHOLD PRICE.

TARIC This is a simplified customs procedure implemented by the E.C. on January 1, 1988. It is a new Community tariff applying to harmonized goods.

See BTN; SINGLE ADMINISTRATIVE DOCUMENT.

tariffs See AIR CARGO; COSTS OF NON-EUROPE; EUROPE WITHOUT FRONTIERS; INTERNAL MARKET; SINGLE EUROPEAN ACT.

taxation In a single market, business decisions should be based on uniform tax considerations. A major problem in cross-border operations is the risk of double taxation. The White Paper proposals aim to remove tax obstacles to cross-frontier expansion. Directives will set up a common taxation system for the members of a group of companies to eliminate double taxation, including a particular type of double taxation that can arise due to non-market-based transfer pricing between firms in a group; to introduce common tax treatment of a group restructuring across frontiers; to harmonize the tax treatment of the carryover of losses from year to year, and to abolish certain taxes on security transactions which distort movements of capital. In March 1990, the Commissioner for Taxation Matters presented three draft laws for simplifying corporate taxes. The first proposed directive aims to abolish a five percent withholding tax imposed by West Germany on the profits made by affiliates of foreign firms. The second would encourage cross-border deals by removing capital gains tax on acquisitions in some E.C. states. The third proposal would set up an arbitration procedure for tax disputes between countries over pricing. In April 1990, the E.C. unveiled a two-stage plan aimed at getting member states to narrow differences in corporate-tax rates. The first step would be tax legislation to encourage firms to do business across national borders. The second would be to explore how the E.C. can reconcile differences in national tax systems with the smooth functioning of the unified market.

See TAX BARRIERS; CARRYOVER OF LOSSES; COMMON TAXATION; DOUBLE TAXATION; INDIRECT TAXATION; WITHHOLDING TAX.

tax barriers In June 1990, E.C. finance ministers agreed to remove several tax barriers facing firms operating on a multinational basis

in the E.C. Three measures are aimed at removing the risk of double taxation for groups of affiliated firms operating in several E.C. states and for firms acquiring a firm in another E.C. member state. The three measures taking effect January 1, 1992 are:

(1) A first directive will eliminate capital-gains taxes when assets are transferred between firms based in different E.C. member states in the event of a merger, corporate split-up, or share swap. Taxation will be deferred until the assets are realized, that is, sold or transferred to a non-E.C. firm.

(2) A second directive will abolish the withholding taxes on dividends paid by a subsidiary to its parent firm based in another E.C. state.

(3) A third measure sets up an "arbitration procedure" to resolve conflicts between tax authorities in different member states. Such conflicts often result in a firm being taxed in two nations on the same operation. When such difficulties arise, the firms will be able to ask for arbitration by a "panel of wise men" who have the power to issue a binding decision.

tax borders See VALUE ADDED TAX.

tax havens In February 1989, the Commission proposed measures to abolish tax havens within the E.C., with a tax of at least 15 percent on interest and dividends earned in one country by residents of another.

tax policies A 1971 resolution proposing the creation of the European monetary union included recommendations for the harmonization of member nations' taxes, including those affecting trade, those for influencing capital movements within the Community, and those for duty-free allowances to citizens crossing Community lines. Presently there is some harmonization of Value Added Tax, customs duties, and levies, and of indirect taxes on the raising of capital that are confined to structures and bases of assessment. The rates of tax remain the national prerogative. Programs for 1992 further advance changes in these areas.

See FINANCE.

tax relief A July 1985 directive amends the rules to increase the amount of tax relief (from VAT and excise duties) available on small consignments of a noncommercial character sent from one private individual to another across internal E.C. frontiers. The directive's purpose is to keep the real value constant while taking cost of living increases into account.

See CONTROL OF INDIVIDUALS.

technologies One purpose of the Single European Act is to create a single market for those services that are linked to rapidly changing innovative technology. As well as proposals for cross-frontier broadcasting and information services, the Community is trying to achieve European standards for advanced equipment. The fragmentation of the Community into separate national markets as a result of varying technical requirements reduces the scope for economies of scale, multiplies the costs of obtaining prototype approvals, and renders less attractive research on a scale sufficient to sustain Europe's competitiveness in international markets. To fulfill the objectives of 1992, the Community will establish rules to ensure the freedom to broadcast across frontiers, open up the market in information services, create a common market for telecommunications services, and introduce guidelines for the operation of electronic payments systems. Also, European standards will be in place for television, information technology, telecommunications equipment, and cellular radios.

See BRITE; TELECOMMUNICATIONS.

TED *See* DATABASES AND DATABANKS OF THE E.C.

TEDIS (Trade Electronic Data Interchange Systems) This is a Community action plan related to the electronic transfer of trade data with objectives of avoiding a proliferation of closed trade electronic data interchange systems and the widespread incompatibility which this would entail; promoting the creation and the establishment of trade electronic data interchange systems which meets the needs of the users, in particular small and medium-sized enterprises; increasing the awareness of the European telematic equipment and services industry to meet user's requirements in this area; and supporting the common use of

international and European standards, where these exist.

See TELECOMMUNICATIONS.

TEE *See* TRANS-EUROP-EXPRESS.

telecommunications No single Community country accounts for more than six percent of the world's telecommuncation market, whereas the United States represents 35 percent. Yet, taken as a whole, the Community has a 20 percent world market. Since 1983 the Community has built up a European telecommunications policy. Action taken includes:

- The 1984 adoption of the first action program;
- The 1984 and 1985 signing of cooperation agreements with the European Conference of Postal and Telecommunications Administrations (CEPT) and with the major European standardization bodies, CEN and Cenelec;
- Between the fall 1984 and the end of 1987, the adoption by the Council of Ministers of 12 directives, decisions, regulations or recommendations;
- The March 29, 1985, judgment of the European Court of Justice in the "British Telecom" case, of fundamental importance for opening up the market for high quality services; and
- The publication by the Commission in 1987 of the Green Paper on the Development of the Common Market for Telecommunications Services and Equipment that opened a broad debate on the adjustment and liberalization of this sector and gave rise to the first Telecommunications Council (1988) which gave strong support to the Green Paper.

The Commission's program provides for the full opening of the terminal equipment market to competition by the end of 1990; progressive opening of the telecommunications services market to competition from 1989 onwards, with all services other than telephone, telex, and data transmission to be opened by the end of 1989; full opening, by the end of 1989, of the market for receiving antennae for satellite broadcasts; progressive alignment of tariffs with costs; and a series of accompanying measures for standardization, including the creation of a European Standards Institute to accelerate development standards and technical specifications and ease certification.

In the spring of 1989, the Commission announced its intention to end postal and telephone monopolies by terminating their exclusive rights over the suppply of telecommunications services by 1991. In June 1989, the Commission adopted controversial legislation aimed at ending state monopolies in certain telecommunications services. The Commission ordered member states to liberalize their telecommunications operations under Article 90 of the Treaty of Rome. The plan forces member states to end national monopolies in computer communications, electronic mail, facsimile transmission and computerized banking and shopping services. At the same time, the Commission adopted a proposal allowing telecommunications equipment certified by one E.C. nation to be sold elsewhere in the Community. Sweden's Asea and Switzerland's Brown Boveri merged into a $17.8 billion electrical giant, and France's Compagnie Generale d'Electricite took control of ITT's telecommunication equipment business, allowing the firm to tie with American Telephone and Telegraph Company for the number one position in the world for telecommunication devices. To break the stalemate over the proposed measures, the E.C. competition commissioner in November 1989 urged consideration of some exceptions to the principle of a free-for-all competitive market. The providing of data-transmission and so-called quality network services would be opened to private operators and to transborder competition. Classic voice services and the facilities would remain in the hands of the big monopolies, most of which are state-owned. The proposal allows temporary exemptions for some nations if the government can prove that competition would put at risk its ability to provide basic services. The Commission also will consider whether national authorities can submit private telecommunications firms to a licensing system, provided that it is nondiscriminatory and not used to lessen competition.

See CADDIA; CHRONOLOGY (APRIL 28, 1988); EUROPEAN RADIO MESSAGING SYSTEM; EUROPEAN TELECOMMUNICATIONS STANDARDS; GREEN PAPER; OPEN NETWORK PROVISION; RACE; RADIO MESSAGING; STAR; TEDIS.

TELEMAN (télémanipulation) This is a $48 million Commission research program running from 1989 to 1993 that is designed to strengthen the scientific and engineering bases used for the design of nuclear remote-handling equipment. It will address basic problems associated with robotic type remote operations using computer assisted teleoperators with increasing degrees of autonomy, questions relating to teleoperation in nuclear environments, and the integration of disciplines that make up robotics. It will also invest most of its resources in the provision of generic building blocks for incorporation in a variety of specialized machines.

télémanipulation *See* TELEMAN.

telematics Since 1974 the European Commission has worked towards a Community policy for reducing existing constraints between member states, developing uniform standards and interoperability of devices, and rationalizing research and development. The Commission provides financial aid for projects that fit in with these objectives. Training, common standards, the establishment of data banks, and the creation of a multipurpose interinstitutional network linking Community industries and the capitals of member nations are Community strategies.

See EURONET DIANE; FINANCE; INDUSTRIAL POLICY; SCIENCE AND TECHNOLOGICAL COMMITTEE; TELECOMMUNICATIONS.

telephone, emergency *See* EMERGENCY TELEPHONE.

television In March 1989, the E.C. trade and industry ministers approved a plan setting a legal framework for television channels to be broadcast throughout the 12 nations. Under the plan, television channels can be broadcast anywhere in the E.C. provided they include a certain European content and meet quality and moral standards. The accord stipulates that E.C. governments should try, "where practical," to ensure that European programs make up a majority of transmissions. The agreement also asks the E.C. to seek ways to encourage local production of programs in countries with a weak production capacity or linguistic restraints. In addition, it calls on broadcasters to reserve, "where practical," at least 10 percent of transmissions for European programs made by independent producers. The United States and Canada have managed to take over 80 percent of the world's audiovisual market while sales of European programs account for only 5 percent of that market.

As of early 1990, the contest for the Pan-European television viewer appears to be between a cable-television service sending signals in many languages across the Continent and a satellite broadcaster that believes English will be the European market's chosen language. In 1979, in addition to government-owned channels, E.C. member states had 28 major commercial channels. In 1989, there were 56 and, by 1995, it is projected to be twice that many or perhaps 200. Estimates based on the passage of the broadcasting directive indicate that the E.C. market for programs will increase from approximately 250,000 hours per year in 1987 to some 400,000 hours per year in the 1990s.

See AUDIO-VISUAL POLICY; CHRONOLOGY (OCTOBER 3, 1989) IN APPENDIX; MEDIA; TECHNOLOGIES.

television without frontiers *See* AUDIO-VISUAL POLICY.

TEMPUS (Trans-European Mobility Scheme for University Studies) A January 1990 Community proposal to provide support for Joint European Projects linking universities and/or enterprises in Central and Eastern European countries with partners in the E.C. The Council of Ministers proposed the establishment of this program to enable the participation of Central and Eastern Europe in education and training programs similar to existing Community programs.

Ten, The The original Six E.E.C. nations plus the Four countries signing the Treaty of Accession would have made up The Ten. Norway failed to sign and it became The Nine.

10–4 *See* TRANSPORT.

tendering rules *See* PUBLIC PROCUREMENT.

territoriality A principle drawing from the application of national law concerning intellectual, industrial, and commercial property does not, in general terms, allow the partitioning of markets within the E.C.

terrorism A pact aimed at fighting international terrorism was signed by E.C. justice ministers in Dublin in December 1979. It states that acts of violence such as kidnapping or airplane hijackings will not be treated as political offenses, and specifies that member states will either prosecute or extradite persons suspected of such actions. The pact eliminated the concept of political asylum or immunity from the legal systems of the signatories. It went into effect in 1981.

testing *See* PRODUCT TESTING.

tests *See* STANDARDS.

textiles The Community's concern with foreign imports led to the first MultiFibre Arrangement (MFA) under the General Agreement on Tariffs and Trade which became effective on January 1, 1974. Its purpose is to extend trade in the textile and clothing industry, to lower barriers, and to stimulate the progressive liberalization of global trade in an systematic and equitable fashion, thereby avoiding the disruption of individual markets and individual lines of manufacture in importing and exporting nations. The extension of the MFA proposed the elimination of an overall import ceiling and differentiation between suppliers, so that imports would be stabilized at stated levels based on the degree of a nation's economic strength, offering the least developed countries more opportunities for export to the Community market.

See COMPETITION POLICY; EXTERNAL TRADE; MULTIFIBRE ARRANGEMENTS.

Thailand In December 1977 Thailand concluded an agreement with the Community on trade in textiles. It is a member of the Association of South East Asian Nations (ASEAN), which concluded a cooperation agreement with the Community in December 1979. In November 1980, the E.C. signed an accord in Bangkok on shipments of Thai manioc (a starchy edible root), where Thailand agreed to gradually reduce its exports of manioc to the Community, contingent on assurances that the reduction would not be replaced by shipments from other Asian countries. The E.C. urged this accord because manioc is used as a cereal substitute, and a grain surplus already existed in the Community.

See ASSOCIATION OF SOUTH EAST ASIAN NATIONS; PACIFIC RIM.

THERMIE (European Technologies for Energy Management) In March 1989, a Council regulation was proposed concerning the promotion of energy technology in Europe. This program covers the areas of energy efficiency, renewable energy sources, the clean use of coal, and oil and gas exploration and development. The proposed program will fund three types of projects (innovation, dissemination, and targeted) and actively diffuse their results to facilitate the repetition of successful projects.

See ENERGY; SPRINT.

THESAURI *See* DATABASES AND DATABANKS OF THE E.C.

third-party financing This vendor financing consists of energy equipment vendors either financing the purchase of their equipment in exchange for a share of future energy cost savings, or underwriting the cost for the purchaser by contractually guaranteeing a level of savings.

Synonymous with ENERGY SERVICE COMPANY FINANCING.

third world Three billion people in underdeveloped or developing countries have an annual income that is lower than the monthly income of people in industrialized nations. The Community's financial aid in the development field represents about 13 percent of the combined efforts of member states, with India the single largest beneficiary. Community policies are to grant generalized preferences, compensation for loss of export earnings, food aid, emergency aid, aid to nongovernmental organizations, and financial and technical cooperation. There is cooperation with all 66 ACP signatories of the 1988 Lomé Convention, agreements with eight Mediterranean nations, and agreements with Latin America and Asia.

See ACP (STATES); GENERALIZED SYSTEM OF PREFERENCES; LESS DEVELOPED COUNTRIES; LOMÉ CONVENTIONS; MEDITERRANEAN POLICY.

Three, The They consist of those nations ratifying the Treaty of Accession: Denmark, the Irish Republic, and the United Kingdom.

three-tier tariff *See* TWO-TIER TARIFF.

three wise men *See* CHRONOLOGY (DECEMBER 4–5, 1978; NOVEMBER 29, 1979).

threshold price This is the minimum import price at which milk items, cereals, and sugar from non-Community nations can be accepted at Community ports. It differs from the target price in that the transport costs are added from the port to the inland destination. Should import prices drop below the threshold price, the difference is secured by agricultural levies.

See AGRICULTURE, COMMON AGRICULTURAL POLICY; BASIC PRICE; GUIDE PRICE; INTERVENTION PRICE; REFERENCE PRICE; SLUICE GATE PRICE; TARGET PRICE.

Tindemans Report At the Paris summit conference in December 1974, the Prime Minister of Belgium Leo Tindemans submitted a comprehensive report on an overall concept of European Union.

See CHRONOLOGY (DECEMBER 9–10, 1974; DECEMBER 29, 1975; NOVEMBER 29 AND 30, 1976).

TIR (Transport International Rontier) This is a carnet customs document issued to international vehicle operators permitting loaded vehicles to cross international borders with minimum formalities.

tires *See* VEHICLES.

tobacco There is a common system of marketing and intervention when the price drops to 80–90 percent of the target price. Excise duties on cigarettes have been harmonized since 1973.

In June 1989, the Commission adopted a proposal for a directive to harmonize member state legislation on tobacco advertising by the end of 1992. It seeks to inform smokers of the risks involved, and to harmonize legislation concerning printed tobacco advertising. In November 1989, the E.C.'s health ministers set limits on the tar content of cigarettes and agreed to impose tough health warnings on all cigarette packs sold in the 12 member states.

A timetable was established for cutting tar per cigarette to 15 milligrams by 1992 and 12 milligrams by 1997 (some French cigarettes, among the strongest sold in the E.C., yield 22.8 milligrams). All packaged cigarettes sold in the E.C. will have to carry specific health warnings beginning on January 1, 1993. The packs will have to carry a general warning: "Tobacco seriously damages health," in addition to specific ones, like: "Smoking causes cancer," "Smoking causes fatal diseases," and "Pregnant women, smoking harms your baby." The new law specified that the warning must cover at least four percent of the package in countries with one official language. If two official languages exist, six percent of the surface must be covered and if three exist, eight percent must be covered. Tar and nicotine levels must also be clearly indicated on the packages. Some 600 billion cigarettes are sold each year in the E.C.

In October 1989, the E.C. approved a directive prohibiting all tobacco ads on TV after October 1991. In May 1990, the E.C. agreed to cut the tar content of cigarettes and moved toward banning some forms of tobacco advertising in all its member states. Britain and West Germany blocked an E.C. bill restricting tobacco ads in the press and on the billboards (a ban on television tobacco advertising already exists in all member states). The health ministers agreed to reduce the maximum tar yield permitted in cigarettes to 15 milligrams by the end of the year 1992 and 12 milligrams a year later, all down from 1990 current levels ranging from 15 to 20 milligrams. Greece would not have to meet the standards until 2004 under a special arrangement intended to give its tobacco growers time to adapt.

See COMMON AGRICULTURAL POLICY; EXCISE DUTIES.

Togo This nation is one of the ACP states and a signatory to the Yaoundé Conventions of 1963 and 1969 and to the Lomé Convention of 1988.

Tokyo Round This was a ministerial meeting of GATT held in Tokyo in September 1973. It initiated the process of securing an agreement on a new set of tariff cuts and other barriers to world trade. Negotiators pre-sented a number of propositions aimed at working out a code of conduct for government purchases among the participating nations, designed to grant favored treatment to developing countries without seeking reciprocal concessions. Other codes included customs valuation, norms and standards, and import licensing practices.

See CHRONOLOGY (SEPTEMBER 12, 1973; DECEMBER 17, 1979); KENNEDY ROUND; MADRID MEETING; MONTREAL ROUND; URUGUAY ROUND.

Tonga Tonga is one of the ACP states and a signatory to the Lomé Convention of 1988.

Torkay Round *See* GENERAL AGREEMENT ON TARIFFS AND TRADE.

tourism In 1985, about 56 percent of Community citizens went on a vacation at least once during the year, with 20 percent going to another Community country. Fifty-two percent went to the sea, 25 percent to the countryside, 23 percent to the moutains and 19 percent to towns and cities. Sixty-eight percent used a car, 14 percent went by train, 13 percent by airplane, and 5 percent by boat. 32 percent stayed at hotels, 21 percent with relatives or friends, 17 percent rented accommodations, 16 percent went camping or caravanning, 7 percent went to their holiday homes, and 5 percent lodged in private houses. Tourism is a prime economic sector, representing about 5.5 percent of the gross domestic product of the Community and 8 percent of private consumption. The Commission's policy on tourism is based on a communication submitted to the Council of Ministers in January 1986. The main themes of Community action to assist tourism in the Community are to improve the seasonal and geographical distribution of tourism, to make better use of financial aid, to improve information and protection for tourists, to improve working conditions in the tourist industry, and to increase the awareness of the sector with further consultation and cooperation.

In 1988, the E.C. Commission proposed regulations for package tour operations in the E.C. nations that would give 150 million tourists better protection, leaving member states at liberty to maintain more stringent rules. The proposal covers not only package vacations per se, but also other forms of package travel, which can be defined as including any combination of travel to and from the holidaymaker's destination, accommodation, meals, excursions, and other services. The Commission expects these rules to be implemented no later than the end of 1990, the "European Tourism Year." A unified market after 1992 will encourage tour operators to sell across borders. More important, their charter airlines will be allowed to pick up passengers anywhere in the 12-country E.C. for the first time. To get ready, the E.C.s vacation packagers are rushing to cut costs and build strategic alliances. A Charter of Tourism Rights is being developed so that the tourist will be better able to compare accurately what all nations offer.

The E.C.'s tourism program for the 1990s contains four elements: improving the quality of services offered by European tourism; promoting European tourism; improving the environment in which firms in the tourism sector operate; and enhancing cooperation between the E.C. and third world countries. Starting January 1, 1993, travelers within the E.C. who book package vacations will be better protected should something go wrong, including giving them the option to withdraw bookings if the price increased before their departure date. There also would be more efficient procedures for refunds and transportation home for E.C. tourists if a travel company were to go out of business while the tourists were on their vacation.

toxic effluent A May 4, 1976, directive attempts to halt the deterioration of the aquatic environment by banning or significantly restricting present and future discharges of harmful substances into rivers, estuaries, or coastal waters. The directive set water quality standards, limiting the amounts that are permitted in rivers or seas for the most dangerous substances (mercury, cadmium, DDT) named in a black-list, with a gray-list (arsenic, lead, copper, plastics) containing less-damaging pollutants.

Two 1973 directives require harmonization of national laws governing the production of detergents and the methods for determining their nonsolvent substances.

See DANGEROUS SUBSTANCES, ENVIRON-

MENT; HARMONIZATION; MARINE POLLUTION; WASTE OILS; WATER.

toxic waste The E.C. Council of Ministers on November 25, 1988, adopted a resolution urging other nations to pass stringent rules on the exports of toxic wastes. In the summer of 1989, the E.C. proposed that producers of toxic waste in Europe could be made liable for damages. The proposal would make companies responsible for damages caused by their waste.

toys In June 1980, the European Commission presented a draft directive for harmonizing safety standards and manufacturers' obligations in the Community to ensure safe children's toys and to remove trade barriers. In September 1982, the European Parliament called for a crackdown on the sale and advertising of war toys because they may represent a physical danger to children and are frequently used as replica weapons in criminal actions. In 1983, the E.C. Commission declared war on ill-made or otherwise dangerous toys that pose a serious health and safety threat to Europe's youngest consumers, requiring member states to subject toys to rigorous tests in approved laboratories. A directive requires warnings to appear on certain types of toys.

See CONSUMER PROTECTION; HARMONIZATION; NON-TARIFF BARRIERS TO TRADE.

tractors and agricultural machinery Without Community-wide harmonized procedures, differing national product regulations and standards prevent the centralization and profitability of the farm machinery section. Proposals to be in place by 1992 include harmonizing technical requirements throughout the Community and ensuring recognition of a single type test. The Commission has the power to update the technical requirements as changes in tractor design and manufacture take place, including the specific area of front-mounted rollover protective structures. Harmonization of Community requirements for these structures is important, both for health and safety considerations, and to ensure that differing national requirements do not constitute barriers to a single Community market in tractors.

See HARMONIZATION, VEHICLES.

Trade Electronic Data Interchange Systems *See* TEDIS.

164

trade fairs More than 700 trade fairs are held each year in the E.C. They are either horizontal, those featuring a diverse range of products and services such as in the Milan Fair; or vertical, those which specialize in a particular industry, such as computers or dental equipment. European fairs provide American firms with access to a $2.4 trillion market which buys roughly $78 billion in U.S. goods and services each year. The most familiar fairs are: the Paris Air Show, showing the latest in aerospace technology; the Hannover Fair, considered to be the world's largest international industrial show; The International Spring Gift Fair at Birmingham, England, England's largest consumer-goods trade exhibition.

trademarks In 1976 the Commission said, "It is clearly in the interest of manufacturers, distributors and consumer[s] in the Common Market that a Community trademark should be created enjoying protection on a uniform basis throughout the E.E.C. territory." There are more than two million trademarks at present in use in the Community, governed by many different systems of law. By 1992, a Community trademark will be applicable throughout the Community. This will remove the current requirement to make separate applications for trademarks in each member state and will ensure that registered trademarks enjoy uniform protection under the legal system of all the member states. A Community Trademark Office will be responsible for registering such actions for a period of ten years from the date of filing, renewable for a further ten years.

See COMMUNITY TRADEMARK, INDUSTRIAL COOPERATION, INTELLECTUAL PROPERTY.

trade surplus The E.C. recorded its first-ever trade surplus in 1986, the result of a steeper fall in the value of imports (down 17 percent) than of exports (down 10 percent), showing a trade surplus of 5 billion ECU (about $5.5 billion).

trade unions Union cooperation is organized via the three major Internationals: the Democratic International Confederation of Free Trade Unions, the Communist-directed World Federation of Trade Unions, and the World Confederation of Labor.

trailers *See* VEHICLES.

train system Construction of a 19,000 mile upgraded, high-speed train system is in progress. The system is expected to cost at least $100 billion and take a quarter of a century to complete, with high-technology trains reaching speeds as high as 185 miles per hour. The Community of European Railways has pooled the interests of 14 Western European railroad firms with the E.C. assisting by subsidizing links where the train may not be profitable. The first phase of the train project is scheduled to be completed by 1995, adding 7,700 miles of high-speed or upgraded track. Including the Channel tunnel and the trains, the cost will be about $60 billion.

See RAILWAYS, TRANSPORT.

Trans-Europ-Express (TEE) Connects major cities in nine European nations by a network of rapid and comfortable trains for which frontier formalities have been lowered to a minimum.

Trans-European Mobility Scheme for University Studies *See* TEMPUS.

transitional period Some of the Treaty of Rome provisions were applied in stages covering several years. Transitional periods were also adapted for new member nations.

transit procedure As a major step towards achieving free movement of goods, a 1987 regulation abolishes the requirement for a guarantee of payment of duties and fiscal charges arising from internal transit operations within the Community. However, it does not apply to high-value goods (those valued in excess of 50,000 ECU) or those subject to high duties or charges. Operators must meet certain conditions to be eligible for a waiver to reduce the risk of incurred charges not being paid. A guarantee waiver may be granted to operators who are regular users and reside in the member state where the waiver is granted. They must be in a healthy financial position, not guilty of any serious infringement of customs or fiscal laws; they must undertake to pay on demand any claims made upon them in respect of their transit operations as soon as possible.

Under present E.C. arrangements, an operator shipping goods must produce a document when goods cross frontiers between member nations, so that any irregularities can be determined. The Commission proposed that this rule by abolished in 1990 and that measures to recover sums due in the case of irregularities be accepted. Because operators presently lodge more than 10 million transit notices a year in the E.C., their abolition will substantially aid the flow of traffic across frontiers.

See CONTROL OF GOODS.

transport The Treaty of Rome demands the creation of a Community common transport policy. Transport represents more than seven percent of the Community GNP. The Community has adopted a two-phase approach applicable to the main transport sectors: road, sea, and air. In the first phase, the objective is to liberalize transport services *between* member states. In the second phase, to be completed by 1992, the objective is to liberalize transport *within* member states by opening up the national markets to nonresident carriers.

Measures in the road transport sector include giving nonresident carriers the freedom to supply goods and passenger transport services within member states while quotas for the international carriage of goods will be phased out. After 20 years of debate, member states have agreed as of July 1, 1990, to distribute a limited number of two-month permits for their national haulers to conduct "cabotage"—the transport of goods within an E.C. nation by a carrier from another. At first there will be a total of 15,000 permits available, increasing by 10 percent each year. This means, for example, that a Dutch transport firm could apply for a permit to haul goods from Rome to Milan. The current ban on cabotage precludes the Dutch transporter who delivers a load in Rome from picking up a new load to drop off in Milan on the return trip. In the inland waterways sector, international transport of goods and passengers will be liberalized and conditions will be established for nonresident carriers to operate services within member states. In the maritime transport sector, member state shipping companies will be free from restrictions on the supply of services between ports within member states and between member states and

third countries. In the air transport sector, increeased competition in services and fares will be introduced while the rights of governments to restrict capacity and access to markets will be limited.

See CHRONOLOGY (SEPTEMBER 16, 1982; MAY 22, 1985); RAILWAYS; SHIPPING REGISTER; TRAIN SYSTEM.

Transport International Rontier See TIR.

traveler's allowances In 1989, the Commission adopted a proposal to substantially increase traveler's allowances from the current 390 ECU to 800 ECU by January 1990, to 1,200 ECU by 1991, and to 1,600 ECU in 1992. Limits will be abolished after January 1993, thereby eliminating any fixed amount of currency brought into another E.C. state.

travelers checks In 1986, Luxembourg issued travelers checks denominated in European Currency Units.

Treaty of Accession This major Treaty was signed on January 22, 1972, by the six members of the Community and Denmark, Ireland, Norway, and the United Kingdom, marking the Communities first enlargement. Norway eventually withdrew and the remaining nine states acceded to the Treaty of Paris and the Treaty of Rome. Denmark, Ireland and the U.K. joined the Community on January 1, 1973. The Greek Treaty of Accession was signed on May 23, 1979, and Greece joined the Community on January 1, 1981. Spain and Portugal applied for membership in 1977 and joined the Community on January 1, 1986.

See EUROPEAN COMMUNITY; GREECE; PORTUGAL; SPAIN; TREATY OF PARIS.

Synonymous with TREATY OF BRUSSELS.

Treaty of Brussels *Synonymous with* TREATY OF ACCESSION.

Treaty of Friendship and Cooperation See CHRONOLOGY (JANUARY 22, 1963) IN APPENDIX.

Treaty of Paris In 1951, this Treaty established the European Coal and Steel Community, the first of the Community institutions. The founder members were Belgium, France, Italy, Luxembourg, the

Netherlands, and the Federal Republic of Germany. Its purpose was to transfer control of the basic materials of war (coal and steel) from individual governments to the E.C.S.C. High Authority.

See EUROPEAN COMMUNITY; INDUSTRIAL POLICY; TREATY OF ROME.

Treaty of Rome On March 25, 1957, two Treaties were signed in Rome. They established the European Economic Community and the European Atomic Energy Community. Its founder members were Belgium, France, Italy, Luxembourg, the Netherlands and the Federal Republic of Germany. The Treaties established the constitutions and tasks of the Communities. The Treaty of Rome has been amended several times.

See EUROPEAN COMMUNITY; INDUSTRIAL POLICY; MERGER TREATY; TREATY OF ACCESSION; TREATY OF PARIS.

Trevi Group *See* DRUG TRAFFICKING.

Trinidad and Tobago Together they formed one of the ACP states and are a signatory to the Lomé Convention of 1988. A protocol annexed to the Convention guarantees the country's sugar exports to the Community.

See CARIBBEAN BASIN; SUGAR.

Tripartite Conference The annual meeting between the Council of Ministers and workers' and employers' organizations seeks to provide a platform for direct contact with Community policy-making on issues of common interest or concern.

See EUROPEAN COMMUNITY.

truck industry Deregulation scheduled for 1993 will radically affect truckers and truck builders. Prohibitions on backhauling will end. Delays for customs inspections will cease because borders will be open, and new shipping hubs will speed service. Such changes will make 30 percent of the E.C. member nations' truck fleets redundant. Most of the larger builders of trucks are merging or forming joint venture partnership with other makers. It is projected that there will be a 10 percent decline in overall demand for new heavy trucks in Europe by 1992.

New heavy diesel trucks sold in the E.C. will have to be 60 percent cleaner by 1997 under a two-stage 1990 plan. Diesel trucks emit 10 times more pollution than other forms of transport. If passed by the Council, the projected standards would be the world's toughest. Emissions would be reduced first by 40 percent, then by 60 percent from the maximum permitted levels set in 1988. First-stage reductions would enter into force for new models on July 1, 1992, and for all new trucks on December 31, 1992. Second-phase cuts would take effect on October 31, 1996, and a year later for all new trucks.

See CAR INDUSTRY; TRANSPORT; VEHICLES.

trucking reform *See* TRANSPORT.

tuberculosis *See* ANIMAL HEALTH AND MEAT INSPECTION.

Tunisia This nation has a cooperation agreement with the Community. It provides free access to the Community market for industrial items and preferential treatment for agricultural products (July 1, 1976).

See MAGHREB AGREEMENT; MEDITERRANEAN POLICY; MNCs.

tunnel *See* EUROPEAN MONETARY UNION; SNAKE.

Turkey This nation signed an association agreement with the E.E.C. on September 12, 1963. The agreement eliminates duties on imports from the E.E.C. according to two timetables—one of twelve years ending in 1985 and one of twenty-two years ending in 1995. Turkey officially requested accession to the Community in April 1987, with the E.C. Commission opening contacts on December 8, 1987.

Tuvalu (formerly Ellice Islands) These islands are one of the ACP states and a signatory to the Lomé Convention of 1988.

twinning Solidarity between citizens of member states and mutual understanding and cooperation has been widely promoted and facilitated by the twinning of towns and cities. It was proposed that the E.C. encourage such measures without usurping local authorities by creating favorable conditions, including providing more information, for their development. The proposal stressed the need for twinnings to be organized between towns or cities with similar features. Participation by all segments of the population should be encouraged. Schools, in particular, should be urged to take part.

two-tier tariff This consists of two sets of rates for the same items in the tariff. The United Kingdom has a full rate for non-Commonwealth nations, and a preferential crate for the Commonwealth. When it was an EFTA member, the U.K. had a three-tier tariff.

See INDUSTRIAL COOPERATION.

typewriters *See* COMPUTERS.

U

UA *See* UNITS OF ACCOUNT.

UCITS (The Collective Investment in Transferable Securities) *See* SECURITIES.

Uganda This nation is one of the ACP states and a signatory to the Lomé Convention of 1988. A protocol annexed to the Convention guarantees the country's sugar exports to the Community.
See ARUSHA CONVENTION, SUGAR.

UK (U.K.) *See* UNITED KINGDOM.

UN The United Nations.

UNCTAD The United Nations Conference on Trade and Development. It was established in 1964 and deals with the fundamental problems affecting the trade of developing nations. It is headquartered in Geneva.

Underdeveloped countries *See* LESS DEVELOPED COUNTRIES, THIRD WORLD.

unemployment In November 1988, there were 15.4 million registered unemployed in the Community, of whom 33.5 percent were under 25 years of age. The unemployment rate in the 12-nation E.C. for the period January–August 1989 was 9.2 percent. The unemployment rate fell to a seasonablly adjusted 8.9 percent in November 1989, down from 9.7 percent in 1988.

UNICE (Union des Industries de la Communauté Européenne) *See* CONFEDERATION OF INDUSTRIES OF THE EUROPEAN COMMUNITY.

unification This is similar to integration but without necessarily involving the creation of common administrative control. It implies total fusion at all essential levels.
Cf. UNITY.

Union des Industries de la Communauté Européenne (UNICE) *See* CONFEDERATION OF INDUSTRIES OF THE EUROPEAN COMMUNITY.

Union of Soviet Socialist Republics (USSR) This nation is a founder member of the Council for Mutual Economic Assistance (COMECON). It first attempted to negotiate with the E.C. through COMECON in 1974. In 1988, Soviet trade with the E.C. amounted to $22.7 billion and with the United States, $3.4 billion. In May 1989, after the two parties established diplomatic ties for the first time, the E.C. proposed a 10-year trade and economic cooperation agreement with the Soviet Union. The E.C. Commission offered to scrap import quotas on some Soviet goods and to increase cooperation in science, technology, transport, energy, and the environment. In return, the E.C. wants better access for its businesses to the Soviet market. On November 27, 1989, the Soviet Union and the E.C. reached agreement on a 10-year trade pact that would ease European quotas for Soviet goods and increase technical cooperation. The agreement also provides for cooperation in numerous areas, including food processing, tourism, banking, insurance, oil and gas, and nuclear energy. The accord was signed by the parties on December 18, 1989. The pact stops short of granting the Soviet Union most-favored-nation status. Foreign Minister Shevardnadze sees this as a step toward a Common European House. This concept was first broached by President Gorbachev in a visit to France in 1985 and reiterated on November 29, 1989, when he called for Russia's admission to the technological and economic activities of the Western industrial nations. In June 1990, the E.C. heads of government, meeting in Dublin, agreed to design a major aid program for the Soviet Union to overcome its deepening economic crisis. The leaders declined to set any specific levels of aid, deciding to wait until two detailed studies on problems in the Soviet economy are completed. The first study would address short-term financing strains, such as the growing payments crisis. The second would attempt to identify ways the West can help the Soviets move away from a centrally planned economy and develop a more efficient and market-oriented economic infrastructure.

See CHRONOLOGY (JANUARY 15–16, 1987; MAY 1989); COUNCIL FOR MUTUAL ECONOMIC ASSISTANCE; EASTERN EUROPE.

United Arab Emirates, The *See* GULF CO-OPERATION COUNCIL.

United Kingdom (U.K.) This nation became a founder member of the European Free Trade Association on November 20, 1959. The U.K. joined the European Community on January 1, 1973, with a five-year transitional period. The decade of the 1980s have been years of economic growth for the United Kingdom. The top rate of income tax was cut to 40 percent, the basic rate was lowered to 25 percent and capital taxes were overhauled. Investment by the English in the E.C. and in the United States has been expanding rapidly, while at the same time, Japanese and American companies have built facilities and plants in the United Kingdom, increasing both employment and the flow of foreign currencies into the country. The Government continues to resist the concept of a single currency and a central bank.

United Nations Development Program. *See* INTERNATIONAL BANK FOR RECONSTRUCTION AND DEVELOPMENT.

United States of America (U.S.) The Community has had a relationship with the United States since 1958 through an agreement with the European Atomic Energy Community, for cooperation on the peaceful uses of atomic energy, and through a 1977 agreement dealing with fisheries off the U.S. coast. The E.C. delegation is represented in the United States in Washington, D.C., and New York City.

The United States is the E.C.'s largest trading partner, and exports and imports between the two account for 36 percent of world trade

and 60 percent of trade between industrialized countries. In 1987, U.S.-E.C. trade totaled $145 billion. Direct investment in each other's markets is estimated at $280 billion, and portfolio investment is even higher. In the late 1960s, United States direct investment in Europe peaked, accounting for 60 percent of total direct investments in the E.C. By the mid-1970s, the United States share of direct investment had fallen to about 30 percent.

The E.C.'s single market program will significantly affect U.S. business through new product standards, new laws and business regulations, stronger growth, and stiffer competition. U.S. exports of goods and services to the E.C. are eight times greater than they were in 1970, climbing from 19 percent of overall U.S. exports to 24 percent. U.S. direct investment in Europe jumped from 15 percent to 40 percent of overall U.S. direct investment abroad. Sales of U.S. subsidiaries in the Community exceed $300 billion annually. In 1987, U.S. exports and imports from the 12 member nations were:

	U.S. exports to E.C. (f.a.s. $ billion)*	U.S. imports from E.C. (c.i.f. $ billion)*
E.C.	60.6	84.9
Belgium-Luxembourg	6.2	4.4
Denmark	0.9	1.9
France	7.9	11.2
Germany	11.9	28.0
Greece	0.4	0.5
Ireland	1.8	1.2
Italy	5.5	11.7
Netherlands	8.2	4.2
Portugal	0.6	0.7
Spain	3.1	3.1
United Kingdom	14.1	18.0

*f.a.s. = free along-side ship, c.i.f. = cost, insurance, and freight.
Source: U.S. Department of Commerce

Five principles are key to Washington's support for the E.C.'s 1992 legislation:

(1) The United States, and other countries, must be given the same open-market opportunities as E.C. nations.

(2) 1992 must reduce existing E.C. protectionism, not convert national barriers into community ones.

(3) Harmonization of technical standards

should be at the most liberal, not the most restrictive, existing national level.

(4) E.C. decision-making should be open; and

(5) Decisions implementing the 1992 program should conform with the multilateral approaches developed in the GATT Round.

The United States is concerned about attempts to apply to foreign investors or exporters the notion of reciprocity, or equivalent access, which would move away from the principle of national treatment. A second issue of concern is recent E.C. action on rules of origin, which are used to define the nationality of a product in dumping cases. Restrictive regulations of origin have the potential to harm U.S. export interests, divert trade from third nations to the E.C. market, or induce investment in the E.C. on noncommercial grounds. In addition, the United States is concerned about the system of quotas or local content requirements. Lastly, standards, certification, and the testing process is an issue of concern. In mid-December 1989, the United States and the E.C. announced that they would begin working in 1990 to formalize a special relationship. It would be an official U.S. consultative role in the E.C., short of membership but closer than that of a trading partner, with periodic meetings of U.S. cabinet members and representatives of the Community.

Units of Account (European Units of Account) (EUA) (UA) These are the financial instruments of the E.C. They are independent of national currencies but linked to them by conversion rates, enabling single common prices to be set for the whole of the Community. Until 1971, it had a gold-based value equivalent to 0.88867088 grams of fine gold. Afterwards such conversions had no relation to the real value of national currencies in the world financial market. The Community developed a new unit—the European Unit of Account (EUA) defined in terms of a "basket" of currencies of the member nations. It varies daily in any one national currency based on movements in all the involved exchange rates. It is used for all Community activities, except the Common Agricultural Policy where the payments retain, in theory, the gold-parity

UA conversion rate, but this is offset by green currencies and monetary compensation amounts to bring currencies into line with the financial market exchange rate. Replaced in March 1979 by the European Currency Unit.

See AGRICULTURE, COMMON AGRICULTURAL POLICY; EUROPEAN CURRENCY UNIT; EUROPEAN MONETARY SYSTEM.

unit trusts In 1976, the Commission proposal on coordinating laws regarding "collective investment undertakings for transferable securities" (CIUTS) was enacted. It regulates the organization and activities of CIUTS, their investment policy, and the information to be freely circulated. Its goal is to provide more uniform safeguards for all savers.

See COMPANY LAW.

unity The ultimate goal of unification. It implies a single governmental and administrative system, and full integration at higher levels.

cf. UNIFICATION.

University Institute, European *See* EUROPEAN UNIVERSITY INSTITUTE.

university research The Commission provides annually a limited number of research grants to young university faculty at the beginning of their careers to carry out research on European integration.

See EDUCATION GRANTS, EUROPEAN UNIVERSITY INSTITUTE, FINANCE, RESEARCH.

Upper Volta Upper Volta is one of the ACP states and a signatory to the Yaoundé Conventions of 1963 and 1969 and of the Lomé Convention of 1988.

Uranium Enrichment, Standing Committee on On May 22, 1973, the Council of Ministers established this Committee as one of the first steps towards establishing a European enrichment plant to cover the requirements of the E.C. It makes up-to-date market surveys on enriched uranium, and examines ways to promote the development of the necessary industrial capacities in the Community and facilitates coordination of measures initiated by member states.

Uruguay This nation has an agreement with the Community on trade in textiles and handmade items.

See LAFTA, LATIN AMERICA.

Uruguay Round On April 8, 1989, 105 nations agreed on greater liberalization of trade in goods and agriculture, as well as extending the General Agreement on Tariffs and Trade's authority to such new areas as trade in services and trade-related intellectual property rights. This marked the halfway point to the scheduled completion of the Round—the GATT seventh—at the end of 1990.

See CHRONOLOGY (APRIL 8, 1989) IN APPENDIX; MADRID MEETING; MONTREAL ROUND.

U.S. (U.S.A.) *See* UNITED STATES OF AMERICA.

U.S.S.R. *See* UNION OF SOVIET SOCIALIST REPUBLICS.

V

vacations *See* TOURISM.

VALOREN A 1986 E.C. research program to improve the economic base of disadvantaged regions of the Community by improving the supply of energy at the local level. VALOREN includes three areas of emphasis: use of local energy resources, the rational use of energy in small and medium-sized enterprises, and the promotion and better use of energy potential at local and regional levels. VALOREN works with capital subventions or interest grants for loans. The beneficiaries are mainly governments and regional bodies.

See ENERGY.

Valorisation and Utilization for Europe *See* VALUE.

VALUE A 1989 E.C. research program to promote the dissemination and utilization of the results of scientific and technical research. It will give special consideration to the needs of small and medium-sized enterprises as regards technical information and support, and promote a common network for computer communications.

See COMPUTERS.

value-added network services *See* TELE-COMMUNICATIONS.

Value Added Tax (VAT) This is a turnover or consumption tax payable on items and services from the activities of a business organization. All Community nations operate a VAT although the rates vary significantly from one nation to another, with France having the highest rate. The VAT assists firms operating within the common market and provides the basis for assessing the VAT element of the "own resources" system for financing the Community budget. The first directive (1967) set the principle of harmonization of legislation concerning turnover taxes. The second directive (1967) identified the structures and procedures for application. A 1970 decision introduced the "own resources" system of financing the budget, including a VAT structure. Another directive (1979) dealt with refunding of VAT to firms operating in a Community nation other than the one in which items and services have been invoiced inclusive of taxes.

An inevitable prerequisite for the abolition of frontier controls by 1992 within intra-Community trade is the termination of the present system under which exported goods are relieved of Value Added Tax and imported goods are subject to it.

The Commission proposed in May 1989 that the E.C. would set a minimum Value Added Tax rate for its member countries of "slightly above" 14 percent, with a rate of between 4 and 9 percent applying to such essentials as food and clothing. In October 1989, E.C. finance ministers agreed in principle to remove border checks on the shipment of goods subject to VAT. They agreed that VAT would continue to be levied in the nation where the items are sold to the consumer and at that state's rate. Checks to make certain that the VAT is paid following export no longer would be required at the border, but to avoid fraud both the seller and purchaser would have to declare the transaction to authorities.

A Value Added Tax Clearing House is envisioned by 1992. In addition, a uniform Value Added Tax after 1992 is expected to make duty-free shopping obsolete for travelers between the 12 E.C. member states, amounting to a loss of $2 billion a year in sales.

In the spring of 1990, the Commission proposed to eliminate border checks for VAT purposes as of January 1, 1993. If passed by the Council of Ministers, VAT would still be charged on goods at the point of consumption rather than at the good's origin. However, instead of routine border checks and the accompanying Single Administrative Document, the proposed system would rely on periodic VAT declaration forms and invoices provided by firms. Except for trade with non-E.C. states, the SAD would be abolished. After 1992 only some 20 percent of the Community's largest traders would have to complete a periodic form requiring 10 pieces of statistical information. The vast majority of firms would have only to supply monthly information on their total intra-Community imports and exports. Individual consumers would be able to purchase goods in the E.C. state of their choice after 1992, paying that member state's VAT rate, without any controls or tax payments at borders. There would be two exemptions, passenger vehicles (cars and motorcycles) and mail-order sales. These would be taxes at the purchaser's home country rate. This interim solution would expire after a four-year transition period, December 31, 1996, at the latest.

See BUDGET, CONTROL OF GOODS; CONTROL OF INDIVIDUALS; DEROGATIONS; EUROPE WITHOUT FRONTIERS; EXCISE DUTIES; FINANCE; FRONTIER BARRIERS; VALUE ADDED TAX EXEMPTION.

value added tax exemption This is a 1988 proposal for a Council directive regarding exemption from Value Added Tax on the final importation of certain goods. The objective is to amend the system of VAT exemption in favor of imports so as to be consistent with certain customs exemptions and in order to introduce specific intra-Community exemptions.

See CONTROL OF INDIVIDUALS; VALUE ADDED TAX.

Vanuatu (formerly New Hebrides) This nation is one of the ACP states and a signatory to the Lomé Convention of 1988.

variable import levy This is a charge levied on certain agricultural items, e.g., some cereals, which is varied so as to raise the price of imports into the Community broadly to the price level that the E.C. desires to maintain. During the transitional stage before completion of the internal market such levies are applied to trade between member states so that Community suppliers will enjoy a preference over other sources of supply. The in-

tra-E.C. levies will be eliminated when the full Common Market stage is reached.

Varoni Plan This was a 10-year plan for industrial expansion in Italy and a protocol of the Treaty of Rome stipulated that this plan should be taken into account in the policy of the E.E.C.

VAT *See* VALUE ADDED TAX.

Vatican City State Although not a member of the Community, in November 1970, the first Papal Nuncio was sent as ambassador to the Community. Monsignor Igino Cardinale was named as the Vatican's special envoy with the functions of permanent observer. All other Vatican representatives are permanent observers or delegates to international organizations.

Vedel Report An April 1972 E.E.C. Commission report advocating a change in the role and power of the European Parliament. Georges Vedel was Professor of Law at the University of Paris and President of an independent commission of the E.E.C. that prepared this study.

vegetables *See* FRUIT AND VEGETABLES, PLANT HEALTH CONTROLS.

vehicle fuel A 1985 directive was passed dealing with the standardization of provisions regarding the duty-free admission of fuel contained in the fuel tanks of commercial motor vehicles. It increased the duty-free fuel allowance of commercial vehicles crossing common frontiers between member states to 600 litres in the case of passenger vehicles and 200 litres in the case of goods vehicles. This will remove controls on ordinary fuel tanks, but problems will still arise when additional tanks are carried.

See CONTROL OF GOODS.

vehicles The Community has attempted a comprehensive E.C. harmonization for passenger cars allowing a car approved in one member state to be marketed in another without having to obtain a new type approval. Since 1970, the Community has adopted over 50 measures harmonizing technical standards and type approval of individual vehicle components in order to bring this about. Adopted proposals have included abolishing the existing 12 national type approvals for motor vehicles and trailers and replacing them with one Community-wide type approval. Less sweeping measures propose to harmonize motor vehicle standards for permissible weights and dimensions, tires (and tire pressure gauges), and safety glass. Measures relating to pollution control cover motorcycle exhaust systems and gasoline and diesel engine emissions. A proposal would extend previous legislation relating to passenger cars to include particulate emissions from diesel engines. In April 1989, the Commission amended its proposals on emission-control standards for small cars. These standards, which would be mandatory in 1993, would be equivalent to the U.S. standards, with a 73 percent reduction in current emission levels.

See DOORS; DRIVING HOURS; GLASS; HORNS; TRACTORS AND AGRICULTURAL MACHINERY; TRUCK INDUSTRY.

Venezuela *See* ANDEAN PACT; LAFTA; LATIN AMERICA.

venture capital In 1976, institutions had invested between $50 million and $75 million in Europe. By 1984, institutional investment had risen to about $7.7 billion; in 1988 to about $18.7 billion, becoming the largest source of venture capital outside the United States. Within the E.C. in 1988 banks accounted for about 25 percent of new venture capital funds, with pension funds (13.4 percent), governments (12.4 percent), and insurance funds (10.1 percent) being the next three largest sources of finance. About 45 percent of the funds are invested in expanding existing businesses; management buy-outs account for another third (35.7 percent). The amount invested in start-ups has remained almost static—about 12 percent. Almost 90 percent of the portfolio holdings are for companies located in the country in which the funds were raised. Twenty percent of the funds are invested in consumer-related industries, while a 17 percent share is invested in the industrial sector. A 14.4 percent share is placed in the computer and electronic-related sector. There is a small increase in funds invested transnationally across Europe. Growth in the size of venture capital funds varied widely among E.C. members between 1986

and 1987. The average was 36 percent, with Belgium (69 percent), France (56 percent) and Spain (78 percent) exceeding this, while the Netherlands (13 percent) and the United Kingdom (7 percent) lagged behind. To encourage the expansion of cross-border ventures, the E.C. formed the Venture Consort in 1983. Tax laws have allowed an increased use of venture capital, which has grown so fast that Europe may soon surpass the $2.5 billion the United States spent in 1988.

See VENTURE CONSORT.

Venture Capital Association *See* VENTURE CONSORT.

Venture Consort The Commission, along with the European Venture Capital Association, launched this pilot project in 1983 to increase financing available to small and medium sized firms involved in new technologies at the first stage of capital formation. The Commission also participates in the distribution of profits. This initiative received $4.2 million since 1985 to help finance 18 transnational projects in eight E.C. member nations. These projects garnered a total equity investment of $42.1 million and generated 1,202 jobs.

See VENTURE CAPITAL.

veterinary products *See* PHARMACEUTICALS.

veterinary surgeons Since December 1990, veterinary surgeons are free to practice their profession anywhere in the Community subject to accepted training standards and the mutual recognition of qualifications. An equivalence in training is not acceptable.

See WORK AND EMPLOYMENT.

veto The right, usually under a Treaty or an Agreement requiring unanimity, of a member-state or its representative to reject an intended act.

Vietnam This nation participates in various bodies of the Council for Mutual Economic Assistance as an observer.

See COUNCIL FOR MUTUAL ECONOMIC ASSISTANCE.

Virgin Islands (British) These islands are a U.K. dependent territory covered by the Lomé Conventions.

See CARIBBEAN BASIN.

Vision 1250 *See* HIGH-DEFINITION TELEVISION.

visitors program *See* EUROPEAN COMMUNITY'S VISITORS PROGRAM.

vocational training *See* EDUCATION; EUROPEAN CENTER FOR THE DEVELOPMENT OF VOCATIONAL TRAINING; EUROTECNET; PETRA; YOUNG WORKERS.

Vocational Training, Advisory Committee on

Von Thunen Landscape This is an idealized series of concentric agricultural zones around a city in which the most specialized farming is nearest the city market followed by less intensive type farming.

voting rights On November 15, 1985, the European Parliament came out in favor of voting rights in local elections being granted in the country of residence to Community nationals living in a member state other than their own. This is consistent with the logic of a People's Europe to promote Community identity. The European Parliament elected in 1984 continues to be aware of the need for progress on a uniform electoral procedure. Once a European electoral procedure is adopted, local electoral law could develop on a reciprocal basis.

Vredeling proposal This is an E.C. Commission directive of 1983 on worker information and consultation rights. It gives workers employed by a European subsidiary of a multinational company the right to be informed and consulted on the company's financial situation, policies, and business decisions likely to affect their livelihoods, such as plant closings or worker lay-offs. A revised draft exempted firms from disclosing "any information whose disclosure would substantially harm the company's prospects or substantially damage its interests."

W

Warsaw Pact The Warsaw Treaty Organization was established in 1955 as a mutual defense alliance of Albania, Bulgaria, Czechoslovakia, the German Republic, Hungary, Poland, Romania, and the U.S.S.R. Albania withdrew in 1968. Events of 1989 may have significant impact on its future.
See EASTERN EUROPE.

waste In 1977, the Community produced around 1.7 billion tons of waste: 90 million tons of household waste, 115 million tons of industrial waste, 200 million tons of sewage sludge, 950 millions tons of agricultural waste, and 300 million tons of waste from its mining industry. The total has been rising by about five percent each year. A 1975 Community directive was adopted to encourage the prevention, recycling, and processing of waste and require governments to guarantee that waste will not endanger human health or damage the environment. Directives were introduced outlining rigid methods for dealing with particular toxic wastes and the management of radioactive wastes. A 1978 directive lists 27 dangerous substances. In June 1990, E.C. environment ministers agreed to tighten controls on the production, transport, and disposal of waste. The measure calls for the E.C. to dispose of waste within its own borders, which would end the much-criticized practice of sending waste to nations in the Third World or Eastern Europe.
See ENVIRONMENT; MARINE POLLUTION; RECYCLING; PAPER, TIRES, AND DRINK CONTAINERS, RECYCLING; TENDERS, WASTE OILS.

waste oils Waste oils account for one-fifth of all industrial pollution. Member nations are required to take measures to prohibit any discharge into surface, ground, or coastal waters and any dumping or processing which may be harmful or cause air pollution exceeding accepted limits. States are required to take needed precautions to guarantee the safe gathering and disposal of these wastes, in the latter case by recycling when feasible.
See ENVIRONMENT; MARINE POLLUTION; TOXIC EFFLUENT; WASTE; WATER.

water Community legislation is directed at protecting the high quality of water supplies, the use of available or potential resources, and at elevating the forecasting of consumer and industrial demand. Two directives (1980) set qualitative criteria for surface waters intended for drinking or for other forms of human consumption. Another directive deals with the quality of bathing water.
See BEACHES; ENVIRONMENT; MARINE POLLUTION; MINERAL WATER; RHINE; TOXIC EFFLUENT.

WCL *See* WORLD CONFEDERATION OF LABOR.

weapons *See* ARMS LEGISLATION.

weighting of votes This is a system by which multiple votes are accorded to the representatives of member-states on the Council and on certain Committees, in order to give expression to the respective numbers of population, territorial sizes, financial powers, and other aspects of comparative national standing of the several member-states.

Werner Report This is a 1970 document prepared by Pierre Werner of Luxembourg. It was presented to the Council of Ministers reiterating the objectives of the economic and monetary union and emphasized the need to take steps at the Community level rather than at national levels, thus paving the way for political union.

Western European Union (WEU) On March 17, 1948, a 50-year treaty "for collaboration in economic, social and cultural matters and for collective self-defense" was signed in

Brussels by the Foreign Ministers of the U.K., France, the Netherlands, Belgium, and Luxembourg, with responsibilities later transfered to the North Atlantic Treaty command.

Western Samoa This nation is one of the ACP states and a signatory to the Lomé Convention of 1988.

West Germany *See* GERMANY, FEDERAL REPUBLIC OF.

WEU *See* WESTERN EUROPEAN UNION.

whale products A 1980 directive established import licenses for all primary whale products including whalemeat, whalebone, nonedible whalemeat, and whale oil and fats. It was waived for Greenland Eskimos and other aboriginal peoples in the Community for whom whale products are an essential part of their culture and/or diets.
See ENVIRONMENT; WILDLIFE.

wheat *See* DURUM WHEAT; GRAIN SECTOR; INTERNATIONAL WHEAT AGREEMENT.

White Paper The White Paper was published in June 1985. It is the European Commission's program for "Completing the Internal Market" and includes over 300 legislative proposals and a timetable for their adoption. Its aim is to weld together the 12 separate national economies into a single market—a single Europe—by 1992. The White Paper program was approved by the European Community Heads of State or Government and given a constitutional basis by the Single European Act of 1986.

By mid-1988 progress had been made towards achieving the White Paper objectives by, among other things, abolishing frontier controls on goods, permitting freedom of movement and establishment for people, and removing barriers or easing restrictions in a variety of services, including financial and transport. Progress was also made in the liberalization of capital movements, the creation of suitable conditions for industrial cooperation, and the removal of fiscal frontiers. Other areas include, but are not limited to, completing the second stage of the liberalization of capital movements, opening the public procurement process, and harmonizing or simplyfying laws on direct and indirect tax-

ation, mergers, banking, insurance, transport, and other areas relating to the commercial life of the E.C. nations. By June 1989 the E.C. Council had definitively adopted 127 measures representing, together with current common positions and partial adoptions, approval of over 50 percent of the program of 279 directives that remained from the original 300 plus. Proposals dealing with academia and cultural aspects of the White Paper program are included in these measures.
See EUROPEAN ROUND TABLE; INTERNAL MARKET; SINGLE EUROPEAN ACT.

WHO World Health Organization.

wildlife The Community is a signatory to the European Wildlife and Natural Habitats, and to the U.N.-sponsored Bonn Convention of 1980 on the conservation of Migratory Species of Wild Animals. An E.C. committee is charged with safeguarding listed endangered species and their habitats. The Directive on the Protection of Wild Birds is an example of European wildlife policy. Seventy-four species of wild birds were originally listed as endangered on the 1979 E.C. birds directive. In 1985, the birds directive was amended and 70 more bird species were added to the list for a total of 144. The E.C. Commission provided 50 percent of required funds to 11 nature conservation projects in 1985.

A ban on whale products was imposed in January of 1981. A Council directive of 1983 bans the importation of products from harp and hooded seal pups.
See ENVIRONMENT.

winding-up *See* BANKING; INSURANCE.

wine In 1970, to encourage intra-Community trade, the six E.E.C. founder members adopted legislation that defined wine and fixed certain prices to regulate output. Each December the Council of Ministers identifies a fixed guide price for wine sales for the following year. The guide price is based on average market prices recorded for the preceding two years and on what price is expected to give farmers a reasonable return for their product. The Council also sets an activating price. When the market price falls to this level certain intervention measures are triggered, the net impact being to withdraw wine from the market, and thus raise prices. A regulation for a common market in wines was adopted in 1980 and includes composition, strength, labeling, assistance for storage, and exports to third-world countries. It also sets rules for controlling output and planting vines in order to maintain the quality and quantity standards, for three fifths of world wine production (accounting for 48 percent of human consumption). By 1984 the Council concluded that the levels of guaranteed prices and market support measures were to be reduced for surplus wine products. By 1992 wine production is expected to reach 145–150 million hectolitres within the E.C., excluding Portugal's output.

See AGRICULTURE, COMMON AGRICULTURAL POLICY; CONSUMER PROTECTION; EXCISE DUTIES.

withholding tax In February 1989, the E.C. Commission proposed levying a minimum 15 percent withholding tax on certain investment income. It would apply only to E.C. residents to curtail tax evasion as capital flows within the E.C. are liberalized. The controversial proposal would impose an automatic 15 percent withholding tax on income from bank deposits and bonds. It would also require greater cooperation among national tax authorities in cases where tax fraud is suspected.

See TAX BARRIER; TAXATION.

women Community directives require national governments to guarantee that the concept of equal pay is a reality; that there is no sex discrimination in securing training and employment, and that in major sectors social security benefits are applied equally to women. Since January 1978, funds from the Social Fund have been used to assist women over 25 to participate in training programs. The 1986–1990 program approved by the Council of Ministers in July 1986 has two main objectives: (1) to consolidate the Community's achievements to date and (2) to promote real change by means of a concrete and pragmatic approach, thus taking into account the specific problems of various categories of women. Efforts are being made to ensure equality in education and training, equality in the workplace, equality in the face of new technology, and equality in social security and social protection. Two specialized services have been created—The Women's Employment and Equality Office and the Women's Information Service which publishes a bi-monthly bulletin "Women of Europe," in nine languages.

See FINANCE; SOCIAL FUND; SOCIAL POLICY; WORK AND EMPLOYMENT.

wool This item is handled as an industrial item in the Community. No system of support prices or duty on wool imports into the Community exist.

See AGRICULTURE, COMMON AGRICULTURAL POLICY.

work and employment The Treaty of Rome provides for the free movement of workers throughout the Community. No discrimination based on nationality regarding employment, remuneration, and other work conditions, except for employment in the public service, is permitted. The European Court of Justice ruled that a member state must not apply any law, regulation, or administrative practice which discriminates against a person from another member nation who desires to form or operate a business.

See ACCOUNTANTS; ARCHITECTS; ASBESTOS; COMPANY LAW; DENTAL PRACTITIONERS; DOCTORS; HAIRDRESSERS; HEALTH AND SAFETY; JOB INFORMATION; LAWYERS; MIDWIVES; NURSES; SOCIAL POLICY; VETERINARY SURGEONS.

worker participation, company assets Following a request of the Tripartite Conference, the Commission published in 1979 a guide on the goals, major problems, and alternatives involved in implementing a harmonized Community policy of profit sharing for workers.

See COMPANY LAW; CORPORATE BREAKUP RULES; VREDELING PROPOSAL; WORK AND EMPLOYMENT.

worker's rights *See* EUROPEAN TRADE UNION CONFEDERATION; SOCIAL CHARTER.

World Bank *Synonymous with* INTERNATIONAL BANK FOR RECONSTRUCTION AND DEVELOPMENT.

World Confederation of Labor (WCL) WCL was created on October 3, 1945, representing union organizations in more than 50 nations. The U.S., U.K., and the Netherlands withdrew in January 1949 when WCL came under complete Communist control.

world profits In its attempt to reform taxes on cross-frontier mergers, the Commission in 1969 argued that all member states should allow companies to opt for a world profits system of taxation. Under such a system, all profits of a company, including the profits of foreign affiliates, would be taxed in its country of domicile. The system would offer firms the additional advantage of being able to deduct any losses of foreign affiliates from their taxable profits. The system would cover all those affiliates of the same parent company operating in the member states.

See CONSOLIDATED PROFITS.

Y

Yaoundé Agreements Yaoundé I was signed in 1963 and Yaoundé II in 1969. They dealt with relations between the Community and former French, Belgian, Dutch, and Italian colonies that wanted to continue their association with the Community following their independence. Conventions outlined duty-free entry for specific exports from the developing nations, including the output of infant industries. A similar arrangement covered exports from the Community into most of the nations. Also created was a European Development Fund for these associated nations. In 1975, the Agreements were replaced by the Lomé Conventions.

See AASM; ASSOCIABLE; EXTERNAL TRADE; LOMÉ CONVENTIONS.

Yemen Arab Republic (North Yemen) A commercial and economic cooperation agreement was begun in the mid 1970s, making Yemen the Community's first contractual link with the region. In 1977, the E.C. granted Yemen aid totalling 13.6 million ECU. Trade between the E.C. and Yemen shows a growing surplus in favor of the Community, with imports from Yemen chiefly coffee, raw hides and skins, and textiles.

YES *See* YOUTH EXCHANGE SCHEME.

young workers The Council of Ministers amended the regulations of the Social Fund permitting aid to create jobs fulfilling a public need. The Fund also provides up to 50 percent of the cost of approved training programs for people under 25 years of age. A Commission decision of 1975 created the Vocational Training Center, guidelines followed in a 1980 resolution.

See EUROPEAN CENTER FOR THE DEVELOPMENT OF VOCATIONAL TRAINING, FINANCE, SOCIAL POLICY, WORK AND EMPLOYMENT.

Youth Exchange Scheme (YES) A program was created for stimulating and improving the exchanges of young people within the E.C. The Commission used 3.5 million ECU of the 1988 budget to begin the program at the end of 1988. The money was used to finance exchanges involving some 25,000 to 30,000 young Europeans between ages 15 and 25.

See CHRONOLOGY (SEPTEMBER 1988) IN APPENDIX; COMETT; EDUCATION; ERASMUS.

Yugoslavia Yugoslavia concluded an agreement with the Council for Mutual Economic Assistance in 1964 whereby it would be able to participate in some of COMECON'S activities. Since 1970, Yugoslavia has had a trading agreement with the Community. It also benefits under the Community Generalized System of Preferences. In 1980, a new agreement was made providing improved preferential access of Yugoslav products to the Community market and financial assistance of 200 million ECU to Yugoslavia over five years in the form of low interest loans from the European Investment Bank. On December 10, 1987 the E.C. and Yugoslavia signed an agreement establishing new trade arrangements, a second protocol on financial cooperation, a protocol of technical adaptation to the Cooperation Agreement consequent on the accession of Spain and Portugal to the Community, and a protocol to the E.C.S.C.-Yugoslavia Agreement also consequent on the accession of Spain and Portugal.

An exchange of information and assistance on energy policy, cooperation in the field of energy planning and saving, and cooperation involving the exchange of experts, professional training, and programs in energy were to run through 1988. Other cooperation programs were in transport, environment, and fisheries, industrial cooperation, and science and technology. In the financial cooperation area an amended trade agreement incorporates in the additional protocols signed on December 10, 1987, and entails improved access to the Community market for Yugoslav industrial goods and greater concession for a wider range of agricultural products. Yugoslav imports from the E.C. in 1987 were valued at 5.0 million ECU, while its exports to the E.C. amounted to 5.3 million ECU. Trade in textiles improved from 1983 to 1985 by 40 percent, with a new textile agreement running until December 31, 1991.

Yugoslavia's first stock exchange opened in the northern city of Ljubljana, with a total capital of $17 million. It will list Yugoslav and foreign companies and publish the closing prices of selected stocks. On January 1, 1990, the dinar will become Eastern Europe's first convertible currency.

Beginning July 1, 1991, a five-year loan plan between the E.C. and Yugoslavia would be 900 million ECU ($1.1 billion) almost double the pre-1991 loan.

See EASTERN EUROPE.

Z

Zaire This nation is one of the ACP states and a signatory to the Yaoundé Conventions of 1963 and 1969 and to the Lomé Convention of 1988.

Zambia This nation is one of the ACP states and a signatory to the Lomé Convention of 1988.

Zimbabwe (formerly Rhodesia) This nation became a signatory to the Lomé Convention in 1988 with special preferential treatment on limited exports of beef, veal, and sugar.

Zollverein Zoll (customs), Verein (union). The customs union created the economic unification of Germany by allowing the expansion of commerce and industry, the improvement of transport and building of railways, and prepared the way for the alignment of commercial and industrial law.

zootechnics *See* ANIMAL HEALTH AND MEAT INSPECTION.

Chronology of the European Community
1957–1990

1957

The Treaties establishing the European Economic Community (E.E.C.) and the European Atomic Energy Community (Euratom) are signed at the capital in Rome. Both Treaties are ratified before the year's end by the Parliaments of all six member countries, with even larger majorities than when the E.C.S.C. Treaty was ratified in 1951. (March 25)

1958

The E.E.C. and Euratom Treaties enter into force. (January 1)

The Members of the E.E.C. and Euratom Commissions are appointed by the governments of the member states. Walter Hallstein becomes President of the E.E.C. Commission and Louis Armand President of the Euratom Commission. (January 7)

The Agriculture Conference in Stresa lays the foundations for the common agricultural policy. (July 3–11)

1959

The first steps are taken in the progressive elimination of customs duties and quotas within the E.E.C. (January 1)

1960

The E.E.C. Council approves the common customs tariff on which the member states are gradually to align their own tariffs during the transitional period. (February 13)

The Convention establishing the European Free Trade Association (EFTA) enters into force. (May 3)

The E.E.C. Council decides to speed up the implementation of the Treaty. (May 12)

The European Parliament approves a draft convention on direct elections (based on a report by Fernand Dehousse). (May 17)

Based on the Stresa Conference and guidelines put forward in November 1959, the Commission sends to the Council its proposals for implementing the common agricultural policy. (June 30)

The European Social Fund Regulation enters into force. (September 20)

The E.E.C. Council approves the basic principles governing the common agricultural policy. (December 19–20)

185

1961

The heads of state or government of the Six decide at a summit meeting in Paris to work toward political union. (February 10–11)

The heads of state or government at a summit meeting in Bonn issue declarations on cultural and political cooperation. They agree to closer political cooperation by the Six and undertake to hold regular meetings to concert their policies. (July 18)

Ireland (July 31), the United Kingdom (August 9), and Denmark (August) apply to join the E.E.C. (July/August)

The first regulation on the free movement of workers within the Community enters into force. (September 1)

The French Government submits a draft treaty establishing a political union of the Six (Fouchet Plan). (November 2)

Accession negotiations begin with the United Kingdom (November 8–9) and Denmark (November 30). (November)

At a ministerial meeting between the E.E.C. member states, the Council and the Associated African States and Madagascar (AASM), the objectives and principles of an association convention are defined. (December 6–7)

Sweden (December 12), Austria (December 12), and Switzerland (December 15) ask that negotiations be started with a view to agreements with the E.E.C. that will be compatible with their neutrality. (December)

1962

The Council finds that the objectives set out in the E.E.C. Treaty for the first stage in the establishment of the common market have been achieved in the main. The second stage begins with effect from January 1. (January 14)

The Council adopts the basic regulations for a common market in agriculture (common organization of the markets in a number of products, European Agricultural Guidance and Guarantee Fund set up). (January 14)

The French Government produces a new version of the Fouchet Plan (January 18)

France's five partners advance an alternative proposal for political union. (February 1)

Spain seeks to open negotiations for association with the E.E.C. (February 9)

At a meeting of foreign ministers, negotiations on political union are abandoned, chiefly because no agreement can be reached on the United Kingdom's participation. (April 17)

Norway applies for membership of the Community. (April 30)

The Six decide a second time to speed up the establishment of the common market. (May 15)

1963

French President de Gaulle declares at a press conference that the United Kingdom is not ready to join the E.E.C. (January 14)

France and the Federal Republic of Germany sign a Treaty of Friendship and Cooperation in Paris. (January 22)

The accession negotiations with the United Kingdom are broken off at the insistence of the French Government; negotiations with the other countries which have applied for membership or association are suspended too. (January 29)

The E.E.C. Council declares its readiness to conclude association agreements with other African countries comparable with the AASM in terms of economic structure and production. (April 2)

The E.E.C. Council proposes regular contacts with the United Kingdom through Western European Union (WEU). (July 11)

The Association Convention between the E.E.C. and 17 African States and Madagascar is signed in Yaoundé, Cameroon. (July 20)

1964

On a proposal from the Commission, the E.E.C. Council agrees to a medium-term economic policy program being prepared for the Community. (April 15)

The Kennedy Round of multilateral tariff negotiations under the General Agreement on Tariffs and Trade (GATT) opens in Geneva. (May 4)

The Yaoundé Convention enters into force. (June 1)

The regulations establishing the first common agricultural market organizations and the European Agricultural Guidance and Guarantee Fund (EAGGF) enter into force. (July 1)

In a memorandum entitled "Initiative 1964," the E.E.C. Commission proposes a timetable for speeding up customs union. (October 1)

The E.E.C. Council for the first time determines common prices for cereals. (December 15)

1965

The E.E.C. Commission puts before the Council its proposals for financing the common agricultural policy and proposals for replacing the member states' contributions to the Community budget by the Community's own resources and reinforcing the European Parliament's budgetary powers. (March 31)

The Six sign the Treaty merging the Executives of the E.E.C., the E.C.S.C., and Euratom, thereby establishing a single Council and a single Commission of the European Communities. (April 8)

Maurice Couve de Murville, French Foreign Minister and President of the E.E.C. Council, breaks off the Council discussions on the Commission's proposals on financing the common agricultural policy, own resources, and Parliament's budgetary powers, noting that the Council has failed to reach agreement on financing arrangements by the appointed time (the January 1962 decisions were taken on the understanding that the new Financial Regulation would take effect on July 1, 1965). (June 30)

The French Government issues a communique stating that the Community is undergoing a "crisis." (July 1)

The French Government informs the member states that it is recalling its Permanent Representative and that the French delegation will not be taking part in meetings of the Council or the Permanent Representatives Committee or in proceedings of committees and working parties that were preparing for economic union or the resumption of earlier negotiations. (July 6)

The E.E.C. Council meets for the first time without France, affirming that it is not prevented from meeting and deliberating by the absence of one delegation. (July 26–27)

At a press conference General de Gaulle voices his concern at the workings of the Community institutions, especially with regard to majority voting in the Council and relations between the Council and the Commission. (September 9)

In a statement from the Council, France's five partners reaffirm their continuing respect for the Treaties, and call on France to resume her place in the

Community institutions. They propose that the Council hold a special meeting, without the Commission, to attempt to resolve the Community's problems. (October 26)

1966

The E.E.C. enters the third and final stage of the common market transitional period: one consequence of this is the replacement of unanimity by majority vote for many Council decisions. (January 1)

The Council holds a special meeting in Luxembourg without the Commission; France takes part. (January 17–18)

Resuming its special meeting in Luxembourg, the Council issues the statements on relations between the Council and the Commission and on majority voting which are commonly called the "Luxembourg Compromise." France resumes its place in the Community institutions. (January 28–29)

The E.E.C. Council sets a firm date (July 1, 1968) for the completion of customs union and the introduction ahead of schedule of the Common Customs Tariff for industrial products. It also adopts a timetable that will bring about free movement of agricultural products by the same date. (May 11)

1967

By adopting Commission proposals for a common system of value-added tax and the procedure for applying it (first and second VAT Directives), the E.E.C. Council embarks on the harmonization of turnover taxes. (February 9)

The governments of the United Kingdom and Ireland (May 10) and Denmark (May 11) make fresh applications to join the Communities. (May)

The Final Act of the Kennedy Round is signed in Geneva by the Commission (for the Community) and the other GATT contracting parties. (June 30)

The Treaty merging the Executives of the European Communities enters into force. (July 1)

The 14-member Commission of the European Communities takes office, with Jean Rey as President. (July 6)

Norway makes a second application to join the Communities. (July 25)

The Swedish Government asks the Six to open negotiations to enable Sweden to take part in the Community in a form which would be compatible with its neutrality. (June 26)

The Commission delivers an Opinion in favor of opening negotiations with a view to the United Kingdom, Ireland, Denmark, and Norway joining the Communities. (September 29)

General de Gaulle at a press conference declares that the United Kingdom is not in a position to join the Community. (November 27)

The Council fails to reach agreement on the reopening of negotiations with the applicant countries. (December 19)

1968

Customs union is completed 18 months ahead of the Treaty schedule: customs duties between member states are removed, and the Common Customs Tariff replaces national customs duties in trade with the rest of the world. (July 1)

The regulation securing complete freedom of movement for workers within the Community is adopted (more than a year ahead of the Treaty schedule). (July 29)

The Commission lays before the Council the "Mansholt Plan" for the reform of agriculture in the Community, which aims to modernize farm structures. (December 18)

1969

The Council resumes examination of the applications for membership from the United Kingdom, Ireland, Denmark, and Norway. (July 23)

The Commission sends the Council a proposal to provide the Community with the instruments it needs to implement a regional development policy. (October 15)

Conference of the heads of state or government at The Hague results in agreement to lay down without delay a definitive financial arrangement for the common agricultural policy, to allocate to the Community its own resources, and to strengthen the budgetary powers of Parliament. They also agree to open negotiations with the four applicant countries, to press forward with economic and monetary union, and to introduce a system of cooperation in foreign affairs. (December 1–2)

The 12-year transitional period provided for in the E.E.C. Treaty for the establishment of the common market ends. (December 31)

1970

The Governors of the Central Banks sign an agreement establishing a system of short-term monetary support within the Community. This takes effect the same day. (February 9)

Honoring the undertakings made at The Hague, the Council adopts definitive arrangements for financing the common agricultural policy and makes a decision on the replacement of financial contributions from member states by the Communities' own resources. The ministers sign a Treaty amending certain budgetary provisions of the treaties establishing the European Communities which gives the European Parliament wider budgetary powers. (April 21–22)

Negotiations with the four countries applying for membership formally open in Luxembourg. (June 30)

A new commission, composed of nine members and presided over by Franco Maria Malfatti, takes office. (July 2)

The working party chaired by Luxembourg Prime Minister Pierre Werner adopts the report on the attainment of stages of economic and monetary union which it had been instructed to draw up by the Council following The Hague Summit. (October 7–8)

The foreign ministers, meeting in Luxembourg, adopt the Davignon report on "the best way of achieving progress in the matter of the political unification of Europe." (October 27)

First "political cooperation" meeting of foreign ministers is held in Munich. (November 19)

1971

The second Yaoundé Convention and Arusha Agreement enter into force. (January 1)

The Council and representatives of the member governments adopt a resolution on the attainment by stages of economic and monetary union, the first stage to start on January 1, 1971. The Council also decides to strengthen coordination of member states' short-term economic policies and cooperation between the central banks, and to set up machinery for medium-term financial assistance. (March 22)

Following the floating of several member states' currencies, the Council introduces a system of monetary compensatory amounts for trade in agricultural products between member states, with the aim of maintaining the unity of the common agricultural market. (May 12)

The Council adopts the Commission's proposals to grant generalized tariff preferences to 91 developing countries. (June 21–22)

The United States Government suspends the convertibility of the dollar into gold. (August 15)

1972

The Treaty and related documents concerning the accession of Denmark, Ireland, Norway, and the United Kingdom to the European Communities are signed in Brussels. (January 22)

Introduction of the currency "snake": the Council of the Communities and the governments of the member states decide to limit the spread between the member states' currencies to a maximum of 2.25 percent. The applicant countries also join the "snake." (March 21)

The Council adopts three Directives on the modernization of agricultural structures, following Commission proposals for the reform of agriculture. (March 24)

The Convention setting up a European University Institute is signed in Florence. (April 19)

The pound sterling and the Irish pound leave the "snake." (June 23)

In Norway's referendum on joining the Community, 53.5 percent vote against. The Norwegian Government asks to negotiate a free-trade agreement with the Community. (September 25)

The nine heads of state or government of the enlarged Community hold a summit conference in Paris. They define new fields of action for the Community (concerning environmental, regional, social and industrial policies, etc.) and ask the Community institutions to draw up the appropriate programs. They reaffirm the determination of member states irreversibly to achieve economic and monetary union. They undertake to transform by 1980 "the whole complex of their relations into a European union." (October 19–21)

1973

Denmark, Ireland, and the United Kingdom formally join the European Communities. (January 1)

Free-trade agreements with Austria, Portugal, Sweden, and Switzerland come into force. Agreements with the other three nonapplicant EFTA countries take effect later (Iceland on April 1, Norway on July 1, Finland on January 1, 1974). (January 1)

The European Parliament convenes for its first session since enlargement. The British Labour Party sends no representatives to Parliament, and the British trade unions do not take the seats allocated to them on the Economic and Social Committee. (January 16)

The Italian lire leaves the "snake." (February 13)

The Council holds a meeting on the monetary situation. The United Kingdom, Ireland, and Italy having decided to let their currencies float independently, the "snake" is retained by the other member states (Belgium, Denmark, France,

Germany, Luxembourg, Netherlands) and now floats against the dollar. (March 11–12)

The Conference on Security and Cooperation in Europe (CSCE) opens in Helsinki. (July 3–7)

The foreign ministers present their second report on political cooperation (Copenhagen report), calling for more active cooperation. The report is subsequently approved by the heads of state or government. (July 23)

A ministerial conference is held between the Community and the AASM, the Commonwealth developing countries referred to in the Act of Accession and certain other African countries, as a prelude to negotiations for what will be the Lomé Convention with the African, Pacific, and Caribbean (ACP) countries. (July 25–26)

The Tokyo Round of multilateral trade negotiations in GATT opens. (September 12)

Yom Kippur War. The Arab oil-producing countries announce that oil exports to certain Western countries will be cut or stopped. The Organization of the Petroleum Exporting Countries (OPEC) decides to raise oil prices substantially. (October 6–27)

The Nine issue a declaration of principles on which to base a peace settlement in the Middle East; this is to guide their policy in the years ahead. (November 6)

The heads of state or government of the member states confer in Copenhagen. On instructions from the Arab Summit in Algiers (November 26–28), the Foreign Ministers of four Arab countries deliver a message to the Conference. The decision is taken to put together the initial components of a common energy policy and set up a European Regional Development Fund by January 1, 1974. The Council then fails to act on these directives, which puts the Community under strain. (December 14–15)

1974

The French franc leaves the "snake." (January 21)

During Britain's election campaign, the Labour Party announces that it will ask for "renegotiation" of the United Kingdom's membership of the Communities. (February 8)

The Council fails to decide on transition to the second phase of economic and monetary union. (February 18)

The newly formed British Government asks for "renegotiation" of the United Kingdom's membership. (April 1)

Portugal's dictatorship, in power since 1928, is overthrown. (April 25)

The Euro-Arab Dialogue opens in Paris. The Community is represented by the Presidents of the Council and the Commission. It is agreed to set up a Euro-Arab General Committee and a number of working groups. (July 31)

Greece asks the Community to "unfreeze" the Association Agreement (confined to routine business since the Colonels' coup d'état). (August 22)

At the invitation of French President Giscard d'Estaing, the heads of state or government of the Nine and the President of the Commission meet for informal talks at the Élysée. France drops its objections to direct election of Parliament and presents a package of proposals on the political organization of Europe. (September 14)

The Council reactivates the Association Agreement with Greece. (September 17)

The United Nations General Assembly grants the Community observer status. (October 11)

191

At the Paris Summit Conference, the heads of state or government make a number of important decisions concerning the Community's institutions:

(a) Parliament to be elected by direct universal suffrage from 1978 onwards;

(b) the heads of state or government to hold regular meetings "in the Council of the Communities and in the context of political cooperation" (subsequently baptized "European Council").

(c) Leo Tindemans, the Belgian Prime Minister, to compile a report on European Union by the end of 1975.

The meeting also produces many policy decisions, including one on the structure and endowment (for the next three years) of the European Regional Development Fund. (December 9–10)

1975

Parliament adopts the new draft convention on the election of its members by direct universal suffrage from 1978 onwards. (January 14)

A joint declaration is signed by Parliament, the Council, and the Commission instituting a conciliation procedure between Parliament and the Council, with the active assistance of the Commission, for Community acts of general application which have appreciable financial implications. (March 4)

The European Council holds its first meeting in Dublin. On the basis of a Commission proposal it works out a solution to the problems raised by the United Kingdom in connection with its contribution to the Community budget, thus paving the way for the conclusion of the "renegotiation" exercise. (March 10–11)

Following the conclusion of the renegotiations, the British Government announces its intention in the House of Commons to organize a referendum on U.K. membership of the Community. (March 18)

The referendum results show a large majority in favor of the United Kingdom remaining a member of the Community: 67.2 percent vote "yes" (68.7 percent in England, 64.8 percent in Wales, 58.4 percent in Scotland and 52.1 percent in Northern Ireland) in a 64.5 percent turn-out. (June 5)

Greece applies to join the European Communities. (June 12)

Reports on European Union are adopted by the Commission on June 25 and by Parliament on July 10, the two reaching similar conclusions. (June/July)

Following the positive outcome to the referendum, 18 British Labour Members take up their seats in the European Parliament. British trade unionists also take their places on the Economic and Social Committee. (July 7)

The French franc rejoins the "snake." (July 10)

The Treaty strengthening the budgetary powers of Parliament and setting up a Court of Auditors is signed in Brussels. (July 22)

In Helsinki the Final Act of the Conference on Security and Cooperation in Europe is signed by the 35 States taking part. Italian Prime Minister Aldo Moro, acting in his capacity as President of the Council, signs on behalf of the Community. (August 1)

Official relations are established with China and a Chinese ambassador is accredited to the Community. (September 16)

The first Tripartite Conference on the economic and social situation is held, attended by Community representatives (Commission and Council), the ministers responsible for economic policy and employment in the member states, and representatives from both sides of industry. (November 18)

Belgian Prime Minister Leo Tindemans transmits his report on European

Union to the other heads of state or government of the Community and to the President of the Commission. (December 29)

1976

The Commission endorses Greece's application for Community membership but expresses the view that there should perhaps be a waiting period before accession in view of the structural changes that will have to take place. (January 28)

The Council favors Greece's application to join the Community; it is agreed that negotiations will open on July 27. (February 9)

The Council for Mutual Economic Assistance (CMEA) proposes an agreement between CMEA and its members, and the Community and its members. (February 16)

The French franc leaves the "snake" again. (March 14)

The ACP-E.E.C. Convention between the Community and 46 African, Caribbean, and Pacific States, signed at Lomé, Togo, on February 28, 1975, enters into force. (April 1)

The Community signs comprehensive agreements with the Maghreb countries (Tunisia on the 25th, Algeria on the 26th and Morocco on the 27th of April). (April 25–27)

The instruments concerning election of Parliament by direct universal suffrage are signed in Brussels. (September 20)

Foreign ministers meeting in The Hague decide that member states will extend fishing limits to 200 miles off their North Sea and North Atlantic coasts from January 1, 1977, and agree on a number of common guidelines and procedures. These decisions, adopted by the Council on November 3, mark the beginnings of the common fisheries policy. (October 30)

Meeting in The Hague, the European Council publishes a statement on the Tindemans Report and calls on the foreign ministers and the Commission to report to it once a year on the results obtained and the progress which can be achieved in the short term towards European Union. (November 29–30)

1977

Cooperation agreements are signed with three Mashrag countries (Egypt, Jordan, and Syria), to be followed by the agreement with Lebanon on May 3). (January 18)

Portugal applies for Community membership. (March 28)

The European Parliament, the Council, and the Commission sign a joint declaration on the respect of fundamental rights. (April 5)

At the third Western Economic Summit in London (the "Downing Street Summit") the Community participates, as such, for the first time in some of the discussions. (May 7–8)

The Council adopts the sixth VAT Directive (establishing a uniform basis of assessment for value-added tax), thus enabling Community own resources arrangements to be operated in full. (May 17)

Customs union is achieved in the enlarged Community. (July 1)

Spain applies for Community membership. (July 28)

The Court of Auditors of the European Communities, replacing the E.E.C. and Euratom Audit Board and the E.C.S.C. Auditor, holds its inaugural meeting in Luxembourg. (October 25)

Commission President Roy Jenkins makes a statement in Florence on the prospects for monetary union. (October 27)

1978

The Community and China sign a trade agreement which comes into force on June 1. (April 3)

The European Council, meeting in Copenhagen, agrees that the first direct elections to the European Parliament will be held between June 7–10, 1979. These dates are endorsed by Parliament and formally approved by the Council on July 25. (April 7–8)

The Commission adopts a favorable Opinion on Portugal's application for Community membership. The Council favors the application on June 6, and negotiations formally open on October 17. (May 19)

The European Council, meeting in Bremen, agrees on a common strategy to achieve a higher rate of economic growth and approves the plan to set up a European Monetary System. (July 6–7)

The Council agrees to create a new Community borrowing and lending instrument. The Commission is empowered to contract loans of up to one billion EUA and on-lend the proceeds to finance energy, industry, and infrastructure projects contributing to priority Community objectives. (October 16)

The Commission adopts a favorable Opinion on Spain's application for Community membership. The Council favors the application on December 19, and negotiations formally open on February 5, 1979. (November 29)

The European Council, meeting in Brussels, decides to set up a European Monetary System based on a European Currency Unit (the ECU). The EMS comprises an exchange and intervention mechanism, credit mechanisms, and a mechanism for the transfer of resources to less prosperous Community countries. Eight member states—Ireland and Italy after a period of reflection—decide to become full members of the EMS. The United Kingdom opts to remain outside the EMS for the time being (despite a limited involvement in some of the credit mechanisms). Because of the link subsequently established by the French Government between the EMS and the phasing-out of monetary compensatory amounts under the common agricultural policy, introduction of the EMS is deferred from the initial target date of early January 1979 to March 13, 1979. (December 4–5)

The European Council also decides to set up a three-man committee to consider essential adjustments to institutional mechanisms and procedures in the context of enlargement. The "three wise men" are Mr. Barend Biesheuvel, former Prime Minister of the Netherlands, Mr. Edmond Dell, former U.K. Minister, and Mr. Robert Marjolin, former Vice-President of the E.E.C. Commission. (December 4–5)

1979

The Commission adopts a memorandum on the accession of the European Communities to the European Convention for the Protection of Human Rights and Fundamental Freedoms. (April 4)

The Treaty and related documents concerning Greece's accession to the Communities are signed in Athens. (May 28)

The first elections to the European Parliament by direct universal suffrage in accordance with electoral procedures adopted by each of the national parliaments take place. (June 7–10)

The European Parliament holds its first part-session in Strasbourg following direct elections. (July 17–20)

The second ACP-E.E.C. Convention governing cooperation between the

Community and 58 African, Caribbean and Pacific countries is signed in Lomé. (October 31)

The "Committee of Three Wise Men" submits to the European Council meeting in Dublin its report suggesting improvements in the efficiency of the Community institutions. (November 29)

The British Government asks for special measures to narrow the wide gap between the amounts the U.K. pays in as own resources and the amounts received under Community policies. (November 29)

Parliament rejects the draft budget for 1980, which will not be adopted until July. (December 13)

The Community signs the agreements reached in the GATT multilateral trade negotiations (Tokyo Round). (December 17)

1980

The Council reaches agreement on a provisional and pragmatic solution to the problem of the British contribution to the Community budget. The Council instructs the Commission to carry out a study, to be completed by June 30, 1981, of the development of Community policies so as to prevent a recurrence of such unacceptable situations. (May 30)

The E.E.C.-Asean Cooperation Agreement comes into force. (October 1)

The Commission finds that the Community's steel industry is in a state of "manifest crisis" (Article 58 of the E.C.S.C. Treaty) and asks for the Council's assent to the introduction of a system of production quotas. Assent is given on October 30 and the Commission adopts its decision introducing production quotas on October 31. (October 6)

1981

Greece becomes the tenth member of the Community. (January 1)

The second ACP-E.E.C. Convention, signed in Lomé on October 31, 1979, comes into force. (January 1)

The Council adopts Community borrowing and lending arrangements enabling up to six billion ECU to be raised to support the balances of payments of member states. This adjusts the smaller-scale mechanism introduced in 1975. (March 16)

The Representatives of the Governments of the member states adopt a resolution providing for the introduction of a European passport with a uniform format. (June 23)

The Commission sends the heads of state or government its report on the mandate it was given on May 30, 1980, centered on three elements: revitalization of the common policies, reform of agricultural policy and budgetary matters. (June 24)

The European Parliament decides, on the initiative of Altiero Spinelli and a large number of members (the "Crocodile Club"), to set up a "permanent institutional committee," chaired by Mr. Spinelli, responsible for drafting amendments to the existing Treaties. (July 7–9)

The foreign ministers approve a report setting out a number of practical improvements in the existing procedure for European political cooperation. (October 13)

The German and Italian Governments submit to the other member states and to the European Parliament and the Commission a draft "Economic Act" and a draft statement on economic integration. (November 6 and 12)

1982

In a referendum held in Greenland, a narrow majority favors seeking withdrawal from the Communities and negotiating a new type of relationship. (February 23)

The Greek Government sends the presidents of the Council and the Commission a memorandum on relations between Greece and the Community, requesting the Community to introduce special provisions in favor of Greece. (March 22)

The presidents of Parliament, the Council, and the Commission sign a joint declaration on improving the budgetary procedure. (June 30)

Parliament avails itself for the first time of the provisions of Article 175 of the E.E.C. Treaty and threatens the Council with an action before the Court of Justice for failure to act in the field of transport policy. The action is brought before the Court in January 1983. (September 16)

1983

After six years of negotiations, agreement is reached on a common fisheries policy. (January 25)

In its response to the Greek memorandum the Commission proposes that the Community should contribute to the development of the Greek economy and the solution of problems specific to Greece through policy measures, rather than through derogations from the Treaties. Specific measures are subsequently introduced, mainly under integrated Mediterranean programs. (March 29)

At the European Council meeting in Stuttgart, the heads of state or government sign the Solemn Declaration on European Union in response to the draft European Act. The European Council produces a working program to secure general agreement on issues that have been blocking the Community for several years: enlargement, financing, adjustment of the common agricultural policy, new policies. (June 17–19)

Despite intensive preparations, the Athens European Council meeting fails to reach agreement on the vital issues facing the Community: financing, adjustment of the common agricultural policy, improving the effectiveness of the structural Funds, and the development of new Community policies. (December 4–6)

1984

The European Parliament adopts by a large majority the draft Treaty establishing European Union, prepared by its Committees on Institutional Affairs (rapporteur/coordinator: Altiero Spinelli). (February 14)

The Council adopts a Decision setting out a European strategic program for R&D in information technology (ESPRIT). (February 28)

At the Fontainebleau European Council meeting, substantial progress is made on a number of difficult issues, notably the reform of the common agricultural policy and the overall solution to the budgetary and financial dispute. The European Council also decides to set up two ad hoc committees, one on institutional affairs (Dooge Committee) and one on the preparation and coordination of action on "a people's Europe" (Adonnino Committee). (June 25–26)

The third ACP-E.E.C. Convention on cooperation between the Community and 65 African, Caribbean, and Pacific countries is signed in Lomé. (December 8)

1985

Greenland leaves the Community but remains associated with it as an overseas territory. (February 1)

The Dooge Committee recommends the convening of an intergovernmental conference to negotiate a draft Treaty for European Union. (March 9)

Meeting in Brussels, the European Council reaches agreement on the integrated Mediterranean program, thus facilitating agreement on the accession of Spain and Portugal. (March 29–30)

In its judgment in Parliament's action against the Council, the Court of Justice finds that the Council is in breach of the Treaty for having failed to ensure freedom to provide services in the sphere of international transport. This judgment is of exceptional importance at two levels: (a) it provides an impetus for progress in transport policy; and (b) it confirms Parliament's right to take action in the Court if it considers that any other institution is not fulfilling its obligations under the Treaties. (May 22)

The instruments of accession of Spain and Portugal are signed. (June 12)

The Commission publishes its White Paper on completing the internal market, which gives details of the measures to be taken to remove all physical, technical, and tax barriers between the member states by 1992. It is welcomed by the European Council, meeting in Milan. (June 14)

In its final report to the European Council, the Adonnino Committee presents both specific immediate proposals and longer-term objectives to make the Community more of a reality for its citizens. (June 20)

The European Council, meeting in Milan, holds a wide-ranging discussion on the convening of an intergovernmental conference to draft a treaty on a common foreign and security policy and to draw up the amendments to the E.E.C. Treaty required for improving the Council's decisionmaking procedures and extending Community activities into new areas. At the end of the meeting, the president concludes that the necessary majority for calling such a conference has been obtained. (June 28–29)

First meeting of the Intergovernmental Conference. The Conference meets six times at the foreign minister level. The Commission takes an active part; Spain and Portugal are also represented. The Commission presents a series of proposals that form the centerpiece of the Conference proceedings. (September 9)

The European Council, meeting in Luxembourg, reaches agreement on a reform of the Community's institutions designed to improve its efficiency and extend its powers and responsibilities, and to provide a legal framework for cooperation on foreign policy. This agreement is finalized in the form of a Single European Act by the foreign ministers meeting in the Intergovernmental Conference on December 16–17. (December 2–3)

1986

Spain and Portugal join the Community. (January 1)

The Single European Act is signed by the Representatives of the Governments of the 12 member states. (January 17 and 28)

The third ACP-E.C. Convention, signed in Lomé on December 8, 1984, comes into force. (May 1)

The European flag adopted by the Community institutions is hoisted for the first time in Brussels to the sound of the European anthem. The flag and the anthem were initially adopted by the Council of Europe and now represent the Community as well. (May 29)

In Punta del Este, Uruguay, ministers of 92 nations agree to a new round of multilateral trade negotiations. (September 15–20)

The Commission adopts a report on voting rights in local elections for Community nationals. (September 17)

The Council agrees to amend its Rules of Procedure so as to facilitate majority voting. Since the Council took a vote on a hundred or so issues in 1986, this constitutes a considerable advance on previous practice. (December 15–16)

1987

The E.C. and the Soviet Union hold their first official talks in a bid to establish formal diplomatic ties. (January 15–16)

In its communication entitled "The Single Act: A New Frontier for Europe" the Commission sets out the conditions for attaining the objectives of the Single Act with proposals for completing the reform of the common agricultural policy, the structural instruments, and the Community's financing rules. (February 15)

Belgium issues the Euro-coin. (March 25)

Turkey makes a formal application to join the European Communities. (April 14)

The E.C. Council of Ministers adopts a new harmonized system of customs classification, replacing the Brussels Tariff Nomenclature (BTN) that was set up in 1950. (July 12)

Norway urged to reconsider E.C. membership. (September 18)

The E.C. Commission adopts proposals for the final stage of a plan to liberalize capital movements within the Community. (October 28)

The E.C. agrees to allow cheaper airfares in Europe. (December 7)

The six nation European Free Trade Association calls for closer cooperation with the European Community for an internal Europe market. (December 14–15)

1988

The E.C. Commission proposes a directive on opening up banking throughout the Community, calling for a Single Community License for banks that will allow any bank authorized to operate in its home country to do business in the rest of Europe as well. (January 13)

The European Parliament votes to back plans for a European "television without frontiers" which would allow people to watch broadcasts from all 12 Community countries. (January 20)

The Commission pledges to enforce an E.C. policy that would give people such as train drivers, teachers, and health service employees the right to work in any member state in the E.C. (March 21)

The E.C. agrees to open up the fast-growing E.C. market for telecommunications equipment to free cross-border competition. (April 28)

The Council adopts the "Youth Exchange Scheme" to stimulate and improve the exchanges of young people within the E.C. (September 21)

The E.C. starts negotiations on the fourth Lomé Convention, the trade and aid pact between the E.C. and 66 African, Caribbean, and Pacific Nations. (October 4)

The Court of First Instance is created, with jurisdiction to hear and determine at first instance certain actions or proceedings brought by individuals. (October 19)

The European Council meeting in Rhodes, Greece, indicated pleasure with the progress toward 1992. (December 2–3)

1989

Jacques Delors is reappointed president of the E.C. Commission (January 1)

E.C. and U.S. officials for trade and agriculture agreed to de-escalate the dispute over the E.C. ban on hormone-treated beef. (February 17–18)

E.C. environmental ministers negotiate a tight schedule for phasing out chlorofluorocarbons by the end of the century. The United States takes similar action the next day. (March 2)

At the Uruguay Round, an agreement of 105 participating nations yields progress in agriculture, trade in services, and intellectual property. (April 8)

The Delors Committee reached unanimous agreement on how to pursue concrete steps toward European monetary union. (April 17)

The E.C. increases relations with Eastern Europe with the signing of an agreement with Bulgaria. (April 18)

E.C. citizens directly elect the European Parliament for the third time in its history. The Socialists are returned as the largest political group. (June 15–18)

Summit of E.C. leaders in Madrid is dominated by a debate on the Delors Committee Report on economic and monetary union. They agree to begin the first stage (of three) toward economic and monetary union in 1990. (June 26–27)

Paris Summit of seven most industrial nations (G-7) entrusts the E.C. Commission with coordinating aid to Poland and Hungary, the two East European nations that are reforming the most rapidly. (July 15)

Austria applies for membership into the European Community. (July 17)

The "new" European Currency Unit (ECU) will now include the Spanish peseta and the Portuguese escudo, and has been revised for the new weights of all component currencies. (September 20)

At a Group of 24 industrialized nations meeting in Brussels, the E.C. announces it will send $325 million in economic aid to Poland and Hungary in 1990. (September 26)

The E.C. recommends that television stations within the Community devote a majority of their broadcasting time to programs made in the E.C. (October 3)

Leaders of the E.C. agreed in Paris to offer substantial aid to Eastern European nations that pursue human rights and free elections, to possibly create a European Development Bank for aid assistance, and to offer associate E.C. membership to Eastern European nations that request it. (November 18)

E.C. transport ministers reach important decisions on opening up the road haulage and airline market sectors to outside competition. (December 4–5)

E.C. member states agree to allow free competition in advanced telecommunications services from the middle of 1990. (December 7)

The 12 member E.C. states meet in Strasbourg, France. A special conference is proposed for 1990 to deal with the issues of a central bank and a common currency. A Social Rights Charter is passed by a vote of 11 to 1. A statement is made dealing with the German people regaining "unity through free self-determination." (December 8–9)

Talks begin between the E.C. and the European Free Trade Association on the formation of a European Economic Space. (December 18)

1990

A treaty is signed by the finance ministers of the two Germanys in Bonn establishing the historical monetary union. (May 18)

The European Bank for Reconstruction and Development (EBRD) is formally established at a treaty ceremony. (May 30)

The E.C. and EFTA began formal negotiations to establish a common economic zone, the European Economic Space. (June 20)

European Community leaders agree in Dublin to design a major aid program for the Soviet Union. (June 26)

European Community leaders agree in Dublin to set December 13 and 14 as the opening dates for conferences on greater economic and political union. (June 26)

East Germany allows a free flow of goods from nations in the E.C. (July 1)

The first stage of the European Monetary Union, as agreed at the European Summit in Madrid in June 1989, begins. (July 1)

The E.C. imposed broad sanctions against Iraq for her invasion of Kuwait. (August 4)

The E.C. approved proposals allowing East Germany temporary exemptions from E.C. laws. (August 21)

The Commission claims sole power to examine corporate mergers within the E.C. (September 21)

The German Democratic Republic officially disappeared with its formal unification into a single Germany. (October 3)

The United Kingdom entered the European Monetary System. (October 8)

E.C. leaders, meeting in Rome, agreed in principle that a common central bank should come into existence on January 1, 1994. (October 28)

INDEX OF MAJOR SUBJECTS

(does **not** include all listings in text)

Institutions and Policies of the European Community

Brussels
Budget
Bulletin of the European Communities
Cabinet
Center for European Policy Studies
Commission, The
Committees
Common Market
Community Patent Convention
Council, The
Council of European Communities
Council of Ministers
Court of Auditors
Court of First Instance
Court of Justice, The European
Currencies of E.C.
Customs Union
CXT
Databases and databanks of the E.C.
E
E.C.
E.C.S.C.
E.E.C.
E.E.C. Six
EMP
EP
EPO
ERP
EUR-6
EUR-9
EUR-10
EUR-12
European Assembly
European Atomic Energy Community
European Coal and Steel Community
  (E.C.S.C.)
European Commission
European Committee for Standardization

European Community (E.C.)
European Community, databases and
  databanks
European Community, statistics
European Company Statute
European Council
European Court of Human Rights
European Court of Justice
European District
European Economic Community
European Information Services
European Parliament
European Parliament, Committees
European Parliament—working methods
European Regional Council
European Standards Institute
EUROSTAT
Father of Europe
Four
Four institutions, The
Framework horizontal directives
Free trade area
Grants and loans
Group of Ten
Harmonization
Industrial policy
Industrial property
Industrial standards
Industry-state aids
Legislative preparation
MEP
Merger Treaty
Nine
Objectives
Opinions
Original Six, The
Paris, Treaty of
Parliament, European
Patent law
PCIJ
People's Europe

Permanent Representatives Committee
Proposals
Quotas
Recommendations
Regional Policy
Regulations
Resolutions
Right of establishment
Rome Treaty
Rules of Competition
Schuman Plan
Six, the
Specific horizontal directives
Standardization
Standards
Strasbourg
Tariffs
Ten, The
Three, The
Trade surplus
Treaty of Accession
Treaty of Brussels
Treaty of Paris
Treaty of Rome
Veto
Worker participation, company assets
Yaoundé Agreements

Green paper
Industrial cooperation
Internal market
Madrid meeting
Market integration
Montreal Round
Non-Europe
Public procurement
Public works contracts
Reciprocity
Rhodes summit
Services
Single Administrative Document
Single customs document
Single European Act
Subsidies
Super 301
TARIC
Taxation
Tax havens
Tax policies
Tax relief
Transit procedure
Value Added Tax
White Paper
Withholding tax

1992 POLICY

Article 100A
Common border posts
Common Customs Tariff
Competition Directorate
Control of goods
Control of individuals
Costs of non-Europe
Cross-border mergers
Customs duties
Delors Committee
Delors, Jacques
Delors Report
Europartnership
European Area of Development
European Economic Interest Grouping
European Economic Unity
European financial area
Europe without frontiers
External dimension
Fortress Europe
Franchisers
Frontier barriers
Government contracts

INDUSTRY APPLICATIONS

Advanced Manufacturing equipment
Aerosol
Aircraft industry
Aircraft sector
Business Cooperation Center
CACTUS
CADDIA
Car industry
Car prices
Certification
Coal
Coal gasification
Conformance testing
Construction products
Dumping
Excise duties
Exclusive dealing arrangements
Footwear
International Organization for
    Standardization
ISO
Medium-sized companies
Mineral water
Pharmaceuticals

Product testing
Shipbuilding
Small and Medium-sized Enterprises
Small businesses
SMEs
Steel
Tankers
Textiles
Toys
Tractors and agricultural machinery
Trade fairs
Trademarks
Transport
Vehicles

BANKING, INSURANCE, FINANCIAL SERVICES, AND INVESTING

Bank for International Settlements (BIS)
Banking
Bankruptcy
BTN
Capital
Capital, free movement of
Central bank
Central banks, The Committee of
  Governors of
CET
Collective Investment in Transferable
  Securities
Collective Investment Undertakings
Commercial agents
Common taxation
Company accounts
Company (group) accounts
Company capitalization
Company law
Competition policy
Consolidated profits
Corporate breakup rules
Corporate statute
Cost savings
Double taxation
Duty-free allowances
EMA
EMS
Eurochecking (Eurochequing)
Eurocheque
Euro-coins
Euro-currency
Euro-dollars
European Co-Production Association
European Currency Unit (ECU)

European Currency Unit bonds
European Currency Unit futures and
  options
European Development Bank
European Guarantee Fund
European Investment Bank (EIB)
European Monetary Agreement (EMA)
European Monetary Cooperation Fund
European Monetary System (EMS)
European Monetary Union (EMU)
European Patent Convention
European Payments Union
European Unit of Account (EUA)
Eurosterling
Exchange-Rate Mechanism (ERM)
Export credit insurance
External trade
Finance
Financial integration
Financial mechanism
Financial services
Fiscal controls
Free movement of capital
General Agreement on Tariffs and Trade
  (GATT)
Generalized System of Preferences (GSP)
Group of 77
GSTP
Incorporation measures
Indirect taxation
Insurance
Intellectual property
Interbourse Data Information System
International Bank for Reconstruction and
  Development
International Monetary Fund (IMF)
Investment
Investment Bank, European
Kennedy Round
Mergers
Mergers, employee protection
Mortgages
Most-Favored Nation
MultiFibre Arrangements
New Community Instrument (NCI)
Public limited companies
Punta del Este
SDRs
Second Banking Coordination Directive
Securities
Snake
Special Drawing Rights
Stabilization of Export Earnings (STABEX)

Stock exchange—listing particulars
Stockholders
Stocks
Tokyo Round
Travelers checks
UCITS
Units of Account (UA)
Unit trusts
Uruguay Round
Venture capital
World Bank

AGRICULTURAL AND ANIMAL POLICIES

Agriculture, Common Agricultural Policy
  (CAP)
Animal health and meat inspection
Article XXXV
Basic price
Common Agricultural Policy (CAP)
Common Agricultural Policy, Accession of
  the Three
Common Fisheries Policy (CFP)
Community preference
Coresponsibility levy
Dairy products
Farm Fund
Fats, oils, and oilseeds
Feedingstuffs
Fertilizers
Fish
Fishery policy
Flax, hemp, and linseed
Food
Food additives
Foodstuffs, labeling
Fruits and vegetables
Fruit jams, jellies, marmalade, and
  chestnut puree
Fruit juices (soft drinks)
Grain sector
Green currencies
Green pound
Guide price
Honey
Hops
Hormones
Maximum guaranteed quantity
Meat inspection
Milk and milk products
Milk, condensed and dried
Monetary Compensatory Amounts
Mountain

Olive oil
Pasta War
Peas and field beans
Pigmeat
Plant health controls
Potatoes
Poultry
Processed fruits and vegetables
Reference price
Rice
Seeds
Sheepmeat
Silk worms
Sluice gate price
Starch
Sugar
Target price
Threshold price
Tobacco
Whale products
Wheat
Wine
Wool

SOCIAL, CONSUMER, AND EDUCATIONAL POLICIES

Accountants
Advertising
AIM
Architects
Artists
Audio-Visual policy
Auditors
Center for Research and Documentation on
  the European Community
Children
Civil protection
COMETT
Community law
Consumer credit
Consumer protection
Contract terms
Cosmetics
Culture
Dental practitioners
Doctors
Driving hours
Driving licenses
Education
Education grants
Engineers
Equality

Equal pay
ERASMUS
Establishment, right of
Euro-license
Euro-lottery
European Cinema and Television Year
European Community Study Organization
    of the U.S.
European Community's Visitors Program
    (ECVP)
European Community Youth Orchestra
    (ECYO)
European Foundation for the Improvement
    of Living and Working Conditions
European Road Safety Year
European Social Fund
Eurydice
Film
Fire safety
Foreign workers
Glass
Hairdressers
Handicapped people
Health and safety
Illiteracy
IRIS
Jurists
Major-accident hazards
Marriage contract
MEDIA
Medical and public health research
Medical practice
Midwives
Migrant workers
Migration
Movies
Nurses
Orphans
Pesticides
Pharmacists
Pilots
Polling
Poverty
Professions
Public opinion polls
Rights
Saccharin
Safety
Self-employed
Social Charter
Social Fund
Social Policy
Symbols

Terrorism
Tourism
Trade Unions
University research
Veterinary surgeons
Voting rights
Women
Work and employment
YES for Europe
Youth for Europe

ENVIRONMENTAL

Air pollution
Asbestos
Cancer
Car pollution
CFCs
Chemicals
Chlorofluorocarbons
Dangerous substances
DRIVE
Environment
Greenhouse effect
Halons
Marine pollution
Noise
PCBs
Pollution
PolyChlorinated Biphenyls
Recycling, paper, tires, and drink
    containers
Recycling, tenders
Toxic effluent
Toxic waste
Vehicle fuel
Waste
Waste oils
Water

SCIENCE, RESEARCH, AND TECHNOLOGY

Apollo
Basic Research in Industrial Technology
    (BRITE)
Biomolecular engineering
Biotechnology
BRITE
Cellular phones
Chips
Computers
Copiers

Data-processing
DELTA
Direct Information Access Network for
  Europe
Energy
ESPRIT
ESRO
ETSI
EUREKA
Euronet
Euronet Diane
European Science Foundation
European Space Agency
European Telecommunications Standards
Forecasting and Assessment in the field of
  Science and Technology
Gas
Green Paper
High-Definition Television (HDTV)
Information Technology
Inter-Institutional Information System
ISDN
IT
JESSI
JET
Joint European Torus
Joint Research Center (JRC)
Memory chips

Mobile telephone
NETT
Next European Torus
Nuclear energy
Nuclear fusion
Oil
Plutonium
RACE
Research
Research and Technological Development
  policy
SCIENCE
Science and technological committee
Semiconductors
Solar energy
Solid fuel
Space
SPRINT
STAR
Technologies
TEDIS
Telecommunications
TELEMAN
Telematics
Television
Television without frontiers
Zootechnics

About the Author

Jerry M. Rosenberg is presently professor at the Graduate School of Management and Department of Business Administration, both at Rutgers University. He has also been a visiting professor at the Middlesex Polytechnic in London, at the John Cabot International College in Rome, and has lectured at the London School of Economics and Political Sciences.

Born in New York City in 1935, Prof. Rosenberg received his B.S. degree from the City College of New York, an M.A. degree from Ohio State University, a Certificate from the Center of Higher Studies in Paris (while on both Fulbright and French Government Awards), and a Ph.D. from New York University.

A member of the European Community Studies Association, he is also a consultant to companies in Western Europe and American firms with European subsidiaries.

Named "America's Foremost Business and Technical Lexicographer," Professor Rosenberg has written nine other reference and nonfiction books. He is a consultant to both the Random House Dictionary and the Oxford English Dictionary since 1984. Professor Rosenberg is married and is the father of two daughters.